# DECISION POINTS

# DECISION POINTS

—

# GEORGE W. BUSH

2 4 6 8 10 9 7 5 3

Published in 2010 by Virgin Books, an imprint of Ebury Publishing
A Random House Group Company
First published in the United States by Crown Publishers in 2010

The Random House Group Limited Reg. No. 954009

Addresses for companies within the Random House Group can be found at
www.randomhouse.co.uk

A CIP catalogue record for this book is available from the British Library

The Random House Group Limited supports The Forest Stewardship Council [FSC],
the leading international forest certification organisation. All our titles that are printed on
Greenpeace-approved FSC-certified paper carry the FSC logo. Our paper procurement policy
can be found at www.rbooks.co.uk/environment

**Mixed Sources**
Product group from well-managed
forests and other controlled sources
www.fsc.org  Cert no. TT-COC-2139
FSC    © 1996 Forest Stewardship Council

Printed and bound in Great Britain by Clays Ltd, St Ives PLC

Hardback ISBN 9780753539668
Trade paperback ISBN 9780753539675

*Front cover photograph by White House/Paul Morse*
*Back cover photograph by Eric Draper*
*Interior Design by Elizabeth Rendfleisch*
*Cover Design by Whitney Cookman*
*Maps by David Lindroth Inc.*
*Frontispiece photograph by White House/Eric Draper*

To buy books by your favourite authors and register for offers,
visit www.rbooks.co.uk

*To the loves of my life:*
*Laura, Barbara, and Jenna*

# CONTENTS

# INTRODUCTION

In the final year of my presidency, I began to think seriously about writing my memoirs. On the recommendation of Karl Rove, I met with more than a dozen distinguished historians. To a person, they told me I had an obligation to write. They felt it was important that I record my perspective on the presidency, in my own words.

"Have you ever seen the movie *Apollo 13*?" the historian Jay Winik asked. "Everyone knows the astronauts make it home in the end. But you're on the edge of your seat wondering how they do it."

Nearly all the historians suggested that I read *Memoirs* by President Ulysses S. Grant, which I did. The book captures his distinctive voice. He uses anecdotes to re-create his experience during the Civil War. I could see why his work had endured.

Like Grant, I decided not to write an exhaustive account of my life or presidency. Instead I have told the story of my time in the White House by focusing on the most important part of the job: making decisions. Each chapter is based on a major decision or a series of related decisions. As a result, the book flows thematically, not in a day-by-day chronology. I do not cover all of the important issues that crossed my desk. Many devoted members of my Cabinet and staff are mentioned briefly or not at all. I value their service, and I will always be grateful for their contributions.

My goals in writing this book are twofold. First, I hope to paint a picture of what it was like to serve as president for eight consequential years. I believe it will be impossible to reach definitive conclusions about my presidency—or any recent presidency, for that matter—for several decades. The passage of time allows passions to cool, results to clarify, and scholars to compare different approaches. My hope is that this book will serve as a resource for anyone studying this period in American history.

Second, I write to give readers a perspective on decision making in a complex environment. Many of the decisions that reach the president's desk are tough calls, with strong arguments on both sides. Throughout the book, I describe the options I weighed and the principles I followed. I hope this will give you a better sense of why I made the decisions I did. Perhaps it will even prove useful as you make choices in your own life.

*Decision Points* is based primarily on my recollections. With help from researchers, I have confirmed my account with government documents, contemporaneous notes, personal interviews, news reports, and other sources, some of which remain classified. There were instances in which I had to rely on my memory alone. If there are inaccuracies in this book, the responsibility is mine.

In the pages that follow, I have done my best to write about the decisions I got right, those I got wrong, and what I would do differently if given the chance. Of course, in the presidency, there are no do-overs. You have to do what you believe is right and accept the consequences. I tried to do that every day of my eight years in office. Serving as president was the honor of a lifetime, and I appreciate your giving me an opportunity to share my story.

# QUITTING

It was a simple question. "Can you remember the last day you didn't have a drink?" Laura asked in her calm, soothing voice. She wasn't threatening or nagging. She did expect an answer. My wife is the kind of person who picks her moments. This was one of them.

"Of course I can," came my indignant response. Then I thought back over the previous week. I'd had a few beers with the guys on Monday night. On Tuesday I'd fixed myself my favorite after-dinner drink: B&B, Benedictine and brandy. I'd had a couple of bourbon and Sevens after I put Barbara and Jenna to bed on Wednesday. Thursday and Friday were beer-drinking nights. On Saturday, Laura and I had gone out with friends. I'd had martinis before dinner, beers with dinner, and B&Bs after dinner. Uh-oh, I had failed week one.

I went on racking my memory for a single dry day over the past few weeks; then the past month; then longer. I could not remember one. Drinking had become a habit.

I have a habitual personality. I smoked cigarettes for about nine years, starting in college. I quit smoking by dipping snuff. I quit that by chewing long-leaf tobacco. Eventually I got down to cigars.

For a while I tried to rationalize my drinking habit. I was nowhere near as bad as some of the drunks I knew in our hometown of Midland, Texas. I didn't drink during the day or at work. I was in good shape and jogged almost every afternoon, another habit.

Over time I realized I was running not only to stay fit, but also to purge my system of the poisons. Laura's little question provoked some big ones of my own. Did I want to spend time at home with our girls or stay out drinking? Would I rather read in bed with Laura or drink bourbon by myself after the family had gone to sleep? Could I continue to grow closer to the Almighty, or was alcohol becoming my god? I knew the answers, but it was hard to summon the will to make a change.

In 1986, Laura and I both turned forty. So did our close friends Don and Susie Evans. We decided to hold a joint celebration at The Broadmoor resort in Colorado Springs. We invited our childhood friends Joe and Jan O'Neill, my brother Neil, and another Midland friend, Penny Sawyer.

The official birthday dinner was Saturday night. We had a big meal, accompanied by numerous sixty-dollar bottles of Silver Oak wine. There were lots of toasts—to our health, to our kids, to the babysitters who were watching the kids back home. We got louder and louder, telling the same stories over and over. At one point Don and I decided we were so cute we should take our routine from table to table. We shut the place down, paid a colossal bar tab, and went to bed.

I awoke the next morning with a mean hangover. As I left for my daily jog, I couldn't remember much of the night before. About halfway through the run, my head started to clear. The crosscurrents in my life came into focus. For months I had been praying that God would show me how to better reflect His will. My Scripture readings had clarified the nature of temptation and the reality that the love of earthly pleasures could replace the love of God. My problem was not only drinking; it was selfishness. The booze was leading me to put myself ahead of others, especially my family. I loved Laura and the girls too much to let that happen. Faith showed me a way out. I knew I could count on the grace of God to help me change. It would not be easy, but by the end of the run, I had made up my mind: I was done drinking.

When I got back to the hotel room, I told Laura I would never have another drink. She looked at me like I was still running on alcohol fumes. Then she said, "That's good, George."

I knew what she was thinking. I had talked about quitting before, and nothing had come of it. What she didn't know was that this time I had changed on the inside—and that would enable me to change my behavior forever.

It took about five days for the freshness of the decision to wear off. As my memory of the hangover faded, the temptation to drink became intense. My body craved alcohol. I prayed for the strength to fight off my desires. I ran harder and longer as a way to discipline myself. I also ate a lot of chocolate. My body was screaming for sugar. Chocolate was an easy way to feed it. This also gave me another motivation for running: to keep the pounds off.

Laura was very supportive. She sensed that I really was going to quit. Whenever I brought up the subject, she urged me to stay with it. Sometimes I talked about drinking again just to hear her encouraging words.

My friends helped, too, even though most of them did not stop drinking when I was around. At first it was hard to watch other people enjoy a cocktail or a beer. But being the sober guy helped me realize how mindless I must have sounded when I drank. The more time passed, the more I felt momentum on my side. Not drinking became a habit of its own—one I was glad to keep.

———

Quitting drinking was one of the toughest decisions I have ever made. Without it, none of the others that follow in this book would have been possible. Yet without the experiences of my first forty years, quitting drinking would not have been possible either. So much of my character, so many of my convictions, took shape during those first four decades. My journey included challenges, struggles, and failures. It is testimony to the strength of love, the power of faith, and the truth that people can change. On top of that, it was one interesting ride.

———

I am the first son of George and Barbara Bush. My father wore the uniform in World War II, married his sweetheart as soon as he came home, and quickly started a new family. The story was common to many young couples of their generation. Yet there was always something extraordinary about George H.W. Bush.

When Pearl Harbor was attacked, Dad was a high school senior. He had been accepted to Yale. Instead he enlisted in the Navy on his eighteenth birthday and became the youngest pilot to earn his wings. Before he shipped off for the Pacific, he fell in love with a beautiful girl named

Barbara Pierce. He immediately told friends he would marry her. As a reminder, he painted her name on the side of his plane.

One morning in September 1944, Dad was flying a mission over Chichi-Jima, an island occupied by the Japanese. His TBM Avenger was struck by enemy fire, but he kept going—diving at two hundred miles per hour—until he had dropped his bombs and hit the target. He shouted for his flight mates to bail out and then did so himself. Alone in the South Pacific, he swam to the tiny rubber raft that had been his seat cushion. When Dad was rescued by a submarine, he was told he could go home. He rejoined his squadron instead. His tour ended just before Christmas, and on January 6, 1945, he married Mother at her family church in Rye, New York.

After the war, Mother and Dad moved to New Haven so he could attend Yale. He was a fine athlete—a first baseman and captain of the baseball team. Mother came to almost every game, even during the spring of 1946, when she was pregnant with me. Fortunately for her, the stadium included a double-wide seat behind home plate designed for former law professor William Howard Taft.

Dad excelled in the classroom, graduating Phi Beta Kappa in just two and a half years. I attended his commencement in Mother's arms, dozing through much of the ceremony. It wouldn't be the last time I slept through a Yale lecture.

Years later, millions of Americans would learn Dad's story. But from the beginning, I knew it by heart. One of my first memories is of sitting on the floor with Mother looking through scrapbooks. She showed me photos from Dad's pilot training in Corpus Christi, box scores from his games in the College World Series, and a famous picture of him with Babe Ruth on the pitcher's mound at Yale Field. I pored over photos from their wedding: the Navy officer and his smiling young bride. My favorite part of the scrapbook was a piece of rubber from the raft that saved Dad's life in the Pacific. I would bug him to tell stories from the war. He refused to brag. But Mother would. She adored him, and so did I. As I got older, there would be others I looked up to. But the truth is that I never had to search for a role model. I was the son of George Bush.

———

When Dad graduated in 1948, most assumed he would head to Wall Street. After all, his father was a partner at a successful investment house. But Dad wanted to make it on his own. So he and Mother loaded up their red Studebaker and moved west. I've always admired them for taking a risk, and I've always been grateful they settled where they did. One of my greatest inheritances is that I was raised in West Texas.

We spent our first year in the blue-collar town of Odessa, where there were few paved streets and frequent dust storms. We lived in a tiny apartment and shared a bathroom with—depending on whom you ask—either one or two prostitutes. Dad's job was on the bottom rung of an oil services company. His duties included sweeping warehouses and painting pump jacks. A fellow worker once asked Dad if he was a college man. Dad told him yes, as a matter of fact, he had gone to Yale. The guy paused a second and replied, "Never heard of it."

After a brief stint in California, we moved back to West Texas in 1950. We settled in Midland, the place I picture when I think of growing up. Midland was twenty miles east of Odessa. Native trees did not exist. The ground was flat, dry, and dusty. Beneath it sat a sea of oil.

Midland was the capital of the Permian Basin, which accounted for about 20 percent of America's oil production in the 1950s. The town had an independent, entrepreneurial feel. There was fierce competition, especially in the oil business. But there was also a sense of community. Anybody could make it, anyone could fail. My friends' parents did all sorts of jobs. One painted houses. One was a surgeon. Another poured cement. About ten blocks away lived a home builder, Mr. Harold Welch. A quarter century passed before I met him and courted his sweet daughter, Laura Lane.

Life in Midland was simple. I rode bikes with pals like Mike Proctor, Joe O'Neill, and Robert McCleskey. We went on Cub Scout trips, and I sold Life Savers door-to-door for charity. My friends and I would play baseball for hours, hitting each other grounders and fly balls until Mother called over the fence in our yard for me to come in for dinner. I was thrilled when Dad came out to play. He was famous for catching pop-ups behind his back, a trick he learned in college. My friends and I tried to emulate him. We ended up with a lot of bruises on our shoulders.

One of the proudest moments of my young life came when I was eleven years old. Dad and I were playing catch in the yard. He fired me a fastball, which I snagged with my mitt. "Son, you've arrived," he said with a smile. "I can throw it to you as hard as I want."

Those were comfortable, carefree years. The word I'd use now is idyllic. On Friday nights, we cheered on the Bulldogs of Midland High. On Sunday mornings, we went to church. Nobody locked their doors. Years later, when I would speak about the American Dream, it was Midland I had in mind.

Amid this happy life came a sharp pang of sorrow. In the spring of 1953 my three-year-old sister Robin was diagnosed with leukemia, a form of cancer that was then virtually untreatable. My parents checked her into Memorial Sloan-Kettering in New York City. They hoped for a miracle. They also knew that researchers would learn from studying her disease.

Mother spent months at Robin's bedside. Dad shuttled back and forth between Texas and the East Coast. I stayed with my parents' friends. When Dad was home, he started getting up early to go to work. I later learned he was going to church at 6:30 every morning to pray for Robin.

My parents didn't know how to tell me my sister was dying. They just said she was sick back east. One day my teacher at Sam Houston Elementary School in Midland asked me and a classmate to carry a record player to another wing of the school. While we were hauling the bulky machine, I was shocked to see Mother and Dad pull up in our family's pea-green Oldsmobile. I could have sworn that I saw Robin's blond curls in the window. I charged over to the car. Mother hugged me tight. I looked in the backseat. Robin was not there. Mother whispered, "She died." On the short ride home, I saw my parents cry for the first time in my life.

Robin's death made me sad, too, in a seven-year-old way. I was sad to lose my sister and future playmate. I was sad because I saw my parents hurting so much. It would be many years before I could understand the difference between my sorrow and the wrenching pain my parents felt from losing their daughter.

The period after Robin's death was the beginning of a new closeness between Mother and me. Dad was away a lot on business, and I spent almost all my time at her side, showering her with affection and trying to cheer her up with jokes. One day she heard Mike Proctor knock on the door and ask if I could come out and play. "No," I told him. "I have to stay with Mother."

For a while after Robin's death I felt like an only child. Brother Jeb, seven years younger than me, was just a baby. My two youngest brothers, Neil and Marvin, and my sister Doro arrived later. As I got older, Mother continued to play a big role in my life. She was the Cub Scout den mother who drove us to Carlsbad Caverns, where we walked among the stalactites and stalagmites. As a Little League mom, she kept score at every game. She took me to the nearest orthodontist in Big Spring and tried to teach me French in the car. I can still picture us riding through the desert with me repeating, "*Ferme la bouche . . . ouvre la fenêtre.*" If only Jacques Chirac could have seen me then.

Along the way, I picked up a lot of Mother's personality. We have the same sense of humor. We like to needle to show affection, and sometimes to make a point. We both have tempers that can flare rapidly. And we can be blunt, a trait that gets us in trouble from time to time. When I ran for governor of Texas, I told people that I had my daddy's eyes and my mother's mouth. I said it to get a laugh, but it was true.

Being the son of George and Barbara Bush came with high expectations, but not the kind many people later assumed. My parents never projected their dreams onto me. If they hoped I would be a great pitcher, or political figure, or artist (no chance), they never told me about it. Their view of parenting was to offer love and encourage me to chart my own path.

They did set boundaries for behavior, and there were times when I crossed them. Mother was the enforcer. She could get hot, and because we had such similar personalities, I knew how to light her fuse. I would smart off, and she would let me have it. If I was smutty, as she put it, I would get my mouth washed out with soap. That happened more than once. Most of the time I did not try to provoke her. I was a spirited boy finding my own way, just as she was finding hers as a parent. I'm only half joking when I say I'm responsible for her white hair.

As I got older, I came to see that my parents' love was unconditional. I know because I tested it. I had two car wrecks when I was fourteen, the legal driving age back then. My parents still loved me. I borrowed Dad's car, carelessly charged in reverse, and tore the door off. I poured vodka in the fishbowl and killed my little sister Doro's goldfish. At times I was surly, demanding, and brash. Despite it all, my parents still loved me.

Eventually their patient love affected me. When you know you have unconditional love, there is no point in rebellion and no need to fear failure. I was free to follow my instincts, enjoy my life, and love my parents as much as they loved me.

One day, shortly after I learned to drive and while Dad was away on a business trip, Mother called me into her bedroom. There was urgency in her voice. She told me to drive her to the hospital immediately. I asked what was wrong. She said she would tell me in the car.

As I pulled out of the driveway, she told me to drive steadily and avoid bumps. Then she said she had just had a miscarriage. I was taken aback. This was a subject I never expected to be discussing with Mother. I also never expected to see the remains of the fetus, which she had saved in a jar to bring to the hospital. I remember thinking: *There was a human life, a little brother or sister.*

Mother checked herself into the hospital and was taken to an exam room. I paced up and down the hallway to steady my nerves. After I passed an older woman several times, she said, "Don't worry, honey, your wife will be just fine."

When I was allowed into Mother's room, the doctor said she would be all right, but she needed to spend the night. I told Mother what the woman had said to me in the hall. She laughed one of her great, strong laughs, and I went home feeling much better.

The next day I went back to the hospital to pick her up. She thanked me for being so careful and responsible. She also asked me not to tell anyone about the miscarriage, which she felt was a private family matter. I respected her wish, until she gave me permission to tell the story in this book. What I did for Mother that day was small, but it was a big deal for me. It helped deepen the special bond between us.

While I was growing up in Texas, the rest of the Bush family was part of a very different world. When I was about six years old, we visited Dad's parents in Greenwich, Connecticut. I was invited to eat dinner with the grown-ups. I had to wear a coat and tie, something I never did in Midland outside of Sunday school. The table was set elegantly. I had never seen so many spoons, forks, and knives, all neatly lined up. A woman dressed in black with a white apron served me a weird-looking red soup with a white blob in the middle. I took a little taste. It was terrible. Soon everyone was looking at me, waiting for me to finish this delicacy. Mother had warned me to eat everything without complaining. But she forgot to tell the chef she had raised me on peanut butter and jelly, not borscht.

I had heard a lot about my paternal grandparents from Dad. My grandfather Prescott Bush was a towering man—six foot four, with a big laugh and a big personality. He was well known in Greenwich as a successful businessman with unquestioned integrity and a longtime moderator of the town assembly. He was also an outstanding golfer who was president of the U.S. Golf Association and once shot sixty-six in the U.S. Senior Open.

In 1950, Gampy, as we all called him, ran for the Senate. He lost by just over a thousand votes and swore off politics. But two years later, Connecticut Republicans persuaded him to try again. This time he won.

When I was ten years old, I went to visit Gampy in Washington. He and my grandmother took me to a gathering at a Georgetown home. As I wandered among the adults, Gampy grabbed my arm. "Georgie," he said, "I want you to meet someone." He led me toward a giant man, the only person in the room as tall as he was.

"I've got one of your constituents here," Gampy said to the man. A huge hand swallowed mine. "Pleased to meet you," said Gampy's colleague, Senate Majority Leader Lyndon B. Johnson.

My grandfather could be a very stern man. He was from the "children should be seen but not heard" school, which was foreign to a chatty little wiseacre like me. He doled out discipline quickly and forcefully, as I found out when he chased me around the room after I had pulled the tail of his favorite dog. At the time, I thought he was scary. Years later, I learned that this imposing man had a tender heart: Mother told me how he had comforted her by choosing a beautiful grave site for Robin in a Greenwich cemetery. When my grandfather died in 1972, he was buried at her side.

Dad loved and respected his father; he adored his mom. Dorothy Walker Bush was like an angel. We called her Ganny, and she was possibly the sweetest person I have ever met. I remember her tucking me into bed when I was little, tickling my back as we said nightly prayers. She was humble, and taught us never to brag. She lived to see Dad become president and died at age ninety-one, a few weeks after his defeat in 1992. Dad was with her in the final moments. She asked him to read to her from the Bible next to her bed. As he opened it, a bundle of old papers slipped out. They were letters Dad had written her years ago. She had cherished them all her life, and wanted them near her at the end.

Mother's parents lived in Rye, New York. Her mother, Pauline Robinson Pierce, died when I was three. She was killed in a car accident when my grandfather Marvin, who was driving, reached down to stop a cup of hot coffee from spilling. The car swerved off the road and hit a stone wall. My little sister was named in my grandmother's memory.

I was very fond of Mother's father, Marvin Pierce, known as Monk. He had lettered in four sports at Miami University of Ohio, which gave him a mythic aura in my young eyes. He was president of McCall's and a distant relative of President Franklin Pierce. I remember him as a gentle, patient, and humble man.

My trips back east taught me two important lessons: First, I could make myself comfortable in just about any environment. Second, I really liked living in Texas. Of course, there was one big advantage to being on the East Coast: I could watch major league baseball. When I was about ten years old, my kind uncle Bucky, Dad's youngest brother, took me to a New York Giants game in the Polo Grounds. I still remember the day I watched my hero, Willie Mays, play the outfield.

Five decades later I saw Willie again, when he served as honorary commissioner for a youth T-ball game on the South Lawn of the White House. He was seventy-five years old, but he still seemed like the Say Hey Kid to me. I told the young ballplayers that day, "I wanted to be the Willie Mays of my generation, but I couldn't hit a curveball. So, instead, I ended up being president."

In 1959 my family left Midland and moved 550 miles across the state to Houston. Dad was the CEO of a company in the growing field of offshore drilling, and it made sense for him to be close to his rigs in the Gulf of Mexico. Our new house was in a lush, wooded area that was often pelted by rainstorms. This was the exact opposite of Midland, where the only kind of storm you got was a dust storm. I was nervous about the move, but Houston was an exciting city. I learned to play golf, made new friends, and started at a private school called Kinkaid. At the time, the differences between Midland and Houston seemed big. But they were nothing compared to what was coming next.

One day after school, Mother was waiting at the end of our driveway. I was in the ninth grade, and mothers never came out to meet the bus— at least mine didn't. She was clearly excited about something. As I got off the bus, she let it out: "Congratulations, George, you've been accepted to Andover!" This was good news to her. I wasn't so sure.

Dad had taken me to see his alma mater, Phillips Academy in Andover, Massachusetts, the previous summer. It sure was different from what I was used to. Most of the dorms were large brick buildings arranged around quads. It looked like a college. I liked Kinkaid, but the decision had been made. Andover was a family tradition. I was going.

My first challenge was explaining Andover to my friends in Texas. In those days, most Texans who went away to high school had discipline problems. When I told a friend that I was headed to a boarding school in Massachusetts, he had only one question: "Bush, what did you do wrong?"

When I got to Andover in the fall of 1961, I thought he might be on to something. We wore ties to class, to meals, and to the mandatory church services. In the winter months, we might as well have been in Siberia. As a Texan, I identified four new seasons: icy snow, fresh snow, melting snow, and gray snow. There were no women, aside from those who worked in the library. Over time, they began to look like movie stars to us.

The school was a serious academic challenge. Going to Andover was the hardest thing I did until I ran for president almost forty years later. I was behind the other students academically and had to study like mad. In my first year, the lights in our dorm rooms went out at ten o'clock, and many nights I stayed up reading by the hall light that shined under the door.

I struggled most in English. For one of my first assignments, I wrote about the sadness of losing my sister Robin. I decided I should come up with a better word than *tears*. After all, I was on the East Coast and should try to be sophisticated. So I pulled out the *Roget's Thesaurus* Mother had slipped into my luggage and wrote, "Lacerates were flowing down my cheeks."

When the paper came back, it had a huge zero on the front. I was stunned and humiliated. I had always made good grades in Texas; this marked my first academic failure. I called my parents and told them I was miserable. They encouraged me to stay. I decided to tough it out. I wasn't a quitter.

My social adjustment came faster than my academic adjustment. There was a small knot of fellow Texans at Andover, including a fellow from Fort Worth named Clay Johnson. We spoke the same language and became close friends. Soon I broadened my circle. For a guy who was interested in people, Andover was good grazing.

I discovered that I was a natural organizer. My senior year at Andover, I appointed myself commissioner of our stickball league. I called myself Tweeds Bush, a play on the famous New York political boss. I named a cabinet of aides, including a head umpire and a league psychologist. We devised elaborate rules and a play-off system. There was no wild card; I'm a purist.

We also came up with a scheme to print league identification cards, which conveniently could double as fake IDs. The plan was uncovered by school authorities. I was instructed to cease and desist, which I did. In my final act as commissioner, I appointed my successor, my cousin Kevin Rafferty.

That final year at Andover, I had a history teacher named Tom Lyons. He liked to grab our attention by banging one of his crutches on the blackboard. Mr. Lyons had played football at Brown University before he was stricken by polio. He was a powerful example for me. His lectures brought historical figures to life, especially President Franklin Roosevelt. Mr. Lyons loved FDR's politics, and I suspect he found inspiration in Roosevelt's triumph over his illness.

Mr. Lyons pushed me hard. He challenged, yet nurtured. He hectored and he praised. He demanded a lot, and thanks to him I discovered a lifelong love for history. Decades later, I invited Mr. Lyons to the Oval Office. It was a special moment for me: a student who was making history standing next to the man who had taught it to him so many years ago.

———

As the days at Andover wound down, it came time to apply to college. My first thought was Yale. After all, I was born there. One time-consuming part of the application was filling out the blue card that asked you to list relatives who were alumni. There was my grandfather and my dad. And all his brothers. And my first cousins. I had to write the names of the second cousins on the back of the card.

Despite my family ties, I doubted I would be accepted. My grades and test scores were respectable but behind many in my class. The Andover dean, G. Grenville Benedict, was a realist. He advised that I "get some good insurance" in case Yale didn't work out. I applied to another good school, the University of Texas at Austin, and toured the campus with Dad. I started to picture myself there as part of an honors program called Plan Two.

At the mailbox one day, I was stunned to find a thick envelope with a Yale acceptance. Mr. Lyons had written my recommendation, and all I could think was that he must have come up with quite a letter. Clay Johnson opened his admissions letter at the same time. When we agreed to be roommates, the decision was sealed.

———

Leaving Andover was like ridding myself of a straitjacket. My philosophy in college was the old cliché: work hard, play hard. I upheld the former and excelled at the latter. I joined the Delta Kappa Epsilon fraternity, played rugby and intramural sports, took road trips to girls' colleges, and spent a lot of time hanging out with friends.

My boisterous spirit carried me away at times. During my senior year, we were at Princeton for a football game. Inspired by the Yale win—and more than a little booze—I led a group onto the field to tear down the goalposts. The Princeton faithful were not amused. I was sitting atop the crossbar when a security guard pulled me down. I was then marched the length of the field and put in a police car. Yale friends started rocking the car and shouting, "Free Bush!"

Sensing disaster, my friend Roy Austin—a big guy from the island of St. Vincent who was captain of the Yale soccer team—yelled at the crowd to move. Then he jumped into the car with me. When we made it to the police station, we were told to leave campus and never return. All these years later I still haven't been back to Princeton. As for Roy, he continued to hone his diplomatic skills. Four decades later, I appointed him ambassador to Trinidad and Tobago.

At Yale, I had no interest in being a campus politician. But occasionally I was exposed to the politics of the campus. The fall of my freshman year, Dad ran for the Senate against a Democrat named Ralph Yarborough. Dad got more votes than any Republican candidate in Texas history, but the national landslide led by President Johnson was too much to overcome. Shortly after the election, I introduced myself to the Yale chaplain, William Sloane Coffin. He knew Dad from their time together at Yale, and I thought he might offer a word of comfort. Instead, he told me that my father had been "beaten by a better man."

His words were a harsh blow for an eighteen-year-old kid. When the story was reported in the newspapers more than thirty years later, Coffin sent me a letter saying he was sorry for the remark, if he had made it. I accepted his apology. But his self-righteous attitude was a foretaste of the vitriol that would emanate from many college professors during my presidency.

Yale was a place where I felt free to discover and follow my passions. My wide range of course selections included Astronomy, City Planning, Prehistoric Archaeology, Masterpieces of Spanish Literature, and, still one of my favorites, Japanese Haiku. I also took a political science course, Mass Communication, which focused on the "content and impact of the mass media." I ended up with a 70, which might explain my shaky relations with the media over the years.

My passion was history, which became my major. I enjoyed listening to the lectures of professors like John Morton Blum, Gaddis Smith, and Henry Turner. One of my first history courses focused on the French Revolution. "My business is the past," Professor Stanley Mellon liked to say. He gave gripping accounts of the Tennis Court Oath, the terror of Robespierre, and the rise of Napoleon. I was appalled by the way the ideas that inspired the Revolution were cast aside when all power was concentrated in the hands of a few.

One of my most memorable courses was History of the Soviet Union, taught by an East German lecturer named Wolfgang Leonhard. Mr. Leonhard had fled Nazi Germany as a boy and grown up in the Soviet Union, where his mother was arrested during Stalin's purges. He was groomed to be a communist official, but he defected to the West. In his thick German accent, he described the show trials, mass arrests, and widespread deprivations. After listening to him, I never thought about the Soviet Union or the communist movement the same way. The class was an introduction to the struggle between tyranny and freedom, a battle that has held my attention for the rest of my life.

My senior year, I took a course called The History and Practice of American Oratory, taught by Professor Rollin G. Osterweis. We read famous American speeches, from the fiery sermons of colonial preacher Jonathan Edwards to President Roosevelt's "Day of Infamy" address after Pearl Harbor. I was struck by the power of words to shape history. I wrote a paper analyzing Georgia journalist Henry W. Grady's speech on the New South and drafted four minutes of remarks nominating Red Sox star Carl Yastrzemski for mayor of Boston. Professor Osterweis taught us how to structure a speech: introduction, three main points, peroration, and conclusion. I've remembered his model all my life, which, as it turned out, has included quite a few speeches.

None of this is to suggest I was a particularly noteworthy student. I think it's fair to say I got more out of the experience than my professors did. John Morton Blum was once asked what he remembered about his famous student George W. Bush. He replied, "I haven't the foggiest recollection of him." But I remember Professor Blum.

———

Graduation came at a tumultuous time. Martin Luther King, Jr., had been assassinated in April of my senior year. Race riots followed in Chicago and Washington, D.C. Then, a few days before commencement, my friends and I were driving back from a trip to upstate New York when we heard on the radio that Bobby Kennedy had been killed. Nobody in the car said a word. There was a sense that everything was coming unglued.

For most of our time at Yale, civil rights dominated the campus discussion. By our senior year, another issue weighed on our minds. The war in Vietnam was escalating, and President Johnson had instituted a draft. We had two options: join the military or find a way to escape the draft. My decision was easy. I was going to serve. I was raised by a dad who had sacrificed for his country. I would have been ashamed to avoid duty.

My attitude toward the war was skeptical but accepting. I was skeptical of the strategy and the people in the Johnson administration executing it. But I accepted the stated goal of the war: to stop the spread of communism. One day in the fall of my senior year, I walked by a recruiting station with a poster of a jet pilot in the window. Flying planes would be an exciting way to serve. I checked in with the recruiter and picked up an application.

When I went home for Christmas, I told my parents about my interest in the Air Force. Dad referred me to a man named Sid Adger, a former pilot who was well connected in the aviation community. He suggested that I consider joining the Texas Air National Guard, which had pilot slots available. Unlike members of the regular Guard, pilots were required to complete a year of training, six months of specialized instruction, and then regular flying to keep up their status.

Serving as a Guard pilot appealed to me. I would learn a new skill. If called, I would fly in combat. If not, I would have flexibility to do other things. At that point in my life, I was not looking for a career. I viewed my first decade after college as a time to explore. I didn't want anchors to hold me down. If something caught my attention, I would try it. If not, I would move on.

This was the approach I had taken to summer jobs. In 1963, I worked on a cattle ranch in Arizona. The foreman was a grizzled fellow named Thurman. He had a saying about well-educated folks he knew: "Book smart, sidewalk stupid." I was determined not to let that phrase apply to me. I spent other summers working on an offshore oil rig in Louisiana, behind the trading desk of a stockbrokerage house, and as a sporting goods salesman at a Sears, Roebuck. I met some fascinating characters along the way: cowboys and Cajuns, roughnecks and roustabouts. I've always felt I received two educations in those years: one from fine schools, and one from solid people.

In the fall of 1968, I reported to Moody Air Force Base in Georgia for pilot training. We started with about one hundred trainees and graduated with about fifty. The washouts were early and frequent. I remember one guy from New York who came back from his first flight in a Cessna 172 looking as green as his flight suit—except for the part on which he had spilled his lunch.

My early experiences in the air were only slightly better. My instructor could smell insecurity, and he did not believe in quiet counseling. On one of my first flights, he suddenly grabbed the yoke, pulled back as hard as he could, and stalled the aircraft. The nose went up, and the plane shuddered. He then shoved the stick forward, and down went the nose. The plane recovered. The trainer had shown me my first stall recovery maneuver. He looked at me and said, "Boy, if you want to be a pilot, you must control this machine and not let it control you."

I took his advice seriously. I mastered the basics of flying, including loops, barrel rolls, and instruments. When Dad came to pin on my wings, I felt a tremendous sense of accomplishment. After flight school, I moved to Houston, where I learned to fly a fighter jet called the F-102 at Ellington Air Force Base. The F-102 was a single-seat, single-engine air interceptor. When you taxied to the end of the runway, put the throttle in afterburner, and felt the engine kick in, it didn't matter who you were or where you came from, you had better pay attention to the moment.

I loved flying, but by 1972, I was getting restless. I was logging my flight hours during the evening or on weekends, and working during the days at an agribusiness. My duties at the office included conducting a study of the mushroom industry in Pennsylvania and visiting plant nurseries that the company had acquired. It was not exactly captivating work.

One day, I got a call from my friend Jimmy Allison, a Midland political operative who had run Dad's successful campaign for the U.S. House of Representatives in 1966. He told me about an opportunity on Red Blount's campaign for the U.S. Senate in Alabama. It sounded interesting, and I was ready to move.

My commanding officer, Lieutenant Colonel Jerry Killian, approved my transfer to Alabama on the understanding that I would put in my required hours there. I informed the Alabama Guard commanders that I would have to miss several meetings during the campaign. They told me I could make them up after the election, which I did. I didn't think much about it for another few decades.

Unfortunately, the record keeping was shoddy, and the documentation of my attendance was not clear. When I entered politics, opponents used the gaps in the system to claim I had not fulfilled my duty. In the late 1990s, I asked a trusted aide, Dan Bartlett, to dig through my records. They showed that I had fulfilled my responsibilities. In 2004, Dan discovered some dental records proving I had been examined at Dannelly Air National Guard Base in Montgomery, Alabama, during the time critics alleged I was absent. If my teeth were at the base, he wisecracked to the press, they could be pretty sure the rest of my body was, too.

I thought the issue was behind us. But as I was landing in Marine One on the South Lawn late one evening in September 2004, I saw Dan's silhouette in the Diplomatic Reception Room. As a general rule, when a senior adviser is waiting to meet the president's chopper, it is not to deliver good news. Dan handed me a piece of paper. It was a typewritten memo on National Guard stationery alleging that I had not performed up to standards in 1972. It was signed by my old commander, Jerry Killian. Dan told me CBS newsman Dan Rather was going to run a bombshell report on *60 Minutes* based on the document.

Bartlett asked if I remembered the memo. I told him I had no recollection of it and asked him to check it out. The next morning, Dan walked into the Oval Office looking relieved. He told me there were indications that the document had been forged. The typeface came from a modern computer font that didn't exist in the early 1970s. Within a few days, the evidence was conclusive: The memo was phony.

I was amazed and disgusted. Dan Rather had aired a report influencing a presidential election based on a fake document. Before long, he was out of a job. So was his producer. After years of false allegations, the Guard questions finally began to abate.

I will always be proud of my time in the Guard. I learned a lot, made lifelong friends, and was honored to wear our country's uniform. I admire and respect those who deployed to Vietnam. Nearly sixty thousand of them never came home. My service was nothing compared to theirs.

—

In 1970, Dad decided to run for the Senate again. We felt good about his chances in a rematch against Ralph Yarborough. But Senator Yarborough had become so unpopular that he lost his primary to Lloyd Bentsen, a conservative Democrat. Dad ran a good race, but again came up short. The lesson was that it was still very tough to get elected as a Republican in Texas.

Soon there was another lesson. Defeat, while painful, is not always the end. Shortly after the 1970 election, President Richard Nixon made Dad ambassador to the United Nations. Then, in 1973, President Nixon asked Dad to head the Republican National Committee. It turned out to be a valuable lesson in crisis management when Dad guided the party through the Watergate scandal.

Mother and Dad were in the White House the day President Nixon resigned and Gerald Ford took the oath of office. Soon after, President Ford offered Dad his pick of ambassadorships in London or Paris, traditionally the two most coveted diplomatic posts. Dad told him he would rather go to China, and he and Mother spent fourteen fascinating months in Beijing. They came home when President Ford asked Dad to head the Central Intelligence Agency. Not a bad run for a twice-defeated Senate candidate. And of course it didn't end there.

I admired Dad's accomplishments. Since my teenage years, I had followed his path closely—Andover and Yale, then service as a military pilot. As I got older, I had an important realization: Nobody was asking me to match Dad's record, and I didn't need to try. We were in completely different situations. By age thirty, he had fought in a war, married, fathered three children, and lost one of them to cancer. When I left the Guard in my late twenties, I had no serious responsibilities. I was spontaneous and curious, searching for adventure. My goal was to establish my own identity and make my own way.

For their part, my parents recognized my buoyant spirit and did not dampen it. They did tell me when I got out of line. One of the sternest conversations I ever had with Dad came when I was twenty years old. I was home from college for the summer and roustabouting on an oil rig for Circle Drilling out of Lake Charles, Louisiana. I worked one week on, one week off. After a lot of hot, hard work, I decided to blow off my last week to spend time with my girlfriend in Houston.

Dad called me into his office. I told him nonchalantly that I had decided to quit my job a week early. He told me the company had hired me in good faith, and I had agreed to work until a certain date. I had a contract and I had violated it. I sat there feeling worse and worse. When he ended with the words "Son, I am disappointed," I was ashamed.

A few hours later, the phone rang at the house. It was Dad. I worried I was going to get another lecture. Instead, he asked, "What are you doing tonight, George?" He told me he had tickets to the Houston Astros game, and he invited me and my girlfriend. I immediately accepted. The experience reinforced the importance of honoring my word. And it showed me the depth of my father's love.

Dad was serious when needed, but our household was full of laughter. Dad loved to tell jokes to us kids: "Have you heard the one about the airplane? Never mind, it's over your head." He came up with nicknames for family and friends. At one point he called me Juney, short for Junior. My brother Neil was known as Whitey, which morphed into Whitney, because of his blond hair. Dad's dear friend James Baker became Bake. In his crowning achievement, Dad dubbed Mother the Silver Fox.

Dad's wonderful sense of humor continued throughout his life. When he was president, he created the Scowcroft Award—named for National Security Adviser Brent Scowcroft—for staff members who fell asleep during meetings. Now, in his eighties, he shares jokes via email, rating each on a scale of one through ten. A few years ago, Dad was recovering from hip surgery at the Mayo Clinic. When the nurse came to check on him, he asked, "Are my testicles black?" She was taken aback. "Excuse me, Mr. President?" He repeated his question, "Are my testicles black?" As she reached for the sheet, he quipped, "I said, 'Are my test results back?'" His medical team roared with laughter.

Over the years there has been a lot of speculation about my relationship with Dad. I suppose that's natural for the first father-and-son presidents in 172 years. The simple truth is that I adore him. Throughout my life I have respected him, admired him, and been grateful for his love. There is an infamous story about me driving home late one night, running over the neighbor's trash can, and then smarting off to Dad. When some people picture that scene, they envision two presidents locked in some epic psychological showdown. In reality, I was a boozy kid, and he was an understandably irritated father. We didn't think much about it until it came up in the newspapers twenty years later.

Moments like these are a reminder that I am not just my father's son. I have a feisty and irreverent streak courtesy of Barbara Bush. Sometimes I went out of my way to demonstrate my independence. But I never stopped loving my family. I think they understood that, even when I got on their nerves.

I finally saw things from my parents' perspective when I had children of my own. My daughter Jenna could be sassy and sharp, just like me. When I was running for governor in 1994, I accidentally shot a killdeer, a protected songbird, on the first day of dove hunting season. The blunder produced headlines but quickly faded. A few weeks before the election, Laura and I campaigned with the girls at the Texas State Fair in Dallas. Twelve-year-old Jenna won a stuffed bird as a prize at a carnival game. With the TV cameras rolling, she held the plush animal in the air. "Look, Dad," she said, giggling. "It's a killdeer!"

In the fall of 1972, I went to visit my grandmother in Florida. My college friend Mike Brooks was in the area, and we played golf. Mike had just graduated from Harvard Business School. He told me I should consider going there. To make sure I got the message, he mailed me an application. I was intrigued enough to fill it out. A few months later, I was accepted.

I wasn't sure I wanted to go back to school or to the East Coast. I shared my doubts with my brother Jeb. I didn't know Jeb very well when he was growing up—he was only eight when I moved out for boarding school—but we grew closer as we got older.

Jeb was always more serious-minded than I was. He was intelligent, focused, and driven in every way. He learned to speak fluent Spanish, majored in Latin American Affairs, and graduated Phi Beta Kappa from the

University of Texas. During his senior year in high school, he lived in Mexico as part of a student exchange program. There he met a beautiful woman named Columba Garnica. They were both young, but it was obvious Jeb was in love. When we went to the Astrodome together, I'd watch the ball game and he'd write letters to Colu. They got married two weeks after his twenty-first birthday.

One night, Jeb and I were having dinner with Dad at a restaurant in Houston. I was working at a mentoring program in Houston's poverty-stricken Third Ward, and Dad and I were having a discussion about my future. Jeb blurted out, "George got into Harvard."

After some thought, Dad said, "Son, you ought to seriously consider going. It would be a good way to broaden your horizons." That was all he said. But he got me thinking. Broadening horizons was exactly what I was trying to do during those years. It was another way of saying, "Push yourself to realize your God-given talents."

For the second time in my life, I made the move from Houston to Massachusetts. The cabdriver pulled up to the Harvard campus and welcomed me to "the West Point of capitalism." I had gone to Andover by expectation and Yale by tradition; I was at Harvard by choice. There I learned the mechanics of finance, accounting, and economics. I came away with a better understanding of management, particularly the importance of setting clear goals for an organization, delegating tasks, and holding people to account. I also gained the confidence to pursue my entrepreneurial urge.

The lessons of Harvard Business School were reinforced by an unlikely source: a trip to visit Mother and Dad in China after graduation. The contrast was vivid. I had gone from the West Point of capitalism to the eastern outpost of communism, from a republic of individual choice to a country where people all wore the same gray clothes. While riding my bike through the streets of Beijing, I occasionally saw a black limo with tinted windows that belonged to one of the party bigwigs. Otherwise there were few cars and no signs of a free market. I was amazed to see how a country with such a rich history could be so bleak.

In 1975, China was emerging from the Cultural Revolution, its government's effort to purify and revitalize society. Communist officials had set up indoctrination programs, broadcast propaganda over omnipresent loudspeakers, and sought to stamp out any evidence of China's ancient history. Mobs of young people lashed out against their elders and attacked the intellectual elite. The society was divided against itself and cascading into anarchy.

China's experience reminded me of the French and Russian revolutions. The pattern was the same: People seized control by promising to promote certain ideals. Once they had consolidated power, they abused it, casting aside their beliefs and brutalizing their fellow citizens. It was as if mankind had a sickness that it kept inflicting on itself. The sobering thought deepened my conviction that freedom—economic, political, and religious—is the only fair and productive way of governing a society.

---

For most of my time at Harvard, I had no idea how I was going to use my business degree. I knew what I did not want to do. I had no desire to go to Wall Street. While I knew decent and admirable people who had worked on Wall Street, including my grandfather Prescott Bush, I was suspicious of the financial industry. I used to tell friends that Wall Street is the kind of place where they will buy you or sell you, but they don't really give a hoot about you so long as they can make money off you.

I was searching for options when my Harvard classmate Del Marting invited me to spend spring break of 1975 at his family's ranch in Tucson, Arizona. On the way out west, I decided to make a stop in Midland. I'd heard from my friend Jimmy Allison, who had become publisher of the *Midland Reporter-Telegram*, that the place was booming. He was right. The energy industry was on the upswing after the 1973 Arab oil embargo. The barriers to entry in the industry were low. I loved the idea of starting a business of my own. I made up my mind: I was headed back to Texas.

I pulled into town in the fall of 1975 with all my possessions loaded into my 1970 Oldsmobile Cutlass. I had a lot to learn, so I sought out mentors. One of the first people I visited was a local lawyer named Boyd Laughlin, affectionately known as Loophole. He set up a meeting with Buzz Mills, a big man with a crew cut and years of experience in the oil business. I found Buzz and his partner, a cigar-chomping man named Ralph Way, playing gin rummy. I couldn't tell how much money they were betting on the game, but it was a hell of a lot more than I had.

Behind their friendly country demeanor was a shrewd understanding of the oil business. I told Buzz and Ralph that I wanted to learn to be a land man. The job of a land man is to travel to county courthouses and research who owns the mineral rights to potential drilling sites. The keys to success in the job are a willingness to read lots of paperwork, a sharp eye for detail, and a reliable car. I started by tagging along with seasoned land men, who showed me how to read title books. Then I made trips on my own, checking courthouse records for day fees. Eventually I bought a few royalties and small working interests in Buzz and Ralph's wells. Compared to the big-time oilmen, I was collecting the crumbs. But I was making a decent living and learning a lot.

I held down costs by living lean. I rented a five-hundred-square-foot alley house that friends described as "a toxic waste dump." One corner of my bed was held together with a necktie. I didn't have a washing machine, so I took my laundry over to Don and Susie Evans's place. Susie and I had known each other since grade school. She married Don, a Houston native with two degrees from the University of Texas, and they moved to Midland to break into the oil business. Don was a down-to-earth, humble guy with a great sense of humor. We ran together, played golf, and forged a lifelong friendship.

In the spring of 1976, Don and another close friend, a Midland orthopedic surgeon named Charlie Younger, suggested I join them for a Willie Nelson concert in Odessa. Of course, we needed a little libation to prepare for the event. We bought hip bottles of bourbon and had a few slugs on the way. When we got to the Ector County Coliseum, we were reminded that no drinking was allowed. We took a couple more gulps, discarded the bottles, and went to our seats.

Charlie decided we needed more alcohol to enjoy the experience fully. To our amazement, he was able to convince a stagehand that Willie Nelson needed some beer. The guy dutifully went out and bought the beer with Charlie's money. Charlie left one case for Willie and snuck one back to us. We hunched over in our seats and drank like thirst-ravaged wanderers. After we had each downed several bottles, Charlie suggested we head up to the stage to thank his new friend. Don wisely stayed behind. Not me.

Over the noise of the band, I heard people yelling my name. A group of Midlanders in the front of the crowd had recognized Charlie and me.

They were shouting for beer. We accommodated them. When the concert ended, Charlie stuffed several longneck bottles under his shirt. As the three of us were walking out, the longnecks slipped and exploded on the floor, one after another. It was as if we had set off an alarm for the authorities. Our steady stride turned into a sprint for the exits, three bozos running for our reputations.

The next day, dozens of folks in Midland told me they had seen me onstage with Willie. There was no editorial commentary until one old boy said I looked like a fool up there. He was right.

—————

I spent Labor Day weekend 1976 at our family's house in Kennebunkport, Maine. That Saturday night, I was at a bar with my sister Doro, Dad's longtime political aide Pete Roussel, and two family friends, Australian tennis star John Newcombe and his wife, Angie. John introduced me to the Aussie tradition of drinking beer with no hands. You put your teeth on the edge of the mug and tilt your head back, and the beer goes down your throat. We had a great old time, until the drive home.

A local policeman, Calvin Bridges, thought it was odd that I was going about ten miles an hour and had two wheels on the shoulder. When I failed the straight-line walk, he took me off to the station. I was guilty and told the authorities so.

I was also embarrassed. I had made a serious mistake. I was fortunate I hadn't done any harm to my passengers, other drivers, or myself. I paid a $150 fine and did not drive in Maine for the proscribed period. The case was closed. Or so I thought.

—————

That fall, I started thinking seriously about settling down. The DUI was part of it, but the feeling had been building for months. My rootless ways were getting a little old. So was I. The big 3-0 had come in the summer. I had pledged that I would spend my first ten years after college experiencing a lot and not getting tied down. That was a promise I had kept. But the decade was almost up.

Back home in Midland in July 1977, my old friend Joe O'Neill invited me over for a burger. I rarely turned down homemade meals. They sure beat the fast food that tended to be my staple. Joe and his wife, Jan, had someone they wanted me to meet: one of Jan's best friends, Laura Welch. I arrived a little late. There in the backyard were Jan and Laura, who was wearing a blue sundress.

She was gorgeous. She had stunning blue eyes and moved so gracefully. She was intelligent and dignified, with a warm and easy laugh. If there is love at first sight, this was it.

Laura and I discovered that we had grown up near each other in Midland and both attended seventh grade at San Jacinto Junior High. We had even lived in the same apartment complex in Houston. She lived on the quiet side, where people sat by the pool and read books. I lived on the side where people played water volleyball till late at night. No wonder our paths had never crossed.

I called Laura the next day, and we agreed to meet again that night. I asked if she wanted to play putt-putt golf. I knew she was my kind of girl when she agreed. Her short game was a little shaky, but she was a lot of fun to be around. My favorable impressions from the previous evening were strengthened. There was only one bad part. Laura had to go back to Austin, where she was a school librarian at Dawson Elementary. I missed her immediately and started visiting her there as often as I could.

We were a perfect match. I'm a talker; Laura is a listener. I am restless; she is calm. I can get a little carried away; she is practical and down-to-earth. Above all, she is genuine and natural. There is no phoniness about her. Her appeal was immediate and constant. In August, I went to visit my family in Kennebunkport, planning to stay for a week. After one night, I flew back to Texas to be with Laura.

A few weeks after we met, Laura introduced me to her parents, Harold and Jenna Welch. Her mom, a kind, sweet, and patient woman, always made me feel welcome. Her dad loved sports and enjoyed putting down a wager or two on football. His hangout was Johnny's Barbecue. The locals called it the Sick Pig because of the awful wooden pig on top of the restaurant. One day Laura's dad introduced me to his friends at the Sick Pig, including Johnny himself. I think I passed muster, because I was offered a screwdriver. I turned it down. It was nine o'clock in the morning.

The courtship moved fast. One weekend Laura and I took a trip to Anne and Tobin Armstrong's ranch in South Texas. Anne was a former U.S. ambassador to Great Britain, and she and Tobin had invited Prince Charles to play polo. Another weekend we visited John and Angie Newcombe at his tennis academy in New Braunfels, in the beautiful Texas Hill Country. This time I kept my hands on the beer mug and off the steering wheel. I was falling hard for Laura. I was not much of a cat person, but I knew our relationship was solid when I bonded with her black-and-white shorthair, Dewey, named for the decimal system.

I've never been afraid to make a decision, and in late September I made a big one. One night in Laura's small Austin rental house, I said, "Let's get married." She said yes right away. Ours had been a whirlwind romance, but we were ready to commit.

Soon after the engagement, Laura and I traveled to Houston, where Jeb and Columba were celebrating the christening of their daughter, Noelle. I introduced Laura to the family. They were as smitten with her as I had been. Laura knew she would be joining a large, competitive family, and that suited her just fine. As an only child, she got a kick out of the boisterous Bush clan.

Our parents checked their schedules, and we picked the first Saturday available, November 5, 1977. We had a small wedding with family and close friends in Midland. The invitations were handwritten by Laura's mom. We had no ushers, no bridesmaids, and no groomsmen. It was just me, Laura, and her dad to walk her down the aisle.

While I couldn't pinpoint it at the time, I believe there is a reason Laura and I never met all those years before. God brought her into my life at just the right time, when I was ready to settle down and was open to having a partner at my side. Thankfully, I had the good sense to recognize it. It was the best decision of my life.

———

Shortly after we got married, Laura and I decided to have children. After a couple of years of trying, it was not happening as easily as we had hoped. We discussed, reflected, prayed, and made the decision to adopt. At first I was uneasy about parenting someone else's child. But the more

I looked into adoption, the more comfortable I became. We had friends who had adopted and loved their children as a precious blessing. And we were fortunate to know about a wonderful agency called the Edna Gladney Home in Fort Worth.

Founded by a Methodist missionary in 1887, Gladney had become one of the premier adoption homes in the world. Laura and I were introduced by phone to the longtime director, Ruby Lee Piester. She invited us to tour the hospital, where we met some of the pregnant women who were near term. I was touched by their selfless decision to bring their children into the world and give them to couples like us.

The application process took several months. First, there was the initial interview, which included a lengthy questionnaire. Fortunately, we passed. In the next stage, Gladney planned to send a representative for a home visit. Laura and I were preparing meticulously. Then, in early 1981, she stunned me with the news that she thought she was pregnant.

Some weeks later we scheduled a trip to a sonogram expert in Houston, a lovely Indian American woman named Srini Malini. I was nervous as she guided the device over Laura's body. She looked at the video monitor and said, "Here is the head, and here is the body. It's a girl!" She moved to get a better angle. Suddenly she shouted, "I see two babies, two beautiful babies! This one is a girl as well. You are going to be the parents of twins." My eyes filled with tears. It was a double blessing. I started calling the sonogram image our first family photo.

When we called the Gladney director to deliver the news, we felt strangely guilty, as if we had been leading her on. She told Laura something so sweet: "Honey, this happens sometimes. Gladney can help a couple have a child one way or another." Ruby Lee was more right than she knew. On the original questionnaire, Laura had checked the box saying we would prefer to adopt twins.

The doctors had warned us that twins can be a high-risk pregnancy. Laura refused to decorate the nursery out of superstition. About seven months into the pregnancy, Laura was diagnosed with preeclampsia, a serious condition that could damage her kidneys and jeopardize the health of the girls. The day after we received this news, Laura checked into Baylor Hospital in Dallas, where her uncle was a surgeon. The doctors told Laura that she should begin bed rest.

I knew Laura had the best possible care, but I was worried. I remembered Mother's miscarriage. I had seen my parents after Robin died. I knew how much it hurt to lose a child. I confessed my anxiety to Laura. I'll never forget her reaction. She looked at me with her blue eyes and said, "George, I am going to bring these girls into the world. They will be born healthy." I marveled at my wife's strength. This quiet, unassuming woman was one tough soul.

Two weeks later, I was in my office in Midland—I had been shuttling back and forth to Dallas—when I got a call from Dr. James Boyd. He was in charge of Laura's care, and he was not big on chitchat. "George," he said, "you are having your children tomorrow. I will deliver them at six in the morning." I asked about Laura's health. He said she would be okay. "What about the girls?" He said, "They will be five weeks premature. They will be fine. But the time to move is now." I called Laura to tell her how thrilled I was. Then I called her parents in Midland, my parents in Washington, a bunch of our friends—and, of course, the airlines.

I've been to some exciting events in my life—presidential inaugurations, speeches in front of huge crowds, throwing out the first pitch at Yankee Stadium—but there was nothing like the moment those girls were born. Laura was in bed and sedated. I stroked her head. Before long, the doctor held up a tiny red body. The baby screamed, and the doctor proclaimed her healthy. A nurse cleaned her and gave her to me. Little Barbara. And then the same for Jenna. We wanted our girls to carry the names of two fine women, so we named them after our mothers.

I had thought about those girls for so long that I could barely believe they were in my arms. It was the day before Thanksgiving 1981. And thankful is exactly how I felt. I was thankful to God for their lives, thankful to the skilled medical team for their excellent care, and thankful to Laura for her determination to carry our girls long enough that they could be born healthy.

Holding Barbara and Jenna for the first time was a moment of incredible clarity. I had been given a blessing and a responsibility. I vowed to be the best father I could possibly be.

Those early months provided a wakeup call. The girls would cry in the middle of the night. I would pick them up, one in each arm, and walk around the house. I wanted to sing them a lullaby, but I didn't really know any. Instead, I usually went with the Yale fight song "Bulldog Bulldog, Bow Wow Wow." That would calm them down, maybe just because they didn't want to hear me sing anymore. Whatever the reason, it worked. I would lay them in their cribs and go back to Laura as one happy dad.

———

As Laura and I were adjusting to life with our new family, I was running a new business. In 1979, I started a small energy exploration company in Midland. I raised money, mostly from the East Coast, to finance drilling in low-risk, low-return oil and gas wells. I made some respectable finds, including some that are still producing. I also drilled my fair share of dry holes. Running a small business taught me a lot, especially that market conditions can change quickly, so you'd better be prepared for the unexpected.

As oil prices softened in 1983, I decided to merge my operations with two entrepreneurs from Cincinnati, Bill DeWitt and Mercer Reynolds. I would be the eyes and ears on the ground in Texas, and they would raise funds back east. The business did well for a couple of years, and we became close friends. But in early 1986, the price of oil plummeted from twenty-six dollars to ten dollars a barrel. A lot of people I knew had borrowed heavily and were now in dire financial jeopardy. Fortunately, we had kept our debt low, and we were able to merge our business into a larger publicly traded company, Harken Energy.

The mid-1980s were gloomy years in Midland. There was a sense of anxiety, and many were searching for purpose. Religion had always been part of my life, but I really wasn't a believer. I was baptized in Yale's nondenominational Dwight Hall Chapel. When I was young my parents took me to First Presbyterian in Midland, St. Martin's Episcopal in Houston, and St. Ann's Episcopal in Kennebunkport.

I went to church at Andover because it was mandatory. I never went at Yale. I did go when I visited my parents, but my primary mission was to avoid irritating Mother. Laura and I were married at First United Methodist in Midland. We started going regularly after the girls were born, because we felt a responsibility to expose them to faith. I liked spending time with friends in the congregation. I enjoyed the opportunity for reflection. Once in a while, I heard a sermon that inspired me. I read the Bible occasionally and saw it as a kind of self-improvement course. I knew I could use some self-improvement. But for the most part, religion was more of a tradition than a spiritual experience. I was listening but not hearing.

In the summer of 1985, we took our annual trip to Maine. Mother and Dad had invited the great evangelical preacher Billy Graham. Dad had asked him to answer some questions from the family after dinner. That was typical of Dad, always willing to share. It would have sent a signal of importance to have had Billy to himself, but that is not George H.W. Bush. He is a generous man, devoid of a big ego. So there we sat, about thirty of us—Laura, my grandmother, brothers and sister, first and second cousins—in the large room at the end of the house on Walker's Point.

The first question was from Dad. He said, "Billy, some people say you have to have a born-again experience to go to heaven. Mother [my grandmother] here is the most religious, kind person I know, yet she has had no born-again experience. Will she go to heaven?" Wow, pretty profound question from the old man. We all looked at Billy. In his quiet, strong voice, he replied, "George, some of us require a born-again experience to understand God, and some of us are born Christians. It sounds as if your mom was just born a Christian."

I was captivated by Billy. He had a powerful presence, full of kindness and grace, and a keen mind. The next day, he asked me to go for a walk around the property. He asked about my life in Texas. I talked to him about the girls and shared my thought that reading the Bible could make me a better person. In his gentle, loving way, Billy began to deepen my shallow understanding of faith. There's nothing wrong with using the Bible as a guide to self-improvement, he said. Jesus' life provides a powerful example for our own. But self-improvement is not really the point of the Bible. The center of Christianity is not the self. It is Christ.

Billy explained that we are all sinners, and that we cannot earn God's love through good deeds. He made clear that the path to salvation is through the grace of God. And the way to find that grace is to embrace Christ as the risen Lord—the son of a God so powerful and loving that He gave His only son to conquer death and defeat sin.

These were profound concepts, and I did not fully grasp them that day. But Billy had planted a seed. His thoughtful explanation had made the soil less firm and the brambles less thick.

Shortly after we got back to Texas, a package from Billy arrived. It was a copy of *The Living Bible*. He had inscribed: "To my friend George W. Bush, May God bless you and Laura always." He included a reference to Philippians 1:6: "And I am certain that God, who began the good work within you, will continue His work until it is finally finished on the day when Christ Jesus returns."

In the early fall, I mentioned my conversation with Billy to Don Evans. He told me he and another Midland friend, Don Jones, had been attending a community Bible study. It met Wednesday nights at First Presbyterian Church. I decided to give it a shot.

Each week, we studied a chapter from the New Testament. At first I was a little skeptical. I had a hard time resisting the temptation to wisecrack. One night the group leader asked, "What is a prophet?" I answered, "That's when revenue exceeds expenses. No one has seen one around here since Elijah."

Soon I started to take the sessions more seriously. As I read the Bible, I was moved by the stories of Jesus' kindness to suffering strangers, His healing of the blind and crippled, and His ultimate act of sacrificial love when He was nailed to the cross. For Christmas that year, Don Evans gave me a Daily Bible, a version split into 365 individual readings. I read it every morning and prayed to understand it more clearly. In time, my faith began to grow.

At first I was troubled by my doubts. The notion of a living God was a big leap, especially for someone with a logical mind like mine. Surrendering yourself to an Almighty is a challenge to the ego. But I came to realize that struggles and doubts are natural parts of faith. If you haven't doubted, you probably haven't thought very hard about what you believe.

Ultimately, faith is a walk—a journey toward greater understanding. It is not possible to prove God's existence, but that cannot be the standard for belief. After all, it is equally impossible to prove He doesn't exist. In the end, whether you believe or don't believe, your position is based on faith.

That realization freed me to recognize signs of God's presence. I saw the beauty of nature, the wonder of my little girls, the abiding love of Laura and my parents, and the freedom that comes with forgiveness—all what the preacher Timothy Keller calls "clues of God." I moved ahead more confidently on my walk. Prayer was the nourishment that sustained me. As I deepened my understanding of Christ, I came closer to my original goal of being a better person—not because I was racking up points on the positive side of the heavenly ledger, but because I was moved by God's love.

———

I realized something else. When Billy started answering questions that night in Maine, I was on my third glass of wine, after a couple of beers before dinner. Billy's message had overpowered the booze. But that was not always the case. I had long been a social drinker. I liked to drink with friends, with meals, at sporting events, and at parties. By my mid-thirties, I was drinking routinely, with an occasional bender thrown in.

We had a saying in West Texas: "Last night he thought he was a ten, when in fact he was an ass." That applied to me more than once. I like to joke around, but alcohol has a way of turning a quip or tease into a slash or insult. What seems funny with booze can sound so stupid later. One summer night we were having dinner in Maine after a great day of fishing and golf. I had worked up a thirst, which I quenched with multiple bourbon and Sevens. As we were eating, I turned to a beautiful friend of Mother and Dad's and asked a boozy question: "So, what is sex like after fifty?"

Everyone at the table looked silently at their food—except for my parents and Laura, who glared at me with disbelief. The lovely woman let out a nervous laugh, and the conversation moved on. When I woke up the next day, I was reminded of what I had said. I instantly felt that morning-after remorse. After I called the woman to apologize, I started asking myself if this was really the way I wanted to lead my life. Years later, when I turned fifty, the good-natured woman sent a note to the Texas Governor's Mansion: "Well, George, how is it?"

Laura saw a pattern developing, too. What seemed hilarious or clever to my friends and me was repetitive and childish to her. She wasn't afraid to tell me what she thought, but she couldn't quit for me. I had to do that on my own. At age forty, I finally found the strength to do it—a strength that came from love I had felt from my earliest days, and from faith that I didn't fully discover for many years.

I haven't had a drop of alcohol since that night at The Broadmoor in 1986. There's no way to know where my life would have headed if I hadn't made the decision to quit drinking. But I am certain that I would not be recording these thoughts as a former governor of Texas and president of the United States.

I've been asked if I consider myself an alcoholic. I can't say for sure. I do know that I have a habitual personality. I was drinking too much, and it was starting to create problems. My ability to quit cold leads me to believe that I didn't have a chemical addiction. Some drinkers are not as fortunate as I was. I admire those who use other methods to quit, such as the twelve-step process of Alcoholics Anonymous.

I could not have quit drinking without faith. I also don't think my faith would be as strong if I hadn't quit drinking. I believe God helped open my eyes, which were closing because of booze. For that reason, I've always felt a special connection to the words of "Amazing Grace," my favorite hymn: "I once was lost, but now am found / was blind, but now I see."

# 2

# RUNNING

The morning of June 12, 1999, was beautiful in Texas. The Rangers were in first place in the American League West. The Dow Jones Industrial Average stood at 10,490. Dad had just celebrated his seventy-fifth birthday by parachuting out of an airplane—successfully. And I was about to make a leap of my own.

After months of soul-searching and countless hours weighing the pros and cons, I was headed to Iowa, site of the first caucus in the 2000 presidential election. I was free from the anxiety of making the decision and eager to begin the journey. Laura and I kissed the girls goodbye, headed to the airport, and boarded a TWA charter bound for Cedar Rapids.

The flight was packed, mostly with journalists. They had filled hours of television and reams of newsprint debating, questioning, and analyzing whether I would run. Now they were going to get the answer. I decided to have a little fun with them. I had christened our plane *Great Expectations*. Shortly after we lifted off, I grabbed the microphone and announced, "This is your candidate. Please stow your expectations securely in the overhead bins, as they may shift during the trip and may fall and hurt someone—especially me."

I often use humor to defuse tension, but I knew I was embarking on a serious undertaking. More than almost any other candidate in history, I understood what running for president would entail. I had watched Dad endure grueling months on the campaign trail, under the constant scrutiny of a skeptical press. I had seen his record distorted, his character attacked, his appearance mocked. I had witnessed friends turn against him and aides abandon him. I knew how hard it was to win. And I knew how much it hurt to lose.

I worried most about our seventeen-year-old daughters, Barbara and

Jenna. I had learned that being the child of a politician is tougher than being a politician yourself. I understood the pain and frustration that comes with hearing your dad called nasty names. I knew how it felt to worry every time you turned on the TV. And I knew what it was like to live with the thought that any innocent slip could embarrass the president of the United States. I had gone through all of this in my forties. If I became president, my girls would be in college when I took office. I could only imagine how much more difficult it would be for them.

I had thought through some big questions. Was I willing to forgo my anonymity forever? Was it right to subject my family to the scrutiny of a national campaign? Could I handle the embarrassment of defeat with the whole country watching? Was I really up to the job?

I believed I knew the answers, but there was no way to be sure.

I did know that I felt a calling to run. I was concerned about the future of the country, and I had a clear vision of where to lead it. I wanted to cut taxes, raise standards in public schools, reform Social Security and Medicare, rally faith-based charities, and lift the sights of the American people by encouraging a new era of personal responsibility. As I said in my speeches, "When I put my hand on the Bible, I will swear to not only uphold the laws of our land, I will swear to uphold the honor and dignity of the office to which I have been elected, so help me God."

My exposure to the presidency had revealed the potential of the job. The two presidents I knew best, Dad and Ronald Reagan, had used their time in office to accomplish historic objectives. President Reagan had challenged the Soviet Union and helped win the Cold War. Dad had liberated Kuwait and guided Europe toward unity and peace.

I had also seen the personal side of the presidency. For all the scrutiny and stress, Dad loved the job. He left office with his honor and values intact. Despite the many pressures, the intensity of the experience brought our family closer together.

The decision process was all-consuming. I thought about it, talked about it, analyzed it, and prayed about it. I had a philosophy I wanted to advance, and I was convinced I could build a team worthy of the presidency. I had the financial security to provide for my family, win or lose. Ultimately, the decisive factors were less tangible. I felt a drive to do more with my life, to push my potential and test my skills at the highest level.

I had been inspired by the example of service my father and grandfather had set. I had watched Dad climb into the biggest arena and succeed. I wanted to find out if I had what it took to join him.

Even if I lost, I would still have a wonderful life. My family loved me. I would be governor of a great state. And I would never have to wonder what might have been. "When my time is up," I would tell friends, "my dance card is going to be full."

My announcement came at a barbecue in the small Iowa town of Amana. I gave my speech in a barn, atop a stage covered with hay in front of a giant cornfield. Congressman Jim Nussle, who would later serve as my Office of Management and Budget director, introduced me by singing "Iowa Stubborn" from *The Music Man*. With Laura at my side, I said, "I'm running for president of the United States. There's no turning back, and I intend to be the next president."

—————

My path to that day was unconventional. I hadn't spent a lifetime planning to run for president. If I had, I probably would have done a few things differently when I was younger. Yet along the journey, I built up the desire and skills to wage and win a presidential campaign. The seeds of that decision, like many others in my life, were planted in the dusty ground beneath the boundless sky of Midland, Texas.

Politics in Midland were conservative. West Texas has an independent spirit and distrust of centralized government. Like much of Texas, Midland had been dominated by the Democratic Party for generations. Midland's sprawling congressional district, which included seventeen counties, had been represented by a Democrat named George Mahon for forty-three years. He was the longest-serving congressman in America. On July 6, 1977—my thirty-first birthday—he announced that he would retire at the end of his term.

By then I had been back in Midland for two years after business school. I was learning the oil business, reconnecting with friends, and generally enjoying life. I was also getting a feel for the political scene.

While I had never considered politics as a profession, I had helped out in all of Dad's campaigns: his Senate race in 1964, his House campaign in 1966, and his second bid for the Senate in 1970. Before I started flight training in 1968, I spent several months as a traveling aide to Congressman Edward Gurney, who was running for the Senate in Florida. The highlight of the experience was a huge rally in Jacksonville where Gurney was endorsed by the tall, tan governor of California, Ronald Reagan. In 1972, I was the political director for Red Blount's Senate campaign in Alabama. In 1976, I volunteered on President Ford's West Texas operation in the Republican primary. I helped him win a total of zero delegates.

The campaign lifestyle was a perfect fit for me in my twenties. I enjoyed moving around and meeting new people. I thrived on the intensity and competition of the races. I liked the finality that came on election day, when the voters picked a winner and we all moved on. I hadn't planned it this way, but by the time Congressman Mahon retired, I was a relatively seasoned political operative.

I started to think about running for the seat. I had the experience to handle the political side of the race. I also felt something stronger pulling me in. I was concerned about the direction of the country. My experiences in business school, China, and the oil business were converging into a set of convictions: The free market provided the fairest way to allocate resources. Lower taxes rewarded hard work and encouraged risk taking, which spurred job creation. Eliminating barriers to trade created new export markets for American producers and more choices for our consumers. Government should respect its constitutional limits and give people the freedom to live their lives.

When I looked at Washington under President Jimmy Carter and the Democratic Congress, I saw the opposite. They had plans to raise taxes, tighten government control over the energy sector, and substitute federal spending for private-sector job creation. I worried about America drifting left, toward a version of welfare-state Europe, where central government planning crowded out free enterprise. I wanted to do something about it. I was having my first experience with the political bug, and it was biting hard.

When I told Mother and Dad about my idea, they were surprised. My decision must have seemed like it had come out of nowhere, but they didn't want to dampen my enthusiasm. Dad asked if I would be willing to listen to advice from a friend of his, former Texas Governor Allan Shivers. "Absolutely," I said. Shivers was a legend. He had been the longest-serving governor in Texas history. He was a conservative Democrat, and his advice would be valuable in a race against Kent Hance, a right-of-center state senator and the likely Democratic nominee.

When I went to see the old governor, he asked me point-blank if I was running for Mr. Mahon's seat. I said I was seriously considering the race. He looked me in the eye and said, "Son, you can't win." There was no encouragement, no nothing. He told me that the district was drawn perfectly to elect Kent Hance. I mumbled something like "I hope you are wrong if I decide to run," and thanked him for his time.

I remember wondering why Dad had introduced me to the governor. Looking back on it, it may have been his way of telling me, without smothering my ambition, that I should be prepared to lose.

The first phase of the campaign was the Republican primary. I made it into a runoff against Jim Reese, a smooth-talking former sportscaster and mayor of Odessa. He had run against George Mahon in 1976 and felt entitled to the nomination in 1978. He was very unhappy that I had outpolled him in the first round of the primary.

Reese had a hard edge, and so did some of his supporters. Their strategy was to paint me as a liberal, out-of-touch carpetbagger. They threw out all kinds of conspiracy theories. Dad was part of a trilateral commission campaign to establish a one-world government. I had been sent by the Rockefeller family to buy up farmland. Four days before the election, Reese produced a copy of my birth certificate to *prove* I had been born back east. How was I supposed to counter that? I responded with a line Dad had once used: "No, I wasn't born in Texas, because I wanted to be close to my mother that day."

Reese received an endorsement and campaign contributions from Ronald Reagan, who was seeking an edge on Dad in the 1980 presidential primary. Despite all the innuendos, I was optimistic about my chances. My strategy was to build up a bulkhead in my home county of Midland. Laura and I attended coffees across town, organized the county block by block, and persuaded friends who had never been involved in politics to help us.* On election night, our grassroots effort in Midland produced a massive turnout. I lost every other county in the district, but took Midland by such a huge margin that I won the nomination.

Dad had predicted that Reagan would call to congratulate me if I won the primary. He did, the next day. He was gracious and volunteered to help in the general election. I was grateful for his call and bore no hard feelings. But I was determined to run the race as my own man. I didn't do any campaigning with Reagan, nor did I do any with Dad.

The race against Reese toughened me as a candidate. I learned I could take a hard punch, keep fighting, and win. My opponent in the general was Kent Hance, the state senator Governor Shivers had warned me about. Hance's strategy was the same as Reese's—turn me into an East Coast outsider—but he executed it with more subtlety and charm.

One of my first TV ads showed me jogging, which I thought emphasized my energy and youth. Hance turned it against me with one line: "The only time folks around here go running is when somebody's chasing 'em."

He also ran a radio ad: "In 1961, when Kent Hance graduated from Dimmitt High School in the Nineteenth Congressional District, his opponent, George W. Bush, was attending Andover Academy in Massachusetts. In 1965, when Kent Hance graduated from Texas Tech, his opponent was at Yale University. And while Kent Hance graduated from University of Texas Law School, his opponent . . . get this, folks . . . was attending Harvard. We don't need someone from the Northeast telling us what our problems are."

Hance was a great storyteller, and he used his skill to pound away with the outsider theme. His favorite story was about a man in a limo who pulled up to a farm where Hance was working. When the driver asked him for directions to the next town, Hance said, "Turn right just past the cattle guard, then follow the road." The punch line came when the driver asked, "Excuse me, but what color uniform will that cattle guard be wearing?" The West Texas crowds loved it. Hance would twist

*Don Evans was the campaign chairman; Joe O'Neill was the treasurer; Robert McCleskey handled the accounting.

the knife by adding, "I couldn't tell if the limo had Massachusetts or Connecticut license plates."

Laura and I moved temporarily to Lubbock, the biggest city in the district, about 115 miles north of Midland. An important hub for the cotton business, Lubbock was home to Texas Tech University. We used the city as our base to campaign in the district's rural counties. Laura and I spent hours in the car together, stumping in towns like Levelland, Plainview, and Brownfield. For someone who didn't particularly care for politics, Laura was a natural campaigner. Her genuineness made it easy for voters to relate to her. After our wedding, we had taken a short trip to Cozumel, Mexico, but we joked that the campaign was our honeymoon.

On the Fourth of July, we campaigned in Muleshoe, in the far northern part of the district. In the May primary, I had received 6 of the 230 votes cast in Bailey County. The way I saw it, I had plenty of room for improvement. Laura and I smiled and waved at the spectators from the back of our white pickup truck. Nobody cheered. Nobody even waved. People looked at us like we were aliens. By the end I was convinced the only supporter I had in Muleshoe was the one sitting next to me.

Election night came, and it turned out that old Governor Shivers was right. I won big in Midland County and in the southern part of the district, but not by enough to offset Hance's margins in Lubbock and elsewhere. The final tally was 53 percent to 47 percent.

I hated losing, but I was glad I'd run. I enjoyed the hard work of politics, meeting people and making my case. I learned that allowing your opponent to define you is one of the biggest mistakes you can make in a campaign. And I discovered that I could accept defeat and move on. That was not easy for someone as competitive as I am. But it was an important part of my maturing.

As for Congressman Kent Hance, he deserved to win that race, and we became good friends. Two gubernatorial and presidential victories later, he is still the only politician ever to beat me. He went on to serve three terms in the House before losing a bid for the Senate. Then he became a Republican and contributed to my campaigns. Kent is now the chancellor of Texas Tech. He says that without him, I would never have become president. He's probably right.

Six months after my campaign ended, I had another race to think about. Dad announced his candidacy for the 1980 presidential election. He was a long shot against Ronald Reagan, but he ran a strong campaign in Iowa and won an upset victory in the caucus. Unfortunately, his hot streak ran out amid the cold winters of New Hampshire. Reagan defeated him there and continued on to the Republican nomination.

There was a lot of speculation about whom Reagan would choose for vice president. At the convention in Detroit, he was in discussions with Gerald Ford about some sort of co-presidency. They agreed it wouldn't work—a good decision. Then Reagan called Dad and asked him to be his running mate—an even better decision.

On election night, the Reagan-Bush ticket crushed Jimmy Carter and Walter Mondale 489 to 49 in the Electoral College. Laura and I flew to Washington for the Inauguration on January 20, 1981, the first time the ceremony was held on the majestic west front of the Capitol. We beamed as Justice Potter Stewart swore in Dad. Then Ronald Reagan repeated the oath administered by Chief Justice Warren Burger.

As a history major, I was thrilled to have a front-row seat. As a son, I was filled with pride. It never crossed my mind that I would one day stand on that platform and hold up my right hand at two presidential inaugurations.

The early 1980s brought tough moments, from a painful recession to the bombing of our Marine barracks in Lebanon, but the Reagan-Bush administration accomplished what it had promised. They cut taxes, regained the edge in the Cold War, and restored American morale. When President Reagan and Dad put their record before the voters in 1984, they won forty-nine of fifty states.

Dad was the logical favorite for the 1988 presidential nomination, but the race would not be easy. He had been so loyal to President Reagan that he had done almost nothing to promote himself. He was also battling the infamous Van Buren factor. Not since Martin Van Buren followed Andrew Jackson into the White House in 1836 had a vice president been elected to succeed the president with whom he had served.

Early in his second term, President Reagan generously allowed Dad to use the presidential retreat at Camp David for a meeting with his campaign team. It was thoughtful of Dad to invite all his siblings and children. I enjoyed meeting his team, although I had some reservations. Dad's top strategist was a young guy named Lee Atwater. A fast-talking, guitar-playing South Carolinian, Lee was considered one of the country's hottest political consultants. No question he was smart. No doubt he had experience. I wanted to know if he was loyal.

When Dad asked if any of the family members had questions, my hand went up. "Lee, how do we know we can trust you, since your business partners are working for other candidates?" I asked. Jeb chimed in: "If someone throws a grenade at our dad, we expect you to jump on it." Our tone was tough, but it reflected our love of Dad and our expectations of his staff—an agenda that put the candidate first and personal ambition second.

Lee said he had known Dad at the Republican National Committee, admired him a lot, and wanted him to win. He added that he was planning to sever his conflicting business connections. Yet it was obvious that our doubts had shaken him. Later in the day, he sought out Jeb and me. If we were so worried, he asked, why didn't one of us move to D.C., help in the campaign, and keep an eye on him and the staff?

The invitation intrigued me. The timing was right. After the downturn in the oil markets, my partners and I had merged our exploration company and found jobs for all the employees. Dad liked the idea, and Laura was willing to give it a try.

At the campaign office in downtown Washington, I had no title. As Dad put it, I already had a good one: son. I focused on fundraising, traveling the country to deliver surrogate speeches, and boosting the morale of volunteers by thanking them on Dad's behalf. From time to time, I also reminded some high-level staffers that they were on a team to advance George Bush's election, not their own careers. I learned a valuable lesson about Washington: Proximity to power is empowerment. Having Dad's ear made me effective.

One of my tasks was to sort through journalists' requests for profile pieces. When Margaret Warner of *Newsweek* told us she wanted to do an interview, I recommended that we cooperate. Margaret was talented and seemed willing to write a fair piece. Dad agreed.

Mother called me the morning the magazine hit the newsstands. "Have you seen *Newsweek*?" Not yet, I told her. "They called your father a wimp!" she growled.

I quickly tracked down a copy and was greeted by the screaming headline: "Fighting the Wimp Factor." I couldn't believe it. The magazine was insinuating that my father, a World War II bomber pilot, was a wimp. I was red-hot. I got Margaret on the phone. She politely asked what I thought of the story. I impolitely told her I thought she was part of a political ambush. She muttered something about her editors being responsible for the cover. I did not mutter. I railed about editors and hung up. From then on, I was suspicious of political journalists and their unseen editors.

After finishing third in Iowa, Dad rallied with a victory in New Hampshire and went on to earn the nomination. His opponent in the general election was the liberal governor of Massachusetts, Michael Dukakis. Dad started the campaign with a great speech at the convention in New Orleans. I was amazed at the power of his words, elegantly written and forcefully delivered. He spoke of a "kinder, gentler" nation, built by the compassion and generosity of the American people—what he called "a thousand points of light." He outlined a strong policy agenda, including a bold pledge: "Read my lips, no new taxes."

I was impressed with Dad's sense of timing. He had managed to navigate perfectly the transition from loyal vice president to candidate. He left the convention leading the polls and charged down the home stretch. On November 8, 1988, the family watched the returns at our friend Dr. Charles Neblett's house in Houston. I knew Dad had won when Ohio and New Jersey, two critical states, broke his way. By the end of the night, he had carried forty states and 426 electoral votes. George H.W. Bush, the man I admired and adored, was elected the forty-first president of the United States.

———

Laura and I enjoyed our year and a half in Washington. But when people suggested that I stay in Washington and leverage my contacts, I never considered it. I had zero interest in being a lobbyist or hanger-on in

Dad's administration. Not long after the election, we packed up for the trip back to Texas.

I had another reason for moving home. Near the end of Dad's campaign, I received an intriguing phone call from my former business partner Bill DeWitt. Bill's father had owned the Cincinnati Reds and was well connected in the baseball community. He had heard that Eddie Chiles, the principal owner of the Texas Rangers, was looking to sell the team. Would I be interested in buying? I almost jumped out of my chair. Owning a baseball team would be a dream come true. I was determined to make it happen.

My strategy was to make myself the buyer of choice. Laura and I moved to Dallas, and I visited Eddie and his wife Fran frequently. I promised to be a good steward of the franchise he loved. He said, "You've got a great name and a lot of potential. I'd love to sell to you, son, but you don't have any money."

I went to work lining up potential investors, mostly friends across the country. When Commissioner Peter Ueberroth argued that we needed more local owners, I went to see a highly successful Fort Worth investor, Richard Rainwater. I had courted Richard before and he had turned me down. This time he was receptive. Richard agreed to raise half the money for the franchise, so long as I raised the other half and agreed to make his friend Rusty Rose co-managing partner.

I went to meet Rusty at Brook Hollow Golf Club in Dallas. He seemed like a shy guy. He had never followed baseball, but he was great with finances. We talked about him being the inside guy who dealt with the numbers, and me being the outside guy who dealt with the public.

Shortly thereafter, Laura and I were at a black-tie charity function. Our plans for the team had leaked out, and a casual acquaintance pulled me aside and whispered: "Do you know that Rusty Rose is crazy? You'd better watch out." At first I blew this off as mindless chatter. Then I fretted. What did "crazy" mean?

I called Richard and told him what I had heard. He suggested that I ask Rusty myself. That would be a little awkward. I barely knew the guy, and I was supposed to question his mental stability? I saw Rusty at a meeting that afternoon. As soon as I entered the conference room, he walked over to me and said, "I understand you have a problem with my mental state. I see a shrink. I have been sick. What of it?"

It turns out Rusty was not crazy. This was his awkward way of laying out the truth, which was that he suffered from a chemical imbalance that, if not properly treated, could drive his bright mind toward anxiety. I felt so small. I apologized.

Rusty and I went on to build a great friendship. He helped me to understand how depression, an illness I later learned had also afflicted Mother for a time in her life, could be managed with proper care. Two decades later in the Oval Office, I stood with Senators Pete Domenici and Ted Kennedy and signed a bill mandating that insurance companies cover treatment for patients with mental illness. As I did, I thought of my friend Rusty Rose.

With Rusty and Richard as part of our ownership group, we were approved to buy the team.* Eddie Chiles suggested that he introduce us to the fans as the new owners on Opening Day 1989. We walked out of the dugout, across the lush green grass, and onto the pitcher's mound, where we joined Eddie and legendary Dallas Cowboys coach Tom Landry, who threw out the first pitch. I turned to Rusty and said, "This is as good as it gets."

Over the next five seasons, Laura and I went to fifty or sixty ball games a year. We saw a lot of wins, endured our fair share of losses, and enjoyed countless hours side by side. We took the girls to spring training and brought them to the park as much as possible. I traveled throughout the Rangers' market, delivering speeches to sell tickets and talking up the ball club with local media. Over time, I grew more comfortable behind the lectern. I learned how to connect with a crowd and convey a clear message. I also gained valuable experience handling tough questions from journalists, in this case mostly about our shaky pitching rotation.

Running the Rangers sharpened my management skills. Rusty and I spent our time on the major financial and strategic issues, and left the

*I am particularly grateful to Commissioner Peter Ueberroth, American League President Bobby Brown, and Jerry Reinsdorf of the Chicago White Sox for their help in navigating the buying process.

baseball decisions to baseball men. When people did not perform, we made changes. It wasn't easy to ask decent folks like Bobby Valentine, a dynamic manager who had become a friend of mine, to move on. But I tried to deliver the news in a thoughtful way, and Bobby handled it like a professional. I was grateful when, years later, I heard him say, "I voted for George W. Bush, even though he fired me."

When Rusty and I took over, the Rangers had finished with a losing record seven of the previous nine years. The club posted a winning record four of our first five seasons. The improvements on the field brought more people to the stands. Still, the economics of baseball were tough for a small-market team. We never asked the ownership group for more capital, but we never distributed cash, either.

Rusty and I realized the best way to increase the long-term value of the franchise was to upgrade our stadium. The Rangers were a major league team playing in a minor league ballpark. We designed a public-private financing system to fund the construction of a new stadium. I had no objection to a temporary sales tax increase to pay for the park, so long as local citizens had a chance to vote on it. They passed it by a margin of nearly two to one.

Thanks to the leadership of Tom Schieffer—a former Democratic state representative who did such a fine job overseeing the stadium project that I later asked him to serve as ambassador to Australia and Japan—the beautiful new ballpark was ready for Opening Day 1994. Over the following years, millions of Texans came to watch games at the new venue. It was a great feeling of accomplishment to know that I had been part of the management team that made it possible. By then, though, a pennant race wasn't the only kind I had on my mind.

---

Shortly after we bought the Rangers in 1989, the campaign for the 1990 Texas gubernatorial election began. Several friends in politics suggested I run. I was flattered but never considered it seriously.

Most of my political involvement focused on Dad. Within months of taking office as president, he was confronted with seismic shifts in the world. With almost no warning, the Berlin Wall came down in November 1989. I admired the way Dad managed the situation. He knew grandstanding could needlessly provoke the Soviets, who needed time and space to make the transition out of communism peacefully.

Thanks to Dad's steady diplomacy at the end of the Cold War—and his strong responses to aggression in Panama and Iraq—the country had tremendous trust in George Bush's foreign policy judgment. But I was worried about the economy, which had started to slow in 1989. By 1990, I feared a recession could be coming. I liquidated my meager holdings and paid off the loan I had taken out to buy my share of the Rangers. I hoped any downturn would end quickly, for the country and for Dad.

Meanwhile, Dad had to decide whether to stand for reelection. "Son, I'm not so sure I ought to run again," he told me as we were fishing together in Maine in the summer of 1991.

"Really?" I asked. "Why?"

"I feel responsible for what happened to Neil," he said.

My brother Neil had served on the board of Silverado, a failed savings and loan in Colorado. Dad believed Neil had been subjected to harsh press attacks because he was the president's son. I felt awful for Neil, and I could understand Dad's anguish. But the country needed George Bush's leadership. I was relieved when Dad told the family he had one last race in him.

The reelection effort got off to a bad start. The first lesson in electoral politics is to consolidate your base. But in 1992, Dad's base was eroding. The primary reason was his reneging on his vow not to raise taxes—the infamous "Read my lips" line from his 1988 convention speech. Dad had accepted a tax increase from the Democratic Congress in return for reining in spending. While his decision benefited the budget, he had made a political mistake.

Pat Buchanan, the far-right commentator, challenged Dad in the New Hampshire primary and came away with 37 percent—a serious protest vote. To make matters worse, Texas billionaire Ross Perot decided to mount a third-party campaign. He preyed on disillusioned conservatives with his anti-deficit, anti-trade rhetoric. One of Perot's campaign centers was across the street from my office in Dallas. Looking out the window was like watching a daily tracking poll. Cadillacs and SUVs lined up to collect Perot bumper stickers and yard signs. I realized Dad would have to fight a two-front battle for reelection, with Perot on one flank and the Democratic nominee on the other.

By the spring of 1992, it was clear who that nominee would be, Governor Bill Clinton of Arkansas. Clinton was twenty-two years younger than Dad—and six weeks younger than me. The campaign marked the beginning of a generational shift in American politics. Up to that point, every president since Franklin Roosevelt had served during World War II, either in the military or as commander in chief. By 1992, Baby Boomers and those younger made up a huge portion of the electorate. They were naturally drawn to support someone of their own generation. Clinton was smart enough to steer away from Dad's strengths in foreign policy. He recognized the economic anxiety in the country and ran on a disciplined message: "It's the economy, stupid."

I stayed in close touch with Dad throughout the election year. By the early summer of 1992, the campaign hadn't gained traction. I told Dad he ought to think about a bold move to shake up the dynamics of the race. One possibility was to replace Vice President Dan Quayle, whom I liked and respected, with a new running mate. I suggested to Dad that he consider Secretary of Defense Dick Cheney. Dick was smart, serious, experienced, and tough. He had done a superb job overseeing the military during the liberation of Panama and the Gulf War. Dad said no. He thought the move would look desperate and embarrass Dan. In retrospect, I don't think Dad would have done better with someone else as his running mate. But I never completely gave up on my idea of a Bush-Cheney ticket.

One change Dad did make was to bring Secretary of State James Baker back to the White House as chief of staff. The campaign ran more smoothly with Baker at the helm. Voters began to focus on Bush versus Clinton. The polls narrowed. Then, four days before the election, Lawrence Walsh, the prosecutor investigating the Iran-Contra scandal of the Reagan administration, dropped an indictment on former defense secretary Caspar Weinberger. The indictment dominated the news and halted the campaign's momentum. Democratic lawyer Robert Bennett, who represented Cap, later called the indictment "one of the greatest abuses of prosecutorial power I have ever encountered." So much for the independence of the independent counsel.

In the final days before the election, my brother Marvin suggested that I campaign with Dad to help keep his spirits high. I agreed to do it, although I was not in the most upbeat mood. I was especially irritated with the press corps, which I thought was cheerleading for Bill Clinton. At one of the final campaign stops, two reporters from the press pool approached me near the steps of Air Force One. They asked about the atmosphere on the plane. The politically astute response would have been some banality like "He feels this hill can be climbed." Instead, I unleashed. I told the reporters I thought their stories were biased. My tone was harsh, and I was rude. It was not my only angry blurt of the campaign. I had developed a reputation in the press corps as a hothead, and I deserved it. What the press did not understand was that my outbursts were driven by love, not politics.

Election night came, and Dad did not win. Bill Clinton won 43.0 percent of the vote. Dad ended up with 37.4 percent. Ross Perot took 18.9 percent, including millions of votes that otherwise would have gone for George Bush. Dad handled the defeat with characteristic grace. He called early in the evening to congratulate Bill, laying the foundation for one of the more unlikely friendships in American political history.

Dad had been raised to be a good sport. He blamed no one; he was not bitter. But I knew he was hurting. The whole thing was a miserable experience. Watching a good man lose made 1992 one of the worst years of my life.

The morning after the election, Mother said, "Well, now, that's behind us. It's time to move on." Fortunately for me, baseball season was never too far away. In the meantime, I trained for the Houston marathon, which I ran on January 24, 1993—four days after Dad left office. I was holding my 8:33-per-mile pace when I passed Mother and Dad's church around mile 19. The 9:30 a.m. service had just ended, and my family was gathered on the curb. I had a little extra spring in my step for the gallery. Dad encouraged me in his typical way. "That's my boy!" he yelled. Mother had a different approach. She shouted, "Keep moving, George! There are some fat people ahead of you!" I finished in three hours, forty-four minutes. I felt ten years younger at the finish line and ten years older the next day.

Just as I had once run to rid my body of alcohol, the marathon helped purge the disappointment I felt about 1992. As the pain began to fade, a new feeling replaced it: the itch to run for office again.

It started gradually. When Laura and I moved back to Texas in 1988, I became more aware of the challenges facing the state. Our education system was in trouble. Children who couldn't read or do math were shuffled through the system without anyone bothering to ask what, or if, they had learned.

The legal climate in our state was a national joke. Texas personal injury lawyers were ringing up huge jury verdicts and driving jobs out of the state. Juvenile crime was growing. And I worried about a culture of "if it feels good, do it" and "if you've got a problem, blame somebody else."

The dividends of that approach were troubling. More babies were being born out of wedlock. More fathers were abdicating their responsibilities. Dependence on welfare was replacing the incentive to work.

My experiences on Dad's campaigns and running the Rangers had sharpened my political, management, and communications skills. Marriage and family had broadened my perspective. And Dad was now out of politics. My initial disappointment at his loss gave way to a sense of liberation. I could lay out my policies without having to defend his. I wouldn't have to worry that my decisions would disrupt his presidency. I was free to run on my own.

I wasn't the only one in the family who reached that conclusion. In the spring of 1993, Jeb told me he was seriously considering running for governor of Florida. In an ironic way, Dad's defeat was responsible for both our opportunities. What had first seemed like the sad end to a great story now looked like the unlikely beginning of two new careers. Had Dad won in 1992, I doubt I would have run for office in 1994, and I almost certainly would not have become president.

The big question was how to get involved. I asked for advice from a close friend, political strategist Karl Rove. I first met Karl in 1973, when Dad was chairman of the Republican National Committee and Karl was the head of the College Republicans. I assumed he would be another one

of the campus politician types who had turned me off at Yale. I soon
recognized that Karl was different. He wasn't smug or self-righteous, and
he sure wasn't the typical suave campaign operator. Karl was like a political mad scientist—intellectual, funny, and overflowing with energy and
ideas.

Nobody I know has read or absorbed more history than Karl. I say
that with confidence because I've tried to keep up. A few years ago, Karl
and I squared off in a book reading contest. I jumped out to an early
lead. Then Karl accused me of gaining an unfair advantage by selecting
shorter works. From that point forward, we measured not only the number of books read, but also their page count and total lateral area. By the
end of the year, my friend had dusted me in all categories.*

Karl didn't just amass knowledge, he used it. He had studied William
McKinley's 1896 election strategy. In 1999, he suggested that I organize a
similar front-porch campaign. It turned out to be a wise and effective approach. I regretted not working with Karl during my congressional run in
1978. I never made that mistake again.

In 1993, Karl and I both saw a political opportunity. The conventional
wisdom was that Texas Governor Ann Richards was guaranteed reelection the next November. Texas's first woman governor since the 1930s,
Ann Richards was a political pioneer. She had a large following among
national Democrats and, many believed, a chance to be president or vice
president someday.

Everyone said the governor was popular, but Karl and I didn't think
she had actually accomplished much. Karl told me his analysis showed
that many Texans—even some Democrats—would be open to a candidate with a serious program to improve the state. That was exactly what
I had in mind.

In a spring 1993 special election, Governor Richards placed a school
funding measure on the ballot. Derisively dubbed "Robin Hood," her plan
redistributed money from rich districts to poor ones. The voters defeated
it by a healthy margin. As Laura and I watched election returns that night,
we listened to an interview by Ann Richards. She was frustrated by the

---

*The final tally was 110 to 95 in books, 40,347 to 37,343 in pages, and 2,275,297 to 2,032,083 in
total square inches.

defeat of the school funding measure and said sarcastically, "We are all, boy, eagerly awaiting any suggestions and ideas that are realistic."

I turned to Laura and said, "I have a suggestion. I might run for governor." She looked at me like I was crazy. "Are you joking?" she asked. I told her I was serious. "But we have such a great life," she said. "You're right," I replied. We were very comfortable in Dallas. I loved my job with the Rangers. Our girls were thriving. Yet I had the political bug again, and we both knew it.

—————

When I brought up the governor's race, I always heard the same thing: "Ann Richards sure is popular." I asked some of Dad's former political strategists for advice. They politely suggested that I wait a few years. When I made up my mind that I was running, Mother's response was to the point: "George," she said, "you can't win."

The good news was that the Republican field was wide open. Nobody wanted to challenge Richards, so I could immediately turn my attention to the general election. I took a methodical approach, laying out a specific, optimistic vision for the state. I focused on four policy issues: education, juvenile justice, welfare reform, and tort reform.

We assembled a skilled and able campaign team.* I made two particularly important hires. First was Joe Allbaugh, an imposing six-foot-four man with a flattop and the bearing of a drill sergeant, who had served as chief of staff to Oklahoma Governor Henry Bellmon. I brought Joe in to run the campaign, and he did a superb job of managing the organization.

We also hired a new communications director, Karen Hughes. I had first met Karen at the state party convention in 1990. "I will be briefing you on your duties," she said crisply. She then delivered my marching orders. There was no doubt this woman was in charge. When she told me her father was a two-star general, it made perfect sense.

---

*The team included my friend Jim Francis as chairman; Don Evans as finance director; Karl Rove as the top strategist; Stanford-educated lawyer Vance McMahon as policy director; former Texas Association of School Boards official Margaret LaMontagne as political director; Dan Bartlett, a recent University of Texas graduate, on the communications team; and Israel Hernandez, a hardworking UT grad who took pressure off Laura and me, as traveling aide.

I stayed in touch with Karen after the convention. She had a warm, outgoing personality and a great laugh. As a former TV correspondent, she knew the media and how to turn a phrase. It was a good sign when she came to hear my announcement speech in the fall of 1993. She was easy to spot because her son Robert was sitting on her shoulders. Karen was my kind of person—one who put family first. The day she signed on with the campaign was one of the best of my political career.

As my campaign started to generate excitement, the national news media got interested. Reporters knew my hothead reputation, and there was a running discussion about when I would finally explode. Ann Richards did her best to set me off. She called me "some jerk" and "shrub," but I refused to spark. Most people failed to understand that there was a big difference between Dad's campaigns and mine. As the son of the candidate, I would get emotional and defend George Bush at all costs. As the candidate myself, I understood that I had to be measured and disciplined. Voters don't want a leader who flails in anger and coarsens the tone of the debate. The best rebuttal to the barbs was to win the election.

In mid-October, Ann Richards and I met for our one televised debate. I had studied the briefing books and practiced during mock debates. A week before the big night, I imposed an advice blackout. I had witnessed some of Dad's debate preps. I knew the candidate could easily get overwhelmed with last-minute suggestions. My favorite old chestnut was "Just be yourself." No kidding. I ordered that all debate advice be filtered through Karen. If she thought it was essential, she would pass it on. Otherwise, I was keeping my mind clear and focused.

On debate night, Karen and I were in the elevator when Ann Richards entered. I shook her hand and said, "Good luck, Governor." In her toughest growl, she said, "This is going to be rough on you, boy."

It was the classic head game. But its effect was opposite to what she intended. If the governor was trying to scare me, I figured she must feel insecure. I gave her a big smile, and the debate went fine. I had seen enough politics to know you can't really win a debate. You can only lose by saying something stupid or looking tired or nervous. In this case, I was neither tired nor nervous. I made my case confidently and avoided any major gaffes.

As usual, the final weeks brought some surprises. Ross Perot weighed in on the race, endorsing Ann Richards. It didn't bother me. I've always thought that endorsements in politics are overrated. They rarely help, and sometimes they hurt. I told a reporter, "She can have Ross Perot. I'll take Nolan Ryan and Barbara Bush." I didn't add that Mother still didn't think I could win.

When the results came in on election night, I was elated. We had pulled off what the *Dallas Morning News* called "once unthinkable." The *New York Times* deemed it "a stunning upset." Dad called me at the Austin Marriott, where my supporters had congregated. "Congratulations, George, on a great win," he said, "but it looks like Jeb is going to lose."

I felt bad for my brother, who had worked so hard and deserved to win. But nothing could dim the thrill I felt as I went to the Marriott ballroom to deliver my victory speech.

———

Inauguration Day was January 17, 1995. As I was getting ready in the hotel room before the ceremony, Mother handed me an envelope. It contained a pair of cufflinks and a letter from Dad:

*Dear George,*

*These cufflinks are my most treasured possession. They were given to me by Mum and Dad on June 9, that day in 1943 when I got my Navy wings at Corpus Christi. I want you to have them now; for, in a sense, though you won your Air Force wings flying those jets, you are again "getting your wings" as you take the oath of office as our Governor.*

He wrote about how proud he was, and how I could always count on his and Mother's love. He concluded:

*You have given us more than we ever could have deserved. You have sacrificed for us. You have given us your unwavering loyalty and devotion. Now it is our turn.*

Dad is not the kind of guy who would say something like that in person. The handwritten note was his style, and his words meant a lot. That morning I felt a powerful connection to the family tradition of service that I was now continuing in my own way.

———

As governor, I didn't need time to plan my agenda. I had spent the last year telling everyone exactly what I wanted to accomplish. I have always believed that a campaign platform is not just something you use to get elected. It is a blueprint for what you do in office.

I had another reason to move fast. In Texas, the legislature meets only 140 days of every two years. My goal was to get all four of my policy initiatives through both houses in the first session.

To make that happen, I needed good relations with the legislature. That started with the lieutenant governor, who serves as president of the state senate, seats committees, and decides on the flow of bills. The lieutenant governor is elected separately from the governor, meaning it is possible for the two top officials to be from opposite parties—as Lieutenant Governor Bob Bullock and I were.

Bullock was a legend in Texas politics. He had served in the powerful post of state comptroller for sixteen years before his election as lieutenant governor in 1990. He ran the senate with a very strong hand. And he had former employees and friends embedded in agencies throughout the government, which allowed him to stay well informed. Bullock had the potential to make my life miserable. On the other hand, if I could persuade him to work with me, he would be an invaluable ally.

A few weeks before the election, Joe Allbaugh had suggested that I meet secretly with Bullock. I slipped away on a quiet afternoon and flew to Austin. Bullock's wife, Jan, opened the door. She is a pretty woman with a warm smile. Then Bullock emerged. He was a wiry man with a weathered look. He had been married five times to four women. Jan was his last wife and the love of his life. He had married her only once. At one time, Bullock had been a heavy drinker. In a famous story, he got drunk and fired his gun into a public urinal. He smoked incessantly, despite the fact that he had lost part of one lung. This was a man who had lived life the hard way. He stuck out his hand and said, "I'm Bullock. Come on in."

He took me into his study. The place looked like a research library. He had stacks of documents, reports, and data. Bullock dropped a huge file on the desk in front of me and said, "Here is a report on juvenile justice." He knew my campaign was based partially on juvenile justice reform and suggested I think about some of his ideas. Then he banged down similar reports for education and welfare reform. We talked for three or four hours. Bullock supported Ann Richards, but he made it clear he would work with me if I won.

The other key legislative player was the speaker of the house, Pete Laney. Like me, Pete came from West Texas. He was a cotton farmer from Hale Center, a rural town between Lubbock and Amarillo that I had visited in my 1978 campaign. Pete was a low-key guy. While Bullock tended to show his cards—and occasionally throw the whole deck at you—Laney kept his hand close to his vest. He was a Democrat with allies on both sides of the aisle.

Shortly after I took office, Pete, Bob, and I agreed to have a weekly breakfast. At first, the meals were a chance to swap stories and help me learn about the legislature. As bills started to wind their way through the system, the breakfasts became important strategy meetings. A couple of months into the session, Bullock had moved a number of important bills through the senate. Most of them were still waiting in the house.

Bullock wanted action, and he let Laney know it. As I ate my breakfast of pancakes, bacon, and coffee, Pete calmly told the lieutenant governor the bills would get done. Bullock was simmering. Before long, he boiled over. He looked straight at me and yelled, "Governor, I am going to f—— you. I am going to make you look like a fool."

I thought for a moment, stood up, walked toward Bullock, and said, "If you are going to f—— me, you better give me a kiss first." I playfully hugged him, but he wriggled away and charged out of the room. Laney and I just laughed. We both understood Bullock's tirade was not aimed at me. It was his way of telling Laney it was time to get his bills out of the house.

Whether Bullock's message had an impact on Laney, I'll never know.

But with all three of us pushing hard, legislation on education, juvenile justice, and welfare reform started moving quickly. The most complicated item on the agenda was tort reform. Reining in junk lawsuits was crucial to stopping jobs from leaving the state. But there was strong opposition from the trial lawyers' bar, which was influential and well funded. I had an ally in David Sibley, a Republican state senator from Waco and the committee chairman who oversaw the issue.

One night early in the session, I invited David over for dinner. We had just started to eat when he got a phone call from Bullock. I listened as a one-way conversation unfolded. David alternated between nodding and staring in stone-faced silence as the lieutenant governor unloaded. Then he said, "He is sitting right here. Would you like to speak to him?" Bullock wanted to have a word. I took the phone.

"Why are you blocking tort reform? I thought you were going to be okay. But no, you're a s—— governor." Bullock fired off a couple of f-bombs and hung up. David knew what had happened. He had seen it before and wasn't sure how I would respond. I laughed and laughed hard. Bullock was tough and earthy, but I had a feeling this would be a passing storm.

Once David realized that I would tolerate the blast, we turned to the tort reform bill. The main difference of opinion was on the size of the cap on punitive damages. I wanted a $500,000 cap; Bullock wanted $1,000,000. David told me that if he could get agreement on this legislation, the other five tort bills that were part of the reform package would move quickly. He suggested a compromise: How about a bill with a $750,000 threshold? No question that would improve the system. I agreed.

David called and told Bullock about the deal. This call was shorter, but once again ended with Sibley passing the phone to me. "Governor Bush," Bullock started in his formal way, "you're going to be one helluva governor. Good night."

———

In 1996, Laura surprised me with a fiftieth birthday party at the Governor's Mansion. She invited family and friends from Midland, Houston, and Dallas; classmates from Andover, Yale, and Harvard; and political folks from Austin, including Bullock and Laney. Laura wasn't the only one with a surprise in store. As the sun set, the toasts began. Bullock headed to the microphone. "Happy birthday," he said with a smile. "You are one helluva governor." He went on, "And Governor Bush, you will be the next president of the United States."

Bullock's prediction shocked me. I had been governor for only eighteen months. President Clinton was still in his first term. I had barely thought about my reelection in 1998. And here was Bullock bringing up 2000. I didn't take him too seriously; Bullock was always trying to provoke. But his comment inspired an interesting thought. Ten years earlier, I had been celebrating my fortieth birthday drunk at The Broadmoor. Now I was being toasted on the lawn of the Texas Governor's Mansion as the next president. This had been quite a decade.

Meanwhile, there was an actual presidential campaign going on. The Republican Party had nominated Senator Bob Dole, a World War II hero who had built a distinguished legislative record. I admired Senator Dole. I thought he would make a good president, and I campaigned hard for him in Texas. But I worried that our party had not recognized the generational politics lesson of 1992: Once voters had elected a president from the Baby Boomer generation, they were not likely to reach back. Sure enough, Senator Dole carried Texas, but President Clinton won reelection.

I went into 1998 feeling confident about my record. I had delivered on each of the four priorities I had laid out in my first gubernatorial campaign. We had also passed the largest tax cut in the history of Texas and made it easier for children in foster care to be adopted by loving families. Many of these laws were sponsored and supported by Democrats. I was honored when Bob Bullock, who had supported Democratic candidates for almost a half century, publicly endorsed my reelection. I was also a little surprised. Bullock was the godfather of one of my opponent's children.

I was determined not to take anything for granted, and I campaigned hard. On election night, I received more than 68 percent of the vote, including 49 percent of Hispanics, 27 percent of African Americans, and 70 percent of independents. I was the first Texas governor elected to consecutive four-year terms.

I also had my eye on another race that night. Jeb became governor of Florida by a convincing margin. I went to his inauguration in January

1999, making us the first pair of brothers to serve at the same time as governors since Nelson and Win Rockefeller more than a quarter century earlier. It was a wonderful moment for our family. It was also a time to think about the future. And I had a big question on my mind.

———

Running for president was a decision that evolved over time. Many urged me to run—some for the sake of the country, others because they hoped to ride the race to glory. I often heard the same comment: "You can win this race. You can be president." I was flattered by the confidence. But my decision would not turn on whether others thought I could win. After all, everyone told me I could never beat Ann Richards. The key question was whether I felt the call to run.

As I pondered the decision, there was a dilemma. Because of the size and complexity of a presidential campaign, you have to start planning early, even if you are not sure whether you want to run. I authorized Karl to start preparing paperwork and recruiting a network of people who would raise money and tend to the grassroots political operation. Once the process started, it created a sense of inevitability. In October 1998, I told *Washington Post* columnist David Broder that I felt like "a cork in a raging river." When I won reelection the next month, the rapids grew even stronger.

I was determined not to get swept away. If I was going to get into the race, I wanted it to be for the right reasons. I can't pinpoint exactly when I made up my mind, but there were moments of clarity along the way. One came during my second inauguration as governor. The morning of the ceremony, we attended a service at First United Methodist Church in downtown Austin. Laura and I had invited Reverend Mark Craig, our friend and pastor from Dallas, to deliver the sermon.

I tried hard to focus on the inauguration, but I couldn't. As we walked into the church, I told Mother I had been struggling with the decision of whether or not to run for president.

"George," she said, "get over it. Make up your mind, and move on." It was good advice, but not too helpful at the time.

Then Mark Craig struck. In his sermon, he spoke about the Book of Exodus, when God calls Moses to action. Moses' first response was disbelief: "Who am I, that I should go to Pharaoh and bring the Israelites out of Egypt?" He had every excuse in the book. He hadn't led a perfect life; he wasn't sure if people would follow him; he couldn't even speak that clearly. That sounded a little familiar.

Mark described God's reassurance that Moses would have the power to perform the task he had been called to do. Then Mark summoned the congregation to action. He declared that the country was starving for moral and ethical leadership. Like Moses, he concluded, "We have the opportunity, each and every one of us, to do the right thing, and for the right reason."

I wondered if this was the answer to my question. There were no mysterious voices whispering in my ears, just Mark Craig's high-pitched Texas twang coming from the pulpit. Then Mother leaned forward from her seat at the other end of the pew. She caught my eye and mouthed, "He is talking to you."

After the service, I felt different. The pressure evaporated. I felt a sense of calm.

———

Laura and I had been discussing the presidential race for eighteen months. She was my sounding board as I talked through the pros and cons. She didn't try to argue me out of the race, nor did she attempt to steer me in. She listened patiently and offered her opinions. I think she always sensed that I would run. As she put it, politics was the family business. Her goal was to make sure I made my decision for the right reasons, not because others were pushing me to run.

If she had objected, she would have told me so, and I would not have run. While she worried about the pressure I would feel as president, she shared my hopes for the country and had confidence I could lead. One night she just smiled at me and said, "I'm in."

Breaking the news to our daughters was more difficult. Barbara and Jenna were seventeen years old, with independent streaks that reminded me a lot of their dad. From the very beginning they had asked me not to run—sometimes joking, sometimes serious, often at the top of their lungs. One of their favorite lines was, "Dad, you're going to lose. You're not as cool as you think you are." Other times they asked, "Why do you want to ruin our lives?"

Those were tough words for a father to hear. I don't know if our daughters really thought I would lose, but I did know they did not want to give up their semi-private lives. One evening I asked Jenna to come out on the back porch of the Governor's Mansion. It was a beautiful Texas night, and the two of us sat and talked for a while. I told her, "I know you think that I'm ruining your life by running for president. But actually, your mom and I are *living* our lives—just like we raised you and Barbara to do."

She told me she had never thought of it that way. The notion of living life to the fullest appealed to her, just as it always had to me. She was not thrilled. But from that point on, I think she and Barbara understood.

Looking back on it a decade later, our daughters appreciated the opportunities that came with the presidency. They traveled with us on international trips, met fascinating and inspirational people like Václav Havel and Ellen Johnson Sirleaf, and learned about public service. Ultimately, Laura and I probably saw Barbara and Jenna more during the presidency than we would have if we had stayed in Texas.

One of our favorite places to spend time with the girls was Camp David. One weekend in the summer of 2007, Laura and I invited Jenna and her boyfriend, Henry Hager, a fine young man from Virginia she'd met on the 2004 campaign. At dinner Friday night, Henry mentioned that he'd like to talk to me the next day. "I'll be available at three o'clock in the presidential cabin," I said.

Henry arrived at the appointed time, clearly well prepared. "Mr. President, I love your daughter," he said, and then began a touching speech. After a couple of minutes, I cut him off. "Henry, the answer is yes, you've got my permission," I said. "Now let's go get Laura." The look on his face said, "Wait, I'm not done with my talking points!"

Laura was as thrilled as I was. Wisely, Henry also asked Barbara's permission. A few weeks later, at Acadia National Park in Maine, he proposed to Jenna. They were married at our ranch in Crawford in May 2008. We had an altar carved out of Texas limestone set on a peninsula in our lake, and our family friend Kirbyjon Caldwell—a wonderful pastor from Houston—officiated at a sunset ceremony. The bride was stunning. Laura and Barbara were radiant. It was one of the joys of my life to walk sweet Jenna down the aisle. After my eight years in the presidency, our family had emerged not only stronger, but bigger, too.

—

After I announced my candidacy in Iowa in June 1999, Laura and I went to Maine to visit Mother and Dad. I gave them an update on the campaign. Then the four of us walked out onto the lawn together. At our back was the beautiful Atlantic Ocean. In front of us was a large group of photographers. Mother got off one of her classic one-liners. She looked at the press corps and asked, "Where were you in '92?"

I laughed. I was amazed by this wonderful woman. She was responsible for so much good in my life. I turned to Dad. My mind went back to my early days spent looking at pictures of him in scrapbooks. Like those old photos, his face was worn. But his spirit was still strong. I told the press what I had known for a lifetime: It was a huge advantage to be the son of George and Barbara Bush. What a journey we had shared. Seven years earlier, Dad's final campaign had ended in defeat. Now I was standing proudly at his side, with a chance to become the forty-third president of the United States.

—

When I got back to Texas, my first stop was Bob and Jan Bullock's house. The years of abuse had taken their toll, and Bob's body was giving out. His skin was losing its color, he was bedridden, and he was wearing an oxygen mask. I gave him a gentle hug. He lifted his mask and picked up a copy of *Newsweek* from his bedside table. My photo was on the cover.

"How come you didn't smile?" he said. I laughed. It was vintage Bullock.

Then he caught me by surprise. "Governor," he said, "will you eulogize me at my funeral?"

He slipped his oxygen mask back on and closed his eyes. I told him about my visit to Iowa and my announcement speech at the barbecue. I'm not sure he heard a word I said. After our extraordinary run together, my unlikely friend and I would both be moving on.

# 3

# PERSONNEL

Dick's face was hard to read. He betrayed no emotion. He stared at the cows grazing under the broiling sun at our ranch in Crawford, Texas.

It was July 3, 2000. Ten weeks earlier, after securing the Republican presidential nomination, I had sent campaign manager Joe Allbaugh to visit Dick Cheney in Dallas. I asked him to find answers to two questions. First, was Dick interested in being a candidate for vice president? If not, was he willing to help me find a running mate?

Dick told Joe he was happy with his life and finished with politics. But he would be willing to lead the VP search committee.

As I expected, Dick did a meticulous, thorough job. In our first meeting, I laid out my top criteria for a running mate. I wanted someone with whom I was comfortable, someone willing to serve as part of a team, someone with the Washington experience that I lacked, and, most important, someone prepared to serve as president at any moment. Dick recruited a small team of lawyers and discreetly gathered reams of paperwork on potential candidates. By the time he came to see me at the ranch in July, we had narrowed the list to nine people. But in my mind, there was always a tenth.

After a relaxed lunch with Laura, Dick and I walked into the yard behind our old wooden ranch house. I listened patiently as Dick talked me through the search committee's final report. Then I looked him in the eye and said, "Dick, I've made up my mind."

———

As a small business owner, baseball executive, governor, and front-row observer of Dad's White House, I learned the importance of properly structuring and staffing an organization. The people you choose to surround you determine the quality of advice you receive and the way your goals are implemented. Over eight years as president, my personnel decisions raised some of the most complex and sensitive questions that reached the Oval Office: how to assemble a cohesive team, when to reshuffle an organization, how to manage disputes, how to distinguish among qualified candidates, and how to deliver bad news to good people.

I started each personnel decision by defining the job description and the criteria for the ideal candidate. I directed a wide search and considered a diverse range of options. For major appointments, I interviewed candidates face to face. I used my time to gauge character and personality. I was looking for integrity, competence, selflessness, and an ability to handle pressure. I always liked people with a sense of humor, a sign of modesty and self-awareness.

My goal was to assemble a team of talented people whose experience and skills complemented each other's and to whom I felt comfortable delegating. I wanted people who agreed on the direction of the administration but felt free to express differences on any issue. An important part of my job was to create a culture that encouraged teamwork and fostered loyalty—not to me, but to the country and our ideals.

I am proud of the many honorable, talented, hardworking people who served in my administration. We had low turnover, little infighting, and close cooperation through some of the most challenging times in our nation's history. I will always be grateful for their dedicated service.

I didn't get every personnel decision right. Prime Minister Margaret Thatcher once said, "I usually make up my mind about a man in ten seconds, and I very rarely change it." I didn't operate quite that fast, but I've always been able to read people. For the most part, this was an advantage. But there were times when I was too loyal or too slow to change. I misjudged how some selections would be perceived. Sometimes I flat out picked the wrong person for the job. Personnel decisions were among my first decisions as president—and my most important.

———

A president's first major personnel decision comes before taking office. The vice presidential selection provides voters with a window into a candidate's decision-making style. It reveals how careful and thorough he or she will be. And it signals a potential president's priorities for the country.

By the time I clinched the Republican nomination in March 2000, I knew quite a bit about vice presidents. I had followed the selection process closely when Dad was discussed as a possible running mate for Richard Nixon in 1968 and Gerald Ford in 1976. I had watched him serve eight years at President Reagan's side. I had observed his relationship with Dan Quayle. And I remembered the vice presidential horror story of my youth, when Democratic nominee George McGovern picked Tom Eagleton to be his running mate, only to learn later that Eagleton had suffered several nervous breakdowns and undergone electroshock therapy.

I was determined not to repeat that mistake, which was one reason I chose someone as careful and deliberate as Dick Cheney to run the vetting process. By early summer, we were focused on the finalists. Four were current or former governors: Lamar Alexander of Tennessee, Tom Ridge of Pennsylvania, Frank Keating of Oklahoma, and John Engler of Michigan. The other five were current or former senators: Jack Danforth of Missouri, Jon Kyl of Arizona, Chuck Hagel of Nebraska, and Bill Frist and Fred Thompson of Tennessee.

I talked through the choices with Dick, Laura, Karl, Karen, and a few other trusted aides. Karen recommended Tom Ridge, a Vietnam veteran from a key swing state. As a fellow chief executive, Tom would be plenty capable of running the country if anything happened to me. He was also pro-choice, which would appeal to moderates in both parties, while turning off some in the Republican base. Others made the case for Chuck Hagel, who sat on the Senate Foreign Relations Committee and would bring foreign policy experience. I was close with Frank Keating and John Engler, and I knew I would work well with either. Jon Kyl was a rock-solid conservative who would help shore up the base. Lamar Alexander, Bill Frist, and Fred Thompson were fine men, and they might help me pull off an upset in Tennessee, the home state of the Democratic nominee, Vice President Al Gore.

I was intrigued by Jack Danforth. An ordained minister, Jack was honest, ethical, and forthright. His voting record over three terms in the Senate was solid. He had earned my respect with his defense of Clarence Thomas during his Supreme Court confirmation hearing in 1991. He was a principled conservative who could also appeal across party lines. As a dividend, he might help carry Missouri, which would be a key battleground state.

I thought seriously about offering the job to Danforth, but I found myself returning again and again to Dick Cheney. Dick's experience was more extensive and diverse than that of anyone else on my list. As White House chief of staff, he had helped President Ford guide the nation through the aftermath of Watergate. He had served more than a decade in Congress and never lost an election. He had been a strong secretary of defense. He had run a global business and understood the private sector. Unlike any of the senators or governors on my list, he had stood next to presidents during the most gut-wrenching decisions that reach the Oval Office, including sending Americans to war. Not only would Dick be a valuable adviser, he would be fully capable of assuming the presidency.

While Dick knew Washington better than almost anyone, he didn't behave like an insider. He allowed subordinates to get credit. When he spoke at meetings, his carefully chosen words carried credibility and influence.

Like me, Dick was a westerner. He enjoyed fishing and spending time outdoors. He had married Lynne Vincent, his high school sweetheart from Wyoming, and he was deeply devoted to their daughters, Liz and Mary. He had a practical mind and a dry sense of humor. He told me he had started at Yale a few years before me, but the university asked him not to come back. Twice. He said he had once filled out a compatibility test designed to match his personality with the most appropriate career. When the results came in, Dick was told he was best suited to be a funeral director.

As I mulled the decision, I called Dad for an outside opinion. I read him the names I was considering. He knew most of the candidates and said they were all fine people. "What about Dick Cheney?" I asked.

"Dick would be a great choice," he said. "He would give you candid and solid advice. And you'd never have to worry about him going behind your back."

By the time Dick came to the ranch to deliver his final report, I had decided to make another run at him. As he finished his briefing, I said, "Dick, you are the perfect running mate."

While I had dropped hints before, he could tell I was serious this time. Finally, he said, "I need to talk to Lynne." I took that as a promising sign. He told me that he had had three heart attacks and that he and Lynne were happy with their life in Dallas. Then he said, "Mary is gay." I could tell what he meant by the way he said it. Dick clearly loved his daughter. I felt he was gauging my tolerance. "If you have a problem with this, I'm not your man," he was essentially saying.

I smiled at him and said, "Dick, take your time. Please talk to Lynne. And I could not care less about Mary's orientation."

Later that day, I talked to a few trusted aides. I didn't want to put all my cards on the table yet. I just told them I was thinking seriously about Cheney. Most were stunned. Karl was opposed. I asked him to come to the Governor's Mansion to make his case. I invited one person to listen in. That would be Dick. I believe in airing out disagreements. I also wanted to cement a relationship of trust between Karl and Dick in case they ended up together in the White House.

Karl gamely delivered his arguments: Cheney's presence on the ticket would add nothing to the electoral map, since Wyoming's three electoral votes were among the most reliably Republican in the country. Cheney's record in Congress was very conservative and included some hot-button votes that would be used against us. Dick's heart condition would raise questions about his fitness to serve. Choosing Dad's defense secretary could make people question whether I was my own man. Finally, Dick lived in Texas, and the Constitution prohibited two residents of the same state from receiving Electoral College votes.

I listened carefully to Karl's objections. Dick said he thought they were pretty persuasive. I didn't. Dick's old congressional record didn't bother me. I considered his experience on Capitol Hill an asset. His lack of impact on the electoral map did not concern me either. I believe voters base their decision on the presidential candidate, not the VP.*

As for Karl's concern about picking Dad's defense secretary, I was

---

*Arguably, my home state provided an exception in 1960, when John F. Kennedy chose Lyndon Johnson as his running mate. There was no similar benefit in 1988, when Michael Dukakis tapped Texas Senator Lloyd Bentsen.

convinced that the benefits of choosing a serious, accomplished running mate would compensate for any perception that I was falling back on Dad for help.

Two concerns did need to be addressed: Dick's health and residency status. Dick agreed to have a medical exam and sent the results to Dr. Denton Cooley, a respected Houston cardiologist. The doctor said Dick's heart would hold up to the stresses of the campaign and the vice presidency. Dick and Lynne would be able to change their voter registration to Wyoming, the state Dick had represented in Congress and still considered home.

The way Dick handled those delicate weeks deepened my confidence that he was the right choice. He never once pushed me to make up my mind. In fact, he insisted that I meet with Jack Danforth before I finalized my decision. Dick and I went to see Jack and his wife, Sally, in Chicago on July 18. We had a relaxed, three-hour visit. My positive impressions of Jack were confirmed. But I had decided on Dick.

A week later, I made the formal offer. As was my habit, I got up around 5:00 a.m. After two cups of coffee, I was anxious to get moving. I managed to wait until 6:22 a.m. before I called Dick. I caught him on the treadmill, which I considered a good sign. He and Lynne came down to Austin for the announcement that afternoon.

Ten years later, I have never regretted my decision to run with Dick Cheney. His pro-life, low-tax positions helped cement key parts of our base. He had great credibility when he announced that "Help is on the way" for the military. His steady, effective answers in the vice presidential debate with Joe Lieberman reassured voters about the strength of our ticket. It gave me comfort to know he would be ready to step in if something happened to me.

The real benefits of selecting Dick became clear fourteen months later. On a September morning in 2001, Americans awoke to an unimaginable crisis. The calm and quiet man I recruited that summer day in Crawford stood sturdy as an oak.

———

The vice presidential selection came at the end of a grueling primary season. The campaign process has a way of stripping the candidates to the core. It exposes strengths and weaknesses to the voters. I didn't realize it at the time, but the grind of the campaign helps a candidate to prepare for the pressures of the presidency. Those intense days also revealed the character of the people around me and laid the groundwork for the personnel decisions I later faced in the White House.

The campaign kicked off with the Iowa caucus, the ultimate grassroots experience. Laura and I traveled the state, shook thousands of hands, and consumed untold gallons of coffee. For all our meticulously planned events, one of the most revealing moments of the campaign came unscripted.

In December 1999, I attended a Republican debate in Des Moines. The moderators were Tom Brokaw of NBC and a local anchor, John Bachman. After covering some predictable topics, Bachman let loose a surprise: "What political philosopher or thinker do you most identify with and why?"

I was third in line to answer. I thought about citing someone like Mill or Locke, whose natural law theory had influenced the Founders. Then there was Lincoln; hard to go wrong with Abe in a Republican debate. I was still thinking when Bachman turned to me: "Governor Bush?" No more time to weigh my options. The words tumbled out of my mouth: "Christ," I said, "because He changed my heart."

Everybody looked stunned. Where had that come from? On the car ride back to the hotel, Mother and Dad checked in. They almost always called after major events. "Fine job, son," Dad said. "I don't think your answer will hurt you too much." "Which answer?" I asked. "You know, that one on Jesus," he said.

At first I hadn't thought about the answer hurting me. I had just blurted out what was in my heart. Upon reflection, however, I understood the note of caution. I was skeptical of politicians who touted religion as a way to get votes. I didn't believe in a Methodist or Jewish or Muslim approach to public policy. It was not the role of government to promote any religion. I hadn't done that as governor of Texas, and I certainly didn't intend to do it as president.

Sure enough, my words prompted an outcry. "There is something unholy about this," one columnist wrote. "W. is just checking Jesus' numbers, and Jesus is polling well in Iowa," another concluded.

The reaction wasn't all negative. My response had connected with many people who had had similar experiences in their own lives and appreciated my speaking openly about faith.

On caucus night, I won Iowa with 40 percent of the vote. After a brief victory celebration, we made the trek to New Hampshire. I knew that the Granite State could be treacherous for front-runners. New Hampshire voters have a history of knocking down the favorite. I felt good about our operation in the state, led by my friend Senator Judd Gregg. I had spent a lot of time in New Hampshire, marching in parades and perfecting my pancake-flipping skills. On primary day, Laura and I settled into our hotel in Manchester to watch the returns. Early in the afternoon, Karl came by with the first exit polls: I was going to lose, and lose badly.

Laura spoke up. "George, do you want to be president?" she asked. I nodded. "Then you'd better not let yourself get defined again," she said.

She was right. I had made the classic front-runner mistake. I had let Senator John McCain of Arizona, the other top contender for the nomination, take the initiative in New Hampshire. He had run an energetic campaign that attracted a lot of independents, which overcame my solid support from fellow Republicans. McCain, a member of Congress since 1983, had managed to define himself as an outsider and me as an insider. He talked about reform at every campaign stop, even though I was the one who had reformed a school system, changed the tort laws, and revamped Texas's approach to welfare. I had to give John credit for a smart, effective campaign. And I had to learn from my mistake.

I went to the gym for a hard workout. On the treadmill, I thought about what to do next. I faced the biggest personnel decision of my young campaign. The conventional playbook called for me to fire a few people and claim a fresh start. I decided to go in the opposite direction. I got the senior staff together and told them I refused to chuck anyone overboard to satisfy the loud voices on TV. One person deserved blame, and that was me. Win or lose, we would finish this race as a team. Then I gave everybody an assignment. Karl called the political directors in upcoming primary states. Joe reassured the campaign staff. Karen reached out to key members of the media. Don Evans bucked up the fundraisers.

I called Policy Director Josh Bolten, who was with the majority of our staff back at campaign headquarters in Austin. "How is everyone holding up?" I asked.

"Most people are in shock," he admitted.

I knew the team would be looking to me for a signal. "Get them together and tell them they ought to hold their heads high because we're going to win this thing," I told Josh.

Looking back on it, the loss in New Hampshire created an opportunity. Voters like to gauge how a candidate responds to adversity. Reagan and Dad showed their resilience after losing Iowa in 1980 and 1988, respectively. Bill Clinton turned his campaign around after defeat in New Hampshire in 1992, as did Barack Obama in 2008. In 2000, I looked at the defeat as a chance to prove I could take a blow and come back. The lesson is that sometimes the best personnel moves are the ones you don't make.

In South Carolina, we picked a new theme to highlight my bipartisan accomplishments in Texas: Reformer with Results. We set up town hall events, where I fielded questions until the audience ran out of things to ask. I worked the phones, enlisting the support of leaders across the state. Then McCain ran an ad questioning my character by comparing me to Bill Clinton. That crossed a line. I went on the air to counterpunch. The response, combined with a well-organized grassroots campaign, paid off. I won South Carolina with 53 percent of the vote, took nine of thirteen primaries on Super Tuesday, and rode the momentum to the nomination.

In early May, John and I met for an hour and a half in Pittsburgh. He was justifiably upset about insulting language some of my supporters had used in South Carolina. I understood his anger and made clear I respected his character. After our meeting, he told reporters I could restore integrity to the White House "more than adequately."

That wasn't the most scintillating endorsement I've ever received, but it was the beginning of reconciliation between John and me. In August, John and his wife, Cindy, hosted us at their beautiful ranch in Sedona, Arizona. It was fun to see Chef McCain behind the grill, relaxed and barbecuing ribs. We campaigned together in 2000 and again in 2004. I respect John, and I was glad to have him at my side.

———

Al Gore was a talented man and an accomplished politician. Like me, he had graduated from an Ivy League school and had a father in politics.

But our personalities seemed pretty different. He appeared stiff, serious, and aloof. It looked like he had been running for president his entire life. He brought together a formidable coalition of big-government liberals, cultural elites, and labor unions. He was plenty capable of engaging in class-warfare populism. He was also vice president during an economic boom. He would be tough to beat.

When I look back on the 2000 campaign, most of it collapses into a blur of handshaking, fundraising, and jousting for the morning headlines. There were two moments when the political merry-go-round stopped. The first came at the Republican National Convention in Philadelphia, which was managed well by Dad's former deputy chief of staff and transportation secretary, Andy Card.

I had attended every convention since 1976, but nothing compared to the feeling when I took center stage. I waited backstage in the dark, listening for the countdown: "Five, four, three, two, one." Then out into the packed arena. At first the scene was disorienting. Light and sound exploded all around me. I could feel the body heat and smell the people. Then the faces came into focus. I saw Laura and the girls, Mother and Dad. All my life, I had been watching George Bush speak. I was struck by the reversal of roles.

"Our opportunities are too great, our lives too short to waste this moment," I said. "So tonight, we vow to our nation we will seize this moment of American promise. We will use these good times for great goals. . . . This administration had its moment, they had their chance. They have not led. We will."

Two months later the campaigns paused again, this time for the debates. Karen Hughes oversaw my preparation team, with Josh Bolten taking the lead on policy. Josh combines a brilliant mind, disarming modesty, and a buoyant spirit. I'll never forget standing at the Ames, Iowa, straw poll in August 1999 watching several hundred motorcycles barrel into town. Among the riders were Governor Tommy Thompson of Wisconsin and Senator Ben Nighthorse Campbell of Colorado. When the lead man hopped down from his shiny blue-and-chrome Iowa-made Victory bike and pulled off his helmet, I was stunned to see Josh, clad in a bandana with our campaign logo. "Governor," he said, "meet the Bikers for Bush."

The first debate was in Boston. In the holding room backstage, I called

Kirbyjon Caldwell, and we prayed over the phone. Kirbyjon asked the Almighty to give me strength and wisdom. His voice gave me such comfort and calm that I made the telephone prayer with Kirbyjon a tradition before major events for the rest of the campaign and during my presidency.

The next voice I heard was that of the moderator, Jim Lehrer of PBS, introducing the candidates. We emerged from our respective corners and met at center stage. Gore deployed the ultra-firm handshake. I suspected he was trying to play a head game, just like Ann Richards had in 1994.

I concentrated on answering the questions, although at times I felt like I was on autopilot. By the time I glanced at my watch—which I had taken off and placed on the lectern to avoid repeating a debate mistake Dad had once made—we were almost done. We gave our closing statements, shook hands again—normal grip this time—and participated in the post-debate stage rush of family, friends, and aides.

Immediately afterward, Karen told me Gore had made a big mistake. He had repeatedly sighed and grimaced while I was talking. That was news to me. I had been so focused on my performance that I had not noticed.

The second and third debates had different formats but similar results. Neither of us made any quotable gaffes. There was one interesting moment in the third debate, at Washington University in St. Louis. The town hall format gave us the freedom to roam the stage. The first question was about the Patients' Bill of Rights. I was giving my answer when I saw Gore heading toward me. He is a big man, and his presence filled my space quickly. Was the vice president about to deliver a chest bump? A forearm shiver? For a split second I thought I was back on the playground at Sam Houston Elementary. I gave him a look of amused disdain and moved on.

I felt good about the debates. I believed my performance had exceeded expectations, and I figured the dramatic moments of the campaign were behind me. I was wrong.

———

Five days before the election, at a routine campaign stop in Wisconsin, Karen Hughes pulled me aside. We walked into a quiet room and she said, "A reporter in New Hampshire called to ask about the DUI." My heart sank. Such negative news at the end of a campaign would be explosive.

I had seriously considered disclosing the DUI four years earlier, when I was called for jury duty. The case happened to involve drunk driving. I was excused from the jury because, as governor, I might later have to rule on the defendant's case as a part of the pardon process. As I walked out of the Austin courthouse, a reporter shouted, "Have you ever been arrested for DUI?" I answered, "I do not have a perfect record as a youth. When I was young, I did a lot of foolish things. But I will tell you this, I urge people not to drink and drive."

Politically, it would not have been a problem to reveal the DUI that day. The next election was two years away, and I had quit drinking. I decided not to raise the DUI for one reason: my girls. Barbara and Jenna would start driving soon. I worried that disclosing my DUI would undermine the stern lectures I had been giving them about drinking and driving. I didn't want them to say, "Daddy did it and he turned out okay, so we can, too."

Laura was traveling with me the day the press uncovered the DUI. She called Barbara and Jenna to tell them before they heard it on TV. Then I went out to the cameras and made a statement: "I was pulled over. I admitted to the policeman that I had been drinking. I paid a fine. And I regret that it happened. But it did. I've learned my lesson."

Not disclosing the DUI on my terms may have been the single costliest political mistake I ever made. Karl later estimated that more than two million people, including many social conservatives, either stayed home or changed their votes. They had been hoping for a different kind of president, somebody who would set an example of personal responsibility.

If I had it to do over, I would have come clean about the DUI that day at the courthouse. I would have explained my mistake to the girls, and held an event with Mothers Against Drunk Driving to issue a strong warning not to drink and drive. All those thoughts ran through my head as I went to bed that night in Wisconsin. So did one more: I may have just cost myself the presidency.

Five days later, the four-point lead I'd held before the DUI revelation evaporated. I campaigned frantically through the final week and went into election day in a dead heat with Gore. That night, our extended family gathered for dinner at the Shoreline Grill in Austin. Toasts flowed freely until the exit polls starting coming in. The networks called Pennsylvania, Michigan, and Florida for Gore. CBS anchor Dan Rather assured his viewers, "Let's get one thing straight right from the get-go. . . . If we say somebody's carried a state, you can pretty much take it to the bank. Book it!"

Our guests who did not know much about politics continued to babble away. "The night is young, anything can happen. . . ." Those who understood the electoral map recognized I had just lost. Jeb and I were furious that the networks had called Florida before the polls closed in the Panhandle, the heavily Republican part of the state that lies in the central time zone. Who knew how many of my supporters had heard that news and decided not to vote? Laura and I slipped out of the dinner without touching our food.

The car ride back to the Governor's Mansion was quiet. There isn't much to say when you lose. I was deflated, disappointed, and a little stunned. I felt no bitterness. I was ready to accept the people's verdict and repeat Mother's words from 1992: "It's time to move on."

Shortly after we got back, the phone rang. I figured this was the first of the consolation calls: "You gave it your best shot. . . ." Instead, it was Karl. He didn't sound dejected; he sounded defiant. He was talking fast. He started spewing information about how the exit polls in Florida had overweighted this county or that precinct.

I cut him off and asked for the bottom line. He said the projections in Florida were mathematically flawed. He then got on the phone to the networks and screamed at the pollsters with the facts. Within two hours, he had systematically proved the major television networks wrong. At 8:55 p.m. central time, CNN and CBS took Florida out of the Gore column. All the others followed.

Laura and I followed the returns from the mansion with Mother, Dad, Jeb, and several top aides. Eventually the Cheneys, Don Evans, and a contingent of other close friends arrived. As the night went on, it became apparent that the outcome of the election would turn on Florida. At 1:15 in the morning, the networks called the state again—this time for me.

Al Gore called shortly after that. He congratulated me graciously and said, "We sure gave them a cliffhanger." I thanked him and said I was headed out to address the twenty thousand hardy souls freezing in the rain at the state capitol. He asked that I wait until he spoke to his supporters in about fifteen minutes. I agreed.

It took time for the meaning of the news to sink in. A few hours earlier I had been getting ready to move on with my life. Now I was preparing to be president of the United States.

Fifteen minutes passed. Then another fifteen. Still no concession speech from Gore. Something was wrong. Jeb got on his laptop and started monitoring the Florida returns. He said my margin was narrowing. At 2:30 a.m., Bill Daley, Gore's campaign chairman, called Don Evans. Don spoke to Daley briefly and handed me the phone. The vice president was on the line. He told me his numbers in Florida had changed since the last call, and thus he was retracting his concession.

I had never heard of a candidate un-conceding. I told him that in Texas, it meant something when a person gave you his word. "You don't have to get snippy about it," he replied. Soon after, the networks put Florida back into the undecided category—their fourth position in eight hours—and threw the outcome of the election into question.

I don't know about snippy, but I was hot. Just when I thought this wild race had ended, we were back at the starting gate. Several folks in the living room advised that I go out and declare victory. I considered it, until Jeb pulled me aside and said, "George, don't do it. The count is too close." The margin in Florida had dwindled to fewer than two thousand votes.

Jeb was right. An attempt to force the issue would have been rash. I told everyone that the election would not be decided that night. Most went to bed. I stayed up with Jeb and Don as they worked the phones to Florida. At one point, Don called the Florida secretary of state, Katherine Harris, to get an update. I heard him yell, "What do you mean you are in bed? Do you understand that the election is in the balance? What's going on?!"

With that, a strange night ended—and an even stranger five weeks began.

———

Of the 105 million ballots cast nationwide, the 2000 election would be determined by several hundred votes in one state. Florida immediately turned into a legal battlefield. Don Evans learned around 4:30 a.m. that Gore's campaign had dispatched a team of lawyers to coordinate a recount. He advised me to do the same. I was confronted with the most bizarre personnel choice of my public life: Whom to send to Florida to ensure that our lead was protected?

There was no time to develop a list or conduct interviews. Don suggested James Baker. Baker was the perfect choice—a statesman, a savvy lawyer, and a magnet for talented people. I called Jim and asked if he would take on the mission. Shortly thereafter, he was bound for Tallahassee.

Laura and I were mentally and physically worn out. We had poured every ounce of our energy into the race. Once it became clear we were in for a lengthy legal process, we spent most of our time decompressing at our ranch in Crawford.

I first saw Prairie Chapel Ranch in February 1998. I had always wanted a place to call my own—a refuge from the busy life—as Dad had in Kennebunkport. When I sold my stake in the Rangers, Laura and I had money to make a purchase.

I was hooked the moment I saw Benny Engelbrecht's 1,583-acre place in McLennan County, almost exactly halfway between Austin and Dallas. The ranch was a combination of flat country suited for cattle grazing and rugged canyons that drained into the middle fork of the Bosque River and Rainey Creek. The view of the limestone cliffs from the bottom of the ninety-foot canyons was stunning. So were the trees—huge native pecans, live oaks, cedar elms, burr oaks, and bois d'arc trees with their green fruits. In all, the place had over a dozen varieties of hardwoods, a rarity for Central Texas.

To win over Laura, I promised to build a home and new roads to access the most scenic parts of the ranch. She found a young architect from the University of Texas named David Heymann, who designed a comfortable one-story house with large windows, each offering a unique view of our property. He utilized geothermal heat and recycled water to minimize the impact on the environment. Most of the construction took place during 2000. Surviving a presidential campaign and a homebuilding project in the same year is the mark of one strong marriage—and a tribute to the patience and skill of Laura Bush.

The ranch was the perfect place to ride out the post-election storm. I checked in regularly with Jim Baker to get updates and provide strategic direction. I decided early on that I would avoid the endless, breathless TV coverage. Instead I took long runs that gave me a chance to think about the future, burned off nervous energy by clearing cedar trees that guzzled water needed by the native hardwoods, and went for hikes by the creek with Laura. If I became president, I wanted to be energized and ready for the transition.

There were some moments of high drama along the way. On December 8, one month and one day after the election, Laura and I were back in Austin. That afternoon, the Florida Supreme Court was scheduled to hand down a decision that Jim Baker was confident would make my victory official.

Laura and I invited our good friends Ben and Julie Crenshaw to watch the announcement. Ben is one of the most accomplished golfers of his era, and one of the most likeable people in professional sports. For the past few weeks, Gentle Ben had joined crowds protesting outside the Governor's Mansion. Some were Gore supporters, but many backed me. One of Ben and Julie's three young daughters carried a poster emblazoned with the words "Sore-Loserman," a play on the Gore-Lieberman ticket. Ben had a homemade pink sign that read "Florida, No More Mulligans."

Ben, Julie, Laura, and I gathered in the living room to await the ruling. I broke my no-TV rule in the hope that I could experience victory in real time. Around three o'clock, the court spokesman walked to the lectern. I prepared to embrace Laura. Then he announced that the court, by a 4–3 vote, had ruled for Gore. The decision mandated a statewide manual recount, yet another mulligan.

Shortly thereafter, Jim Baker called to ask if I wanted to appeal to the U.S. Supreme Court. He and Ted Olson, an outstanding lawyer Jim had recruited, felt we had a strong case. They explained that appealing the decision was a risky move. The U.S. Supreme Court might not agree to hear the case, or they could rule against us. I told Jim to make the appeal. I was prepared to accept my fate. The country needed closure, one way or the other.

On December 12, thirty-five days after the election, Laura and I were lying in bed when Karl called and insisted that we turn on the TV. I listened intently as Pete Williams of NBC News deciphered the Supreme Court's verdict. By a vote of 7–2, the justices found that Florida's chaotic, inconsistent recount procedure had violated the equal protection clause of the Constitution. Then, by a vote of 5–4, the Court ruled that there was no fair way to recount the votes in time for Florida to participate in the Electoral College. The election results would stand. By a tally of 2,912,790 to 2,912,253, I had won Florida. I would be the forty-third president of the United States.

My first response was relief. The uncertainty had inflicted a heavy toll on the country. After all the ups and downs, I didn't have the emotional capacity to rejoice. I had hoped to share my victory with twenty thousand people at the state capitol on election night. Instead, I probably became the first person to learn he had won the presidency while lying in bed with his wife watching TV.

———

For the first 140 years of American history, presidential inaugurations were held on March 4. A president elected in early November had about 120 days to prepare for his administration. In 1933, the Twentieth Amendment changed Inauguration Day to January 20, shortening the average transition to about 75 days. When the 2000 election was finally resolved in *Bush v. Gore*, I had 38 days.

My first big decision was how I wanted the White House to function. That was a question I had pondered before. In 1991, Dad asked me to study the operation of his White House. After interviewing all his senior staffers, a common theme emerged: People were dissatisfied. Most felt that Chief of Staff John Sununu had denied them access to the Oval Office and limited the flow of information to Dad. I had always liked John, but my job was not to debate the case; it was to report the findings. I did so several days before Thanksgiving of 1991. Dad concluded that he needed to make a change. He asked me to notify John, which I did in an awkward conversation. He submitted his resignation shortly thereafter.

I was determined to avoid that problem in my White House. I wanted a structure that was tight enough to ensure an orderly flow of information but flexible enough that I could receive advice from a variety of sources. It was important that advisers felt free to express concerns to me directly, without passing through a filter. Plus it would be easier to convince key members of my Texas political family to move to Washington if they would have regular access to me.

The key to creating this structure was to hire an experienced, confident chief of staff who would not feel threatened by my relationships with his subordinates. Ironically, I found the perfect man in John Sununu's deputy, Andy Card. When I visited Dad's White House, I would often kick back in Andy's office to get a candid update on how things were going. Andy was perceptive, humble, loyal, and hardworking. He had served under every chief of staff during both the Reagan and Bush presidencies. He had the sound judgment and steady temperament I needed, along with a caring heart and a good sense of humor. I was convinced he was the right person to lead my White House staff.

A couple of weeks before the election, I met discreetly with Andy in Florida. It was clear he thought I was asking him to lead the transition. "No, I'm talking about The Big One," I said. I explained that he would be the only chief of staff, but that I would also rely heavily on Texans like Karl, Karen, Al Gonzales, Harriet Miers, Clay Johnson, and Dan Bartlett for advice. Andy agreed to the job, so long as I informed him of any decisions I made outside his presence. I announced his selection in late November, making him the first official member of my White House team.

The next important position to fill was national security adviser. I knew from watching Dad's close relationship with Brent Scowcroft that it was crucial to find someone highly capable and completely trustworthy.

On a trip to Maine in the summer of 1998, Dad introduced me to Condoleezza Rice, who had served as a Soviet specialist on his National Security Council staff. The daughter of an African American minister from segregated Birmingham, Alabama, Condi had a Ph.D. from the University of Denver and had become provost of Stanford at age thirty-eight. She immediately struck me as a smart, thoughtful, energetic woman.

Over the next two and a half years, Condi and I met frequently to discuss foreign policy. One summer day in 1999, Condi, Laura, and I were hiking on the ranch. As we started to climb up a steep grade, Condi launched into a discourse on the history of the Balkans. Laura and I were huffing and puffing. Condi kept going, explaining the disintegration of Yugoslavia and the rise of Milosevic. That trail is now known as Balkan Hill. I decided that if I ended up in the Oval Office, I wanted Condi Rice by my side.

The first selection for the Cabinet was easy. Colin Powell would be secretary of state. I had first met Colin at Camp David in 1989, when he was chairman of the Joint Chiefs of Staff. He and Dick Cheney had come to brief Dad on the surrender of Panamanian dictator Manuel Noriega. Colin was wearing his Army uniform. In contrast to the formality of his dress, he was good-natured and friendly. He spoke to everyone in the room, even bystanders like the president's children.

Colin was widely admired at home and had a huge presence around the world. He would credibly defend American interests and values, from a stronger NATO to freer trade. I believed Colin could be the second coming of George Marshall, a soldier turned statesman.

The two key national security positions left were secretary of defense and director of central intelligence. More than a decade after the Berlin Wall fell, much of the Defense Department was still designed for fighting the Cold War. I had campaigned on an ambitious vision to transform the military. I planned to realign our force structure and invest in new technologies such as precision weapons and missile defense. I knew there would be resistance within the Pentagon, and I needed a tenacious, innovative secretary to lead the effort.

My top candidate was Fred Smith, the founder and chief executive of FedEx. Fred graduated from Yale two years ahead of me, earned the Silver Star as a Marine in Vietnam, and built his company into one of the world's most successful businesses. He loved the military and would bring an organizational mind to the Pentagon. Andy Card called Fred, learned he was interested in the job, and invited him to Austin. I was prepared to offer Fred the position, but before he made the trip, he was diagnosed with a heart condition. He had to bow out to focus on his health.

We considered a variety of other names for secretary of defense, including Dan Coats, a fine senator from Indiana. Then Condi threw out an interesting idea: How about Don Rumsfeld?

Don had been secretary of defense twenty-five years earlier, during the Ford administration. He had since served on a number of influential national security commissions. I had been considering Rumsfeld for CIA, not Defense. When I interviewed him, Don laid out a captivating vision for transforming the Defense Department. He talked about making our forces lighter, more agile, and more rapidly deployable. And he was a strong proponent of a missile defense system to protect against rogue states like North Korea and Iran.

Rumsfeld impressed me. He was knowledgeable, articulate, and confident. As a former secretary of defense, he had the strength and experience to bring major changes to the Pentagon. He would run the bureaucracy, not let it run him. Dick Cheney, who had been Don's deputy when he was chief of staff in the Ford White House, recommended him strongly.

There was one awkward issue. Some believed that Don had used his influence to persuade President Ford to appoint Dad to run the CIA in 1975 as a way of taking him out of contention for the vice presidency. I had no way of knowing if this was true. But whatever disagreements he and Dad might have had twenty-five years earlier did not concern me, so long as Don could do the job. Don went on to become both the youngest and oldest person to serve as secretary of defense.

With Rumsfeld going to the Pentagon, I no longer had a leading candidate for the CIA. I had great respect for the Agency as a result of Dad's time there. I had been receiving intelligence briefings as president-elect for a few weeks when I met the sitting director, George Tenet. He was the opposite of the stereotypical CIA director you read about in spy novels— the bow-tied, Ivy League, elite type. Tenet was a blue-collar guy, the son of Greek immigrants from New York City. He spoke bluntly, often colorfully, and obviously cared deeply about the Agency.

Retaining Bill Clinton's CIA director would send a message of continuity and show that I considered the Agency beyond the reach of politics. I asked Dad to sound out some of his CIA contacts. He told me Tenet was highly respected within the ranks. As George and I got to know each other, I decided to stop looking for a replacement. The cigar-chomping, Greek-to-the-core director agreed to stay.

For the most part, the national security team functioned smoothly in the early years of the administration. The economic team did not. The problem was partly the result of a personnel mismatch. As president, I had three key economic advisers: the National Economic Council director, the Council of Economic Advisers chairman, and the secretary of the treasury. I chose Larry Lindsey, an accomplished economist and senior adviser on my campaign, to lead the NEC. Glenn Hubbard, another thoughtful economist, chaired the CEA. They did a fine job designing the tax cuts I had proposed during the campaign. The legislation passed with a strong bipartisan majority.

My treasury secretary did not share the same enthusiasm for tax cuts. Paul O'Neill had come recommended by Dick, Clay Johnson, and others on the team. His strong résumé included success at the Office of Management and Budget and as the CEO of Alcoa, a Fortune 100 company. I felt that his practical business experience would command respect on Wall Street and Capitol Hill.

Unfortunately, things started going wrong from the start. Paul belittled the tax cuts, which of course got back to me. He and I met regularly, but never clicked. He didn't gain my confidence, nor did he build credibility with the financial community, Congress, or his colleagues in the administration. I was hoping for a strong treasury secretary—a leader like Jim Baker or Bob Rubin—who would advance my economic policies in speeches and on TV. By late 2002, nearly two million Americans had lost jobs in the past year, and Paul wasn't conveying our determination to get them back to work. Instead, he used his meetings in the Oval Office to talk about tangential topics, like his plan to improve workplace safety at the U.S. Mint.

I did not want to repeat Dad's mistake of 1992, when he was perceived as disengaged on the economy. I decided that a shakeup of the economic team was the best way to signal that my administration was serious about confronting the slowdown affecting everyday Americans. For the change to be credible, it had to be sweeping. Larry Lindsey had done a fine job, and it was not easy to ask him to move on. He understood the need for a fresh start and handled the news professionally. Paul did not take it as well. I was disappointed that he departed on bad terms, but glad I made the decision when I did.

———

The next summer, I received a surprising invitation to make another change. Every week, Dick Cheney and I ate lunch together, just the two of us. Jimmy Carter and Walter Mondale had started the tradition, and it had continued ever since. I liked the relaxed setting and the chance to hear whatever Dick had on his mind. While I had similar meetings with other top aides, Dick was the only one on a regular schedule. I didn't look at the vice president as another senior adviser. He had put his name on the ballot and gotten elected. I wanted him to be comfortable with all the issues on my desk. After all, it could become his at any moment.

Dick and I ate in a small dining room off the Oval Office. The room's decorations included a bronze bull sculpture given to me by some East Texas friends and a landscape painting that reminded me of the Maine coast. The dominant piece of art in the room was a portrait of John Quincy Adams, the only other son of a president to hold the office. I hung it as an inside joke with Dad. One day early in my presidency, he was teasing me about the special kinship between W and Q. I wanted him to have to look Q in the face the next time he felt the urge to needle. I had read a fair amount about Quincy. I admired his abolitionist principles, although I wasn't crazy about his campaign to exclude Texas from the Union. Nevertheless, I kept the portrait up for the rest of my time in the White House.

In mid-2003, Dick opened one of our weekly lunches with a startling comment. He said, "Mr. President, I want you to know that you should feel free to run for reelection with someone else. No hard feelings." I asked about his health. He said his heart was fine. He just thought I should have the option to refashion the ticket. His offer impressed me. It was so atypical in power-hungry Washington. It confirmed the reasons I'd picked Dick in the first place.

I did consider his offer. I talked to Andy, Karl, and a few others about the possibility of asking Bill Frist, the impressive Tennessee senator who had become majority leader, to run with me instead. We all expected 2004 to bring another close election. While Dick helped with important parts of our base, he had become a lightning rod for criticism from the media and the left. He was seen as dark and heartless—the Darth Vader of the administration. Dick didn't care much about his image—which I liked—but that allowed the caricatures to stick. One myth was that Dick was actually running the White House. Everyone inside the building, including the vice president, knew that was not true. But the impression was out there. Accepting Dick's offer would be one way to demonstrate that I was in charge.

The more I thought about it, the more strongly I felt Dick should stay. I hadn't picked him to be a political asset; I had chosen him to help me do the job. That was exactly what he had done. He accepted any assignment I asked. He gave me his unvarnished opinions. He understood that I made the final decisions. When we disagreed, he kept our differences private. Most important, I trusted Dick. I valued his steadiness. I enjoyed being around him. And he had become a good friend. At one of our lunches a few weeks later, I asked Dick to stay, and he agreed.

———

As the 2004 election approached, I grew concerned about the growing discord within the national security team. In most administrations, there is natural friction between the diplomats at State and the warriors at Defense. Secretary of State George Shultz and Secretary of Defense Caspar Weinberger famously battled throughout the Reagan administration. President Ford replaced Defense Secretary James Schlesinger largely because he couldn't get along with Henry Kissinger. I didn't mind some creative tension in the organization. Differences of opinion among advisers helped clarify tough decisions. The key was that disagreements had to be aired respectfully, and my decisions had to be accepted as final.

After the successful liberation of Afghanistan, the territorial squabbles between State and Defense seemed tolerable. But when the debate over Iraq intensified, high-level officials within the respective departments started sniping at each other viciously. Colin and Don were always respectful to each other in my presence. Over time I realized they were like a pair of old duelers who kept their own pistols in their holsters, but let their seconds and thirds fire away.

A memorable example came during one of Don Rumsfeld's televised press briefings, which he had been holding almost daily since the war in Afghanistan started. Don's handling of the press was fun to watch. He was an expert at parrying reporters' questions, and he jousted with exuberance and flair. I liked to tease him about his stardom in the early-afternoon TV slot. "You're a matinee idol for the over-sixty crowd," I told him. He took the ribbing in stride.

In January 2003, a Dutch television reporter asked Don why America's European allies were not more supportive of our calls to hold Saddam Hussein to account. "You're thinking of Europe as Germany and France," Don said. "I don't. I think that's old Europe."

I agreed with Don's point. The new democracies of Central and Eastern Europe understood the nightmare of tyranny firsthand and supported action against Saddam Hussein. But that sensible argument is not what made the news. Don's characterization of Germany and France as "old Europe" ignited a wave of protest.

Colin was furious. He was trying to persuade the Germans and French to join our cause at the United Nations, and he felt Don had crossed into his lane in a way that complicated his diplomatic mission. His subordinates clearly felt the same way. Policy disputes that once took place behind closed doors started spilling out in the press.

It irritated me to read headlines like "A White House Divided: The Bush Administration's Civil War" and "Bush's Next Role: Mediator in Disputes over Running Postwar Iraq." I announced at NSC meetings that the squabbling and leaks were damaging our credibility and giving ammunition to our critics. I spoke to Don and Colin individually. I asked Dick and Condi to work behind the scenes. I instructed Condi's skillful deputy, Steve Hadley, to tell the seconds and thirds to cool it. Nothing worked.

---

In the spring of 2004, Don came to me with serious news. In defiance of their orders and military law, American soldiers had severely mistreated detainees at an Iraqi prison called Abu Ghraib. I felt sick, really sick. This was not what our military or our country stood for. While the perpetrators were court-martialed, America's reputation took a severe hit. I considered it a low point of my presidency.

I also felt blindsided. Don had told me the military was investigating reports of abuse at the prison, but I had no idea how graphic or grotesque the photos would be. The first time I saw them was the day they were aired by *60 Minutes II*. I was not happy with the way the situation had been handled. Neither was the team at the White House. People started talking to the press and pointing fingers, mostly at my secretary of defense. When Don got word of the stories, he gave me a handwritten note: "Mr. President, I want you to know that you have my resignation as secretary of defense anytime you feel it would be helpful to you."

I called Don that night and told him I would not accept his resignation. I didn't blame him for the misconduct of the soldiers at Abu Ghraib, and I didn't want to turn him into a scapegoat. I needed the problem fixed, and I wanted him to do it. Four days later, Don sent another, longer letter. He wrote,

> *During recent days, I have given a good deal of thought to the situation, testified before Congress, and considered your views. I have great respect for you, your outstanding leadership in the global war on terror and your hopes for our country. However, I have concluded that the damage from the acts of abuse that happened on my watch, by individuals for whose conduct I am ultimately responsible, can best be responded to by my resignation.*

I respected Don for repeating his offer. It was clear his earlier message had not been a mere formality; he was serious about leaving. It was a testament to his character, his loyalty to the office, and his understanding of the damage Abu Ghraib was causing. I seriously considered accepting his advice. I knew it would send a powerful signal to replace the leader of the Pentagon after such a grave mistake. But a big factor held me back: There was no obvious replacement for Don, and I couldn't afford to create a vacuum at the top of Defense.

While I decided not to accept Don's resignation, the spring of 2004 marked the end of my tolerance for the squabbling within the national security team. What started as creative tension had turned destructive.

The stories about the feuds were fueling the impression of disarray within the administration and making me furious. I concluded that the animosity was so deeply embedded that the only solution was to change the entire national security team after the 2004 election.

Colin Powell made it easier for me. That same spring of 2004, he told me he was ready to move on. He had served three tough years and was naturally fatigued. He was also a sensitive man who had been wounded by the infighting and discouraged by the failure to find weapons of mass destruction in Iraq. I asked Colin to stay through the election, and I was grateful that he agreed.

The early notification gave me plenty of time to think about a successor. I admired Colin, but it sometimes seemed like the State Department he led wasn't fully on board with my philosophy and policies. It was important to me that there be no daylight between the president and the secretary of state. After six years together in the White House and on the campaign, I had grown very close to Condi Rice. She could read my mind and my moods. We shared a vision of the world, and she wasn't afraid to let me know when she disagreed with me.

Condi's range of talents was impressive. I had watched her brief members of Congress and the press on sensitive national security issues. She was a talented pianist who had played with Yo-Yo Ma. She inspired people with her story of growing up in the segregated South. And she knew how to handle some of the biggest personalities in the world.

I saw that in March 2001, when I held a meeting on North Korea policy to prepare for my visit the next day with South Korean President Kim Dae-jung, my first with an Asian head of state. The previous administration had offered concessions to North Korean dictator Kim Jong-il in return for a pledge to abandon his nuclear weapons program. The policy had not worked, and I told the team we were going to change it. From then on, North Korea would have to change its behavior *before* America made concessions.

At 5:15 the next morning, I read the *Washington Post*. One story opened, "The Bush administration intends to pick up where the Clinton administration left off in negotiations with North Korea over its missile programs, Secretary of State Colin L. Powell said yesterday."

I was stunned. I figured the reporter must have misquoted Colin, because the story was the exact opposite of what we had discussed at the meeting. I called Condi. Like me, she is an early riser, but she had not yet seen the paper. I gave her a summary of the *Post* story and said, "By the time Colin gets to the White House for the meeting, this had better be fixed."

I had given Condi a daunting assignment. She had to instruct the secretary of state, a world-famous former general a generation older than she, to correct his quote. Later that morning, Colin came bounding into the Oval Office and said, "Mr. President, don't worry, it's all been cleared up."

The next year, I asked Condi to take on a similar mission with the vice president. It was August 2002, and I was thinking through my decision on whether to seek a UN resolution to send weapons inspectors back to Iraq. Dick gave a speech at the Veterans of Foreign Wars Convention in which he said, "A return of inspectors would provide . . . false comfort that Saddam was somehow 'back in his box.'" That made it sound like my decision had been made. But I was still considering my options. I asked Condi to make clear to Dick that he had gotten out in front of my position. She made the call and, to Dick's credit, it never happened again.

I prepared to announce Condi's nomination as secretary of state shortly after the 2004 election. To fill the national security adviser post, I decided to promote her outstanding deputy, Steve Hadley, a humble and thoughtful lawyer whose advice was always crisp, discreet, and uncolored by any personal agenda. Then, out of nowhere, Andy informed me that Colin had expressed second thoughts about leaving. I considered Colin a friend and appreciated his achievements, especially his work to rally a strong coalition in the war on terror and lay the groundwork for future peace between the Israelis and Palestinians. But I had already decided on Condi.

I've always wondered if one of the reasons Colin hesitated to leave is that he expected Don Rumsfeld to go, too. He was right to assume that. I had planned to make a change at Defense as part of a new national security team. Late in 2004, I asked Andy to approach Fred Smith again to see if he would consider the job. I had seen Fred, and he looked perfectly fine. The problem this time was not Fred's health; it was his oldest daughter's. Wendy had been born with a fatal genetic heart condition, and he needed to spend time with her. Sadly, she died in 2005.

I considered other possible replacements at Defense. I thought about sending Condi to the Pentagon, but I decided she would be a better secretary of state. I considered Senator Joe Lieberman of Connecticut, but I didn't think he was the right fit, either. At one point, I reached out to Jim Baker. Had he accepted, Jim could have claimed a historic triple crown as the first person ever to serve as secretary of state, treasury, and defense. But he was enjoying his retirement and had no interest in returning to Washington.

The reality is that there aren't many people capable of leading the military during a complex global war. Don Rumsfeld was one of the few. He had valuable experience and shared my view of the war on terror as a long-term ideological struggle. At times, Don frustrated me with his abruptness toward military leaders and members of my staff. I felt he'd made a mistake by skipping the retirement ceremony of General Eric Shinseki, the four-star Army chief of staff who stepped down in 2003 after an honorable career. Don's decision helped feed the false impression that the general had been fired for policy disagreements over Iraq.*

Still, I liked Don. He respected the chain of command. He and his wife, Joyce, devoted themselves to our troops and frequently visited military hospitals without seeking press attention. Don was doing a superb job transforming the military, the mission that initially attracted me to him. He had increased our arsenal of unmanned aerial vehicles, made our forces more expeditionary, expanded the military's broadband capacity so we could make better use of real-time data links and imagery, begun bringing home troops from former Cold War outposts such as Germany, and invested heavily in the Special Forces, especially in the integration of intelligence and special operations.

Despite his tough external veneer, Don Rumsfeld was a decent and caring man. One day he and I were in the Oval Office. He had just finished briefing me on a military operation, and I had a few minutes before my next meeting. I asked casually how his family was doing. He did not answer at first. Eventually he got out a few words, but then he broke down in tears. He explained to me that his son, Nick, was battling a seri-

---

*I later heard that General Shinseki's staff had not invited Don to attend. I think he should have gone anyway.

ous drug addiction. Don's pain was deep, his love genuine. Months later, I asked how Nick was doing. Don beamed as he explained that his son had gone through rehab and was well. It was touching to see Don's pride in his son's character and strength.

I felt for Don again in the spring of 2006, when a group of retired generals launched a barrage of public criticism against him. While I was still considering a personnel change, there was no way I was going to let a group of retired officers bully me into pushing out the civilian secretary of defense. It would have looked like a military coup and would have set a disastrous precedent.

As 2006 wore on, the situation in Iraq worsened dramatically. Sectarian violence was tearing the country apart. In the early fall, Don told me he thought we might need "fresh eyes" on the problem. I agreed that change was needed, especially since I was seriously contemplating a new strategy, the surge. But I was still struggling to find a capable replacement.

One evening in the fall of 2006, I was chatting with my high school and college friend Jack Morrison, whom I had appointed to the President's Foreign Intelligence Advisory Board (PFIAB). I was worried about the deteriorating conditions in Iraq and mentioned Don Rumsfeld's comment about needing fresh eyes.

"I have an idea," Jack said. "What about Bob Gates?" He told me he had met with Gates recently as part of his PFIAB work.

Why hadn't I thought of Bob? He had been CIA director in Dad's administration and deputy national security adviser to President Reagan. He had successfully run a large organization, Texas A&M University. He served on the Baker-Hamilton Commission, which was studying the problems in Iraq. He would be ideal for the job.

I immediately called Steve Hadley and asked him to feel out Bob. We had tried to recruit him as director of national intelligence the previous year, but he had declined because he loved his job as president of A&M. Steve reported back the next day. Bob was interested.

I was pretty sure I had found the right person for the job. But I was concerned about the timing. We were weeks away from the 2006 midterm elections. If I were to change defense secretaries at that point, it would look like I was making military decisions with politics in mind. I decided to make the move after the election.

The weekend before the midterms, Bob drove from College Station, Texas, to the ranch in Crawford. We met in my office, a secluded one-story building about a half-mile from the main house. I felt comfortable around Bob. He is a straightforward, unassuming man with a quiet strength. I promised him access to me anytime he needed it. Then I told him there was something else he needed to know before taking the job: I was seriously considering a troop increase in Iraq. He was open to it. I told him I knew he had a great life at A&M, but his country needed him. He accepted the job on the spot.

I knew Dick would not be happy with my decision. He was a close friend of Don's. As always, Dick told me what he thought. "I disagree with your decision. I think Don is doing a fine job. But it's your call. You're the president." I asked Dick to deliver the news to his friend, which I hoped would soften the blow.

Don handled the change like the professional he is. He sent me a touching letter. "I leave with great respect for you and for the leadership you have provided during a most challenging time for our country," he wrote. ". . . It has been the highest honor of my long life to have been able to serve our country at such a critical time in our history."

———

Replacing the secretary of defense was one of two difficult personnel changes I made in 2006. The other was changing chiefs of staff. With the environment in Washington turning sour, Andy Card reminded me often that there were only a handful of positions in which a personnel move would be viewed as significant. His job was one of them. In early 2006, Andy often brought up the possibility of his departure. "You can do it easily and it could change the debate," he said. "You owe it to yourself to consider it."

Around the same time, Clay Johnson asked to see me. Clay had served with me every day since I took office as governor in 1995. When we sat down for lunch that day, he asked me how I thought the White House was functioning. I told him I was a little unsettled. I had been hearing complaints from staff members. From the perch of the presidency, though, it was hard to tell whether the gripes were petty grievances or evidence of a serious problem.

Clay gave me a look that showed there wasn't much doubt in his mind. Then he pulled a pen out of his pocket, picked up his napkin, and sketched the organizational chart of the White House. It was a tangled mess, with lines of authority crossing and blurred. His point was clear: This was a major source of the unrest. Then he said, "I am not the only one who feels this way." He told me that several people had spontaneously used the same unflattering term to describe the White House structure: It started with "cluster" and ended with four more letters.

Clay was right. The organization was drifting. People had settled into comfort zones, and the sharpness that had once characterized our operation had dulled. The most effective way to fix the problem was to make a change at the top. I decided it was time to take Andy up on his offer to move on.

The realization was painful. Andy Card was a loyal, honorable man who led the White House effectively through trying days. On a trip to Camp David that spring, I went to see Andy and his wife Kathi at the bowling alley. They are one of those great couples whose love for each other is so obvious. They knew I wasn't there for bowling. My face must have betrayed my anguish. I started by thanking Andy for his service. He cut me off and said, "Mr. President, you want to make a change." I tried to explain. He wouldn't let me. We hugged and he said he accepted my decision.

I was uncomfortable creating any large vacancy without having a replacement lined up. So before I had my talk with Andy, I had asked Josh Bolten to come see me. I respected Josh a lot, and so did his colleagues. Since his days as policy director of my campaign, he had served as deputy chief of staff for policy and director of the Office of Management and Budget. He knew my priorities as well as anyone. My trust in him was complete.

When I asked Josh if he would be my next chief of staff, he did not jump at the offer. Like most at the White House, he admired Andy Card and knew how hard the job could be. After thinking about it, he agreed that the White House needed restructuring and refreshing. He told me that if he took the job, he expected a green light to make personnel changes and clarify lines of authority and responsibility. I told him that was precisely why I wanted him. He accepted the job and stayed to the end, which made him one of the first staffers I hired for my campaign and the last I saw in the Oval Office—with ten full years in between.

Shortly after taking over, Josh moved forward with a number of changes, including replacing the White House press secretary with Tony Snow, a witty former TV and radio host who became a dear friend until he lost his valiant battle with cancer in 2008. The trickiest move was redefining Karl's role. After the 2004 election, Andy had asked Karl to become deputy chief of staff for policy, the top policy position in the White House. I understood his rationale. Karl is more than a political adviser. He is a policy wonk with a passion for knowledge and for turning ideas into action. I approved his promotion because I wanted to benefit from Karl's expertise and abilities. To avoid any misperceptions, Andy made clear that Karl would not be included in national security meetings.

By the middle of 2006, Republicans were in trouble in the upcoming midterm elections, and the left had unfairly used Karl's new role to accuse us of politicizing policy decisions. Josh asked Karl to focus on the midterms and continue to provide strategic input. To take over the day-to-day policy operations, Josh brought in his deputy from OMB— Joel Kaplan, a brilliant and personable Harvard Law graduate who had worked for me since 2000.

I worried about how Karl would interpret the move. He had developed a thick skin in Washington, but he was a proud, sensitive man who had absorbed savage attacks on my behalf. It was a tribute to Karl's loyalty and Josh's managerial skill that they made the new arrangement work until Karl left the White House in August 2007.

———

While White House staff and Cabinet appointments are crucial to decision making, they are temporary. Judicial appointments are for life. I knew how proud Dad was to have appointed Clarence Thomas, a wise, principled, humane man. I also knew he was disappointed that his other nominee, David Souter, had evolved into a different kind of judge than he expected.

History is full of similar tales. John Adams famously called Chief Justice John Marshall—who served on the bench for thirty years after Adams left office—his greatest gift to the American people. On the other hand, when Dwight Eisenhower was asked to name his biggest mistakes as president, he answered, "I made two and they're both sitting on the Supreme Court."

Shortly after the 2000 election was decided, I asked my White House counsel, Alberto Gonzales, and his team of lawyers to develop a list of candidates for the Supreme Court. Al was an impressive second-generation American who had worked his way through Rice University and Harvard Law School and earned my trust when I was governor. I told him the Supreme Court list should include women, minorities, and people with no previous experience on the bench. I made clear there should be no political litmus test. The only tests in my mind were personal integrity, intellectual ability, and judicial restraint. I was concerned about activist judges who substituted their personal preferences for the text of the law. I subscribed to the strict constructionist school: I wanted judges who believed the Constitution meant what it said.

For more than eleven years, the same nine justices had sat together on the Court, the longest such streak in modern history. On June 30, 2005, Harriet Miers—who had replaced Al Gonzales as White House counsel when he became attorney general—was informed that the Supreme Court would be forwarding a letter for me from one of the justices. We all assumed it was from Chief Justice William Rehnquist, who was eighty years old and sick. But the next morning Harriet called me with a surprise. "It's O'Connor," she said.

I had met Justice Sandra Day O'Connor many times over the years. The first female justice in the history of the Court, she had an engaging, straightforward personality. I was fond of Sandra and called her immediately after I received her letter. She told me it was time for her to go take care of her beloved husband, John, who was suffering from Alzheimer's.

While the vacancy was not the one I expected, we were prepared to fill it. Harriet's team prepared a thick binder that contained the biographies of eleven candidates, as well as detailed analyses of their writings, speeches, and judicial philosophies. I had a trip to Europe scheduled in early July, and the long hours on Air Force One made for good reading time. After studying the binder, I narrowed the list down to five impressive judges: Samuel Alito, Edith Brown Clement, Michael Luttig, John Roberts, and J. Harvie Wilkinson.

Each came to meet me in the White House residence. I tried to put them at ease by giving them a tour of the living area. Then I took them to the family sitting room that overlooks the West Wing. I had read the summaries of their legal opinions; now I wanted to read the people. I was looking for someone who shared my judicial philosophy, and whose values wouldn't change over time. I went into the interviews hoping one person would stand apart.

One did. John Roberts flew in from London, where he was teaching for the summer. I knew Roberts's record: top of his class at Harvard and Harvard Law School, law clerk to Justice Rehnquist, dozens of cases argued before the Supreme Court. Roberts had been nominated to the D.C. Circuit Court of Appeals in 1992, but he wasn't confirmed before the election. I had nominated him to a seat on the same court in 2001. He was confirmed in 2003 and had established a solid record. Behind the sparkling résumé was a genuine man with a gentle soul. He had a quick smile and spoke with passion about the two young children he and his wife, Jane, had adopted. His command of the law was obvious, as was his character.

I talked about the decision with Dick, Harriet, Andy, Al, and Karl. They liked Roberts, but he was not at the top of all lists. Dick and Al backed Luttig, who they felt was the most dedicated conservative jurist. Harriet supported Alito because he had the most established judicial record. Andy and Karl shared my inclination toward Roberts. I solicited opinions from others, including some of the younger lawyers in the White House. One was Brett Kavanaugh, whom I had nominated to the D.C. Circuit Court of Appeals. Brett told me that Luttig, Alito, and Roberts would all be solid justices. The tiebreaker question, he suggested, was which man would be the most effective leader on the Court—the most capable of convincing his colleagues through persuasion and strategic thinking.

I believed Roberts would be a natural leader. I didn't worry about him drifting away from his principles over time. He described his philosophy of judicial modesty with a baseball analogy that stuck with me: "A good judge is like an umpire—and no umpire thinks he is the most important person on the field."

On Tuesday, July 19, I called John to offer him the job. We made the announcement that night in the East Room. Everything went according to plan until, during my primetime televised speech, four-year-old Jack Roberts slipped out of his mother's grip and started dancing around the floor. We later learned he was imitating Spider-Man. I saw him out of the corner of my eye, and it took all my concentration to continue my remarks. Eventually Jane reclaimed little Jack. The audience had a good laugh, and Jack's family got slide-show material for life.

In early September, three days before Roberts's confirmation hearing was scheduled to begin, Karl called me late on a Saturday night. Laura and I were in bed, and nobody calls with good news at that hour. Karl told me the chief justice had just died. Rehnquist was one of the greats. He had served thirty-three years on the Supreme Court, nineteen of them in the center chair. He had conducted Dad's swearing-in as president in 1989 and mine in 2001. As my Second Inauguration approached, Rehnquist was ailing with thyroid cancer. He hadn't been seen in public for weeks. But when it came time to read the oath of office, his voice boomed loud and clear: "Repeat after me: I, George Walker Bush, do solemnly swear . . ."

I now had two vacancies on the Court to fill. I decided that John Roberts's leadership ability made him a perfect fit for chief justice. John excelled at his hearing, was confirmed by a wide majority, and came back to the East Room for his swearing-in. The moment showed what unlikely turns life can take. John Roberts, who thirteen years earlier assumed that his chance to be a judge had passed, was now chief justice of the United States.

———

With O'Connor's seat still vacant, I felt strongly that I should replace her with a woman. I didn't like the idea of the Supreme Court having only one woman, Justice Ruth Bader Ginsburg. Laura agreed—and shared her views with the press.

This was a rare occasion when Laura's advice spilled out into the public, but far from the only time I relied on her thoughtful counsel. Laura had an instinctive feel for the pulse of the country. She wasn't involved in every issue, and she didn't want to be. She picked areas that appealed to her—including education, women's health, rebuilding the Gulf Coast after Katrina, AIDS and malaria, and freedom in Burma and Afghanistan.

I instructed Harriet and the search committee to draw up a new list with more women. The candidates she found were impressive. But there were frustrating roadblocks. When I asked for a more thorough vetting of one well-qualified woman judge, it turned out that her husband had a financial problem that would jeopardize her confirmation. A top choice on the list was Priscilla Owen, a former justice on the Texas Supreme Court. Priscilla was one of the first people I nominated for a federal appeals court position in 2001. Unfortunately, Democrats made her a target. She was finally confirmed in the spring of 2005 as part of a bipartisan compromise. I thought she would make a fine member of the Supreme Court. But a number of senators, including Republicans, told me the fight would be bloody and ultimately she would not be confirmed.

Two other messages came from our consultations on Capitol Hill. The first was that I should think about picking a lawyer from outside the bench. The second was that I seriously consider my White House counsel, Harriet Miers. Several senators had been very impressed by Harriet as she shepherded John Roberts through his interviews on Capitol Hill.

I liked the idea of nominating Harriet. She had been a legal pioneer in Texas—the first woman president of a major Texas law firm, the Dallas Bar Association, and the State Bar of Texas. She had been elected to the Dallas City Council, directed the Texas Lottery Commission, and served nearly five years in top White House positions. There was no doubt in my mind that she shared my judicial philosophy and that her outlook would not change. She would make an outstanding justice.

I asked Harriet if she had any interest in the job. She was surprised—more like shocked—but she said she would serve if I asked. I raised the idea with other members of the search group. Harriet's colleagues loved and respected her, and some thought she would be a good choice. Others argued that it was too risky to pick someone with no established record on the bench, or that we would be accused of cronyism. Several told me bluntly that she was not the right choice. None told me to expect the firestorm of criticism we received from our supporters.

The decision came down to Harriet and Priscilla Owen. I decided to go with Harriet. I knew her better. I thought she had a better chance to be confirmed. And she would bring a unique perspective to the Court as someone outside the judicial fraternity. Initially, a number of senators and judges praised the selection. Their voices, however, were quickly drowned out. On the right, initial whispers of disbelief turned to howls of incredulity. How could I name someone with so little experience? How could they trust the judicial philosophy of someone they didn't know?

It seemed to me that there was another argument against Harriet, one that went largely unspoken: How could I name someone who did not run in elite legal circles? Harriet had not gone to an Ivy League law school. Her personal style compounded the doubts. She is not glib. She is not fancy. She thinks hard before she speaks—a trait so rare in Washington that it was mistaken for intellectual slowness. As one conservative critic condescendingly put it, "However nice, helpful, prompt, and tidy she is, Harriet Miers isn't qualified to play a Supreme Court justice on *The West Wing*, let alone to be a real one."

All of these criticisms came from so-called friends. When the left started criticizing Harriet, too, I knew the nomination was doomed. After three terrible weeks, I got a call in my office in the Treaty Room, where I was working late in the evening. The White House operator told me Harriet was on the phone. In a steady, composed voice, she informed me that she thought it best that she withdraw from consideration for the Supreme Court. As much as it pained me, I agreed.

While I know Harriet would have made a fine justice, I didn't think enough about how the selection would be perceived by others. I put my friend in an impossible situation. If I had it to do over again, I would not have thrown Harriet to the wolves of Washington.

The morning after the announcement, Harriet reported to work, just like on any other day. She went office to office in the West Wing, lifting the spirits of the many colleagues, junior and senior, who were saddened to see a person they admired treated so wrongly. When she came to the Oval Office, I said, "Thank goodness you withdrew. I still have a great lawyer." She smiled and said, "Mr. President, I am ready to lead the search for your next nominee."

I had to get the next pick right. While the idea of selecting a woman still appealed to me, I could not find any as qualified as Sam Alito. Sam is as reserved as they come. When we first sat down for the interview, he seemed ill at ease. I tried the old common-ground icebreaker—in this case, baseball. Sam is a huge Philadelphia Phillies fan. As we talked about the game, his body language changed. He opened up a little about his life and the law. He was scholarly, but practical. He had been a federal prosecutor in New Jersey before moving to the Third Circuit Court of Appeals in 1990. His opinions were well grounded and tightly argued. There was no doubt he would adhere strictly to the Constitution.

Four days after Harriet withdrew, I met with Sam in the Oval Office and offered him the job. He accepted. Our supporters were elated. Our critics knew they would not be able to block Sam's confirmation, but they subjected him to a nasty hearing anyway. They tried to paint him as a racist, a radical, a bigot, anything they could think of—all based on zero evidence. I was disgusted by the demagoguery. As one senator recounted the false charges, Sam's wife, Martha Ann, broke into tears. Her reaction was so genuine that even some Democrats realized they had gone too far.

After the Senate confirmed Sam to the Court, I invited him and his family to the White House for his swearing-in. Before we went out for the ceremony, I had a moment alone with Sam. I thanked him for enduring the hearings and wished him well on the Court. Then I said, "Sam, you ought to thank Harriet Miers for making this possible." He replied, "Mr. President, you're exactly right."

The most emotional personnel decision I had to make was the last one of my presidency. The roots of my dilemma stretched back to the summer of 2003. Our troops in Iraq had not found the weapons of mass destruction we all expected, and the media's scramble for a scapegoat had commenced. In my 2003 State of the Union address, I had cited a British intelligence report that Iraq sought to buy uranium from Niger. The single sentence in my five-thousand-word speech was not a major point in the case against Saddam. The British stood by the intelligence.* Yet those sixteen words became a political controversy and a massive distraction.

In July 2003, former ambassador Joseph Wilson wrote a *New York Times* column alleging that the administration had ignored his skeptical findings when he traveled to Africa to investigate the Iraq-Niger connection. There were serious questions about the accuracy and thoroughness of Wilson's report, but his charge became a prime talking point for critics of the war. Shortly after Wilson's op-ed, longtime Washington columnist Bob Novak reported that Wilson had been sent to Niger not by Dick Cheney or any senior member of the administration, as Wilson had suggested, but on the recommendation of his wife, Valerie Plame, who worked at the CIA.

Then it came out that Wilson's wife's position was classified. Critics alleged that someone in my administration had committed a crime by intentionally leaking the identity of a CIA operative. The Justice Department named a special prosecutor to investigate.

I was inherently skeptical of special prosecutors. I remembered how Lawrence Walsh had politicized his investigation of Iran-Contra during the 1992 campaign. But an intelligence leak was a serious matter, and I directed my staff to cooperate fully. U.S. Attorney Patrick Fitzgerald interviewed most of the team, including me. Early in the process, Deputy Secretary of State Richard Armitage informed Fitzgerald that he had provided Novak with the information about Plame. Nevertheless, the special prosecutor continued to investigate.

Over the course of more than two years, Fitzgerald brought numerous administration officials before a grand jury, including Dick's chief of staff, Scooter Libby. After two appearances by Scooter, Fitzgerald produced an indictment for perjury, obstruction of justice, and making false statements. Scooter went to trial and was convicted. In June 2007 he was sentenced to thirty months in prison.

I faced an agonizing decision. I could let Scooter go to jail. I could use my power under the Constitution to grant him a pardon. Or I could commute his sentence, meaning his conviction would stand but his prison sentence would not. Some in the White House, led by the vice

* In 2004, the nonpartisan Butler Report concluded that the statement was "well-founded."

president, pushed aggressively for a pardon. Their argument was that the investigation should never have proceeded after Fitzgerald had identified Novak's source. On the other hand, most advisers believed that the jury verdict was correct and should remain in place.

I decided it would send a bad message to pardon a former staff member convicted of obstructing justice, especially after I had instructed the staff to cooperate with the investigation. But the punishment Scooter had received did not fit the crime. The protracted investigation and trial had already caused personal, professional, and financial damage for Scooter and his family. In early July 2007, I announced my decision: "I respect the jury's verdict. But I have concluded that the prison sentence given to Mr. Libby is excessive. Therefore, I am commuting the portion of Mr. Libby's sentence that required him to spend thirty months in prison."

The reaction from the left was blistering. "President Bush's action today tells America that it's okay to lie, mislead, and obstruct justice, as long as you are loyal to his administration," one congressman said. Another said, "I call on House Democrats to reconsider impeachment proceedings." Not everyone in the White House liked the decision, either. Dick continued to advocate a full pardon.

One of the biggest surprises of my presidency was the flood of pardon requests at the end. I could not believe the number of people who pulled me aside to suggest that a friend or former colleague deserved a pardon. At first I was frustrated. Then I was disgusted. I came to see massive injustice in the system. If you had connections to the president, you could insert your case into the last-minute frenzy. Otherwise, you had to wait for the Justice Department to conduct a review and make a recommendation. In my final weeks in office, I resolved that I would not pardon anyone who went outside the formal channels.

In the closing days of the administration, Dick pressed his case that Scooter should be pardoned. Scooter was a decent man and dedicated public servant, and I understood the ramifications for his family. I asked two trusted lawyers to review the case from top to bottom, including the evidence presented at the trial for and against Scooter. I also authorized them to meet with Scooter to hear his side of the story. After careful analysis, both lawyers told me they could find no justification for overturning the jury's verdict.

I spent our last weekend at Camp David wrestling with the decision. "Just make up your mind," Laura told me. "You're ruining this for everyone." Ultimately, I reached the same conclusion I had in 2007: The jury verdict should be respected. In one of our final meetings, I informed Dick that I would not issue a pardon. He stared at me with an intense look. "I can't believe you're going to leave a soldier on the battlefield," he said. The comment stung. In eight years, I had never seen Dick like this, or even close to this. I worried that the friendship we had built was about to be severely strained, at best.

A few days later, I talked to another person about the pardon process. On the ride up Pennsylvania Avenue on Inauguration Day, I told Barack Obama about my frustrations with the pardon system. I gave him a suggestion: announce a pardon policy early on, and stick to it.

After President Obama's Inauguration, Laura and I choppered to Andrews Air Force Base. Our final event before boarding the plane home to Texas was a farewell ceremony in front of three thousand friends, family, and former staff. Dick had agreed to introduce me. He had injured his back moving boxes, so Lynne had to push him onto the stage in a wheelchair. Dick grabbed the microphone. I had no idea what he would say. I hoped he would be able to get past the disappointment he felt. His words were heartfelt and kind: "Eight and a half years ago, I began a partnership with George Bush that has truly been a special honor. . . . If I have one regret, it is only that these days have ended and that all the members of this fine team, now, must go their own way."

The man I picked that hot day in July remained steady to the end. Our friendship had survived.

# 4

# STEM CELLS

I n the heart of central London sat a thirty-four-story gray building. One floor contained a large, open space known as the Fertilizing Room. Inside, technicians meticulously mixed eggs and sperm in test tubes to produce the next generation. The hatchery served as the lifeblood of a new world government, which had mastered the formula for engineering a productive and stable society.

That scene was not the creation of Jay Lefkowitz, the bright lawyer reading aloud to me in the Oval Office in 2001. It came from Aldous Huxley's 1932 novel, *Brave New World*. With the recent breakthroughs in biotechnology and genetics, the book now seemed chillingly relevant. So did its lesson: For all its efficiency, Huxley's utopian world seemed sterile, joyless, and empty of meaning. The quest to perfect humanity ended in the loss of humanity.

In April of that same year, another piece of writing turned up in the Oval Office. Describing what she called a "wrenching family journey," the author urged me to support the "miracle possibilities" of embryonic stem cell research to provide cures for people like her husband, who was suffering from Alzheimer's. She closed, "Mr. President, I have some personal experience regarding the many decisions you face each day. . . . I'd be very grateful if you would take my thoughts and prayers into your consideration on this critical issue. Most sincerely, Nancy Reagan."

The juxtaposition of Mrs. Reagan's letter and the Huxley novel framed the decision I faced on stem cell research. Many felt the federal government had a responsibility to fund medical research that might help save the lives of people like President Reagan. Others argued that supporting the destruction of human embryos could take us off a moral cliff toward an uncaring society that devalued life. The contrast was stark, and I faced a difficult decision.

———

"Sometimes our differences run so deep it seems we share a continent, but not a country," I said in my Inaugural Address on January 20, 2001. "We do not accept this, and we will not allow it. Our unity, our union, is the serious work of leaders and citizens in every generation. And this is my solemn pledge: I will work to build a single nation of justice and opportunity."

After a luncheon with dignitaries at the Capitol, Laura and I made our way to the White House as part of the official Inaugural parade. Pennsylvania Avenue was lined by well-wishers, along with a few pockets of protesters. They carried big signs with foul language, hurled eggs at the motorcade, and screamed at the top of their lungs. I spent most of the ride in the presidential limo behind thick glass windows, so their shouting came across in pantomime. While I couldn't make out their words, their middle fingers spoke loudly: The bitterness of the 2000 election was not going away anytime soon.

Laura and I watched the rest of the parade from the reviewing stand at the White House. We waved to the marchers from every state and were thrilled to see high school bands from Midland and Crawford. After the parade, I went to check out the Oval Office. As I walked over from the residence, the room looked like it was glowing. Its bright lights and gold drapes stood out in vivid contrast from the dark winter sky.

Each president decorates the Oval Office in his own style. I hung several Texas paintings, including Julian Onderdonk's renditions of the Alamo, a West Texas landscape, and a field of bluebonnets—a daily reminder of our ranch in Crawford. I also brought a painting called *Rio Grande* from an El Paso artist and friend, Tom Lea, and a scene of a horseman charging up a hill by W.H.D. Koerner. The name of the piece, *A Charge to Keep*, echoed a Methodist hymn by Charles Wesley, which we sang at my first inauguration as governor. Both the painting and hymn reflect the importance of serving a cause larger than oneself.

I decided to keep the Rembrandt Peale portrait of George Washington that Dad and Bill Clinton had placed over the mantel. I added busts of Abraham Lincoln, Dwight Eisenhower, and Winston Churchill—a gift on loan from the British government courtesy of Prime Minister Tony Blair. I had told Tony that I admired Churchill's courage, principle, and sense of humor—all of which I thought were necessary for leadership. (My favorite example of Churchill's wit was his reply when Franklin Roosevelt caught him coming out of the tub on a visit to the White House in December 1941. "I have nothing to hide from the president of the United States!" he said.) After 9/11, I realized the three busts had something in common: All depicted wartime leaders. I certainly didn't have that in mind when I chose them.

One space on the wall was reserved for the president's most influential predecessor. I chose Lincoln. He'd had the most trying job of any president, preserving the Union. Some asked why I didn't put Dad's portrait in that spot. "Number forty-one hangs in my heart," I said. "Sixteen is on the wall."

The centerpiece of the Oval Office was the Resolute desk. I had chosen the desk because of its historical significance. Its story began in 1852, when Queen Victoria dispatched the HMS *Resolute* to search for the British explorer John Franklin, who had been lost looking for the Northwest Passage. The *Resolute* was trapped in ice near the Arctic and abandoned by its crew. In 1855 it was discovered by an American whaling ship, which sailed the *Resolute* back to Connecticut. The vessel was purchased by the U.S. government, refitted, and returned to England as a goodwill gift to the queen. When the *Resolute* was decommissioned two decades later, Her Majesty had several ornate desks made out of its timbers, one of which she gave to President Rutherford B. Hayes.

Most presidents since Hayes have used the Resolute desk in one capacity or another. Franklin Roosevelt commissioned a front panel door with a carved presidential seal, which some historians believe was intended to hide his wheelchair. Little John F. Kennedy, Jr., poked his head out that door in the most famous Oval Office photo ever taken. Dad had used the Resolute in his upstairs office in the residence, while Bill Clinton returned it to the Oval. Sitting behind the historic desk was a reminder—that first day and every day—that the institution of the presidency is more important than the person who holds it.

Andy Card was with me as I took my place at the Resolute for the first time. My first Oval Office decision was to replace the desk chair—a bizarre contraption that vibrated when plugged in—with something more practical. Then the door to the Rose Garden swung open. I looked up and saw Dad.

"Mr. President," he said. He was wearing a dark suit, his hair still wet from the hot bath he'd taken to thaw out.

"Mr. President," I replied.

He stepped into the office, and I walked around the desk. We met in the middle of the room. Neither of us said much. We didn't need to. The moment was more moving than either of us could have expressed.

———

On my ninth day as president, my domestic policy team gathered in the Oval Office. Everyone was on time. That was what I expected. Timeliness is important to make sure an organization does not get sloppy. The chief briefer that day was Margaret Spellings, a smart and feisty mother of two. Margaret had served with me in Austin and moved to Washington as my top domestic policy adviser. She covered a variety of topics that day, including a new initiative for people with disabilities and an election reform commission chaired by former Presidents Ford and Carter. Then she launched into a discussion of embryonic stem cell research. "The Clinton administration issued new legal guidelines that interpret the Dickey Amendment to permit federal funding for embryonic stem cell research. We have several options going forward—"

That's as far as she got before I cut her off. "First of all," I asked, "what exactly is a stem cell?" I learn best by asking questions. In some cases, I probe to understand a complex issue. Other times, I deploy questions as a way to test my briefers' knowledge. If they cannot answer concisely and in plain English, it raises a red flag that they may not fully grasp the subject.

As usual, Margaret was well prepared. She started by explaining the science. Embryonic stem cells are a special medical resource because they can transform into a wide variety of different cell types. Just as the stem of a vine grows into many distinct branches, embryonic stem cells have the capacity to grow into nerve cells for the brain, muscle tissues for the heart, or other organs. These cells offered a possible way to treat ailments from juvenile diabetes to Alzheimer's to Parkinson's. The technology was new, and the science was unproven. But the potential was significant. However, the only way to extract embryonic stem cells is to destroy the embryo. This raised a moral dilemma: Could the destruction of one human life be justified by the hopes of saving others?

Congress's answer seemed clear. Every year since 1995, the House and Senate had passed legislation banning the use of federal funds for research in which human embryos were destroyed. The law was known as the Dickey Amendment after its sponsor, Congressman Jay Dickey of Arkansas.

In 1998, a researcher at the University of Wisconsin isolated an individual embryonic stem cell for the first time. As the cell divided, it created a multitude of other cells—called a line—that could be used for research. Soon after, the Clinton administration adopted a novel interpretation of the Dickey Amendment. Lawyers argued that taxpayer dollars could be used to support stem cell research on lines derived from destroyed embryos so long as the destruction itself was funded by private sources. The National Institutes of Health prepared to award grants under those terms, but President Clinton's term ended before any funds were distributed. The immediate decision facing me was whether to allow those grants to proceed.

———

It was clear this would be more than a funding dispute. The moral questions were profound: Is a frozen embryo a human life? If so, what responsibilities do we have to protect it?

I told Margaret and Deputy Chief of Staff Josh Bolten that I considered this a far-reaching decision. I laid out a process for making it. I would clarify my guiding principles, listen to experts on all sides of the debate, reach a tentative conclusion, and run it past knowledgeable people. After finalizing a decision, I would explain it to the American people. Finally, I would set up a process to ensure that my policy was implemented.

To run the process, Josh tapped Jay Lefkowitz, the general counsel of the Office of Management and Budget, the agency that would oversee my funding policy. Jay was a thoughtful and lively lawyer from New York with a serious commitment to his Jewish faith and a dry sense of humor. I liked him immediately. That was good, because we were going to spend a lot of time together.

Jay loaded me up with background reading. He included articles from medical journals, writings on moral philosophy, and legal analyses. The reading he sent spanned the spectrum of viewpoints. In *Science* magazine, bioethicist Dr. Louis Guenin argued, "If we spurn [embryonic stem cell research], not one more baby is likely to be born. If we conduct research, we may relieve suffering."

Those on the other side of the debate argued that government support for the destruction of human life would cross a moral line. "Embryonic stem cell research takes us onto a path that would transform our perception of human life into a malleable, marketable natural resource—akin to a cattle herd or copper mine—to be exploited for the benefit of the born and breathing," bioethics expert Wesley J. Smith wrote in *National Review*.

At its core, the stem cell question harked back to the philosophical clash between science and morality. I felt pulled in both directions. I had no interest in joining the Flat Earth Society. I empathized with the hopes for new medical cures. I had lost a sister to childhood leukemia. I had served on the board of the Kent Waldrep National Paralysis Foundation, an advocacy group led by a former Texas Christian University football player who had suffered a spinal cord injury. I believed in the promise of science and technology to alleviate suffering and disease. During my presidential campaign, I had pledged to follow through on the commitment Congress made in the late 1990s to double funding for the National Institutes of Health.

At the same time, I felt that technology should respect moral boundaries. I worried that sanctioning the destruction of human embryos for research would be a step down the slippery slope from science fiction to medical reality. I envisioned researchers cloning fetuses to grow spare body parts in a laboratory. I could foresee the temptation of designer babies that enabled parents to engineer their very own blond-haired basketball player. Not far beyond that lies the nightmare of full-scale human cloning. I knew these possibilities would sound fanciful to some people. But once science started heading down that path, it would be very hard to turn back.

The stem cell question overlapped with the abortion debate. It seems hard to believe now, but abortion was not a major political issue when I was young. I don't remember it coming up much during Dad's early campaigns or in conversations at Andover or Yale. That changed in 1973 when the Supreme Court, in a decision Justice Byron White called "an exercise in raw judicial power," deemed abortion a right protected by the Constitution.

The abortion issue is difficult, sensitive, and personal. My faith and conscience led me to conclude that human life is sacred. God created man in His image and therefore every person has value in His eyes. It seemed to me that an unborn child, while dependent on its mother, is a separate and independent being worthy of protection in its own right. When I saw Barbara and Jenna on the sonogram for the first time, there was no doubt in my mind they were distinct and alive. The fact that they could not speak for themselves only enhanced society's duty to defend them.

Many decent and thoughtful people disagreed, including members of my family. I understood their reasons and respected their views. As president, I had no desire to condemn millions as sinners or dump new fuel on raging cultural fires. I did feel a responsibility to voice my pro-life convictions and lead the country toward what Pope John Paul II called a culture of life. I was convinced that most Americans agreed we would be better off with fewer abortions. One of my first acts in the White House was to reinstate the so-called Mexico City Policy, which prevented federal funding for groups that promote abortion overseas. I supported state laws requiring parental notification for minors seeking abortions. And

I supported, signed, and defended a bill banning the grisly practice of partial-birth abortion.

Laura and I were also strong supporters of adoption. After having difficulty conceiving children, it was hard for us to imagine anyone rejecting what we considered a precious gift. Yet as the father of daughters, I could envision the dilemma facing a scared teenager with an unplanned pregnancy. Adoption was such a positive alternative to abortion, a way to save one life and brighten two more: those of the adoptive parents. I was pleased to sign legislation increasing funding for crisis pregnancy counseling centers, as well as to expand tax credits to offset the costs of adoption.

In the long run, I hoped a change in hearts would lead to a change in law, as new technologies like 3-D ultrasounds help more Americans recognize the humanity of unborn babies. I also hoped political leaders would continue to speak out for a culture that values all innocent human life. Bob Casey, the late Democratic governor of Pennsylvania, said it well: "When we look to the unborn child, the real issue is not when life begins, but when love begins."

———

Beginning in the spring of 2001, Margaret, Jay, and Karl Rove—who was in close touch with advocacy groups on both sides of the issue—invited a series of distinguished scientists, ethicists, religious thinkers, and advocates to discuss embryonic stem cell research. The conversations fascinated me. The more I learned, the more questions I had. When I delivered the commencement address at Notre Dame, I brought up embryonic stem cell research with Father Ed "Monk" Malloy, the president of the university. When I spoke at Yale the next day, I raised the topic with Dr. Harold Varmus of the Memorial Sloan-Kettering Cancer Center. At a birthday party for a doctor in the White House Medical Unit, I asked all the physicians there what they thought. As word got out that I was seeking opinions, I was bombarded with input from Cabinet secretaries, staffers, outside advisers, and friends.

Of course, I asked Laura for her advice. Her father had died of Alzheimer's, her mother had suffered from breast cancer, and she held out great hope for the possibility of new cures. But she worried that advocacy groups would overpromise what embryonic stem cell research could achieve, leaving desperate families with dashed hopes.

Members of the scientific community presented two main arguments in favor of funding embryonic stem cell research. First was the medical potential. Researchers told me there were millions of Americans suffering from diseases that might be alleviated through treatments derived from embryonic stem cells. Experts believed that only a few stem cell lines would be needed to explore the science and determine its value. "If we had ten to fifteen lines, no one would complain," Irv Weissman, a prominent researcher from Stanford, told the *New York Times*.

A research team from the National Institutes of Health told me that several dozen stem cell lines were already under development. They also reported some preliminary research into alternative ways of deriving stem cells without destroying embryos. Their unanimous opinion was that denying federal support for embryonic stem cell research would result in a missed opportunity. Taxpayer dollars were important not only as a source of financing, they explained, but also as a seal of approval for scientific innovation.

The scientists' second point was a practical one: Most of the embryos used to derive the stem cells would likely be discarded anyway. The primary source of these embryos was In Vitro Fertilization (IVF) clinics. When a couple signed up for IVF, doctors usually fertilized more eggs than they implanted in the prospective mother. As a result, some embryos would be left after the treatment was complete. They were usually frozen and stored by the fertility clinic. Since these so-called spare embryos were not going to be used to conceive children, scientists argued, didn't it make sense to use them for research that could potentially save lives?

One of the groups most actively supporting embryonic stem cell research was the Juvenile Diabetes Research Foundation. In July 2001, I invited representatives from the organization to the Oval Office. Among the delegation were two friends of mine, Woody Johnson and Mike Overlock. Both men were political backers, and both had children suffering from diabetes. They were passionate, compelling advocates with an unmistakable devotion to their children. But their certainty about a rapid embryonic stem cell breakthrough surprised me. When I pointed out that the science was unproven and that there could be alternatives to embryo destruction, it was obvious that the advocacy group had left no room for doubt in their minds. The meeting was a window into the passions the issue could generate.

That same day, I also met representatives of National Right to Life. They opposed any research that destroyed embryos. They pointed out that each tiny stem cell cluster had the potential to grow into a person. In fact, all of us had started our lives in this early state. As evidence, they pointed to a new program run by Nightlight Christian Adoptions. The agency secured permission from IVF participants to place their unused frozen embryos up for adoption. Loving mothers had the embryos implanted in them and carried the babies—known as snowflakes—to term. The message was unmistakable: Within every frozen embryo were the beginnings of a child.

Many of the bioethicists I met took the same position. They acknowledged that most embryos frozen in IVF clinics would not become children. Yet they argued that there was a moral difference between allowing embryos to die naturally and proactively ending their lives. Sanctioning the destruction of life to save life, they argued, crossed into dangerous moral territory. As one put it, "The fact that a being is going to die does not entitle us to use it as a natural resource for exploitation."

I heard some opinions that surprised me. Dr. Dan Callahan, a thoughtful ethicist, told me he was pro-choice on abortion but against embryonic stem cell research. He believed there was a moral distinction between aborting a baby for the direct benefit of its mother and destroying an embryo for the vague and indirect purpose of scientific research. Dr. Benjamin Carson, one of the world's most respected surgeons, told me that stem cell research could be valuable, but that scientists should focus on alternatives to embryo destruction, such as collecting stem cells from the blood of umbilical cords. On the other hand, Orrin Hatch and Strom Thurmond, two of the most staunchly pro-life members of the Senate, supported federal funding for embryonic stem cell research because they thought the benefit of saving lives outweighed the cost of destroying embryos.

In July 2001, I visited Pope John Paul II at his beautiful summer residence, Castel Gandolfo. Swiss Guards in full regalia escorted us through a series of rooms and into the reception area. Pope John Paul II was one of the great figures in modern history. A survivor of Nazi and communist rule in his native Poland, he had become the first non-Italian pope in 455 years. With his call "Be Not Afraid," he rallied the conscience of Central and Eastern Europe to bring down the Iron Curtain. As the distinguished Cold War historian John Lewis Gaddis later wrote, "When John Paul II kissed the ground at the Warsaw airport on June 2, 1979, he began the process by which communism in Poland—and ultimately everywhere else in Europe—would come to an end."

By 2001, the Holy Father's vigor and energy had given way to frailty. His movements were deliberate, his speech soft and slow. Yet his eyes sparkled. He was filled with an unmistakable spirit. He gingerly walked Laura, our daughter Barbara, and me to a balcony, where we marveled at gorgeous Lake Albano below. He and I then retired to a simple meeting room, where we discussed a variety of issues, including stem cell research. He understood the promise of science—the Holy Father himself was stricken with Parkinson's. Yet he was firm in his view that human life must be protected in all its forms. I thanked him for his example of principled leadership. I explained that the Catholic Church's steadfast support of life provided a firm moral foundation on which pro-life politicians like me could take a stand. I told him I hoped the Church would always be a rock in the defense of human dignity.

When the Holy Father passed away in 2005, Laura, Dad, Bill Clinton, and I flew together to his funeral in Rome. It was the first time an American president had attended the funeral of a pope, let alone brought two of his predecessors. Shortly after we arrived, we went to pay our respects to the Holy Father while he was lying in state. As we knelt at the communion rail to pray over his body, Laura turned to me and said, "Now is the time to pray for miracles." An unexpected impulse came over me. I prayed for Peter Jennings, the ABC News anchor who was dying of cancer.

The funeral mass was incredibly moving. The crowd in St. Peter's Square cheered, sang, and carried banners celebrating the Holy Father's life. After a homily by Cardinal Joseph Ratzinger—who eleven days later emerged from the conclave as Pope Benedict XVI—a group of Church officials carried the Holy Father's casket up the stairs toward St. Peter's Basilica. Just before entering the doors, they turned to face the crowd and lifted the coffin for a last time. As they did, the clouds parted and the sun shined through onto the simple wooden box.

———

After several months of listening and reflecting, I was close to a decision on stem cell research. A defining moment came in a conversation with Leon Kass on July 10. Leon was a highly respected physician and philosophy professor at the University of Chicago. He had written and taught in fields as diverse as evolutionary biology, literature, and the Bible. He struck me as a thoughtful and wise man.

I told Leon I had been wrestling with the decision. Embryonic stem cell research seemed to offer so much hope. Yet it raised troubling moral concerns. I wondered if it was possible to find a principled policy that advanced science while respecting the dignity of life.

Leon's logical mind went to work. He argued that embryos—even those long frozen—had the potential for life and thus deserved some form of respect. "One goes with a heavy heart if we use these things," he said. "We at least owe them the respect not to manipulate them for our own purposes. We are dealing with the seeds of the next generation."

I shared an idea: What if I authorized federal funding for embryonic stem cell research—but solely for existing stem cell lines? The embryos used to create those lines had been destroyed. There was no way to get them back. It seemed logical to let scientists use them to pursue treatments that might save other lives. But that raised another question: If I allowed federal funding for research that relied on destroyed embryos, would I be tacitly encouraging further destruction?

Leon said he believed that funding research on already destroyed embryos would be ethical, with two conditions. I must reaffirm the moral principle that had been violated—in this case, the dignity of human life. And I must make clear that federal funds would not be used in the further destruction of embryos. So long as I did both, he said, the policy would pass the ethical test. "If you fund research on lines that have already been developed," he said, "you are not complicit in their destruction."

The conversation with Leon crystallized my thinking. I decided that the government would fund research on stem cell lines derived from embryos that had already been destroyed. At the same time, I would ask Congress to increase federal funding for alternative sources of stem cells that brought no ethical controversy. And I would draw a firm moral line: Federal tax dollars would not be used to support the destruction of life for medical gain. I also created a new presidential bioethics council, composed of experts from all backgrounds and chaired by Leon Kass.

The next step was to announce the decision to the American people. Karen suggested a rare primetime speech to the nation. When the president addresses the nation in primetime, he usually speaks as commander in chief. In this case, I would be speaking as educator in chief. I liked the idea. Stem cell research was a serious issue for the nation, but an obscure one for most citizens—as it had been for me in January. Explaining my decision would be almost as important as making it.

On August 9, 2001, I addressed a nationwide network TV audience from Crawford, Texas—definitely a first in presidential history. The night before the speech, Laura and I had dinner with Jay, Karen and her son Robert, and a family friend, Fort Worth interior designer Ken Blasingame. I asked Jay to say a prayer before we began the meal. He delivered some thoughtful words. As he finished, we all kept our heads bowed, waiting for the amen. After a few seconds of hanging, Jay told us that Jewish prayers don't always end with amen. It was a fitting conclusion to a process filled with learning.

"Good evening," I began my address, "I appreciate you giving me a few minutes of your time tonight so I can discuss with you a complex and difficult issue, an issue that is one of the most profound of our time." I outlined the dilemma: "While we must devote enormous energy to conquering disease," I said, "it is equally important that we pay attention to the moral concerns raised by the new frontier of human embryo stem cell research. Even the most noble ends do not justify any means."

Near the end, I pivoted to my decision:

*Embryonic stem cell research offers both great promise and great peril. So I have decided we must proceed with great care. . . . I have concluded that we should allow federal funds to be used for research on these [existing] stem*

*cell lines, where the life-and-death decision has already been made. Lead-*
*ing scientists tell me research on these sixty lines has great promise that*
*could lead to breakthrough therapies and cures. This allows us to explore*
*the promise and potential of stem cell research without crossing a funda-*
*mental moral line, by providing taxpayer funding that would sanction or*
*encourage further destruction of human embryos that have at least the*
*potential for life. . . . I have made this decision with great care, and I pray*
*it is the right one.*

For weeks before the speech, I had felt a sense of anxiety. I had constantly questioned my assumptions and weighed the options again and
again. With the decision made, I felt a sense of calm. I didn't know what
the reaction would be. We hadn't commissioned a focus group or taken
a poll. Just as we had waited for the amen at the end of Jay's prayer, we
settled in to await the response.

———

Reaction to my stem cell decision poured in quickly. Many politicians
and activists on both sides praised the policy as reasonable and balanced.
While some scientists and advocacy groups responded with disappointment, many welcomed the unprecedented federal funding as a vote of
confidence in their work. The head of the Juvenile Diabetes Research
Foundation issued a statement saying, "We applaud the president for
supporting embryonic stem cell research." My friend Kent Waldrep, the
paralyzed TCU football player on whose advocacy board I used to sit,
told a reporter, "It does everything the scientific community needs and I
think a little bit more."

To the degree that I faced criticism, it came from the right. One conservative activist compared my decision to Nazi conduct during the Holocaust. Another said, "I am ashamed of our president, who compromises
and gives my generation the . . . mentality that human life can be picked
apart, abused, and destroyed." The spokesman for the U.S. Conference
of Catholic Bishops said, "I seem to be the only man in America who is
against the president's policy."

His loneliness did not last long. The tone of the debate quickly became heated and harsh. Looking back, it is clear that a toxic pair of factors had converged: money and politics.

Many of the first to turn against the policy were scientists. By providing some federal funding, I had whetted their appetite for more. In the spring of 2002, I addressed a major complaint by allowing privately funded embryonic stem cell research to be conducted at facilities that received federal dollars. It was an important step, but it did not satisfy the scientists, who constantly demanded more.

Advocacy groups quickly followed. Their high hopes for new cures had led them to make unrealistic promises. They seemed to feel that limiting the number of stem cells available for research would delay breakthroughs. They recruited well-meaning Hollywood stars to tug at heartstrings. They also discovered that the issue could help them raise large amounts of money. Some who had initially supported my decision transformed into vocal critics.

Politicians recognized that they, too, could capitalize on the issue. By 2004, Democrats had concluded that stem cell research was a political winner. It allowed them to open a new front in the abortion debate while also claiming the mantle of compassion. Candidates across the country ran TV ads that highlighted the benefits of embryonic stem cell research without mentioning that the science was unproven, the morality was in doubt, and ethical alternatives existed.

The Democratic presidential nominee, Senator John Kerry, campaigned hard on the issue. Kerry frequently criticized what he called a "ban" on embryonic stem cell research. I pointed out that there was no such ban. To the contrary, I was the first president in history to fund embryonic stem cell research. Plus, there were no restrictions on funding from the private sector.

Nonetheless, Kerry's campaign used stem cell research as the foundation for a broader attack, labeling my positions "anti-science." The charge was false. I had supported science by funding alternative stem cell research, promoting clean energy development, increasing federal spending on technology research, and launching a global AIDS initiative. Yet the demagoguery continued all the way up to the election. The low point came in October, when Kerry's running mate, Senator John Edwards, told a political rally in Iowa that if Kerry became president, "people like Christopher Reeve* will get up out of that wheelchair and walk again."

———

The stem cell debate was an introduction to a phenomenon I witnessed throughout my presidency: highly personal criticism. Partisan opponents and commentators questioned my legitimacy, my intelligence, and my sincerity. They mocked my appearance, my accent, and my religious beliefs. I was labeled a Nazi, a war criminal, and Satan himself. That last one came from a foreign leader, Venezuelan President Hugo Chavez. One lawmaker called me both a loser and a liar. He became majority leader of the U.S. Senate.

In some ways, I wasn't surprised. I had endured plenty of rough politics in Texas. I had seen Dad and Bill Clinton derided by their opponents and the media. Abraham Lincoln was compared to a baboon. Even George Washington became so unpopular that political cartoons showed the hero of the American Revolution being marched to a guillotine.

Yet the death spiral of decency during my time in office, exacerbated by the advent of twenty-four-hour cable news and hyper-partisan political blogs, was deeply disappointing. The toxic atmosphere in American politics discourages good people from running for office.

Over time, the petty insults and name-calling hardened into conventional wisdom. Some have said I should have pushed back harder against the caricatures. But I felt it would debase the presidency to stoop to the critics' level. I had run on a promise to change the tone in Washington. I took that vow seriously and tried to do my part, but I rarely succeeded.

The shrill debate never affected my decisions. I read a lot of history, and I was struck by how many presidents had endured harsh criticism. The measure of their character, and often their success, was how they responded. Those who based decisions on principle, not some snapshot of public opinion, were often vindicated over time.

George Washington once wrote that leading by conviction gave him

*The famous actor who played Superman, Reeve was confined to a wheelchair after a horse-riding accident. Sadly, he died in October 2004, one day before Edwards's statement.

"a consolation within that no earthly efforts can deprive me of." He continued: "The arrows of malevolence, however barbed and well pointed, never can reach the most vulnerable part of me."

I read those words in *Presidential Courage*, written by historian Michael Beschloss in 2007. As I told Laura, if they're still assessing George Washington's legacy more than two centuries after he left office, this George W. doesn't have to worry about today's headlines.

———

Far from the yelling on the TV sets and the campaign trail, my stem cell policy quietly moved forward in the labs. For the first time in history, scientists received federal grants to support embryonic stem cell research.

Scientists also used new federal funding for alternative stem cell research to explore the potential of adult bone marrow, placentas, amniotic fluid, and other non-embryonic sources. Their research yielded new treatments for patients suffering from dozens of diseases—free of moral drawbacks. For example, doctors discovered a way to collect stem cells harmlessly from the blood of umbilical cords to treat patients suffering from leukemia and sickle-cell anemia.

Much of this research was overseen by Dr. Elias Zerhouni, the talented Algerian American I appointed to lead the NIH. I had put Elias in a tough position. He felt trapped between a president he had agreed to serve and the scientific community of which he was part. He did not agree with my embryonic stem cell policy. Yet he was more interested in new cures than in politics. He funded the alternative stem cell sources aggressively, and a good deal of credit for the breakthroughs in the field belongs to Dr. Zerhouni and his team of professionals at the NIH.

Unfortunately, most members of Congress paid more attention to politics than to the scientific discoveries. As the 2006 elections approached, Democrats made clear they would again use the issue as a political weapon. A U.S. Senate candidate in Missouri persuaded Michael J. Fox, who suffers from Parkinson's, to attack her opponent in statewide TV ads. Some Republicans who had initially supported the policy feared for their seats and changed their minds. In July 2006, the House and Senate considered a bill that would overturn my stem cell policy by permitting federal funding for research that destroyed human life.

Five and a half years into the presidency, I had yet to veto a piece of legislation. I had worked closely with our congressional majorities to pass bills I could accept. But as the stem cell bill was working its way through Congress, I had made clear I would veto it. When it reached my desk, I did.

I was hit with all sorts of labels, "stubborn" being one of the most polite. But I would not change my position. If I abandoned my principles on an issue like stem cell research, how could I maintain my credibility on anything else?

I thought a lot about how to send the right signal about the veto. I wanted a vivid way to show that my position was grounded in my reverence for life, not any aversion to science. When Karl Zinsmeister, my domestic policy adviser, suggested inviting a group of snowflake babies to the White House, I thought the idea was perfect. Each had come from a frozen embryo that, rather than being destroyed for research, was implanted in an adoptive mother.

I gave my veto speech in the East Room with twenty-four excited children and their parents onstage. One of the little wigglers was fourteen-month-old Trey Jones. He started life as an embryo fertilized by Dave and Heather Wright of Macomb, Michigan. The couple had undergone IVF treatment, which helped them bring three beautiful children into the world. They gave permission for their remaining frozen embryos to be adopted, instead of being destroyed for research.

In Cypress, Texas, J. J. and Tracy Jones were praying for a child. Through Nightlight Christian Adoptions, they were paired with the Wright family embryos. The result was the smiling, blond-haired boy named Trey whom I held in my arms at the White House. Thanks to the miracle of science and the compassion of two families, Trey had a loving home and a hopeful life ahead of him.

A few weeks after the event, I received a touching letter from J. J. Jones. He described the "pain of infertility" and how blessed he and Tracy felt to have their "precious Trey who some describe as a leftover destined to be either destroyed or used for research." He also informed me that Trey would soon have a sibling, the product of another frozen embryo he and Tracy had adopted.

Congress's response to my veto was not so warm. The Democratic sponsor of the bill erupted with a statement claiming that my veto was based on "cynical political gain." It was hard to see how, since most polls showed my stem cell stance was not popular. As punishment for my veto, Democrats refused to pass legislation supporting research into alternative sources of stem cells. The message was that if they couldn't fund stem cell research that destroyed embryos, they would prefer to fund none at all. So much for their passionate desire to see new cures.

When Democrats won control of the House and Senate, they decided to make another run at overturning my policy. Speaker Nancy Pelosi announced that it was one of her top priorities. They sent me another bill in June 2007; I sent it back again with my veto. Thanks to the courage of many Republicans on Capitol Hill, the veto held.

———

Five months later, Americans awoke to an unexpected headline on the front page of the *New York Times*: "Scientists Bypass Need for Embryo to Get Stem Cells." The article described how two teams of researchers, one in Wisconsin and one in Japan, had reprogrammed an adult skin cell to behave like an embryonic stem cell. By adding just four genes to the adult cell, scientists were able to replicate the medical promise of embryonic stem cells without moral controversy.

The discovery reverberated throughout the scientific community. Fervent advocates of embryonic stem cell research hailed the breakthrough as "a spectacular advance" and "ethically uncomplicated." Ian Wilmut, the Scottish scientist who cloned Dolly the sheep, announced that he would no longer pursue the cloning of human embryos, but would instead use this new technique.

I was thrilled by the news. This was the scientific breakthrough that I had hoped for when I made my announcement in 2001. Charles Krauthammer, one of the most insightful columnists in America and a respectful critic of my stem cell decision in 2001, wrote, "The verdict is clear: Rarely has a president—so vilified for a moral stance—been so thoroughly vindicated."

In the years to come, our nation will face more dilemmas about bio-ethics, from cloning to genetic engineering. History will judge the character of our country in large part by the way we answer these challenges to human dignity. I have faith, as I did when I announced my stem cell decision in 2001, that science and ethics can coexist. With thoughtful policy, we can usher in the new cures that Nancy Reagan hoped for, without moving toward the world foreseen by Aldous Huxley.

———

After my address to the nation on stem cell research in August 2001, several commentators called it the most important decision of my presidency. That was true at the time, but not for long.

# 5

# DAY OF FIRE

On Tuesday, September 11, 2001, I awoke before dawn in my suite at the Colony Beach and Tennis Resort near Sarasota, Florida. I started the morning by reading the Bible and then went downstairs for a run. It was pitch-black as I began my jog around the golf course. The Secret Service agents had grown accustomed to my exercise routine; the locals must have found this run in the dark a little bizarre.

Back at the hotel, I took a quick shower, ate a light breakfast, and skimmed the morning papers. The biggest story was that Michael Jordan was coming out of retirement to rejoin the NBA. Other headlines focused on the New York mayoral primary and a suspected case of mad cow disease in Japan.

Around 8:00 a.m., I received the Presidential Daily Briefing. The PDB, which combined highly classified intelligence with in-depth analysis of geopolitics, was one of the most fascinating parts of my day. The September 11 briefing, delivered by a bright CIA analyst named Mike Morell, covered Russia, China, and the Palestinian uprising in the West Bank and Gaza Strip.

Shortly after the PDB, we left for a visit to Emma E. Booker Elementary School to highlight education reform.

On the short walk from the motorcade to the classroom, Karl Rove mentioned that an airplane had crashed into the World Trade Center. That sounded strange. I envisioned a little propeller plane horribly lost. Then Condi called. I spoke to her from a secure phone in a classroom that had been converted into a communications center for the traveling White House staff. She told me the plane that had just struck the Trade Center tower was not a light aircraft. It was a commercial jetliner.

I was stunned. That plane must have had the worst pilot in the world.

How could he possibly have flown into a skyscraper on a clear day? Maybe he'd had a heart attack. I told Condi to stay on top of the situation and asked my communications director, Dan Bartlett, to work on a statement promising the full support of federal emergency management services.

I greeted Booker's principal, a friendly woman named Gwen Rigell. She introduced me to the teacher, Sandra Kay Daniels, and her roomful of second-graders. Mrs. Daniels led the class through a reading drill. After a few minutes, she told the students to pick up their lesson books. I sensed a presence behind me. Andy Card pressed his head next to mine and whispered in my ear.

"A second plane hit the second tower," he said, pronouncing each word deliberately in his Massachusetts accent. "America is under attack."

———

My first reaction was outrage. Someone had dared attack America. They were going to pay. Then I looked at the faces of the children in front of me. I thought about the contrast between the brutality of the attackers and the innocence of those children. Millions like them would soon be counting on me to protect them. I was determined not to let them down.

I saw reporters at the back of the room, learning the news on their cell phones and pagers. Instinct kicked in. I knew my reaction would be recorded and beamed throughout the world. The nation would be in shock; the president could not be. If I stormed out hastily, it would scare the children and send ripples of panic throughout the country.

The reading lesson continued, but my mind raced far from the classroom. Who could have done this? How bad was the damage? What did the government need to do?

Press Secretary Ari Fleischer positioned himself between the reporters and me. He held up a sign that read "Don't say anything yet." I didn't plan to. I had settled on a plan of action: When the lesson ended, I would leave the classroom calmly, gather the facts, and speak to the nation.

About seven minutes after Andy entered the classroom, I returned to the hold room, into which someone had wheeled a television. I watched in horror as the footage of the second plane hitting the south tower replayed in slow motion. The huge fireball and explosion of smoke were worse than I had imagined. The country would be shaken, and I needed to get on TV right away. I scribbled out my statement longhand. I wanted to assure the American people that the government was responding and that we would bring the perpetrators to justice. Then I wanted to get back to Washington as quickly as possible.

"Ladies and gentlemen, this is a difficult moment for America," I began. ". . . Two airplanes have crashed into the World Trade Center in an apparent terrorist attack on our country." There was an audible gasp from the audience of parents and community members, who were expecting a speech on education. "Terrorism against our nation will not stand," I said. I closed by asking for a moment of silence for the victims.

Later, I learned that my words had echoed Dad's promise that "this aggression will not stand" after Saddam Hussein invaded Kuwait. The repetition was not intentional. In my notes, I had written, "Terrorism against America will not succeed." Dad's words must have been buried in my subconscious, waiting to surface during another moment of crisis.

———

The Secret Service wanted to get me to Air Force One, and fast. As the motorcade charged down Florida Route 41, I called Condi from the secure phone in the limo. She told me there had been a third plane crash, this one into the Pentagon. I sat back in my seat and absorbed her words. My thoughts clarified: The first plane could have been an accident. The second was definitely an attack. The third was a declaration of war.

My blood was boiling. We were going to find out who did this, and kick their ass.

The shift to wartime was visible at the airport. Agents carrying assault rifles surrounded Air Force One. Two of the flight attendants stood at the top of the stairs. Their faces betrayed their fear and sadness. I knew millions of Americans would be feeling the same way. I hugged the flight attendants and told them it would be okay.

I stepped into the presidential cabin and asked to be alone. I thought about the fear that must have seized the passengers on those planes and the grief that would grip the families of the dead. So many people had lost their loved ones with no warning. I prayed that God would comfort the suffering and guide the country through this trial. I thought of the lyrics from one of my favorite hymns, "God of Grace and God of Glory": "Grant us wisdom, grant us courage, for the facing of this hour."

While my emotions might have been similar to those of most Americans, my duties were not. There would be time later to mourn. There would be an opportunity to seek justice. But first I had to manage the crisis. We had suffered the most devastating surprise attack since Pearl Harbor. An enemy had struck our capital for the first time since the War of 1812. In a single morning, the purpose of my presidency had grown clear: to protect our people and defend our freedom that had come under attack.

The first step of any successful crisis response is to project calm. That was what I had tried to do in Florida. Next, we needed to sort out the facts, take action to secure the nation, and help the affected areas recover. Over time, we had to devise a strategy to bring the terrorists to justice so they would not strike again.

I called Dick Cheney as Air Force One climbed rapidly to forty-five thousand feet, well above our typical cruising altitude. He had been taken to the underground Presidential Emergency Operations Center— the PEOC—when the Secret Service thought a plane might be coming at the White House. I told him that I would make decisions from the air and count on him to implement them on the ground.

Two big decisions came quickly. The military had dispatched Combat Air Patrols—teams of fighter aircraft assigned to intercept unresponsive airplanes—over Washington and New York. Air-to-air intercepting was what I had trained to do as an F-102 pilot in the Texas Air National Guard thirty years earlier. In that era, we assumed the targeted aircraft would be a Soviet bomber. Now it would be a commercial airliner full of innocent people.

We needed to clarify the rules of engagement. I told Dick that our pilots should contact suspicious planes and try to get them to land peacefully. If that failed, they had my authority to shoot them down. Hijacked planes were weapons of war. Despite the agonizing costs, taking one out could save countless lives on the ground. I had just made my first decision as a wartime commander in chief.

Dick called back a few minutes later. Condi, Josh Bolten, and senior members of the national security team had joined him in the PEOC. They had been informed that an unresponsive plane was headed toward Washington. Dick asked me to confirm the shootdown order I had given. I did. I later learned that Josh Bolten had pushed for clarification to ensure that the chain of command was respected. I thought back to my days as a pilot. "I cannot imagine what it would be like to receive this order," I told Andy Card. I sure hoped no one would have to execute it.

The second decision was where to land Air Force One. I felt strongly that we should return to Washington. I wanted to be in the White House to lead the response. It would reassure the nation to see the president in the capital that had been attacked.

Shortly after we took off from Sarasota, Andy and Eddie Marinzel, the wiry athletic Secret Service agent from Pittsburgh who led my detail on 9/11, started to throw cold water on the idea. They said conditions in Washington were too volatile, the danger of attack too high. The FAA believed six planes had been hijacked, meaning three more could be in the air. I told them I was not going to let terrorists scare me away. "I'm the president," I said firmly. "And we're going to Washington."

They stood their ground. I hated the image of terrorists putting me on the run. But as much as I wanted to get back, I recognized that part of my responsibility was to ensure the continuity of government. It would be an enormous propaganda victory for the enemy if they took out the president. The military aide and Secret Service agents recommended that we divert the plane to Barksdale Air Force Base in Louisiana, where we could refuel. I relented. A few minutes later, I felt Air Force One bank hard to the west.

———

One of my greatest frustrations on September 11 was the woeful communications technology on Air Force One. The plane had no satellite television. We were dependent on whatever local feeds we could pick up. After a few minutes on a given station, the screen would dissolve into static.

I caught enough fleeting glimpses of the coverage to understand the horror of what the American people were watching. Stranded people were jumping to their deaths from the top floors of the World Trade Center towers. Others hung out of windows, hoping to be rescued. I felt their agony and despair. I had the most powerful job in the world, yet I felt powerless to help them.

At one point, the television signal held steady long enough for me to see the south tower of the World Trade Center collapse. The north tower fell less than thirty minutes later. I had held out hope that the desperate souls trapped on the upper floors would have time to escape. Now there was no chance.

The collapse of the towers magnified the catastrophe. Fifty thousand people worked in the buildings on a typical business day. Some had been evacuated, but I wondered how many were left. Thousands? Tens of thousands? I had no idea. But I was certain that I had just watched more Americans die than any president in history.

I kept up-to-date on the latest developments by calling Dick and Condi in the PEOC. We tried to establish an open line, but it kept dropping. In the years ahead, Deputy Chief of Staff Joe Hagin oversaw major upgrades to the communications systems of the PEOC, Situation Room, and Air Force One.

When we did receive information, it was often contradictory and sometimes downright wrong. I was experiencing the fog of war. There were reports of a bomb at the State Department, a fire on the National Mall, a hijacked Korean airliner bound for the United States, and a call-in threat to Air Force One. The caller had used the plane's code name, Angel, which few people knew. The most bizarre report came when I was informed of a high-speed object flying toward our ranch in Crawford. All of this information later proved to be false. But given the circumstances, we took every report seriously.

One report I received proved true. A fourth plane had gone down somewhere in Pennsylvania. "Did we shoot it down, or did it crash?" I asked Dick Cheney. Nobody knew. I felt sick to my stomach. Had I ordered the death of those innocent Americans?

When the fog lifted, I learned about the heroism aboard Flight 93. After hearing about the earlier attacks in phone calls to loved ones on the ground, the passengers had decided to storm the cockpit. In some of the last words recorded from the doomed flight, a man named Todd Beamer can be heard rallying the passengers into action by saying, "Let's roll." The 9/11 Commission later concluded that the revolt of the passengers aboard Flight 93 may have spared either the Capitol or the White House from destruction. Their act of courage ranks among the greatest in American history.

———

I had been trying to reach Laura all morning. She had been scheduled to testify before a Senate committee in support of our education initiative around the same time the planes struck the World Trade Center towers. I placed several calls, but the line kept dropping. I couldn't believe that the president of the United States couldn't reach his wife in the Capitol Building. "What the hell is going on?" I snapped at Andy Card.

I finally connected with Laura as Air Force One descended into Barksdale. Laura's voice is always soothing, but it was especially comforting to hear that day. She told me she had been taken to a safe location by the Secret Service. I was very relieved when she told me she had spoken to Barbara and Jenna, both of whom were fine. Laura asked when I was coming back to Washington. I told her that everyone was urging me not to return, but that I would be there soon. I had no idea whether that was true, but I sure hoped so.

Landing at Barksdale felt like dropping onto a movie set. F-16s from my old unit at Ellington Air Force Base in Houston had escorted us in. The taxiway was lined with bombers. It made for a striking scene, the power of our mighty Air Force on display. I knew it was only a matter of time before I put that power to use against whoever had ordered this attack.

There was no presidential motorcade assembled at Barksdale, so the commanding officer, General Tom Keck, had to improvise. The agents hustled me down the stairs of the plane and into a vehicle, which blasted off down the runway at what felt like eighty miles an hour. When the man behind the wheel started taking turns at that speed, I yelled, "Slow down, son, there are no terrorists on this base!" It was probably the closest I came to death that day.

I connected with Don Rumsfeld on a secure phone in General Keck's office at Barksdale. Don had been hard to track down because he had become a first responder at the Pentagon. After the plane hit, he ran outside and helped emergency workers lift victims onto stretchers.

I told Don that I considered the attacks an act of war and approved his decision to raise the military readiness level to DefCon Three for the first time since the Arab-Israeli War of 1973. American military installations around the world heightened security precautions and prepared to respond immediately to further orders. I told Don our first priority was to make it through the immediate crisis. After that, I planned to mount a serious military response. "The ball will be in your court and [Joint Chiefs Chairman] Dick Myers's court to respond," I told him.

By 11:30 Louisiana time, it had been almost three hours since I had spoken to the country. I was worried people would get the impression that the government was disengaged. Laura had expressed the same concern. I taped a brief message explaining that the government was responding and that the nation would meet the test. The sentiment was right, but the setting—a sterile conference room at a military base in Louisiana—did not inspire much confidence. The American people needed to see their president in Washington.

I pressed Andy on when we could head back to the White House. The Secret Service agents felt it was still too uncertain. Dick and Condi agreed. They recommended that I go to the Strategic Command at Offutt Air Force Base in Nebraska. It had secure housing space and reliable communications. I resigned myself to delaying my return once again. As we boarded the plane at Barksdale, the Air Force loaded pallets of extra food and water into the belly. We had to be ready for any possibility.

———

After we arrived at Offutt, I was taken to the command center, which was filled with military officers who had been taking part in a planned exercise. Suddenly, a voice crackled over the sound system. "Mr. President, a nonresponsive plane is coming in from Madrid. Do we have authority to shoot it down?"

My first reaction was *When is this going to end?* Then I outlined the rules of engagement I had approved earlier. My mind ran through the worst-case scenarios. What were the diplomatic ramifications of shooting down a foreign plane? Or what if we were too late and the terrorists had already hit their target?

The voice on the loudspeaker returned. "The flight from Madrid," he intoned, "has landed in Lisbon, Portugal."

*Thank God*, I thought. It was another example of the fog of war.

We moved to the communications center, where I had called a national security meeting by videoconference. I had thought carefully about what I wanted to say. I started with a clear declaration. "We are at war against terror. From this day forward, this is the new priority of our administration." I received an update on the emergency response. Then I turned to George Tenet. "Who did this?" I asked.

George answered with two words: al Qaeda.

---

Before 9/11, most Americans had never heard of al Qaeda. I had received my first briefing on the terrorist network as a presidential candidate. Arabic for "the base," al Qaeda was a fundamentalist Islamic terror network hosted and supported by the Taliban government in Afghanistan. Its leader was Osama bin Laden, a radical Saudi from a wealthy family who had been expelled from the kingdom when he opposed the government's decision to allow American troops to be there during the Gulf War. The group held extremist views and considered it their duty to kill anyone who stood in their way.

Al Qaeda had a penchant for high-profile attacks. Three years earlier, the terrorists had carried out simultaneous bombings of two American embassies in East Africa that killed more than two hundred and wounded more than five thousand. They were also behind the attack on the USS *Cole* that claimed the lives of seventeen American sailors off the coast of Yemen in October 2000. By the afternoon of 9/11, the intelligence community had discovered known al Qaeda operatives on the passenger manifests of the hijacked planes.

The CIA had been worried about al Qaeda before 9/11, but their intelligence pointed to an attack overseas. During the late spring and early summer of 2001, we had hardened security at embassies abroad, increased cooperation with foreign intelligence services, and issued warnings through the FAA about possible hijackings on international flights. In the first nine months of my presidency, we had helped disrupt terrorist threats to Paris, Rome, Turkey, Israel, Saudi Arabia, Yemen, and other places.

During the summer, I had asked the CIA to reexamine al Qaeda's capabilities to attack inside the United States. In early August, the Agency delivered a Presidential Daily Briefing that reiterated bin Laden's long-standing intent to strike America, but could not confirm any concrete plans. "We have not been able to corroborate some of the more sensational threat reporting, such as that . . . bin Laden wanted to hijack a U.S. aircraft," the PDB read.*

On 9/11, it was obvious the intelligence community had missed something big. I was alarmed by the lapse, and I expected an explanation. But I did not think it was appropriate to point fingers or fix blame in the middle of the crisis. My immediate concern was that there could be more al Qaeda operatives in the United States.

I looked into the video screen in the Offutt bunker and told George Tenet to get his ears up, a term for listening to all the intelligence and running down every lead.

I also made clear that I planned to use the military in this war when the time was right. Our response would not be a pinprick cruise missile strike. As I later put it, we would do more than put "a million-dollar missile on a five-dollar tent." When America responded to these attacks, it would be deliberate, forceful, and effective.

———

There was one more issue to cover on the videoconference: when to return to Washington? Secret Service Director Brian Stafford told me the capital was still not safe. This time, I put my foot down. I had decided to speak to the nation, and there was no way I was going to do it from an underground bunker in Nebraska.

*The source of the reporting, a foreign intelligence service, remains classified.

On the flight back, Andy and CIA briefer Mike Morell came to see me in the conference room. Mike told me that the French intelligence service had provided reports of other operatives—so called sleeper cells—in the United States planning a second wave of attacks. It was a chilling phrase, "second wave." I believed America could overcome the September 11 attacks without further panic. But a follow-on strike would be very difficult to bear. It was one of the darkest moments of the day.

As I was watching TV coverage on the flight home, I saw a photo of Barbara Olson. Barbara was a talented TV commentator and the wife of Solicitor General Ted Olson, who argued my side in the Florida recount case before the Supreme Court. She had been aboard American Airlines Flight 77, the plane that hit the Pentagon. She was my first personal connection to the tragedy. I reached Ted on the phone. He was calm, but I could sense the shock and devastation in his voice. I told him how sorry I felt. He told me how Barbara had called him from the hijacked flight and calmly relayed information. She was a patriot to the end. I vowed to Ted that we would find those responsible for her death.

The flight home also gave me a chance to check in with my parents. Mother and Dad had spent the night of September 10 at the White House and then left early on the morning of the eleventh. They had been in the air when news of the attacks came. The operator connected me with Dad. I could tell he was anxious. He wasn't worried about my safety—he trusted the Secret Service to protect me—but he was concerned about the stress I would be feeling. I tried to put his mind at ease. "I'm just fine," I said.

Dad put Mother on the phone. "Where are you?" I asked.

"We're at a motel in Brookfield, Wisconsin," she replied.

"What in the world are you doing there?"

"Son," she retorted, "you grounded our plane!"

In an extraordinary feat, Transportation Secretary Norm Mineta and the FAA had overseen the safe landing of four thousand flights in just over two hours. I was hopeful that the terror from the skies was over.

I started thinking about what I should say to the country when I spoke from the Oval Office that night. My first instinct was to tell the American people that we were a nation at war. But as I watched the carnage on TV, I realized that the country was still in shock. Declaring war could further contribute to the anxiety. I decided to wait one day.

I did want to announce a major decision I had made: The United States would consider any nation that harbored terrorists to be responsible for the acts of those terrorists. This new doctrine overturned the approach of the past, which treated terrorist groups as distinct from their sponsors. We had to force nations to choose whether they would fight the terrorists or share in their fate. And we had to wage this war on the offense, by attacking the terrorists overseas before they could attack us again at home.

I also wanted the speech to convey my sense of moral outrage. The deliberate murder of innocent people is an act of pure evil. Above all, I wanted to express comfort and resolve—comfort that we would recover from this blow, and resolve that we would bring the terrorists to justice.

Air Force One touched down at Andrews Air Force Base in Maryland just after 6:30 p.m. I moved quickly to Marine One, which lifted off for the ten-minute helicopter flight to the South Lawn. The chopper banked left and right in an evasive pattern. I felt no fear. I knew the Marine pilots of HMX-1 would get me home.

I looked out on an abandoned, locked-down Washington. In the distance I saw smoke rising from the Pentagon. The symbol of our military might was smoldering. I was struck by how skilled and ruthless the al Qaeda pilot must have been to fly directly into the low-lying building. My mind drifted back over history. I was looking at a modern-day Pearl Harbor. Just as Franklin Roosevelt had rallied the nation to defend freedom, it would be my responsibility to lead a new generation to protect America. I turned to Andy and said, "You're looking at the first war of the twenty-first century."

———

My first stop after landing on the South Lawn was the Oval Office. I read over a draft of my speech and modified a few lines. Then I went down to the PEOC, part of a hardened underground structure built during the early Cold War to withstand a substantial attack. The bunker is manned by military personnel around the clock and contains enough food, water, and electric power to sustain the president and his family for long periods of time. At the center of the facility is a conference room with a large wood table—a subterranean Situation Room. Laura was waiting for me there. We didn't have a lot of time to talk, but we didn't need to. Her hug was more powerful than any words.

I went back upstairs, practiced my speech, and then headed to the Oval Office.

"Today, our fellow citizens, our way of life, our very freedom, came under attack in a series of deliberate and deadly terrorist acts," I began. I described the brutality of the attack and the heroism of those who had responded. I continued: "I've directed the full resources of our intelligence and law enforcement communities to find those responsible and to bring them to justice. We will make no distinction between the terrorists who committed these acts and those who harbor them."

I closed with Psalm 23: "Even though I walk through the valley of the shadow of death, I will fear no evil, for You are with me." I felt the speech was much better than the statements I made in Florida and Louisiana. Still, I knew I would have to do more to rally the nation in the days ahead.

After the speech, I returned to the PEOC to meet with my national security team. I wanted to catch up on the latest developments and plan the next day's response. I told them we had been given a mission that none of us had sought or expected, but the country would rise to meet it. "Freedom and justice will prevail," I said.

The meeting ended around 10:00 p.m. I had been up since before dawn and going full speed all day. Carl Truscott, the head of the Presidential Protective Division, told us we would be sleeping in a small room off the PEOC conference room. Against the wall was an old couch with a fold-out bed inside. It looked like Harry Truman himself had put it there. I could envision a restless night battling the cramped mattress and the steel supporting rods. The next day would bring important decisions, and I needed sleep to think clearly. "There is no way I'm sleeping there," I told Carl.

He knew I was not budging. "Sleep in the residence," he said. "We will come get you if there are any problems."

Sleep did not come easily. My mind replayed the images of the day: the planes hitting the buildings, the towers crumbling, the Pentagon in flames. I thought of the grief so many families must be feeling. I also thought about the heroism—the flight attendants on the hijacked planes who calmly called supervisors to report their status and the first responders who raced toward the flames at the World Trade Center and the Pentagon.

Just as I was about to doze off, I saw a figure silhouetted at the bedroom door. He was breathing heavily and shouting: "Mr. President, Mr. President, the White House is under attack! Let's go!"

I told Laura we needed to move fast. She didn't have time to put in her contact lenses, so she held on to me. I grabbed her robe and guided her with one arm while I scooped up Barney, our Scottish terrier, with the other. I called Spot, our English springer spaniel, to follow. I was barefoot and wearing running shorts and a T-shirt. We must have made quite a sight.

The Secret Service hustled us out of the residence and down to the underground shelter. I heard the slam of a heavy door and the sound of a pressurized lock as we entered the tunnel. The agents rushed us through another door. *Bang, hiss.* We hustled down the final corridor, past the staff seated outside, and into the PEOC.

After a few minutes, an enlisted man walked into the conference room. "Mr. President," he said matter-of-factly, "it was one of ours." An F-16 fighter had flown down the Potomac squawking the wrong transponder signal. A day that started with a run on a golf course had ended with a scramble to the bunker to escape a possible attack on the White House.

———

When I woke up on September 12, America was a different place. Commercial aircraft were grounded. Armed vehicles patrolled the streets of Washington. A wing of the Pentagon had been reduced to rubble. The New York Stock Exchange was closed. New York's Twin Towers were gone. The focus of my presidency, which I had expected to be domestic policy, was now war. The transformation showed how quickly fate can shift, and how sometimes the most demanding tasks a president faces are unexpected.

The psyche of the nation had been shaken. Families stocked up on gas masks and bottled water. Some fled cities for the countryside, fearing that downtown buildings could be targets. Others who worked in skyscrapers couldn't bring themselves to go back to work. Many refused to board a plane for weeks or months. It seemed almost certain that there would be another attack.

There is no textbook on how to steady a nation rattled by a faceless enemy. I relied on instincts and background. My West Texas optimism helped me project confidence. Occasionally, I spoke a little too bluntly, such as when I said I wanted bin Laden "dead or alive." The people around me helped a lot during those trying days. The team at the White House was steady and a source of inspiration. Laura was a rock of stability and love. My brother Marvin and sister Doro, both of whom lived in the Washington area, stopped by frequently for meals. Mother and Dad offered constant support. My family gave me comfort and helped me clear my mind.

I also drew strength from my faith, and from history. I found solace in reading the Bible, which Abraham Lincoln called "the best gift God has given to man." I admired Lincoln's moral clarity and resolve. The clash between freedom and tyranny, he said, was "an issue which can only be tried by war, and decided by victory." The war on terror would be the same.

I set three goals for the days immediately following the attacks. First, keep the terrorists from striking again. Second, make clear to the country and the world that we had embarked on a new kind of war. Third, help the affected areas recover and make sure the terrorists did not succeed in shutting down our economy or dividing our society.

I went to the Oval Office on September 12 at my usual time, around 7:00 a.m. The first order of the day was to return phone calls from the many world leaders who had offered their sympathy. My first call was with Prime Minister Tony Blair of Great Britain. Tony began by saying he was "in a state of shock" and that he would stand with America "one hundred percent" in fighting terror. There was no equivocation in his voice. The conversation helped cement the closest friendship I would form with any foreign leader. As the years passed and the wartime decisions grew tougher, some of our allies wavered. Tony Blair never did.

Every leader who called expressed support. Jean Chrétien of Canada said simply, "We are there," a promise that had been upheld by Canadian citizens who welcomed thousands of stranded Americans after their flights were diverted. Silvio Berlusconi of Italy told me he had "cried like a little boy and could not stop," and pledged his cooperation. Jiang Zemin of China, Gerhard Schroeder of Germany, and Jacques Chirac of France promised to help in any way they could. Junichiro Koizumi, prime minister of the nation that struck America at Pearl Harbor, called the events of September 11 "not an attack against just the United States but an attack against freedom and democracy." For the first time in NATO's fifty-two-year history, the members of the alliance voted to invoke Article 5 of the charter: An attack on one is an attack on all.

The coalition of the willing in the war against terror was forming, and—for the time being—everyone wanted to join.

After my calls, I had a CIA briefing and convened an NSC meeting in the Cabinet Room. George Tenet confirmed that bin Laden was responsible for the attacks. Intelligence intercepts had revealed al Qaeda members congratulating one another in eastern Afghanistan. I made clear this would be a different kind of war. We faced an enemy that had no capital to call home and no armies to track on the battlefield. Defeating them would require the full resources of our national power, from gathering intelligence to freezing terrorists' bank accounts to deploying troops.

The meeting gave me an opportunity to speak to the press. I was ready to make the declaration I had postponed the night before. "The deliberate and deadly attacks which were carried out yesterday against our country were more than acts of terror," I said. "They were acts of war."

A half hour later, I met with the congressional leadership from both parties. I laid out two concerns. The first was complacency. It seemed hard to imagine at the time, when the pain of 9/11 was so fresh, but I knew the public would eventually move on. As elected leaders, we had a responsibility to stay focused on the threat and fight the war until we had prevailed.

My second concern was about backlash against Arab and Muslim Americans. I had heard reports of verbal harassment against people who appeared to be Middle Eastern. I was mindful of the ugly aspects of America's history during war. In World War I, German Americans were shunned, and in some extreme cases jailed. In World War II, President

Roosevelt supported placing huge numbers of Japanese Americans in internment camps. One was Norm Mineta, who had been interned as a ten-year-old boy. Seeing him in the Cabinet Room that morning was a powerful reminder of the government's responsibility to guard against hysteria and speak out against discrimination. I made plans to convey that message by visiting a mosque.

Members of Congress were united in their determination to protect the country. Senator Tom Daschle, the Democratic majority leader, issued one cautionary note. He said I should be careful about the word *war* because it had such powerful implications. I listened to his concerns, but I disagreed. If four coordinated attacks by a terrorist network that had pledged to kill as many Americans as possible was not an act of war, then what was it? A breach of diplomatic protocol?

One of the last people to speak was Robert Byrd, the eighty-three-year-old Democratic senator from West Virginia. He had served through the Cuban Missile Crisis, the Vietnam War, the end of the Cold War, and countless other challenges. His eloquent words inspired the room. "Despite Hollywood and TV," he said, "there is an army of people who believe in divine guidance and the Creator. . . . Mighty forces will come to your aid."

———

Late in the afternoon of September 12, I made the short trip across the Potomac to the Pentagon. The building was smoldering, and there were still bodies inside. Don Rumsfeld and I walked the crash site and thanked the work crews for their devotion. At one point, a team of workers atop the building unfurled a giant American flag. It was a sign of defiance and resolve, exactly what the nation needed to see. One of the last groups I met was the morgue team. Joe Hagin brought them over. They were covered in dust after performing the saddest duty of all. I told them how much I appreciated the dignity they brought to their work.

The experience at the Pentagon convinced me I needed to go to New York as soon as possible. Joe told me there were some serious problems with that idea. The Secret Service wasn't sure the area was secure. The advance teams did not have time to prepare for a presidential event. No one knew what the environment at Ground Zero would be like. These were valid concerns, but I had made up my mind. I wanted New Yorkers to know that they were not alone. I took the attack as personally as they did. There was no substitute for telling them face to face.

I decided to break the news Thursday morning. Ari Fleischer had suggested that we invite the press into the Oval Office to witness my phone call with New York Governor George Pataki and Mayor Rudy Giuliani. "I can't tell you how proud I am of the good citizens of your part of the world, and the extraordinary job you all are doing," I said. Then I dropped the surprise. "You've extended me a kind invitation to come to New York City. I accept; I'll be there tomorrow afternoon."

I agreed to take a few questions from the press after the call. They asked about the safety of the aviation system, the whereabouts of bin Laden, and what I was requesting from Congress. The last question came from a reporter for the *Christian Science Monitor*: "Could you give us a sense as to what kind of prayers you are thinking and where your heart is . . . ?"

I had managed to suppress my emotion in public for the past two days, but this question brought it to the surface. I had been thinking about Ted Olson's grief-stricken voice. I pictured the exhausted morgue team. I thought about the innocent children who had died, and those who had lost their mom or dad. The sorrow that had accumulated burst forth. My eyes filled with tears and my throat caught. I paused briefly as the cameras clicked rapidly. I regained my composure, put my hand down on the Resolute desk, and leaned forward. "Well, I don't think about myself right now. I think about the families, the children. I am a loving guy, and I am also someone, however, who has got a job to do. And I intend to do it."

Later that day, Laura and I went to the Washington Hospital Center to visit victims from the Pentagon. Some had been burned over huge portions of their bodies. I asked one if he was an Army Ranger. Without missing a beat, he answered, "No, sir, I'm Special Forces. My IQ is too high to be a Ranger." Everyone in the room—his wife, his doctors, Laura, and me—cracked up. It felt good to laugh. I left the hospital inspired by the courage of the wounded and the compassion of the doctors and nurses.

Andy Card was waiting in the South Lawn driveway when we returned from the hospital. Before I could get out of the limo, he opened the door and jumped in. He told me there had been a bomb threat to the White House. The Secret Service had relocated the vice president, and they wanted to evacuate me, too. I told the agents to double-check the intelligence and send home as many of the White House staff as possible. But I was staying put. I was not going to give the enemy the pleasure of seeing me hustled around to different locations again. The Secret Service extended the security perimeter of the White House. We made it through the day. When we went to bed, I thought, *Another day with no attack. Thank God.*

———

Nearly three thousand innocent men, women, and children were killed on September 11. I felt it was important for the country to mourn together, so I set aside Friday as a National Day of Prayer and Remembrance. I knew September 14 would be a grueling and emotional day. I did not expect it to be the most inspiring one of my life.

A little after 7:00 a.m., Andy Card met me in the Oval Office for my national security briefing. The CIA believed that there were more al Qaeda operatives in the United States and that they wanted to attack America with biological, chemical, or nuclear weapons. It was hard to imagine anything more devastating than 9/11, but a terrorist attack with weapons of mass destruction would qualify.

I asked FBI Director Bob Mueller and Attorney General John Ashcroft to update me on the progress of the FBI's investigation of the hijackers. Bob told me they had identified most of the terrorists and determined when they'd entered the country, where they'd stayed, and how they'd executed the plot. It was an impressive piece of investigation. But it wasn't enough.

"What are you doing to stop the next attack?" I asked. People nervously shifted in their seats. I told Bob I wanted the Bureau to adopt a wartime mentality. We needed to disrupt attacks before they happened, not just investigate them after they took place. At the end of the meeting, Bob affirmed, "That's our new mission, preventing attacks." Over the years ahead, he fulfilled his promise and carried out the most fundamental transformation of the FBI in its century-long history.

After a phone call with Prime Minister Ariel Sharon of Israel, a leader who understood what it meant to fight terror, I began my first Cabinet meeting since the terrorist attacks. As I stepped into the room, the team broke out in sustained applause. I was surprised, and I choked up at their heartfelt support. The tears flowed for the second time in two days.

We started the Cabinet meeting with a prayer. I asked Don Rumsfeld to lead it. He offered moving words about the victims of the attacks and asked for the "patience to measure our lust for action." The moment of silence after the prayer gave me time to collect my emotions. I thought about the speech I would soon give at the National Cathedral. Apparently Colin Powell did, too. The secretary of state slipped me a note.

"Dear Mr. President," he wrote. "When I have to give a speech like this, I avoid those words that I know will cause me to well up, such as Mom and Pop." It was a thoughtful gesture. Colin had seen combat; he knew the powerful emotions we were all feeling and wanted to comfort me. As I began the meeting, I held up the note and joked, "Let me tell you what the secretary of state just told me. . . . 'Dear Mr. President, Don't break down!'"

———

The National Cathedral is an awesome structure, with 102-foot ceilings, elegant buttresses, and sparkling stained glass. On September 14 the pews were filled to capacity. Former Presidents Ford, Carter, Bush, and Clinton were there with their wives. So was almost every member of Congress, the whole Cabinet, the Joint Chiefs of Staff, the justices of the Supreme Court, the diplomatic corps, and families of the victims. One person not there was Dick Cheney. He was at Camp David to ensure the continuity of government, a reminder of the ongoing threat.

I had asked Laura and Karen Hughes to design the program, and they did a fine job. The speakers included religious leaders of many faiths: Imam Muzammil Siddiqi of the Islamic Society of North America, Rabbi Joshua Haberman, Billy Graham, Cardinal Theodore McCarrick, and Kirbyjon Caldwell. Near the end of the service, my turn came. As I climbed the steps to the lectern, I whispered a prayer: "Lord, let your light shine through me."

The speech at the cathedral was the most important of my young presidency. I had told my speechwriters—Mike Gerson, John McConnell, and Matthew Scully—that I wanted to accomplish three objectives: mourn the loss of life, remind people there was a loving God, and make clear that those who attacked our nation would face justice.

"We are here in the middle hour of our grief," I began. "So many have suffered so great a loss, and today we express our nation's sorrow. We come before God to pray for the missing and the dead, and for those who love them. . . . To the children and parents and spouses and families and friends of the lost, we offer the deepest sympathy of the nation. And I assure you, you are not alone."

I scanned the crowd. Three soldiers sitting to my right had tears cascading down their faces. So did my lead advance woman, Charity Wallace. I was determined not to fall prey to the contagion of crying. There was one place I dared not look: the pew where Mother, Dad, and Laura were seated. I continued:

*Just three days removed from these events, Americans do not yet have the distance of history. But our responsibility to history is already clear: to answer these attacks and rid the world of evil. War has been waged against us by stealth and deceit and murder. This nation is peaceful, but fierce when stirred to anger. This conflict was begun on the timing and terms of others. It will end in a way, and at an hour, of our choosing. . . .*

*God's signs are not always the ones we look for. We learn in tragedy that His purposes are not always our own. Yet the prayers of private suffering, whether in our homes or in this great cathedral, are known and heard, and understood. . . . This world He created is of moral design. Grief and tragedy and hatred are only for a time. Goodness, remembrance, and love have no end. And the Lord of life holds all who die, and all who mourn.*

As I took my seat next to Laura, Dad reached over and gently squeezed my arm. Some have said the moment marked a symbolic passing of the torch from one generation to another. I saw it as the reassuring touch of a father who knew the challenges of war. I drew strength from his example and his love. I needed that strength for the next stage of the journey: the visit to the point of attack, lower Manhattan.

———

The flight north was quiet. I had asked Kirbyjon Caldwell to make the trip with me. I had seen the footage of New York on television, and I knew the devastation was overwhelming. It was comforting to have a friend and a man of faith by my side.

Governor Pataki and Mayor Giuliani greeted me at McGuire Air Force Base in New Jersey. They looked spent. The governor had been working tirelessly since Tuesday morning, allocating state resources and rallying the troops under his command. And rarely had a man met his moment in history more naturally than Rudy Giuliani did on September 11. He was defiant at the right times, sorrowful at the right times, and in command the entire time.

I boarded the chopper with George and Rudy. On the flight into the city, the Marine pilots flew over Ground Zero. My mind went back to the helicopter flight on the evening of September 11. The Pentagon had been wounded, but not destroyed. That was not the case with the Twin Towers. They were gone. There was nothing left but a pile of rubble. The devastation was shocking and total.

The view from the air was nothing compared to what I saw on the ground. George, Rudy, and I piled into a Suburban. We had just started the drive to the disaster site when something on the side of the road caught my eye. It appeared to be a lumbering gray mass. I took a second look. It was a group of first responders covered head to toe in ash.

I asked the driver to stop. I walked over, started shaking hands, and thanked the men for all they had done. They had been working nonstop. Several had tears running down their faces, cutting a path through the soot like rivulets through a desert. The emotion of the encounter was a harbinger of what was to come.

As we approached Ground Zero, I felt like I was entering a nightmare. There was little light. Smoke hung in the air and mixed with suspended particles of debris, creating an eerie gray curtain. We sloshed through puddles left behind by the morning rain and the water used to fight the fires. There was some chatter from the local officials. "Here is where the old headquarters stood. . . . There is where the unit regrouped." I tried to listen, but my mind kept returning to the devastation, and to those who ordered the attacks. They had hit us even harder than I had comprehended.

We had been walking for a few minutes when George and Rudy led us down into a pit where rescue workers were digging through the rubble for survivors. If the rest of the site was a nightmare, this was pure hell. It seemed darker than the area up top. In addition to the heavy soot in the air, there were piles of shattered glass and metal.

When the workers saw me, a line formed. I shook every hand. The workers' faces and clothes were filthy. Their eyes were bloodshot. Their voices were hoarse. Their emotions covered the full spectrum. There was sorrow and exhaustion, worry and hope, anger and pride. Several quietly said, "Thank you" or "God bless you" or "We're proud of you." I told them they had it backward. I was proud of them.

After a few minutes, the mood started to turn. One soot-covered firefighter told me that his station had lost a number of men. I tried to comfort him, but that was not what he wanted. He looked me square in the eye and said, "George, find the bastards who did this and kill them." It's not often that people call the president by his first name. But that was fine by me. This was personal.

The more time I spent with the workers, the more raw emotions rose to the surface. To most of these men and women, I was a face they had seen on TV. They didn't know me. They hadn't seen me tested. They wanted to make sure I shared their determination. One man yelled, "Do not let me down!" Another shouted straight at my face, "Whatever it takes!" The bloodlust was palpable and understandable.

Andy Card asked if I wanted to say something to the crowd. I decided I should. There was no stage, no microphone, and no prepared remarks. Andy pointed me to a mound of metal. I looked at Secret Service agent Carl Truscott, who nodded that it was safe to climb up. An older fire-

My grandparents, Prescott and Dorothy Walker Bush, campaigning for the U.S. Senate in Connecticut.

The Navy officer and his beautiful young bride. When Dad went to war, he painted "Barbara" on the side of his plane.

On Dad's shoulders at Yale, age nine months.

On a trip with Mother in the desert.

A typical Midland day, playing baseball until sunset.

With my sister, Robin, on her last Christmas, 1952.

Home in Houston on a break from Andover. Because of the age difference, I felt more like an uncle than a brother to my siblings in those days.

Laura and I got married three months after Joe and Jan O'Neill's barbecue in Midland. It was the best decision of my life.

We were preparing to adopt when we found out Laura was pregnant with twins.

Barbara Bush and Jenna Welch holding their namesakes.

In the Rangers' dugout with our girls. Owning a ballclub was my dream, and I was certain it was the best job I'd ever have.

Before my Inauguration as governor, Dad gave me the cufflinks his parents had given him when he earned his wings as a Navy pilot. *Dallas Morning News/David Woo*

With Lieutenant Governor Bob Bullock, my unlikely Democratic partner in Austin. *Associated Press/Harry Cabluck*

Kissing the First Lady of Texas at my second Inauguration as governor. *Dallas Morning News/ David Woo*

Whistlestop campaigning with Dick Cheney, a valuable addition to the ticket and a steady, principled vice president. *Associated Press/Eric Draper*

With brother Jeb on election night 2000, when things were looking good.
*Time Magazine/Brooks Kraft*

Karl Rove was like a political mad scientist—intellectual, funny, and overflowing with energy and ideas.
*White House/Eric Draper*

With my two closest foreign policy advisers, National Security Adviser Steve Hadley and Secretary of State Condi Rice.
*White House/Paul Morse*

With my communications team, (*from left*) Dan Bartlett, Dana Perino, and Tony Snow.
*White House/Eric Draper*

Having coffee with John Roberts in the West Sitting Hall the morning after his nomination in 2005.
*White House/ Eric Draper*

Talking with the Reverend
Billy Graham, who deepened
my understanding of faith.
*White House/Paul Morse*

Visiting Pope John Paul II
at Castel Gandolfo in 2001.
The Holy Father urged me
to defend the sanctity of life.
*White House/Eric Draper*

Holding Trey Jones, a snowflake baby born from a frozen
embryo that otherwise could
have been destroyed for
research. *White House/
Kimberlee Hewitt*

During a second-grade reading exercise on September 11, 2001, Chief of Staff Andy Card whispered into my ear, "A second plane hit the second tower. America is under attack." *Associated Press/ Doug Mills*

On the phone with Dick Cheney aboard Air Force One on 9/11. I authorized the shootdown of a hijacked commercial jetliner but prayed our pilots wouldn't have to execute my order. *White House/Eric Draper*

Back at the White House on 9/11, editing my address to the nation with (*from left*) White House Counsel Al Gonzales, Condi Rice, Counselor Karen Hughes, Press Secretary Ari Fleischer, and Andy Card. *White House/Paul Morse*

Visiting the Pentagon on September 12, 2001, with Secretary of Defense Don Rumsfeld.
*White House/Eric Draper*

At the National Cathedral on September 14, 2001. "This conflict was begun on the timing and terms of others," I said. "It will end in a way, and at an hour, of our choosing."
*White House/Eric Draper*

Huddling with New York City Mayor Rudy Giuliani (*left*) and New York Governor George Pataki at McGuire Air Force Base just before we choppered to Ground Zero. *White House/Paul Morse*

With rescue workers amid the wreckage of the towers. "George, find the bastards who did this and kill them," one shouted at me. Another yelled, "Whatever it takes!" *White House/Eric Draper*

Holding the badge of Port Authority police officer George Howard, who died at the World Trade Center.
*White House/Eric Draper*

Opening Game Three of the 2001 World Series at Yankee Stadium. "Don't bounce it, they'll boo you," Yankees shortstop Derek Jeter had warned me. *White House/Eric Draper*

Meeting with Dick Cheney, Colin Powell, Don Rumsfeld, and the national security team at Camp David the Saturday after 9/11. *White House/Eric Draper*

In the Blue Room, informing British Prime Minister Tony Blair that we would deploy ground troops to Afghanistan. *White House/Eric Draper*

Working in the Treaty Room, where I announced the opening stage of the war in Afghanistan on October 7, 2001. *White House/Joyce Boghosian*

By 2006, Pakistani President Pervez Musharraf (*left*) and Afghan President Hamid Karzai were barely on speaking terms. I tried to bring them together through personal diplomacy.
*White House/Eric Draper*

Addressing the Tenth Mountain Division, which helped drive al Qaeda and the Taliban from power in Afghanistan, at Fort Drum in 2002. *White House/Paul Morse*

Presenting Dan and Maureen Murphy with the Medal of Honor earned by their son, Navy SEAL Lieutenant Michael Murphy, who sacrificed his life to call in help for his men in Afghanistan. *White House/Joyce Boghosian*

At the ranch with General Tommy Franks, who commanded the liberations of Afghanistan and Iraq. *White House/Susan Sterner*

"You've got to try everything you can to avoid war," Dad told me in a conversation about Iraq in late 2002. "But if the man won't comply, you don't have any other choice." *White House/Eric Draper*

fighter was standing atop the pile. I put out my hand, and he pulled me up next to him. His name was Bob Beckwith.

Nina Bishop, a member of the advance team, had tracked down a bullhorn that I could use to address those assembled. She thrust it into my hands. The crowd was able to see me atop the mound, which I later learned was a crumpled fire truck. My first instinct was to console. I told them that America was on bended knee in prayer for the victims, the rescuers, and the families.

People shouted, "We can't hear you." I shot back, "I can hear you!" It got a cheer. I had been hoping to rally the workers and express the resolve of the country. Suddenly I knew how. "I can hear you. The rest of the world hears you," I said, prompting a louder roar. "And the people who knocked these buildings down will hear all of us soon!" The crowd exploded. It was a release of energy I had never felt before. They struck up a chant of "USA, USA, USA!"

---

I had spent a fair amount of time in New York over the years. But it wasn't until September 14, 2001, that I got a sense of the city's real character. After the visit to Ground Zero, we drove three miles north to the Javits Center. I was amazed by the number of people on the West Side Highway waving flags and cheering. "I hate to break it to you, Mr. President," Rudy joked, "but none of these people voted for you."

At the Javits Center, I walked into a staging area for first responders from across the country. I greeted firemen and rescuers from states as far away as Ohio and California. Without being asked, they had come to the city to serve as reinforcements. I thanked them on behalf of the nation and urged them to continue their good work.

The building's parking garage had been converted into a gathering place for about two hundred family members of missing first responders. The people in the room spanned all ages, from elderly grandmothers to newborn babies. Many were living the same nightmare: Their loved ones had last been seen or heard near the World Trade Center. They wanted to know if they had survived.

I had just seen the debris of the towers. I knew it would be a miracle if anyone emerged. Yet the families refused to give up hope. We prayed together and wept together. Many people asked for pictures or autographs. I felt awkward signing autographs in a time of grief, but I wanted to do anything I could to ease their pain. I asked each family to tell me a little bit about their missing loved one. Then I said, "I'll sign this card, and then when your dad [or mom or son or daughter] comes home, they'll believe that you really met the president."

As I came to the last corner of the room, I saw a family gathered around a seated woman. I sat down next to the woman, who told me her name was Arlene Howard. Her son was a Port Authority police officer who'd had September 11 off but volunteered to help as soon as he heard about the attacks. He had last been seen rushing into the dust and smoke three days earlier.

As I was getting ready to say goodbye, Arlene reached into her purse and held out her hand. It contained a metal object. "This is my son's badge. His name is George Howard. Please remember him," she said as she pressed the badge into my hand. I promised I would.

———

I served 2,685 days as president after Arlene gave me that badge. I kept it with me every one of them. As the years passed, most Americans returned to life as usual. That was natural and desirable.

It meant the country was healing and people felt safer. As I record these thoughts, that day of fire is a distant memory for some of our citizens. The youngest Americans have no firsthand knowledge of the day. Eventually, September 11 will come to feel more like Pearl Harbor Day— an honored date on the calendar and an important moment in history, but not a scar on the heart, not a reason to fight on.

For me, the week of September 11 will always be something more. I still see the Pentagon smoldering, the towers in flames, and that pile of twisted steel. I still hear the voices of the loved ones searching for survivors and the workers yelling, "Do not let me down!" and "Whatever it takes!" I still feel the sadness of the children, the agony of the burn victims, and the torment of the broken families. I still marvel at the bravery of the firefighters, and the compassion of strangers, and the matchless courage of the passengers who forced down that plane.

September 11 redefined sacrifice. It redefined duty. And it redefined my job. The story of that week is the key to understanding my presidency. There were so many decisions that followed, many of them controversial and complex. Yet after 9/11, I felt my responsibility was clear. For as long as I held office, I could never forget what happened to America that day. I would pour my heart and soul into protecting the country, whatever it took.

6

———

# WAR FOOTING

On October 17, 2001, I boarded Air Force One for my first trip out of the country since 9/11. We were headed to Shanghai for the Asia Pacific Economic Cooperation summit, a gathering of twenty-one leaders from Pacific Rim nations. The Secret Service was anxious about the trip. For weeks, we had received chilling intelligence reports about potential follow-up attacks. Yet strengthening America's relationships in the Far East was one of my top priorities, and I wanted my fellow world leaders to see firsthand my determination to battle the terrorists.

As Air Force One touched down at the Shanghai airport, I thought back to the dusty, bicycle-filled city I had visited with Mother in 1975. This time we made the forty-five-minute drive to downtown Shanghai on a modern highway. We sped past a sparkling new section of the city called Pudong. I later learned the government had moved roughly one hundred thousand people off the land to enable the construction. The skyscrapers and neon lights reminded me of Las Vegas. For Shanghai, the Great Leap Forward had finally arrived.

The next morning, I squeezed into a blue tent at the Ritz-Carlton with Colin Powell, Condi Rice, Andy Card, and the CIA briefer. The structure was designed to protect the national security briefing from potential eavesdroppers. We turned on a video monitor and Dick Cheney's face popped up from New York City. He was wearing white tie and tails for his speech at the Alfred E. Smith Memorial Foundation Dinner, an annual charity event organized by the Catholic archdiocese.

As soon as I saw Dick, I could tell something was wrong. His face was as white as his tie.

"Mr. President," he said, "one of the bio-detectors went off at the White

House. They found traces of botulinum toxin. The chances are we've all been exposed."

The CIA had briefed me on botulinum toxin. It was one of the world's most poisonous substances. Nobody said a word. Finally, Colin asked, "What's the time of exposure?" Was he doing the mental math, trying to figure out how long it had been since he was last in the White House?

Deputy National Security Adviser Steve Hadley explained that the FBI was testing the suspicious substance on mice. The next twenty-four hours would be crucial. If the mice were still scurrying around, feet down, we would be fine. But if the mice were on their backs, feet up, we were goners. Condi tried to lighten the mood. "Well," she said, "this is one way to die for your country."

I went to the summit meetings and awaited the test results. The next day, Condi got a message that Steve was trying to reach her. "I guess this is the call," she said. After a few minutes, Condi came back with the news.

"Feet down, not feet up," she said. It was a false alarm.

———

Years later, incidents like the botulinum toxin scare can seem fanciful and far-fetched. It's easy to chuckle at the image of America's most senior officials praying for lab mice to stay upright. But at the time, the threats were urgent and real. Six mornings a week, George Tenet and the CIA briefed me on what they called the Threat Matrix, a summary of of potential attacks on the homeland. On Sundays, I received a written intelligence briefing. Between 9/11 and mid-2003, the CIA reported to me on an average of 400 specific threats each month. The CIA tracked more than twenty separate alleged large-scale attack plots, ranging from possible chemical and biological weapons operations in Europe to potential homeland attacks involved sleeper operatives. Some reports mentioned specific targets, including major landmarks, military bases, universities, and shopping malls. For months after 9/11, I would wake up in the middle of the night worried about what I had read.

I peppered my briefers with questions. How credible was each threat? What had we done to follow up on a lead? Each piece of information was like a tile in a mosaic. In late September, FBI Director Bob Mueller inserted a big tile when he told me there were 331 potential al Qaeda operatives inside the United States. The overall image was unmistakable: The prospect of a second wave of terrorist attacks against America was very real.

Prior to 9/11, many had viewed terrorism primarily as a crime to be prosecuted, as the government had after the bombing of the World Trade Center in 1993. After 9/11, it was clear that the attacks on our embassies in East Africa and on the USS *Cole* were more than isolated crimes. They were a warm-up for September 11, part of a master plan orchestrated by Osama bin Laden, who had issued a religious edict, known as a fatwa, calling the murder of Americans "an individual duty for every Muslim who can do it in any country in which it is possible to do it."

On 9/11, it was obvious the law enforcement approach to terrorism had failed. Suicidal men willing to fly passenger planes into buildings were not common criminals. They could not be deterred by the threat of prosecution. They had declared war on America. To protect the country, we had to wage war against the terrorists.

The war would be different from any America had fought in the past. We had to uncover the terrorists' plots. We had to track their movements and disrupt their operations. We had to cut off their money and deprive them of their safe havens. And we had to do it all under the threat of another attack. The terrorists had made our homefront a battleground. Putting America on a war footing was one of the most important decisions of my presidency.

My authority to conduct the war on terror came from two sources. One was Article II of the Constitution, which entrusts the president with wartime powers as commander in chief. The other was a congressional war resolution passed three days after 9/11. By a vote of 98 to 0 in the Senate and 420 to 1 in the House, Congress declared:

*That the President is authorized to use all necessary and appropriate force against those nations, organizations, or persons he determines planned, authorized, committed, or aided the terrorist attacks that occurred on September 11, 2001, or harbored such organizations or persons, in order to prevent any future acts of international terrorism against the United States by such nations, organizations, or persons.*

In the years ahead, some in Congress would forget those words. I never did. I woke up every morning thinking about the danger we faced and the responsibilities I carried. I was also keenly aware that presidents had a history of overreaching during war. John Adams signed the Alien and Sedition Acts, which banned public dissent. Abraham Lincoln suspended *habeas corpus* during the Civil War. Franklin Roosevelt ordered Japanese Americans interned during World War II. When I took the oath of office, I swore to "preserve, protect, and defend the Constitution." My most solemn duty, the calling of my presidency, was to protect America—within the authority granted to me by the Constitution.

———

The immediate task after 9/11 was to harden our nation's defenses against a second attack. The undertaking was daunting. To stop the enemy, we had to be right 100 percent of the time. To harm us, they had to succeed only once.

We implemented a flurry of new security measures. I approved the deployment of National Guard forces to airports, put more air marshals on planes, required airlines to harden cockpit doors, and tightened procedures for granting visas and screening passengers. Working with state and local governments and the private sector, we increased security at seaports, bridges, nuclear power plants, and other vulnerable infrastructure.

Shortly after 9/11, I appointed Governor Tom Ridge of Pennsylvania to a new senior White House position overseeing our homeland security effort. Tom brought valuable management experience, but by early 2002, it had become clear that the task was too large to be coordinated out of a small White House office. Dozens of different federal agencies shared responsibility for securing the homeland. The patchwork approach was inefficient, and there was too much risk that something would slip through the seams. One egregious example came in March 2002, when the Immigration and Naturalization Service (INS) mailed a letter notifying a Florida flight school that it had granted student visas to Mohamed Atta and Marwan al Shehhi. The person opening the letter must have been shocked. Those were the two pilots who had flown airplanes into the Twin Towers on 9/11.

I was shocked, too. As I told the press at the time, "I could barely get

my coffee down." The sloppy error exemplified the need for broader reform. INS, a branch of the Justice Department, wasn't the only agency
struggling with its new homeland security responsibilities. The Customs
Service, reporting to the Treasury Department, faced the enormous task
of securing the nation's ports. They shared that responsibility with the
Coast Guard, which was part of the Transportation Department.

Democratic Senator Joe Lieberman of Connecticut had been making
the strong case for creating a new federal department that unified our
homeland security efforts. I liked and respected Joe. He was a solid legislator who had put the bitterness of the 2000 election behind him and
understood the urgency of the war on terror. Initially I was wary of his
idea for a new department. A big bureaucracy would be cumbersome. I
was also anxious about a massive reorganization in the midst of crisis. As
J.D. Crouch, later my deputy national security adviser, put it: "When you
are in the process of beating swords into plowshares, you can't fight and
you can't plow."

Over time, I changed my mind. I recognized that having one department focused on homeland security would align authority and responsibility. With the agencies accountable for protecting the country under
one roof, there would be fewer gaps and less redundancy. I also knew
there was a successful precedent for restructuring the government in
wartime. At the dawn of the Cold War in 1947, President Harry Truman
had consolidated the Navy and War departments into a new Department
of Defense. His reforms strengthened the military for decades to come.

I decided the reorganization was worth the risk. In June 2002, I addressed the nation from the White House to call on Congress to create a
new Department of Homeland Security.

Despite support from many lawmakers, the bill faced rough sledding.
Democrats held up the legislation by insisting that the new department
grant its employees extensive collective bargaining rights that did not
apply in any other government agency. I was frustrated that Democrats
would delay an urgent security measure to placate labor unions.

Republican candidates took the issue to the voters in the 2002 midterm elections, and I joined them. On election day, our party picked up
six seats in the House and two in the Senate. Karl Rove reminded me that

the only other president to pick up seats in both the House and Senate in his first midterm election was Franklin Roosevelt.

Within weeks of the election, the homeland security bill passed. I didn't have to search long for my first secretary of the new department. I nominated Tom Ridge.

———

On October 2, 2001, a tabloid photo editor named Bob Stevens was admitted to a Florida hospital with a high fever and vomiting. When doctors examined him, they discovered that he had inhaled a lethal bacteria, anthrax. Three days later, he was dead.

More employees at the tabloid turned up sick, along with people who opened the mail at NBC, ABC, and CBS News. Envelopes laced with white powder arrived at the Senate office of Tom Daschle. Several Capitol Hill staffers and postal workers got sick. So did a New York City hospital worker and a ninety-four-year-old woman in Connecticut. Ultimately, seventeen people were infected. Tragically, five died.

One of the letters containing anthrax read:

*09-11-01*
*YOU CAN NOT STOP US.*
*WE HAVE THIS ANTHRAX.*
*YOU DIE NOW.*
*ARE YOU AFRAID?*
*DEATH TO AMERICA.*
*DEATH TO ISRAEL.*
*ALLAH IS GREAT.*

I was struck by a sickening thought: Was this the second wave, a biological attack?

I had been briefed on the horrifying consequences of a bioweapons attack. One assessment concluded that a "well-executed smallpox attack by a state actor on the New York City metropolitan area" could infect 630,000 people immediately and 2 to 3 million people before the outbreak was contained. Another scenario contemplated the release of bioweapons on subway lines in four major cities during rush hour. Some 200,000 could be infected initially, with 1 million victims overall. The economic costs could "range from $60 billion to several hundred billion or more, depending on the circumstances of the attack."

As the anthrax news broke, panic spread across the country. Millions of Americans were afraid to open their mailboxes. Office mailrooms shut down. Mothers rushed to the hospital to order anthrax tests for children suffering from a common cold. Deranged hoaxsters mailed packages laced with talcum powder or flour, which exacerbated people's fears.

The Postal Service tested samples of mail for anthrax at more than two hundred sites across the country. Mail at the White House was rerouted and irradiated for the rest of my presidency. Thousands of government personnel, including Laura and me, were advised to take Cipro, a powerful antibiotic.

The biggest question during the anthrax attack was where it was coming from. One of the best intelligence services in Europe told us it suspected Iraq. Saddam Hussein's regime was one of few in the world with a record of using weapons of mass destruction, and it had acknowledged possession of anthrax in 1995. Others suspected that al Qaeda was involved. Frustratingly, we had no concrete evidence and few good leads.*

One month after 9/11, I held a primetime televised press conference from the White House. Earlier that day, we had raised the terror alert level in response to reports about a senior Taliban official warning of another major attack on America.

"You talk about the general threat toward Americans," Ann Compton of ABC News said. ". . . What are Americans supposed to look for?"

A CIA briefing on the threat of terrorists spraying anthrax over a city from a small plane was fresh in my mind. "Ann," I said, "if you find a person that you've never seen before getting in a crop duster that doesn't belong to [him], report it."

---

*In 2010, after an exhaustive investigation, the Justice Department and FBI concluded that Dr. Bruce Ivins, a U.S. government scientist who committed suicide in 2008, had executed the anthrax attack alone.

My line got a laugh, but behind the humor was a maddening reality: We believed more attacks were coming, but we didn't know when, where, or from whom. Striking the right balance between alerting and alarming the public remained a challenge for the rest of the administration. As time passed, some critics charged that we inflated the threat or manipulated alert levels for political benefit. They were flat wrong. We took the intelligence seriously and did the best we could to keep the American people informed and safe.

———

"This is the worst we've seen since 9/11," George Tenet said in a grave voice as he pulled out his half-chewed cigar at a late October intelligence briefing. He cited a highly reliable source warning that there would be an attack on either October 30 or 31 that was bigger than the World Trade Center attack.

After several false alarms, we believed this could be the real deal. Dick Cheney and I agreed that he should move to a safe place outside Washington—the famous undisclosed location—to ensure continuity of government. The Secret Service recommended that I leave, too. I told them I was staying put. Maybe this was a little bravado on my part. Mostly it was fatalism. I had made my peace. If it was God's will that I die in the White House, I would accept it. Laura felt the same way. We were confident the government would survive an attack, even if we didn't.

I did have one good reason to leave Washington for a few hours. The New York Yankees had invited me to throw out the first pitch at Game Three of the World Series. Seven weeks after 9/11, it would send a powerful signal for the president to show up in Yankee Stadium. I hoped my visit would help lift the spirits of New Yorkers.

We flew to New York on Air Force One and choppered into a field next to the ballpark. I went to a batting cage to loosen up my arm. A Secret Service agent strapped a bulletproof vest to my chest. After a few warm-up pitches, the great Yankees shortstop Derek Jeter dropped in to take some swings. We talked a little. Then he asked, "Hey President, are you going to throw from the mound or from in front of it?"

I asked what he thought. "Throw from the mound," Derek said. "Or else they'll boo you." I agreed to do it. On his way out, he looked over his shoulder and said, "But don't bounce it. They'll boo you."

Nine months into the presidency, I was used to being introduced to a crowd. But I'd never had a feeling like I did when Bob Sheppard, the Yankees legendary public address announcer, belted out, "Please welcome the president of the United States." I climbed the mound, gave a wave and a thumbs-up, and peered in at the catcher, Todd Greene. He looked a lot farther away than sixty feet, six inches. My adrenaline was surging. The ball felt like a shot put. I wound up and let it fly.

The noise in the stadium was like a sonic boom. "USA, USA, USA!" I thought back to the workers at Ground Zero. I shook hands with Todd Greene, posed for a photo with the managers, Joe Torre of the Yankees and Bob Brenly of the Arizona Diamondbacks, and made my way to George Steinbrenner's box. I was the definition of a relieved pitcher. I was thrilled to see Laura and our daughter Barbara. She gave me a big hug and said, "Dad, you threw a strike!"

We flew back to Washington late that night and waited out the next day. October 31 passed without an attack.

———

Putting the country on a war footing required more than just tightening our physical defenses. We needed better legal, financial, and intelligence tools to find the terrorists and stop them before it was too late.

One major gap in our counterterrorism capabilities was what many called "the wall." Over time, the government had adopted a set of procedures that prevented law enforcement and intelligence personnel from sharing key information.

"How can we possibly assure our citizens we are protecting them if our own people can't even talk to each other?" I said in one meeting shortly after the attacks. "We've got to fix the problem."

Attorney General John Ashcroft took the lead in writing a legislative proposal. The result was the USA PATRIOT Act.* The bill eliminated the

---

*Congress named the law the Uniting and Strengthening America by Providing Appropriate Tools Required to Intercept and Obstruct Terrorism Act.

wall and allowed law enforcement and intelligence personnel to share information. It modernized our counterterrorism capabilities by giving investigators access to tools like roving wiretaps, which allowed them to track suspects who changed cell phone numbers—an authority that had long been used to catch drug traffickers and mob bosses. It authorized aggressive financial measures to freeze terrorist assets. And it included judicial and congressional oversight to protect civil liberties.

One provision created a little discomfort at home. The PATRIOT Act allowed the government to seek warrants to examine the business records of suspected terrorists, such as credit card receipts, apartment leases, and library records. As a former librarian, Laura didn't like the idea of federal agents snooping around libraries. I didn't, either. But the intelligence community had serious concerns about terrorists using library computers to communicate. Library records had played a role in several high-profile cases, such as the Zodiac gunman murders in California. The last thing I wanted was to allow the freedom and access to information provided by American libraries to be utilized against us by al Qaeda.

Lawmakers recognized the urgency of the threat and passed the PATRIOT Act 98 to 1 in the Senate and 357 to 66 in the House. I signed the bill into law on October 26, 2001. "We took time to look at it, we took time to read it, and we took time to remove those parts that were unconstitutional and those parts that would have actually hurt liberties of all Americans," Democratic Senator Patrick Leahy of Vermont said. His Democratic colleague, Senator Chuck Schumer of New York, added, "If there is one key word that underscores this bill, it is 'balance.' In the new post–September 11 society that we face, balance is going to be a key word. . . . Balance and reason have prevailed."

Over the next five years, the PATRIOT Act helped us break up potential terror cells in New York, Oregon, Virginia, and Florida. In one example, law enforcement and intelligence authorities shared information that led to the arrest of six Yemeni Americans in Lackawanna, New York, who had traveled to a terrorist training camp in Afghanistan and met with Osama bin Laden. Five pled guilty to providing material support to al Qaeda. The other admitted to unlawful transactions with al Qaeda.

Some claimed the Lackawanna Six and others we arrested were little more than "small-town dupes" with fanciful plots "who had no intention of carrying out terrorist acts." I always wondered how the second-guessers could be so sure. After all, in August 2001, the idea that terrorists commanded from caves in Afghanistan would attack the World Trade Center and the Pentagon on U.S. commercial airplanes would have seemed pretty far-fetched. For me, the lesson of 9/11 was simple: Don't take chances. When our law enforcement and intelligence professionals found people with ties to terrorist networks inside the United States, I would rather be criticized for taking them into custody too early than waiting until it was too late.

As the freshness of 9/11 faded, so did the overwhelming congressional support for the PATRIOT Act. Civil liberties advocates and commentators on the wings of both parties mischaracterized the law as a stand-in for everything they disliked about the war on terror. Key provisions of the PATRIOT Act, such as the authority to conduct roving wiretaps, were set to expire in 2005. I pushed hard for their reauthorization. As I told Congress, the threat had not expired, so the law shouldn't, either.

Lawmakers delayed and complained. But when they finally held a vote, they renewed the PATRIOT Act by a margin of 89 to 10 in the Senate and 251 to 174 in the House. In early 2010, key provisions of the PATRIOT Act were authorized again by the heavily Democratic Congress.

My one regret about the PATRIOT Act is its name. When my administration sent the bill to Capitol Hill, it was initially called the Anti-Terrorism Act of 2001. Congress got clever and renamed it. As a result, there was an implication that people who opposed the law were unpatriotic. That was not what I intended. I should have pushed Congress to change the name of the bill before I signed it.

———

As part of the 9/11 investigation, we discovered that two hijackers who had infiltrated the United States, Khalid al Mihdhar and Nawaf al Hazmi, had communicated with al Qaeda leaders overseas more than a dozen times before the attack. My immediate question was: Why hadn't we intercepted the calls? If we had heard what Mihdhar and Hazmi were saying, we might have been able to stop the attacks of 9/11.

The man with the answers was Mike Hayden, the three-star Air Force general who led the National Security Agency. If the intelligence community is the brains of national security, the NSA is part of the gray matter. The agency is filled with smart, techno-savvy experts and code breakers, along with analysts and linguists. Mike told me the NSA had the capability to monitor those al Qaeda phone calls into the United States before 9/11. But he didn't have the legal authority to do it without receiving a court order, a process that could be difficult and slow.

The reason was a law called the Foreign Intelligence Surveillance Act. Written in 1978, before widespread use of cell phones and the Internet, FISA prohibited the NSA from monitoring communications involving people inside the United States without a warrant from the FISA court. For example, if a terrorist in Afghanistan contacted a terrorist in Pakistan, NSA could intercept their conversation. But if the same terrorist called someone in the United States, or sent an email that touched an American computer server, NSA had to apply for a court order.

That made no sense. Why should it be tougher to monitor al Qaeda communications with terrorists inside the United States than with their associates overseas? As Mike Hayden put it, we were "flying blind with no early warning system."

After 9/11, we couldn't afford to fly blind. If al Qaeda operatives were calling into or out of the United States, we damn sure needed to know who they were calling and what they were saying. And given the urgency of the threats, we could not allow ourselves to get bogged down in the court approval process. I asked the White House counsel's office and the Justice Department to study whether I could authorize the NSA to monitor al Qaeda communications into and out of the country without FISA warrants.

Both told me I could. They concluded that conducting surveillance against our enemies in war fell within the authorities granted by the congressional war resolution and the constitutional authority of the commander in chief. Abraham Lincoln had wiretapped telegraph machines during the Civil War. Woodrow Wilson had ordered the interception of virtually every telephone and telegraph message going into or out of the United States during World War I. Franklin Roosevelt had allowed the military to read and censor communications during World War II.

Before I approved the Terrorist Surveillance Program, I wanted to ensure there were safeguards to prevent abuses. I had no desire to turn the NSA into an Orwellian Big Brother. I knew that the Kennedy brothers had teamed up with J. Edgar Hoover to listen illegally to the conversations of innocent people, including Martin Luther King, Jr. Lyndon Johnson had continued the practice. I thought that was a sad chapter in our history, and I wasn't going to repeat it.

On the morning of October 4, 2001, Mike Hayden and the legal team came to the Oval Office. They assured me the Terrorist Surveillance Program had been carefully designed to protect the civil liberties of innocent people. The purpose of the program was to monitor so-called dirty numbers, which intelligence professionals had reason to believe belonged to al Qaeda operatives. Many had been found in the cell phones or computers of terrorists captured on the battlefield. If we inadvertently intercepted any portion of purely domestic communications, the violation would be reported to the Justice Department for investigation. To be sure the program was used only as long as necessary, it had to be regularly reassessed and reapproved.

I gave the order to proceed with the program. We considered going to Congress to get legislation, but key members from both parties who received highly classified briefings on the program agreed that the surveillance was necessary and that a legislative debate was not possible without exposing our methods to the enemy.

I knew the Terrorist Surveillance Program would prove controversial one day. Yet I believed it was necessary. The rubble at the World Trade Center was still smoldering. Every morning I received intelligence reports about another possible attack. Monitoring terrorist communications into the United States was essential to keeping the American people safe.

———

On December 22, a British passenger named Richard Reid tried to blow up an American Airlines flight carrying 197 people from Paris to Miami by detonating explosives in his shoes. Fortunately, an alert flight attendant noticed his suspicious behavior, and passengers overwhelmed him before he could light the fuse. The plane was diverted to Boston, where Reid was marched off in handcuffs. He later told questioners that his goal was to cripple the U.S. economy with an attack during the holiday season. He pled guilty to eight counts of terrorist activity, leading to a life sentence at the federal supermax prison in Florence, Colorado.

The foiled attack had a big impact on me. Three months after 9/11, it was a vivid reminder that the threats were frighteningly real. Airport screeners began requiring passengers to remove their shoes at checkpoints. I recognized that we were creating an inconvenience, but I felt it was worth it to prevent a copycat attack. I knew my policy was being implemented fully when Laura's eighty-two-year-old mom had to take off her shoes before her Christmas flight from Midland to Washington. I sure hoped I wouldn't be nearby if they asked Mother to do the same.

The near-miss over the Atlantic highlighted a broader gap in our approach to the war on terror. When Richard Reid was arrested, he was swiftly placed into the U.S. criminal justice system, which entitled him to the same constitutional protections as a common criminal. But the shoe bomber was not a burglar or bank robber; he was a foot soldier in al Qaeda's war against America. He had emailed his mother two days before his attempted attack: "What I am doing is part of the ongoing war between Islam and disbelief." By giving this terrorist the right to remain silent, we deprived ourselves of the opportunity to collect vital intelligence on his plan and his handlers.

Reid's case made clear we needed a new policy for dealing with captured terrorists. In this new kind of war, there is no more valuable source of intelligence on potential attacks than the terrorists themselves. Amid the steady stream of threats after 9/11, I grappled with three of the most critical decisions I would make in the war on terror: where to hold captured enemy fighters, how to determine their legal status and ensure they eventually faced justice, and how to learn what they knew about future attacks so we could protect the American people.

Initially, most captured al Qaeda fighters were held for questioning in battlefield prisons in Afghanistan. In November, CIA officers went to interrogate Taliban and al Qaeda prisoners detained at a primitive nineteenth-century Afghan fortress, Qala-i-Jangi. A riot ensued. Using weapons smuggled onto the complex, enemy fighters killed one of our officers, Johnny "Mike" Spann, making him the first American combat death in the war.

The tragedy highlighted the need for a secure facility to hold captured terrorists. There were few options, none particularly attractive. For a while, we held al Qaeda detainees on Navy ships in the Arabian Sea. But that was not a viable long-term solution. Another possibility was to send the terrorists to a secure base on a distant island or U.S. territory, such as Guam. But holding captured terrorists on American soil could activate constitutional protections they would not otherwise receive, such as the right to remain silent. That would make it much more difficult to get urgently needed intelligence.

We decided to hold detainees at a remote naval station on the southern tip of Cuba, Guantanamo Bay. The base was on Cuban soil, but the United States controlled it under a lease acquired after the Spanish-American War. The Justice Department advised me that prisoners brought there had no right of access to the U.S. criminal justice system. The area surrounding Guantanamo was inaccessible and sparsely populated. Holding terrorists in Fidel Castro's Cuba was hardly an appealing prospect. But as Don Rumsfeld put it, Guantanamo was the "least worst choice" available.

At Guantanamo, detainees were given clean and safe shelter, three meals a day, a personal copy of the Koran, the opportunity to pray five times daily, and the same medical care their guards received. They had access to exercise space and a library stocked with books and DVDs. One of the most popular was an Arabic translation of *Harry Potter*.

Over the years, we invited members of Congress, journalists, and international observers to visit Guantanamo and see the conditions for themselves. Many came away surprised by what they found. A Belgian official inspected Guantanamo five times and called it a "model prison" that offered detainees better treatment than Belgian prisons. "I have never witnessed acts of violence or things which shocked me in Guantanamo," he said. "One should not confuse this center with Abu Ghraib."

While our humane treatment of Guantanamo detainees was consistent with the Geneva Conventions, al Qaeda did not meet the qualifications for Geneva protection as a legal matter. The purpose of Geneva was to provide incentives for nation-states to fight wars by an agreed set of rules that protect human dignity and innocent life—and to punish warriors who do not. But the terrorists did not represent a nation-state. They had not signed the Geneva Conventions. Their entire mode of operation—intentionally killing the innocent—defied the principles of Geneva. And if al Qaeda captured an American, there was little chance they would treat him humanely.

This was confirmed with gruesome clarity in late January 2002, when terrorists in Pakistan abducted *Wall Street Journal* reporter Daniel Pearl. They alleged he was a CIA spy and tried to blackmail the United States into bargaining for his release. America has a longstanding policy of not negotiating with terrorists, and I continued it. I knew that if I accepted one terrorist's demands, it would only encourage more kidnappings. Our military and intelligence assets were searching urgently for Pearl, but they couldn't make it in time. In his final moments, Danny Pearl said, "My father is Jewish, my mother is Jewish, I am Jewish." Then his al Qaeda captors slit his throat.

As I made my decision on Geneva protection, I also decided to create a legal system to determine the innocence or guilt of detainees. George Washington, Abraham Lincoln, William McKinley, and Franklin Roosevelt had faced similar dilemmas of how to bring captured enemy combatants to justice during wartime. All had reached the same conclusion: a court operated by the military.

On November 13, 2001, I signed an executive order establishing military tribunals to try captured terrorists. The system was based closely on the one created by FDR in 1942, which tried and convicted eight Nazi spies who had infiltrated the United States. The Supreme Court had unanimously upheld the legality of those tribunals.

I was confident the military tribunals would provide a fair trial. Detainees were entitled to the presumption of innocence, representation by a qualified attorney, and the right to present evidence that would "have probative value to a reasonable person." For practical national security reasons, they were not allowed to view classified information that would expose intelligence sources and methods. Convicting a defendant required agreement of two thirds of the tribunal. The detainee could appeal the tribunal's decision or sentence to the secretary of defense and to the president.

Inherent in my tribunals decision—and many others in the new war—

was the tension between protecting the American people and upholding civil liberties. Maintaining our values was critical to our position in the world. We could neither lead the free world nor recruit new allies to our cause if we did not practice what we preached. I believed military tribunals struck the right balance, upholding the rule of law while protecting the country.

———

On March 28, 2002, I could hear excitement in George Tenet's voice. He reported that Pakistani police—with a hand from the FBI and CIA—had launched a takedown operation against several al Qaeda safe houses in the Pakistani city of Faisalabad. They netted more than two dozen operatives, including Abu Zubaydah.

I had been hearing reports about Zubaydah for months. The intelligence community believed he was a trusted associate of Osama bin Laden and a senior recruiter and operator who had run a camp in Afghanistan where some of the 9/11 hijackers had trained. He was suspected of involvement in previous plots to destroy targets in Jordan and blow up Los Angeles International Airport. The CIA believed he was planning to attack America again.

Zubaydah had been severely wounded in a gun battle prior to his arrest. The CIA flew in a top doctor, who saved his life. The Pakistanis then turned him over to our custody. The FBI began questioning Zubaydah, who had clearly been trained on how to resist interrogation. He revealed bits and pieces of information that he thought we already knew. Frighteningly, we didn't know much. For example, we received definitive information about a new alias for Khalid Sheikh Mohammed, who Zubaydah also confirmed had masterminded the 9/11 attacks.

Then Zubaydah stopped answering questions. George Tenet told me interrogators believed Zubaydah had more information to reveal. If he was hiding something more, what could it be? Zubaydah was our best lead to avoid another catastrophic attack. "We need to find out what he knows," I directed the team. "What are our options?"

One option was for the CIA to take over Zubaydah's questioning and move him to a secure location in another country where the Agency could have total control over his environment. CIA experts drew up a list of interrogation techniques that differed from those Zubaydah had successfully resisted. George assured me all interrogations would be performed by experienced intelligence professionals who had undergone extensive training. Medical personnel would be on-site to guarantee that the detainee was not physically or mentally harmed.

At my direction, Department of Justice and CIA lawyers conducted a careful legal review. They concluded that the enhanced interrogation program complied with the Constitution and all applicable laws, including those that ban torture.

I took a look at the list of techniques. There were two that I felt went too far, even if they were legal. I directed the CIA not to use them. Another technique was waterboarding, a process of simulated drowning. No doubt the procedure was tough, but medical experts assured the CIA that it did no lasting harm.

I knew that an interrogation program this sensitive and controversial would one day become public. When it did, we would open ourselves up to criticism that America had compromised our moral values. I would have preferred that we get the information another way. But the choice between security and values was real. Had I not authorized waterboarding on senior al Qaeda leaders, I would have had to accept a greater risk that the country would be attacked. In the wake of 9/11, that was a risk I was unwilling to take. My most solemn responsibility as president was to protect the country. I approved the use of the interrogation techniques.

The new techniques proved highly effective. Zubaydah revealed large amounts of information on al Qaeda's structure and operations. He also provided leads that helped reveal the location of Ramzi bin al Shibh, the logistical planner of the 9/11 attacks. The Pakistani police picked him up on the first anniversary of 9/11.

Zubaydah later explained to interrogators why he started answering questions again. His understanding of Islam was that he had to resist interrogation only up to a certain point. Waterboarding was the technique that allowed him to reach that threshold, fulfill his religious duty, and then cooperate. "You must do this for all the brothers," he said.

On March 1, 2003, George Tenet told a spy story suitable for a John le Carré novel. Information gleaned through the interrogations of Abu Zubaydah and Ramzi bin al Shibh, combined with other intelligence, had helped us draw a bead on a high-ranking al Qaeda leader. Then a brave foreign agent recruited by the CIA led us to the door of an apartment complex in Pakistan. "I want my children free of these madmen who distort our religion and kill innocent people," the agent later said.

Pakistani forces raided the complex and hauled out their target. It was the chief operating officer of al Qaeda, the murderer of Danny Pearl, and the mastermind of 9/11: Khalid Sheikh Mohammed.

I was relieved to have one of al Qaeda's senior leaders off the battlefield. But my relief did not last long. Agents searching Khalid Sheikh Mohammed's compound discovered what one official later called a "mother lode" of valuable intelligence. Khalid Sheikh Mohammed was obviously planning more attacks. It didn't sound like he was willing to give us any information about them. "I'll talk to you," he said, "after I get to New York and see my lawyer."

George Tenet asked if he had permission to use enhanced interrogation techniques, including waterboarding, on Khalid Sheikh Mohammed. I thought about my meeting with Danny Pearl's widow, who was pregnant with his son when he was murdered. I thought about the 2,973 people stolen from their families by al Qaeda on 9/11. And I thought about my duty to protect the country from another act of terror.

"Damn right," I said.

Khalid Sheikh Mohammed proved difficult to break. But when he did, he gave us a lot. He disclosed plans to attack American targets with anthrax and directed us to three people involved in the al Qaeda biological weapons program. He provided information that led to the capture of Hambali, the chief of al Qaeda's most dangerous affiliate in Southeast Asia and the architect of the Bali terrorist attack that killed 202 people. He provided further details that led agents to Hambali's brother, who had been grooming operatives to carry out another attack inside the

United States, possibly a West Coast version of 9/11 in which terrorists flew a hijacked plane into the Library Tower in Los Angeles.

Years later, the *Washington Post* ran a front-page story about Khalid Sheikh Mohammed's transformation. Headlined "How a Detainee Became an Asset," it described how Mohammed "seemed to relish the opportunity, sometimes for hours on end, to discuss the inner workings of al-Qaeda and the group's plans, ideology and operatives. . . . He'd even use a chalkboard at times." The intelligence he provided, which proved vital to saving American lives, almost certainly would not have come to light without the CIA's enhanced interrogation program.

Of the thousands of terrorists we captured in the years after 9/11, about a hundred were placed into the CIA program. About a third of those were questioned using enhanced techniques. Three were waterboarded. The information the detainees in the CIA program revealed constituted more than half of what the CIA knew about al Qaeda. Their interrogations helped break up plots to attack American military and diplomatic facilities abroad, Heathrow Airport and Canary Wharf in London, and multiple targets in the United States. Experts in the intelligence community told me that without the CIA program, there would have been another attack on the United States.

After we implemented the CIA program, we briefed a small number of lawmakers from both parties on its existence. At the time, some were concerned we weren't pushing hard enough. But years later, once the threat seemed less urgent and the political winds had shifted, many lawmakers became fierce critics. They charged that Americans had committed unlawful torture. That was not true. I had asked the most senior legal officers in the U.S. government to review the interrogation methods, and they had assured me they did not constitute torture. To suggest that our intelligence personnel violated the law by following the legal guidance they received is insulting and wrong.

The CIA interrogation program saved lives. Had we captured more al Qaeda operatives with significant intelligence value, I would have used the program for them as well.

On the morning of March 10, 2004, Dick Cheney and Andy Card greeted me with a startling announcement: The Terrorist Surveillance Program would expire at the end of the day.

"How can it possibly end?" I asked. "It's vital to protecting the country." Two and a half years had passed since I authorized the TSP in October 2001. In that time, the NSA had used the program to uncover key details about terrorist plots and locations. NSA Director Mike Hayden later said publicly that the program had been "successful in detecting and preventing attacks inside the United States" and that it was his "professional judgment that we would have detected some of the 9/11 al Qaeda operatives in the United States" if it had been operational before the attacks.

Andy explained the situation. While John Ashcroft had regularly recommended the renewal of the TSP since 2001, the Justice Department had raised a legal objection to one component of the program.

"Why didn't I know about this?" I asked. Andy shared my disbelief. He told me he had just learned about the objection the previous night. The legal team must have thought the disagreement could be settled without presidential involvement. I told Andy to work with Ashcroft and White House Counsel Alberto Gonzales to solve the problem. In the meantime, I had to fly to Cleveland to deliver a speech on trade policy.

When I got back, I checked in with Andy. Little progress had been made. The Justice Department was sticking to its objection. My lawyers weren't budging, either. They were convinced the program was legal.

"Where the hell is Ashcroft?" I asked.

"He's in the hospital," Andy replied.

That was news to me. I called John, who I discovered was recovering from emergency gallbladder surgery. I told him I was sending Andy and Al to talk to him about an urgent matter. They drove to the hospital with the TSP reauthorization order. When they got back, they told me Ashcroft hadn't signed. The only way to allow the program to continue was to override the Justice Department's objection. I didn't like the idea, but I saw no other alternative. I signed an order keeping the TSP alive based on my authority as head of the executive branch.

I went to bed irritated and had a feeling I didn't know the full story. I intended to get it.

———

"Mr. President, we've got a major problem," Andy told me when I got to the Oval Office on the morning of March 12. "Jim Comey is the acting attorney general, and he's going to resign because you extended the TSP. So are a bunch of other Justice Department officials."

I was stunned. Nobody had told me that Comey, John Ashcroft's deputy, had taken over Ashcroft's responsibilities when he went in for surgery. If I had known that, I never would have sent Andy and Al to John's hospital room.

I asked to speak to Comey privately after the morning FBI briefing, which he attended in John Ashcroft's place. I hadn't spent a lot of time with Jim, but I knew he had a distinguished record as a prosecutor in New York. I started by explaining that I had an obligation to do what was necessary to protect the country. I felt the TSP was essential to that effort. He explained his concerns about the problematic aspect of the program. "I just don't understand why you are raising this at the last minute," I said.

He looked shocked. "Mr. President," he said, "your staff has known about this for weeks." Then he dropped another bomb. He wasn't the only one planning to resign. So was FBI Director Bob Mueller. I was about to witness the largest mass resignation in modern presidential history, and we were in the middle of a war.

I called Bob into the Oval Office. I had come to know him well over the past two and a half years. He was a good and decent man, a former Princeton hockey star who had served in the Marines and led the U.S. Attorney's Office in San Francisco. Without hesitation, he agreed with Comey. If I continued the program over the Justice Department's objection, he said, he couldn't serve in my administration.

I had to make a big decision, and fast. Some in the White House believed I should stand on my powers under Article II of the Constitution and suffer the walkout. Others counseled that I accept Justice's objections, modify the program, and keep the administration intact.

I was willing to defend the powers of the presidency under Article II. But not at any cost. I thought about the Saturday Night Massacre in October 1973, when President Richard Nixon's firing of Watergate prosecutor

Archibald Cox led his attorney general and deputy attorney general to resign. That was not a historical crisis I was eager to replicate. It wouldn't give me much satisfaction to know I was right on the legal principles while my administration imploded and our key programs in the war on terror were exposed in the media firestorm that would inevitably follow.

I decided to accommodate the Justice Department's concern by modifying the part of the program they found problematic, while leaving the TSP in place. Comey and Mueller dropped their resignation threats. The surveillance program continued to produce results, and that was the most important thing.

I was relieved to have the crisis over, but I was disturbed it had happened at all. I made clear to my advisers that I never wanted to be blindsided like that again. I did not suspect bad intentions on anyone's part. One of the toughest questions every White House faces is how to manage the president's time and when to bring policy disputes to his desk. The standoff over the surveillance program was a case of bad judgment. There was no shortage of disagreements in the years ahead, but nothing like this ever happened again.

———

One of my favorite books is the fine historian David McCullough's biography of President Harry Truman. I admired Truman's toughness, principle, and strategic vision. "I felt like the moon, the stars, and all the planets had fallen on me," he said when he took office suddenly in the final months of World War II. Yet the man from Missouri knew how to make a hard decision and stick by it. He did what he thought was right and didn't care much what the critics said. When he left office in 1953, his approval ratings were in the twenties. Today he is viewed as one of America's great presidents.

After she became secretary of state, Condi gave me a biography of Truman's secretary of state, Dean Acheson. Both books reminded me how Truman's decisions in the late 1940s and early 1950s laid the foundation for victory in the Cold War and helped shape the world I inherited as president. Truman forged the NATO alliance; signed the National Security Act of 1947, which created the CIA, the National Security Council, and the Defense Department; fought an unpopular war that enabled the rise of a democratic ally in South Korea; and pledged assistance to all countries resisting communist takeover, the Truman Doctrine.

As in Truman's era, we were in the early years of a long struggle. We had created a variety of tools to deal with the threats. I made it a high priority of my second term to turn those tools into institutions and laws that would be available to my successors.

In some areas, we were off to a good start. The Department of Homeland Security, while prone to the inefficiencies of any large bureaucracy, was an improvement over twenty-two uncoordinated agencies. The FBI had created a new National Security Branch focused on preventing terrorist attacks. The Defense Department had established a new Northern Command with the sole responsibility to defend the homeland. The Treasury Department had adopted an aggressive new approach to disrupting terrorist financing. We had recruited more than ninety countries to a new Proliferation Security Initiative aimed at stopping international trafficking of materials related to weapons of mass destruction. Based in part on the recommendation of the 9/11 Commission, we had created a new National Counterterrorism Center and appointed a director of national intelligence—the largest reform of the intelligence community since Truman created the CIA.

In other areas, we had work to do. Some of our most important tools in the war on terror, including the TSP and the CIA interrogation program, were based on the broad authority of Article II and the congressional war resolution. The best way to ensure they remained available after I left office was to work with Congress to codify those programs into law. As Justice Robert Jackson explained in a landmark opinion in 1952, a president has the most authority when he is acting with the explicit support of Congress.

The challenge was how to present the TSP and the CIA interrogation program to Congress without exposing details to the enemy. I believed it was possible, but we would have to work closely with members of Congress to structure the debate in a way that did not reveal critical secrets. We were developing a strategy to do that. Then two events forced our hand.

"The *New York Times* is on the surveillance story again," Steve Hadley told me in December 2005. The previous year, the *Times* had considered running a story exposing the TSP. Condi and Mike Hayden had talked the paper out of revealing the key elements of the program.

I asked the *Times* publisher, Arthur Sulzberger, Jr., and editor, Bill Keller, to come see me on December 5, 2005. It was a rare request, and I appreciated their willingness to speak face to face. They arrived around 5:00 p.m. Steve Hadley, Andy Card, Mike Hayden, and I greeted them in the Oval Office. We sat by the fireplace beneath the portrait of George Washington. I told them the nation was still in danger, and their newspaper was on the verge of increasing that danger by revealing the TSP in a way that could tip off our enemies. Then I authorized General Hayden to walk them through the program.

Mike is a calming personality. He is not a macho guy who tries to intimidate people with the stars on his shoulders. He talked about his long career in intelligence and his natural suspicion about any program that could result in collecting information on U.S. citizens. He outlined the safeguards in place, the numerous legal reviews, and the results the program had produced.

Mike's briefing lasted about thirty minutes. I watched the *Times* men closely. They were stone-faced. I told them they could ask Mike any question they wanted. They didn't have many. I looked directly at Sulzberger and strongly urged that he withhold the story for national security reasons. He said he would consider my request.

Ten days later, Bill Keller called Steve to say the *Times* was going forward with the story. We had no chance for a closing argument. They had posted it on their website before Keller placed the call.

I was disappointed in the *Times* and angry at whoever had betrayed their country by leaking the story. The Justice Department opened a criminal investigation into the disclosure of classified information. As of the summer of 2010, nobody had been prosecuted.

The left responded with hysteria. "He's President George Bush, not King George Bush," one senator blustered. "The Bush administration seems to believe it is above the law," another said. One immediate effect of the leak was to derail the renewal of the PATRIOT Act, which was set to be reauthorized by Congress. "We killed the PATRIOT Act," Senate Minority Leader Harry Reid, who had voted for the law in 2001, bragged at a political rally.

Ultimately the PATRIOT Act was renewed, but the leak created a bigger problem. Telecommunications companies suspected of helping the government operate the TSP faced massive class-action lawsuits. That was unfair. Companies that had agreed to do their patriotic duty to help the government keep America safe deserved to be saluted, not sued. One thing was sure: Any hope of future cooperation from the telecom industry was gone unless we could provide legal immunity.

In early 2006, I began outreach to key legislators on a bill modernizing the Foreign Intelligence Surveillance Act. The new legislation provided explicit authority for the kind of surveillance we had conducted under the TSP, as well as liability protection for telecom companies.

The debate continued in fits and starts for two years. Fortunately, I had two persuasive advocates: Director of National Intelligence Mike McConnell, a clear-thinking former Navy admiral, and Attorney General Mike Mukasey, a tough-minded federal judge from New York. They spent hours on Capitol Hill explaining the need to close the gaps in our intelligence capabilities as well as the safeguards we had in place to prevent abuses.

Finally, both houses of Congress held a vote in the summer of 2008. The House passed the bill 293 to 129. In the Senate, it received 69 votes. The legislation essentially ended the debate over the legality of our surveillance activities. Congress had shown bipartisan support for a law that provided even more flexibility than we'd had under the Terrorist Surveillance Program.

---

The second event that forced our hand came in June 2006, when the Supreme Court ruled in *Hamdan v. Rumsfeld*.

The decision was the culmination of more than four years of litigation involving the military tribunals I had authorized in November 2001. It had taken two and a half years for the Defense Department to work out the procedures and start the first trial. No doubt it was a complex legal and logistical undertaking. But I detected a certain lack of enthusiasm for the project. With all the pressures in Afghanistan and Iraq, it never seemed like the tribunals were a top priority.

Lawyers advocating for the detainees moved with more urgency. In 2004, the Navy-appointed lawyer for Salim Hamdan—Osama bin Laden's driver, who had been captured in Afghanistan—challenged the fairness of the tribunal. The appeals court upheld the validity of the tribunals as a system of wartime justice. But in June 2006, the Supreme Court overturned that ruling. The Court decided that, unlike Franklin Roosevelt and other predecessors, I needed explicit authorization from Congress to establish the tribunals.

The ruling also affected the CIA interrogation program. In his majority opinion, Justice John Paul Stevens ruled that a part of the Geneva Conventions known as Common Article III—written exclusively for "armed conflict not of an international character"—somehow applied to America's war with al Qaeda. The provision prohibited "outrages upon personal dignity," a vague phrase that could be interpreted to mean just about anything. As a result, CIA lawyers worried that intelligence personnel who questioned terrorists could suddenly face legal jeopardy. The CIA informed me that it had to suspend the interrogation program that had yielded so much lifesaving information.

I disagreed strongly with the Court's decision, which I considered an example of judicial activism. But I accepted the role of the Supreme Court in our constitutional democracy. I did not intend to repeat the example of President Andrew Jackson, who said, "John Marshall has made his decision, now let him enforce it!" Whether presidents like them or not, the Court's decisions are the law of the land.

Similar to the TSP leak, the Supreme Court decision made clear it was time to seek legislation codifying the military tribunal system and CIA interrogation program. I took the issue to the people with a series of speeches and statements. The most dramatic came in the East Room of the White House in September 2006. As a way to highlight the stakes of passing the bill, I announced that we would transfer Khalid Sheikh Mohammed and

thirteen other high-ranking al Qaeda detainees from CIA custody overseas to Guantanamo, where they would face trial under the new tribunals
Congress would create.

"This bill makes the president a dictator," one congressman proclaimed.
Other lawmakers compared the conduct of our military and CIA professionals to the Taliban and Saddam Hussein.

I was confident the American people had better judgment. Most
Americans understood the need for intelligence professionals to have the
tools to get information from terrorists planning attacks on our country. And they did not want Guantanamo detainees brought to the United
States and tried in civilian courts with the same constitutional rights as
common criminals.

Within a month of my East Room speech, Congress passed the Military Commissions Act of 2006 by a comfortable bipartisan majority. It
contained everything we asked for, including authority for the tribunals
to restart and for a president to use enhanced interrogation techniques,
should he choose to do so.

As I listened to my last CIA briefing the morning before President
Obama's Inauguration, I reflected on all that had happened since 9/11: the
red alerts and the false alarms, the botulinum toxin we thought would
kill us, and the plots we had disrupted. Years had passed, but the threat
had not. The terrorists had struck Bali, Jakarta, Riyadh, Istanbul, Madrid, London, Amman, and Mumbai. My morning intelligence reports
made clear that they were determined to attack America again.

After the shock of 9/11, there was no legal, military, or political blueprint for confronting a new enemy that rejected all the traditional rules
of war. By the time I left office, we had put in place a system of effective
counterterrorism programs based on a solid legal and legislative footing.

Of course, there are things I wish had come out differently. I am frustrated that the military tribunals moved so slowly. Even after the Military Commissions Act was passed, another lawsuit delayed the process
again. By the time I left office, we had held only two trials.

The difficulty of conducting trials made it harder to meet a goal I had set early in my second term: closing the prison at Guantanamo in a responsible way. While I believe opening Guantanamo after 9/11 was necessary, the detention facility had become a propaganda tool for our enemies and a distraction for our allies. I worked to find a way to close the prison without compromising security. By the time I left office, the number of detainees at Guantanamo had dropped from nearly 800 to fewer than 250. My hope is that many of those remaining will stand trial for their crimes. Some of the hardened, dangerous terrorists at Guanta-namo may be very difficult to try. I knew that if I released them and they killed Americans, the blood would be on my hands. Deciding how to handle them is the toughest part of closing Guantanamo.

In retrospect, I probably could have avoided some of the contro-versy and legal setbacks by seeking legislation on military tribunals, the TSP, and the CIA enhanced interrogation program as soon as they were created. If members of Congress had been required to make their de-cisions at the same time I did—in the immediate aftermath of 9/11—I am confident they would have overwhelmingly approved everything we requested. Yet in the case of the TSP and the CIA program, the risk of exposing operational details to the enemy was one I could not take until we had a better handle on the security situation.

I have been troubled by the blowback against the intelligence com-munity and Justice Department for their role in the surveillance and in-terrogation programs. Our intelligence officers carried out their orders with skill and courage, and they deserve our gratitude for protecting our nation. Legal officials in my administration did their best to resolve complex issues in a time of extraordinary danger to our country. Their successors are entitled to disagree with their conclusions. But criminal-izing differences of legal opinion would set a terrible precedent for our democracy.

From the beginning, I knew the public reaction to my decisions would be colored by whether there was another attack. If none happened, what-ever I did would probably look like an overreaction. If we were attacked again, people would demand to know why I hadn't done more.

That is the nature of the presidency. Perceptions are shaped by the clarity of hindsight. In the moment of decision, you don't have that ad-vantage. On 9/11, I vowed that I would do what it took to protect America, within the Constitution and laws of our nation. History can debate the decisions I made, the policies I chose, and the tools I left behind. But there can be no debate about one fact: After the nightmare of September 11, America went seven and a half years without another successful terrorist attack on our soil. If I had to summarize my most meaningful accomplishment as president in one sentence, that would be it.

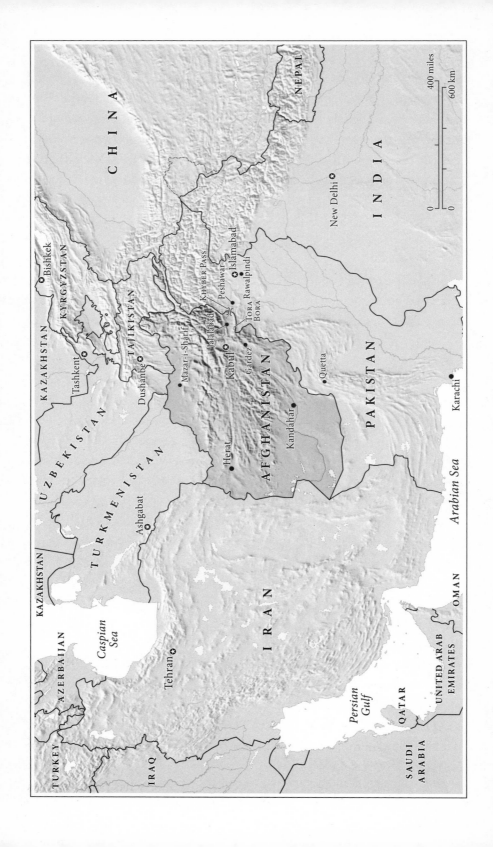

# 7

# AFGHANISTAN

The Treaty Room was one of my favorite places in the White House. Spacious and stately, it sits on the second floor between the Lincoln Bedroom and the Yellow Oval Room. Before the construction of the West Wing, the Treaty Room was the presidential office. Its name dates back to 1898, when President William McKinley chose it to sign the treaty ending the Spanish-American War.

The dominant piece of furniture is a large, dark walnut desk, where the treaty was signed and the cabinet of President Ulysses S. Grant met. I used the desk to edit speeches, read briefing papers, and make phone calls, usually in the evening after I had come back from the Oval Office.

Opposite the desk was a large oil painting, *The Peacemakers*. It shows President Lincoln aboard the *River Queen* steamer with General Grant, General William Tecumseh Sherman, and Rear Admiral David Porter in the final month of the Civil War. Lincoln is consulting with his military commanders on the strategy to defeat the Confederacy and establish a just and lasting peace. Before 9/11, I saw the scene as a fascinating moment in history. After the attack, it took on a deeper meaning. The painting reminded me of Lincoln's clarity of purpose: He waged war for a necessary and noble cause.

Just after noon on Sunday, October 7, 2001, I walked into the Treaty Room to address the nation. Hours earlier, long-range bombers had taken off from Whiteman Air Force Base in Missouri. American and British submarines in the Arabian Gulf had launched their Tomahawk missiles. And Navy fighter planes had lifted off the decks of the USS *Carl Vinson* and the USS *Enterprise*.

"On my orders," I said, "the United States military has begun strikes against al Qaeda terrorist training camps and military installations of the Taliban regime in Afghanistan."

I felt the gravity of the decision. I knew the war would bring death and sorrow. Every life lost would devastate a family forever. At the end of my speech, I quoted a letter I had received from a fourth-grade girl with a father in the military. "As much as I don't want my dad to fight," she wrote, "I'm willing to give him to you."

My anxiety about the sacrifice was mitigated by the urgency of the cause. Removing al Qaeda's safe haven in Afghanistan was essential to protecting the American people. We had planned the mission carefully. We were acting out of necessity and self-defense, not revenge.

I looked out the window of the Treaty Room. In the distance I could see the Jefferson Memorial, where the words of the Declaration of Independence are carved into the wall: "We hold these truths to be self-evident, that all men are created equal." Across the Potomac sat the scarred Pentagon. For twenty-six days after 9/11, we had planned and prepared. Now the wait was over. America's counterattack was under way. The liberation of Afghanistan had begun.

———

Sending Americans to war is the most profound decision a president can make. I saw that in 1989, when Laura, the girls, and I spent Christmas at Camp David. On December 20, Dad had deployed twenty-seven thousand troops to Panama to remove dictator Manuel Noriega and restore democracy.

Operation Just Cause was a success. The dictator was deposed quickly. American casualties were few. Most were in a celebratory mood. But not Dad. For the wounded and the families of the fallen—and for their commander in chief—the cost of battle was painfully high.

I was standing next to Mother and Dad at a Christmas Eve caroling session when the Navy chaplain walked over. He said, "Sir, I've just returned from Wilford Hall in San Antonio, where the wounded troops lie. I told the boys that if they had a message for the president, I'd be seeing you tonight."

He continued: "They said, 'Please tell the president we're proud to serve a great country, and we're proud to serve a great man like George Bush.'" Dad's eyes filled with tears.

The poignant moment gave me an up-close look at the personal toll of sending troops into combat. But nothing prepared me for the feeling when I was the president who gave the order.

———

As I knew from my visits during Dad's time in office, Camp David is one of the great privileges afforded the president. Nestled in Maryland's Catoctin Mountains about seventy miles from Washington, the 200-acre site is a thirty-minute helicopter ride from the White House. It feels much more removed than that. The retreat is run by the Navy and protected by the Marines. It consists of rustic cabins, a gym and swimming pool, a bowling alley, a chipping green, and scenic trails through the woods for hiking and biking. The atmosphere fosters reflection and clear thinking.

The presidential cabin is known as Aspen. Its interior is simple but comfortable. The wooden structure has three bedrooms, a perfect size for our family; a sunlit living room where I watched football with my brother Marvin and friends; and a stone fireplace beside which Laura and I liked to read at night.

About a quarter mile down the hill is Laurel, a large lodge with a spacious dining area, a small presidential office, and a wood-paneled conference room that Jimmy Carter used when he negotiated the Camp David Peace Accords.

That was where my national security team gathered on Saturday morning, September 15, to start developing the battle plan for Afghanistan. The mood was somber, serious, and focused. With me at the big oak table were the top national security officials from across the government.* Together they had decades of crisis management experience.

---

*Vice President Dick Cheney, Secretary of State Colin Powell, Defense Secretary Don Rumsfeld and Deputy Secretary Paul Wolfowitz, Attorney General John Ashcroft and FBI Director Bob Mueller, Treasury Secretary Paul O'Neill, CIA Director George Tenet and Deputy Director John McLaughlin, Joint Chiefs of Staff Chairman Hugh Shelton and Vice Chairman Dick Myers, White House Chief of Staff Andy Card, National Security Adviser Condi Rice and Deputy National Security Adviser Steve Hadley, White House Counsel Alberto Gonzales, and Chief of Staff to the Vice President I. Lewis "Scooter" Libby.

The first key presentation that morning came from CIA Director George Tenet. Six months earlier, at my direction, George and the National Security Council had started developing a comprehensive strategy to destroy the al Qaeda network. In the four days between 9/11 and the Camp David meeting, the CIA team had beefed up their plan. George proposed that I grant broader authority for covert actions, including permission for the CIA to kill or capture al Qaeda operatives without asking for my sign-off each time. I decided to grant the request.

The heart of the CIA plan was a new offensive in Afghanistan, where 9/11 had been planned. The roots of the terrorist presence in Afghanistan traced back to 1979, when the Soviet Union invaded and installed a communist puppet regime. Afghan tribes, along with a band of hard-core Islamic fighters known as the Mujahideen, rose up against the foreign occupation. With assistance from the United States, Pakistan, and Saudi Arabia, the rebels inflicted fifteen thousand casualties and drove out the Soviets in 1989. Two years later, the superpower collapsed.

Free of the communist occupiers, the Afghan people had a chance to rebuild their country. But the U.S. government no longer saw a national interest in Afghanistan, so it cut off support. America's noninvolvement helped create a vacuum. Tribal warriors who had defeated the Soviets turned their guns on one another. Ultimately, the Taliban, a group of Islamic fundamentalists, seized power. They imposed a fanatical, barbaric brand of Islam that prohibited girls from going to school, required men to grow beards of a certain length, and forbade women from leaving their homes without a male relative as an escort. The simplest pleasures—singing, clapping, and flying kites—were banned.

The Taliban's rules were enforced by brutal religious police. A 1998 State Department report described a woman struggling to carry two small children and a load of groceries on a street in Mazar-i-Sharif. When her body-length burqa slipped from her face, she was beaten with a car antenna. Petty thieves were taken to the national soccer stadium to have their limbs hacked off.

Homosexuals were stoned to death, as was anyone suspected of adultery. Shortly after the Taliban seized Kabul, they kidnapped the former president of Afghanistan from his UN compound. After beating and castrating him, they hung his body from a lamppost. In Bamiyan Province,

home to the minority Hazaras, the Taliban massacred at least 170 innocent civilians in January 2001. Later that year, they dynamited two cherished 1,500-year-old Buddha sculptures.

There were some who received warm hospitality from the Taliban.
Shortly after taking power, the radical mullahs offered sanctuary to
Osama bin Laden, the founder of al Qaeda. Between 1996 and 2001, bin
Laden established camps in Afghanistan that trained an estimated ten
thousand terrorists. In return, bin Laden drew on his personal fortune
to fund the Taliban. By 9/11, Afghanistan was not only a state sponsor of
terror, but a state sponsored by terror.

While the Taliban's ideology was rigid, its control of the country was
not. In a small section of northern Afghanistan, a group of tribal commanders called the Northern Alliance held the allegiance of the local
population. On September 9, 2001, bin Laden operatives assassinated the
Northern Alliance's beloved leader, Ahmad Shah Massoud. His murder
galvanized the Alliance to cooperate with America. We shared an enemy
and a determination to end Taliban rule.

George's plan called for deploying CIA teams to arm, fund, and join
forces with the Northern Alliance. Together they would form the initial
thrust of the attack. By mating up our forces with the local opposition, we
would avoid looking like a conqueror or occupier. America would help the
Afghan people liberate themselves.

———

We would not act alone. Colin Powell had done an impressive job rallying countries to our coalition. Some, such as Great Britain and Australia, offered to deploy forces. Others, including Japan and South Korea,
pledged humanitarian aid and logistical support. South Korea later sent
troops. Key Arab partners, such as Jordan and Saudi Arabia, shared sensitive intelligence on al Qaeda's operations.

The most pivotal nation we recruited was Pakistan. No country wielded
more influence in Afghanistan than its eastern neighbor. On 9/11, Pakistan
was one of only three countries that recognized the Taliban. Saudi Arabia
and the United Arab Emirates were the other two.

Some in Pakistan may have sympathized with the Taliban's ideology.

But the primary motive was to counterbalance India, Pakistan's bitter archrival. So long as Pakistan held the loyalty of Afghanistan's government, it would never be encircled.

Pakistan had a troubled history with the United States. After our close cooperation in the Cold War, Congress suspended aid to Pakistan—including coveted F-16s America had promised to sell them—out of concern over the government's nuclear weapons program. In 1998, Pakistan conducted a secret nuclear test, incurring further sanctions. A year later, General Pervez Musharraf overthrew the democratically elected government in a coup. By 2001, America had cut off virtually all aid to Pakistan.

On September 13, Colin called President Musharraf and made clear he had to decide whose side he was on. He presented a list of nonnegotiable demands, including condemning the 9/11 attacks, denying al Qaeda safe haven in Pakistan, sharing intelligence, granting us overflight rights, and breaking diplomatic relations with the Taliban.

Musharraf faced intense internal pressure. Turning against the Taliban was unthinkable for hardliners in his government and intelligence service. I called Musharraf from Camp David during a break in the war council meeting. "I want to thank you for listening to our sad nation's requests, and I look forward to working with you to bring these people to justice," I said.

"The stakes are high," Musharraf told me. "We are with you."

Our relationship with Pakistan would prove complex. But in four days we had turned Afghanistan's pivotal neighbor from a supporter of the Taliban to a partner in removing them from power.

—

The next presentation came from the military. Don Rumsfeld called on Joint Chiefs Chairman Hugh Shelton, an Army Ranger in his final month on the job, and Vice Chairman Dick Myers, the Air Force general I had nominated to take his place. They walked me through three options.

The first was the Pentagon's contingency plan, the preexisting strategy to be used in an emergency. It called for cruise missile strikes on al Qaeda camps in Afghanistan. The plan could be executed immediately, with no risk to American troops.

The second option was to combine cruise missile strikes with manned bomber attacks. This would allow us to hit more targets, while exposing our pilots to limited risk.

The third and most aggressive option was to employ cruise missiles, bombers, and boots on the ground. This was mostly a theoretical option; the military would have to develop the details from scratch.

General Shelton stressed that it would take time and delicate diplomacy to insert our forces into a mountainous, landlocked country. We would need basing rights, overflight permission, and search-and-rescue capability—not to mention good weather and good luck.

A wide-ranging discussion followed. George Tenet warned that a retaliatory strike on our homeland was likely. "We can't deter them if they've already planned a second round," he said. "I expect they have some chemical and biological weapons," he added ominously.

Dick Cheney worried that the war could spill over into Pakistan, causing the government to lose control of the country and potentially its nuclear arsenal. As Deputy National Security Adviser Steve Hadley rightly put it, that would be "the nightmare scenario."

At one point, Deputy Defense Secretary Paul Wolfowitz suggested that we consider confronting Iraq as well as the Taliban. Before 9/11, Saddam Hussein's brutal dictatorship was widely considered the most dangerous country in the world. The regime had a long record of supporting terrorism, including paying the families of Palestinian suicide bombers. Saddam's forces fired routinely at American and British pilots patrolling the no-fly zones imposed by the United Nations. And Iraq had defied more than a decade's worth of UN resolutions demanding that it prove it had destroyed its weapons of mass destruction.

"Dealing with Iraq would show a major commitment to antiterrorism," Don Rumsfeld said.

Colin cautioned against it. "Going after Iraq now would be viewed as a bait and switch," he said. "We would lose the UN, the Islamic countries, and NATO. If we want to do Iraq, we should do it at a time of our choosing. But we should not do it now, because we don't have linkage to this event."

George Tenet agreed. "Don't hit now. It would be a mistake," he said. "The first target needs to be al Qaeda."

Dick Cheney understood the threat of Saddam Hussein and believed we had to address it. "But now is not a good time to do it," he said. "We would lose our momentum. Right now people have to choose between the United States and the bad guys."

I welcomed the vigorous debate. Listening to the discussion and divergent views helped clarify my options. I wasn't going to make a decision on the spot. That would come the next day.

———

Sunday, September 16, was a day of reflection. Laura and I went to services at Camp David's beautiful Evergreen Chapel. Started during the Reagan administration and finished during Dad's, the chapel was a special place for my family. The first wedding performed there was between my sister Doro and her fine husband, Bobby Koch.

At 10:00 a.m. that first Sunday after 9/11, late summer light streamed through the serene woods and into the chapel. Navy and Marine Corps personnel and family members joined us in worship, as did members of the national security team who had stayed over from the meetings the day before.

Camp David was blessed to have a fine pastor, Navy Chaplain Bob Williams. His sermon that Sunday was touching and comforting. He asked the questions so many of us had struggled with: "Why? . . . How could this happen, God?"

Bob said the answer was beyond our power to know. "Life is sometimes a maze of contradictions and incongruities," he acknowledged. Yet we could take comfort in knowing that God's plan would prevail. He quoted a passage from St. Ignatius of Loyola: "Pray as if it all depends upon God, for it does. But work as if it all depends upon us, for it does."

After the service, Laura and I boarded Marine One for the flight back to Washington. By that afternoon I had reached one of the defining decision points in my presidency: We would fight the war on terror on the offense, and the first battlefront would be Afghanistan.

My decision was a departure from America's policies over the past two decades. After Hezbollah terrorists bombed our Marine barracks and embassy in Lebanon in 1983, President Reagan withdrew our forces. When terrorist warlords in Somalia shot down an American Black Hawk heli-copter in 1993, President Clinton pulled our troops out. In 1998, al Qaeda's bombing of two American embassies in East Africa prompted President Clinton to launch cruise missiles at al Qaeda sites in Afghanistan. But the training camps had been largely abandoned, and the long-distance strike came across as impotent and ineffectual. When al Qaeda blew up the USS *Cole* off the coast of Yemen, America mounted almost no response at all.

My predecessors made their decisions in a different era. After al Qaeda killed nearly three thousand people in the United States, it was clear the terrorists had interpreted our lack of a serious response as a sign of weak-ness and an invitation to attempt more brazen attacks. Al Qaeda mes-sages frequently cited our withdrawals as evidence that Americans were, in the words of bin Laden, "paper tigers" who could be forced to "run in less than twenty-four hours."

After 9/11, I was determined to change that impression. I decided to employ the most aggressive of the three options General Shelton had laid out. Cruise missile and manned bomber attacks would be part of our response, but they were not enough. Dropping expensive weapons on sparsely populated camps would not break the Taliban's hold on the country or destroy al Qaeda's sanctuary. It would only reinforce the ter-rorists' belief that they could strike us without paying a serious price. This time we would put boots on the ground, and keep them there until the Taliban and al Qaeda were driven out and a free society could emerge.

Unless I received definitive evidence tying Saddam Hussein to the 9/11 plot, I would work to resolve the Iraq problem diplomatically. I hoped unified pressure by the world might compel Saddam to meet his international obligations. The best way to show him we were serious was to succeed in Afghanistan.

The next morning, I convened the National Security Council in the Cabinet Room. "The purpose of this meeting is to assign tasks for the first wave of the war on terrorism," I said. "It starts today."

——

Shortly after 9/11, Denny Hastert, the reliable and steady speaker of the House, had suggested that I address a joint session of Congress, as

President Franklin Roosevelt had done after Pearl Harbor. I liked the idea but wanted to wait until I had something to say. Now I did. We scheduled the speech for September 20.

I knew the American people had a lot of questions: Who attacked us? Why do they hate us? What will the war look like? What is expected of the average citizen? The answers would form the outline of my address.

I decided to invite a special guest to join me for the speech, British Prime Minister Tony Blair. A few hours before I left for Capitol Hill, Tony came to the White House for dinner. I pulled him into a quiet corner of the State Floor to give him an update on the war plans, including my decision to deploy ground troops. He reiterated that Great Britain would be at our side. America's closest ally in the wars of the last century would be with us in the first war of a new century.

As the moment to deliver the speech approached, Tony said, "You don't seem the least bit nervous, George. Don't you need some time alone?" I hadn't thought about it until he mentioned it. I didn't need to be alone. I had taken time to make a careful decision, and I knew what I wanted to say. Plus, I appreciated the company of my friend.

The environment in the House chamber felt different from the National Cathedral on September 14. There was a mix of energy, anger, and defiance. I later learned that more than eighty-two million people were watching on TV, the largest audience ever for a presidential speech.

"In the normal course of events, presidents come to this chamber to report on the state of the Union," I began. "Tonight, no such report is needed. It has already been delivered by the American people. . . . My fellow citizens, we have seen the state of our Union—and it is strong."

I ran through the questions and answers—the identity of the terrorists, their ideology, and the new kind of war we would wage. "Our response involves far more than instant retaliation and isolated strikes," I said. "Americans should not expect one battle, but a lengthy campaign, unlike any other we have ever seen. It may include dramatic strikes, visible on TV, and covert operations, secret even in success. . . . Every nation, in every region, now has a decision to make. Either you are with us, or you are with the terrorists."

I laid out an ultimatum to the Taliban: "They will hand over the terrorists, or they will share in their fate." We had little hope that Afghan-istan's leaders would heed it. But exposing their defiance to the world would firm up our justification for a military strike. As I approached the conclusion, I said:

*[In] our grief and anger we have found our mission and our moment. . . . We will rally the world to this cause by our efforts, by our courage. We will not tire, we will not falter, and we will not fail.*

*It is my hope that in the months and years ahead, life will return al-most to normal. We'll go back to our lives and routines, and that is good. Even grief recedes with time and grace. But our resolve must not pass. Each of us will remember what happened that day, and to whom it hap-pened. We'll remember the moment the news came—where we were and what we were doing. Some will remember an image of a fire, or a story of rescue. Some will carry memories of a face and a voice gone forever.*

*And I will carry this: It is the police shield of a man named George Howard, who died at the World Trade Center trying to save others. It was given to me by his mom, Arlene, as a proud memorial to her son. It is my reminder of lives that ended, and a task that does not end.*

*I will not forget this wound to our country or those who inflicted it. I will not yield; I will not rest; I will not relent in waging this struggle for freedom and security for the American people.*

The next day, September 21, I immersed myself in the war planning. Dealing with the military as commander in chief was a new experience. The officers' dress uniforms with the rows of ribbons highlighted their military expertise, which was a whole lot more extensive than mine.

Seven months earlier, Laura and I had held a dinner at the White House for military leaders and their wives. I hoped to break down some of the formality and get to know the generals and admirals on a personal level, so they would feel free to give me candid opinions and I would feel more comfortable asking for them.

One of the commanders I met was General Tommy Franks, who

came to the White House with his wife, Cathy. Tommy had a chestful of medals, including multiple Bronze Stars and Purple Hearts from Vietnam. As a one-star general, he had commanded troops in the Gulf War. In 2000, he assumed the top post at Central Command, a theater stretching from the Horn of Africa to Central Asia, including Afghanistan.

"General, I understand you're from Midland, Texas," I said.

"Yes, Mr. President, I am," he said with a warm smile and a West Texas drawl.

"I hear you went to high school with Laura," I added.

"Yes, sir, graduated one year before her," he answered. "But don't worry, Mr. President, I never dated her."

I let out a big laugh. That was an interesting thing to say to your new commander in chief. I had a feeling Tommy and I were going to get along just fine.

Tommy made clear the mission in Afghanistan would not be easy. Everything about the country screamed trouble. It is remote, rugged, and primitive. Its northern half is home to ethnic Tajiks, Uzbeks, Hazaras, Turkmen, and others. The southern half is dominated by Pashtuns. Tribal, ethnic, and religious rivalries date back centuries. Yet for all their differences, the people of Afghanistan have a way of banding together against foreigners. They drove out the British in the nineteenth century. They drove out the Soviets in the twentieth century. Even Alexander the Great failed to conquer the country. Afghanistan had earned a foreboding nickname: Graveyard of Empires.

Tommy's war plan, later code-named Operation Enduring Freedom, included four phases. The first was to connect the Special Forces with the CIA teams to clear the way for conventional troops to follow. Next we would mount a massive air campaign to take out al Qaeda and Taliban targets, and conduct humanitarian airdrops to deliver relief to the Afghan people. The third phase called for ground troops from both America and coalition partners to enter the country and hunt down remaining Taliban and al Qaeda fighters. Finally, we would stabilize the country and help the Afghan people build a free society.

I viewed my role as making sure the plan was comprehensive and consistent with the strategic vision—in this case, removing the Taliban, denying sanctuary to al Qaeda, and helping a democratic government emerge. I asked Tommy a lot of questions: How many troops would we need? What kind of basing would be available? How long would it take to move everyone? What level of enemy resistance did he expect?

I did not try to manage the logistics or the tactical decisions. My instinct was to trust the judgment of the military leadership. They were the trained professionals; I was a new commander in chief. I remembered the Vietnam-era photos of Lyndon Johnson and Defense Secretary Robert McNamara poring over maps to pick bombing targets for routine missions. Their micromanagement had an impact throughout the chain of command. When I was in flight school, one of my instructors who had flown in Vietnam complained that the Air Force was so restricted that the enemy could figure out exactly when and where they would be flying. The reason, as he put it, was that "the politicians did not want to piss people off."

———

One area where Tommy needed help was in lining up support from Afghanistan's neighbors. Without logistical cooperation from Uzbekistan and Tajikistan, we would not be able to move our troops into Afghanistan. I didn't know the leaders of these former Soviet republics. But Russia still had tremendous influence in the region, and I knew Vladimir Putin.

Putin and I had met for the first time that June in a Slovenian palace once used by the communist leader Tito. My goal at the summit had been to cut through any tension and forge a connection with Putin. I placed a high priority on personal diplomacy. Getting to know a fellow world leader's personality, character, and concerns made it easier to find common ground and deal with contentious issues. That was a lesson I had picked up from Dad, who was one of the great practitioners of personal diplomacy. Another was Abraham Lincoln. "If you would win a man to your cause," Lincoln once said, "first convince him that you are his friend."

The summit with Putin started with a small meeting—just Vladimir and me, our national security advisers, and the interpreters. He seemed a little tense. He opened by speaking from a stack of note cards. The first topic was the Soviet-era debt of the Russian Federation.

After a few minutes, I interrupted his presentation with a question: "Is it true your mother gave you a cross that you had blessed in Jerusalem?"

A look of shock washed over Putin's face as Peter, the interpreter, delivered the line in Russian. I explained that the story had caught my attention in some background reading—I didn't tell him it was an intelligence briefing—and I was curious to learn more. Putin recovered quickly and told the story. His face and his voice softened as he explained that he had hung the cross in his dacha, which subsequently caught on fire. When the firefighters arrived, he told them all he cared about was the cross. He dramatically re-created the moment when a worker unfolded his hand and revealed the cross. It was, he said, "as if it was meant to be."

"Vladimir," I said, "that is the story of the cross. Things are meant to be." I felt the tension drain from the meeting room.

After the meeting, a reporter asked if Putin was "a man that Americans can trust." I said yes. I thought of the emotion in Vladimir's voice when he shared the story of the cross. "I looked the man in the eye," I said, ". . . I was able to get a sense of his soul." In the years ahead, Putin would give me reasons to revise my opinion.

Three months after our meeting in Slovenia, Putin was the first foreign leader to call the White House on September 11. He couldn't reach me on Air Force One, so Condi spoke to him from the PEOC. He assured her that Russia would not increase its military readiness in response to our move to DefCon Three, as the Soviet Union would have done automatically during the Cold War. When I talked to Vladimir the next day, he told me he had signed a decree declaring a minute of silence to show solidarity with the United States. He ended by saying, "Good will triumph over evil. I want you to know that in this struggle, we will stand together."

On September 22, I called Putin from Camp David. In a long Saturday-morning conversation, he agreed to open Russian airspace to American military planes and use his influence with the former Soviet republics to help get our troops into Afghanistan. I suspected he would be worried about Russia being encircled, but he was more concerned about the terrorist problem in his neighborhood. He even ordered Russian generals to brief their American counterparts on their experience during their Afghanistan invasion in the 1980s.

It was an amazing conversation. I told Vladimir I appreciated his willingness to move beyond the suspicions of the past. Before long, we had our agreements with the former Soviet republics.

———

In late September, George Tenet reported that the first of the CIA teams had entered Afghanistan and linked up with the Northern Alliance. Tommy Franks told me he would be ready to deploy our Special Forces soon. I threw out a question to the team that had been on my mind: "So who's going to run the country?"

There was silence.

I wanted to make sure the team had thought through the postwar strategy. I felt strongly that the Afghan people should be able to select their new leader. They had suffered too much—and the American people were risking too much—to let the country slide back into tyranny. I asked Colin to work on a plan for a transition to democracy.

On Friday, October 5, General Dick Myers told me the military was ready to launch. I was ready, too. We had given the Taliban more than two weeks to respond to the ultimatum I had delivered. The Taliban had not met any of our demands. Their time was up.

Don Rumsfeld was on his way back from the Middle East and Central Asia, where he had finalized several important basing agreements. I waited for him to return before I gave the official order. On Saturday morning, October 6, I spoke to Don and Dick Myers by secure videoconference from Camp David. I asked one last time if they had everything they needed. They did.

"Go," I said. "This is the right thing to do."

I knew in my heart that striking al Qaeda, removing the Taliban, and liberating the suffering people of Afghanistan was necessary and just. But I worried about all that could go wrong. The military planners had laid out the risks: mass starvation, an outbreak of civil war, the collapse of the Pakistani government, an uprising by Muslims around the world, and the one I feared most—a retaliatory attack on the American homeland.

When I boarded Marine One the next morning to return to Washington, Laura and a few key advisers knew I had given the order, but virtually no one else did. To preserve the secrecy of the operation, I went

ahead with my previously announced schedule, which included attending a ceremony at the National Fallen Firefighters Memorial in Emmits-
burg, Maryland. I spoke about the 343 New York City firefighters who
had given their lives on 9/11, by far the worst day in the history of American firefighting. The casualties ranged from the chief of the department,
Pete Ganci, to young recruits in their first months on the job.

The memorial was a vivid reminder of why America would soon be in
the fight. Our military understood, too. Seven thousand miles away, the first
bombs fell. On several of them, our troops had painted the letters *FDNY*.

———

The first reports out of Afghanistan were positive. In two hours of aerial bombardment, we and our British allies had wiped out the Taliban's
meager air defense system and several known al Qaeda training camps.
Behind the bombs, we dropped more than thirty-seven thousand rations
of food and relief supplies for the Afghan people, the fastest delivery of
humanitarian aid in the history of warfare.

After several days, we ran into a problem. The air campaign had destroyed most of the Taliban and al Qaeda infrastructure. But we were
having trouble inserting our Special Forces. They were grounded at a
former Soviet air base in Uzbekistan, separated from their landing zone
in Afghanistan by fifteen-thousand-foot-high mountains, freezing temperatures, and blinding snowstorms.

I pressed for action. Don and Tommy assured me they were moving
as fast as possible. But as the days passed, I became more and more frustrated. Our response looked too much like the impotent air war America
had waged in the past. I worried we were sending the wrong message to
the enemy and to the American people. Tommy Franks later called those
days a period "from hell." I felt the same way.

Twelve days after I announced the start of the war, the first of the Special Forces teams finally touched down. In the north, our forces linked
up with the CIA and Northern Alliance fighters. In the south, a small
team of Special Forces raided Taliban leader Mullah Omar's headquarters in Kandahar.

Months later, I visited Fort Bragg in North Carolina, where I met members of the Special Forces team that had led the raid. They gave me a brick from the remnants of Mullah Omar's compound. I kept it in the private study next to the Oval Office as a reminder that we were fighting this war with boots on the ground—and that the Americans in those boots were courageous and skilled.

———

The arrival of our troops did not quiet doubts at home. On October 25, Condi told me the slow pace of operations, which was producing a drumbeat of criticism in the media, was affecting the national security team. The war was only eighteen days old, but some were already talking about alternative strategies.

In times of uncertainty, any indication of doubt from the president ripples throughout the system. At a National Security Council meeting the next morning, I said, "I just want to make sure that all of us did agree on this plan, right?" I went around the table and asked every member of the team. They all agreed.

I assured the team that we had the right strategy. Our plan was well conceived. Our military was capable. Our cause was just. We shouldn't give in to second-guessing or let the press panic us. "We're going to stay confident and patient, cool and steady," I said.

I could sense the relief in the room. The experience reminded me that even the most accomplished and powerful people sometimes need to be reassured. As I later told journalist Bob Woodward, the president has to be the "calcium in the backbone."

I was glad we had stiffened our spines when I saw the *New York Times* on October 31. Reporter Johnny Apple had written an article headlined "A Military Quagmire Remembered: Afghanistan as Vietnam." His opening sentence read, "Like an unwelcome specter from an unhappy past, the ominous word 'quagmire' has begun to haunt conversations among government officials and students of foreign policy, both here and abroad."

In some ways, this was predictable. The reporters of my generation tend to see everything through the prism of Watergate or Vietnam. Still, I was amazed the *Times* couldn't wait even a month to tag Afghanistan with the Vietnam label.

The differences between the two conflicts were striking. The enemy in Afghanistan had just murdered three thousand innocent people on American soil. At the time we had almost no conventional forces in Afghanistan, compared to the hundreds of thousands that had been in Vietnam. America was unified behind our troops and their mission. And we had a growing coalition at our side.

None of those distinctions mattered to the media. The debate about the so-called quagmire continued on the editorial pages and cable TV. I shrugged it off. I knew most Americans would be patient and supportive, so long as we delivered results.

———

In early November, results arrived. Supported by CIA officers and Special Forces, Northern Alliance generals moved toward Taliban positions. The Afghan warriors led the ground attacks, while our Special Forces used GPS units and laser guidance systems to direct airstrikes. Northern Alliance fighters and our Special Forces mounted a cavalry charge and liberated the strategic city of Mazar-i-Sharif. Residents poured into the streets in celebration. The most modern weaponry of the twenty-first century, combined with a horse charge reminiscent of the nineteenth century, had driven the Taliban from their northern stronghold.

I was relieved. While I had confidence in our strategy and dismissed the quagmire talk, I had felt some anxiety. There was no way to know for sure whether our approach would succeed. The fall of Mazar reassured me. "This thing might just unravel like a cheap suit," I told Vladimir Putin.

It unraveled fast. Within days, almost every major city in the north fell. The Taliban fled Kabul for mountain hideouts in the east and south. Women came out of their homes. Children flew kites. Men shaved off their beards and danced in the streets. One man listened to music—banned under the Taliban—with a cassette player pressed to his ear. "We are free!" he shouted. A woman teacher said, "I'm happy because I believe now the doors of the school will be open for girls."

I was overjoyed by the scenes of liberation. So was Laura. The Saturday after Kabul fell, she delivered the weekly radio address, the first time a First Lady had ever done so. The Taliban regime, she said, "is now in retreat across much of the country, and the people of Afghanistan—especially women—are rejoicing. Afghan women know, through hard experience, what the rest of the world is discovering. . . . The fight against terrorism is also a fight for the rights and dignity of women."

Laura's address prompted positive responses from around the world. The most meaningful came from Afghan women. Expanding opportunity in Afghanistan, especially for women and girls, became a calling for Laura. In the years to come, she met with Afghan teachers and entrepreneurs, facilitated the delivery of textbooks and medicine, supported a new U.S.-Afghan Women's Council that mobilized more than $70 million in private development funds, and made three trips to the country. Just as I was feeling more comfortable as commander in chief, she was gaining her footing as First Lady.

———

With northern Afghanistan liberated, our attention turned to the south. George Tenet reported that an anti-Taliban movement was coalescing around a Pashtun leader, Hamid Karzai. Karzai was not a typical military commander. He grew up near Kandahar, earned a college degree in India, spoke four languages, and served in the Afghan government before it was taken over by the Taliban.

Two days after our bombing campaign began, Karzai hopped on a motorcycle in Pakistan, crossed the border, and rallied several hundred men to take Tarin Kot, a small city near Kandahar. The Taliban discovered Karzai's presence and sent troops to kill him. With his position about to be overrun, the CIA dispatched a helicopter to pick him up. After a brief period, Karzai returned to lead the resistance. He was joined in late November by a contingent of Marines. The remaining Taliban officials fled Kandahar. The city fell on December 7, 2001, the sixtieth anniversary of Pearl Harbor, two months to the day after my speech in the Treaty Room.

———

Driven out of their strongholds, the remnants of the Taliban and al Qaeda fled to Afghanistan's rugged eastern border with Pakistan. In early 2002,

Tommy Franks mounted a major assault called Operation Anaconda. Our troops, joined by coalition partners and Afghan forces, squeezed out the remaining al Qaeda and Taliban fighters in eastern Afghanistan. CIA officers and Special Forces crawled through the caves, calling in airstrikes on terrorist hideouts and putting a serious dent in al Qaeda's army.

I hoped I would get a call with the news that Osama bin Laden was among the dead or captured. We were searching for him constantly and received frequent but conflicting information on his whereabouts. Some reports placed him in Jalalabad. Others had him in Peshawar, or at a lake near Kandahar, or at the Tora Bora cave complex. Our troops pursued every lead. Several times we thought we might have nailed him. But the intelligence never panned out.

Years later, critics charged that we allowed bin Laden to slip the noose at Tora Bora. I sure didn't see it that way. I asked our commanders and CIA officials about bin Laden frequently. They were working around the clock to locate him, and they assured me they had the troop levels and resources they needed. If we had ever known for sure where he was, we would have moved heaven and earth to bring him to justice.

Operation Anaconda marked the end of the opening phase of the battle. Like any war, our campaign in Afghanistan had not gone perfectly. But in six months, we had removed the Taliban from power, destroyed the al Qaeda training camps, liberated more than twenty-six million people from unspeakable brutality, allowed Afghan girls to return to school, and laid the foundation for a democratic society to emerge. There had been no famine, no outbreak of civil war, no collapse of the government in Pakistan, no global uprising by Muslims, and no retaliatory attack on our homeland.

———

The gains came at a precious cost. Between the start of the war and Operation Anaconda, twenty-seven brave Americans were killed. I read each name, usually in my early morning briefings at the Resolute desk. I imagined the pain their families felt when the military officer appeared at their door. I prayed that God would comfort them amid their grief.

Early in the war, I decided to write letters to the family members of Americans lost on the battlefield. I wanted to honor their sacrifice, express my sorrow, and extend the gratitude of the country. As I sat down to write on November 29, 2001, I remembered a letter Abraham Lincoln had written in 1864 to Lydia Bixby, a Massachusetts woman who was believed to have lost five sons in the Civil War.

"I feel how weak and fruitless must be any word of mine which should attempt to beguile you from the grief of a loss so overwhelming," Lincoln wrote. "But I cannot refrain from tendering you the consolation that may be found in the thanks of the Republic they died to save. I pray that our Heavenly Father may assuage the anguish of your bereavement, and leave you only the cherished memory of the loved and lost, and the solemn pride that must be yours to have laid so costly a sacrifice upon the altar of freedom."

My letter was addressed to Shannon Spann, the wife of Mike Spann, the CIA officer killed in the prison uprising at Mazar-i-Sharif and the first battlefield death of the war:

*Dear Shannon,*

*On behalf of a grateful nation, Laura and I send our heartfelt sympathy to you and your family on the loss of Mike. I know your heart aches. Our prayers are with you all.*

*Mike died in a fight against evil. He laid down his life for a noble cause—freedom. Your children must know that his service to our nation was heroic and brave.*

*May God bless you, Shannon, your children, and all who mourn the loss of a good and brave man.*

*Sincerely,*
*George W. Bush*

I sent letters to the families of every service member who laid down his or her life in the war on terror. By the end of my presidency, I had written to almost five thousand families.

In addition to my correspondence, I met frequently with family members of the fallen. I felt it was my responsibility to comfort those who had lost a loved one. When I traveled to Fort Bragg in March 2002, I met the families of servicemen killed during Operation Anaconda. I was apprehensive. Would they be angry? Would they be bitter? I was ready to share tears, to listen, to talk—whatever I could do to ease their pain.

One of the widows I met was Valerie Chapman. Her husband, Air Force Technical Sergeant John Chapman, had bravely attacked two al Qaeda bunkers in remote mountains during an enemy ambush, helping to save his teammates before laying down his own life. Valerie told me John loved the Air Force. He had enlisted when he was nineteen and had served for seventeen years.

I crouched down so that I was eye level with John and Valerie's two daughters—Madison, age five, and Brianna, age three. I pictured my own girls at that age. My heart broke at the thought that they would grow up without their dad. I told them he was a good man who had served with courage. I fought back tears. If the little girls remembered anything of the meeting, I wanted it to be how much I respected their father, not a weepy commander in chief.

As the meeting wrapped up, Valerie handed me a copy of her husband's memorial pamphlet. "If anyone ever tells you this is the wrong thing to do," she said intently, "you look at this." She had written a note on the pamphlet:

"John did his job, now you do yours."

I remembered her words, and others like them, every time I made decisions about the war.

———

Over time, the thrill of liberation gave way to the daunting task of helping the Afghan people rebuild—or, more accurately, build from scratch. Afghanistan in 2001 was the world's third-poorest country. Less than 10 percent of the population had access to health care. More than four out of five women were illiterate. While Afghanistan's land area and population were similar to those of Texas, its annual economic output was comparable to that of Billings, Montana. Life expectancy was a bleak forty-six years.

In later years, Afghanistan would often be compared with Iraq. But the two countries started from vastly different points. At the time of its liberation, Afghanistan's per capita GDP was less than a third of Iraq's. The infant mortality rate in Afghanistan was more than twice as high. Helping the Afghan people join the modern world would clearly be a long, arduous undertaking.

When I ran for president, I never anticipated a mission like this. In the fall of 2000, Al Gore and I debated the most pressing issues facing America. Not once did the words *Afghanistan, bin Laden,* or *al Qaeda* come up. We did discuss nation building. "The vice president and I have a disagreement about the use of troops," I said in the first debate. ". . . I would be very careful about using our troops as nation builders."

At the time, I worried about overextending our military by undertaking peacekeeping missions as we had in Bosnia and Somalia. But after 9/11, I changed my mind. Afghanistan was the ultimate nation building mission. We had liberated the country from a primitive dictatorship, and we had a moral obligation to leave behind something better. We also had a strategic interest in helping the Afghan people build a free society. The terrorists took refuge in places of chaos, despair, and repression. A democratic Afghanistan would be a hopeful alternative to the vision of the extremists.

The first step was to empower a legitimate leader. Colin Powell worked with UN officials on a process for the Afghan people to select an interim government. They decided to hold a traditional Afghan gathering called a *loya jirga*, or grand council. Afghanistan was not a safe enough place to convene the meeting, so Chancellor Gerhard Schroeder of Germany generously offered to host the council in Bonn.

After nine days of deliberations, the delegates selected Hamid Karzai to serve as chairman of the interim authority. When Karzai arrived in Kabul for his inauguration on December 22—102 days after 9/11—several Northern Alliance leaders and their bodyguards greeted him at the airport. As Karzai walked across the tarmac alone, a stunned Tajik warlord asked where all his men were. Karzai responded, "Why, General, you are my men. All of you who are Afghans are my men."

Five weeks later, I looked Hamid Karzai in the eye for the first time. Forty-four years old with sharp features and a salt-and-pepper beard, Karzai cut a distinctive figure. He wore a shimmering green cape over his gray tunic, along with a pointed cap made of goatskin that was traditional in his southern Afghan tribe.

"Mr. Chairman, welcome to America," I said, "and welcome to the Oval Office." I experienced some fascinating moments in that office over the years. Opening the door for the leader of a free Afghanistan four months after 9/11 ranks among them.

"On behalf of me and my people, thank you, Mr. President," Karzai said. "The United States liberated Afghanistan from the Soviet Union in the 1980s. And now you have liberated us again from the Taliban and al Qaeda.

"We are independent and we will stand on our own two feet," he said, "but we need your help. The most common question I hear from my ministers and others in Afghanistan is whether the United States will continue to work with us."

I assured Karzai that he could count on America as a partner, and that we would not abandon his country again. We talked about the hunt for the remaining Taliban and al Qaeda operatives, the need to train an Afghan army and police force, and the importance of constructing roads, health clinics, and schools.

The next night, I saw Karzai again, in the House of Representatives for my State of the Union address. Laura sat next to him. One row back was Karzai's vice chairman—and Afghanistan's new minister of women's affairs—Dr. Sima Samar.

———

Karzai's immediate task was to show that life would improve with the Taliban gone. To support him, I sent Zalmay Khalilzad, a talented Afghan American on the National Security Council staff, to serve as my special envoy and, later, as American ambassador. Zal and Karzai used hundreds of millions of dollars in American aid to build infrastructure, train teachers, print textbooks, and extend electricity and clean water to Afghanistan's rural population. One program funded by the U.S. Agency for International Development, USAID, helped more than three million Afghan children return to school. That was three times the number who had attended under the Taliban. About a million of the new students were girls.

From the beginning, we sought to bring as many nations as possible into the rebuilding effort. A multilateral approach would defray the financial burden and invest nations around the world in the ideological struggle against extremists. Prime Minister Junichiro Koizumi of Japan hosted an international donors' conference in January 2002. The Tokyo meeting yielded $4.5 billion in pledges. America and several key allies decided to divvy up responsibility for helping to build Afghan civil society. We took the lead in training a new Afghan National Army. Germany focused on training the national police. Great Britain adopted a counternarcotics mission. Italy worked to reform the justice system. Japan launched an initiative to disarm and demobilize warlords and their militias.

Basic security was a necessary precondition for political and economic gains. So as part of the Bonn process, we supported the creation of an International Security Assistance Force, known as ISAF, under the auspices of the United Nations. In the fall of 2002, NATO agreed to take command of ISAF, which contained nearly five thousand troops from twenty-two countries. We also had eight thousand American troops under the command of Tommy Franks training the Afghan security forces and conducting operations against the remnants of al Qaeda and the Taliban.

At the time, thirteen thousand troops seemed like the right amount. We had routed the Taliban with far fewer, and it seemed that the enemy was on the run. I agreed with our military leaders that we did not need a larger presence. We were all wary of repeating the experience of the Soviets and the British, who ended up looking like occupiers.

This strategy worked well at first. But in retrospect, our rapid success with low troop levels created false comfort, and our desire to maintain a light military footprint left us short of the resources we needed. It would take several years for these shortcomings to become clear.

In June 2002, Afghans gathered for a second *loya jirga* to select a transitional government. This time security was good enough to host the conference in Kabul. The delegates chose Karzai to head the new government, and he appointed cabinet ministers from a variety of ethnic and religious backgrounds. I made it a priority to check in regularly with Karzai. I knew he had a daunting task, and I wanted to lift his spirits and assure him of our commitment. I offered advice and made requests, but I was careful not to give him orders. The best way to help him grow as a leader was to treat him like one.

The young government made progress. In September 2003, President Karzai told me that pay for the average Afghan had increased from one dollar to three dollars a day—a major improvement, but also a reminder of how primitive the country remained. The government's biggest accomplishment was drafting a new constitution, which was ratified by a third *loya jirga* in January 2004. A country that three years earlier had forced women to paint the windows of their homes black now protected basic rights such as freedom of speech and assembly. The constitution established an independent judiciary and bicameral legislature, and it mandated that women account for 25 percent of the House of the People.

The next step was to hold the first free presidential election in Afghanistan's history, which was scheduled for October 9, 2004. The Taliban and al Qaeda pledged to kill voters, candidates, and election officials. U.S., NATO, and UN officials helped train election workers and secure voting stations. I hoped the Afghan people would express their desire for liberty at the polls. In truth, nobody knew what to expect.

When dawn broke, the world witnessed an amazing sight. Across the country, Afghans had lined up overnight, eager to vote. At the front of the line outside the first polling station to open was a nineteen-year-old girl. "I cannot explain my feelings, just how happy I am," she said. "I would never have thought I would be able to vote in this election."

Across the country, turnout exceeded eight million, nearly 80 percent of the voting-age population. Every major ethnic and religious group participated, as did millions of women. The polls stayed open two extra hours to accommodate the huge crowds.

Condi gave me the news early in the morning in Missouri, where I'd debated John Kerry the night before. I was pleased with the results, but not surprised. I believe the human desire for freedom is universal. History shows that, when given the chance, people of every race and religion take extraordinary risks for liberty. In one village, a toothless man in a black turban said, "It is like independence day, or freedom day. We are bringing security and peace to this country."

When the ballots were tallied, Hamid Karzai became the freely elected president. History has a way of dulling memories. But I will always remember the joy and pride I felt that first election day, when the people of Afghanistan—the land where 9/11 was conceived—cast their ballots for a future of freedom.

———

In September 2005, the Afghan people went to the polls again, this time to choose a national legislature. More than 2,700 candidates put their names forward for 249 seats. Nearly 7 million voters turned out, despite Taliban threats and calls for a boycott. The new National Assembly included 68 women and representatives of almost every ethnic group.

Dick Cheney represented the United States at the assembly's inaugural session in December 2005. The ceremony opened with an emotional speech from the nation's former king, ninety-one-year-old Zahir Shah. "I thank God that today I am participating in a ceremony that is a step towards rebuilding Afghanistan after decades of fighting," he said. "The people of Afghanistan will succeed!"

I shared his optimism. Four years after the fall of the Taliban, the country had elected a president and a parliament. But I recognized the elections were only a first step. Democracy is a journey that requires a nation to build governing institutions such as courts of law, security forces, an education system, a free press, and a vibrant civil society. Afghanistan had made some hopeful progress. Some 5 million children, including 1.5 million girls, were back in school. The economy was growing at an average rate of more than 15 percent per year. A much-anticipated new highway from Kabul to Kandahar had been completed. Four million of 7 million refugees had returned home.

On the surface, it seemed we were making progress. But trouble lurked underneath. In June 2005, a four-man Navy SEAL team operating high in the mountains was ambushed by the Taliban. The team leader, Lieutenant Michael Murphy, moved into an exposed position to call in help for his three fellow wounded SEALs. He stayed on the line long enough to relay his teammates' location before suffering fatal wounds. When a Special Forces chopper arrived to extract the SEALs, Taliban fighters shot it down. Nineteen Americans were killed, making it the deadliest day of the war in Afghanistan and the worst for the SEALs since World War II. One SEAL, Petty Officer First Class Marcus Luttrell, lived to tell the story in his riveting book, *Lone Survivor*.

Two years later, I presented the Medal of Honor to Lieutenant Michael Murphy's parents in the East Room of the White House. We talked about their son, a talented athlete and honors graduate of Penn State whose one brush with trouble came when he intervened in a schoolyard fight to protect a disabled child. In our meeting before the ceremony, they gave me a gold dog tag with Mike's name, photo, and rank engraved on it. I put it on under my shirt and wore it during the ceremony.

As the military aide read the Medal of Honor citation, I looked into the audience. I saw a group of Navy SEALs in their dress blues. These battle-hardened men had tears streaming down their cheeks. As I later told Daniel and Maureen Murphy, I gained strength from having a reminder of Mike next to my heart.

———

The devastating attack on the SEALs was a harbinger of trouble to come. In 2005 and 2006, Taliban militants killed road-building crews, burned down schools, and murdered teachers in provinces near the Pakistan border. In September 2006, a Taliban suicide bomber assassinated the governor of Paktia Province near his office in Gardez. The next day, another suicide bomber struck the governor's funeral, killing six mourners.

My CIA and military briefings included increasingly dire reports about Taliban influence. The problem was crystallized by a series of color-coded maps I saw in November 2006. The darker the shading, the more attacks had occurred in that part of Afghanistan. The 2004 map was lightly shaded. The 2005 map had darker areas in the southern and eastern parts of the country. By 2006, the entire southeastern quadrant was black. In just one year, the number of remotely detonated bombs had doubled. The number of armed attacks had tripled. The number of suicide bombings had more than quadrupled.

It was clear we needed to adjust our strategy. The multilateral approach to rebuilding, hailed by so many in the international community, was failing. There was little coordination between countries, and no one devoted enough resources to the effort. The German initiative to build the national police force had fallen short. The Italian mission to reform the justice system had failed. The British-led counternarcotics campaign showed results in some areas, but drug production had boomed in fertile southern provinces like Helmand. The Afghan National Army that America trained had improved, but in an attempt to keep the Afghan government from taking on an unsustainable expense, we had kept the army too small.

The multilateral military mission proved a disappointment as well. Every member of NATO had sent troops to Afghanistan. So had more than a dozen other countries. But many parliaments imposed heavy restrictions—known as national caveats—on what their troops were permitted to do. Some were not allowed to patrol at night. Others could not engage in combat. The result was a disorganized and ineffective force, with troops fighting by different rules and many not fighting at all.

Failures in the Afghan government contributed to the problem. While I liked and respected President Karzai, there was too much corruption. Warlords pocketed large amounts of customs revenue that should have gone to Kabul. Others took a cut of the profits from the drug trade. The result was that Afghans lost faith in their government. With nowhere else to turn, many Afghans relied on the Taliban and ruthless extremist commanders like Gulbuddin Hekmatyar and Jalaluddin Haqqani. A CIA report quoted one Afghan as saying, "I don't care who is in power, as long as they bring security. Security is all that matters."

The stakes were too high to let Afghanistan fall back into the hands of the extremists. I decided that America had to take on more of the responsibility, even though we were about to undertake a major new commitment in Iraq as well.

"Damn it, we can do more than one thing at a time," I told the national security team. "We cannot lose in Afghanistan."

In the fall of 2006, I ordered a troop increase that would boost our force levels from twenty-one thousand to thirty-one thousand over the next two years. I called the 50 percent increase a "silent surge."* To help the Afghan government extend its reach and effectiveness, we more than doubled funding for reconstruction. We increased the number of Provincial Reconstruction Teams, which brought together military personnel and civilian experts to ensure that security gains were translated into meaningful improvements in everyday life. We also increased the size of the Afghan National Army, expanded our counternarcotics effort, improved intelligence efforts along the Pakistan border, and sent civilian experts from the U.S. government to help Afghan ministries strengthen their capacity and reduce corruption.

I urged our NATO allies to match our commitment by dropping caveats on their troops and adding more forces. Several leaders responded, including Stephen Harper of Canada, Anders Fogh Rasmussen of Denmark, and Nicolas Sarkozy of France. The British and Canadians fought especially bravely and suffered significant casualties. America was fortunate to have them at our side, and we honor their sacrifice as our own.

Other leaders told me bluntly that their parliaments would never go along. It was maddening. Afghanistan was supposed to be a war the world had agreed was necessary and just. And yet many countries were sending troops so heavily restricted that our generals complained they just took up space. NATO had turned into a two-tiered alliance, with some countries willing to fight and many not.

———

The adjustments in our strategy improved our ability to take on the insurgents. Yet the violence continued. The primary cause of the trouble did not originate in Afghanistan or, as some suggested, in Iraq. It came from Pakistan.

For most of my presidency, Pakistan was led by President Pervez Musharraf. I admired his decision to side with America after 9/11. He held parliamentary elections in 2002, which his party won, and spoke

*The surge in Iraq attracted much more attention.

about "enlightened moderation" as an alternative to Islamic extremism. He took serious risks to battle al Qaeda. Terrorists tried to assassinate him at least four times.

In the months after we liberated Afghanistan, I told Musharraf I was troubled by reports of al Qaeda and Taliban forces fleeing into the loosely governed, tribal provinces of Pakistan—an area often compared to the Wild West. "I'd be more than willing to send our Special Forces across the border to clear out the areas," I said.

He told me that sending American troops into combat in Pakistan would be viewed as a violation of Pakistani sovereignty. A revolt would likely ensue. His government would probably fall. The extremists could take over the country, including its nuclear arsenal.

In that case, I told him, his soldiers needed to take the lead. For several years, the arrangement worked. Pakistani forces netted hundreds of terrorists, including al Qaeda leaders like Khalid Sheikh Mohammed, Abu Zubaydah, and Abu Faraj al Libbi. Musharraf also arrested A.Q. Khan, the revered father of the Pakistani nuclear bomb, for selling components from the country's program on the black market. As Musharraf often reminded me, Pakistani forces paid a high price for taking on the extremists. More than fourteen hundred were killed in the war on terror.

In return for Pakistan's cooperation, we lifted the sanctions, designated Pakistan a major non-NATO ally, and helped fund its counterterrorism operations. We also worked with Congress to provide $3 billion in economic aid and opened our markets to more Pakistani goods and services.

Over time, it became clear that Musharraf either would not or could not fulfill all his promises. Part of the problem was Pakistan's obsession with India. In almost every conversation we had, Musharraf accused India of wrongdoing. Four days after 9/11, he told me the Indians were "trying to equate us with terrorists and trying to influence your mind." As a result, the Pakistani military spent most of its resources preparing for war with India. Its troops were trained to wage a conventional battle with its neighbor, not counterterrorism operations in the tribal areas. The fight against the extremists came second.

A related problem was that Pakistani forces pursued the Taliban much less aggressively than they pursued al Qaeda. Some in the Pakistani intelligence service, the ISI, retained close ties to Taliban officials. Others wanted an insurance policy in case America abandoned Afghanistan and India tried to gain influence there. Whatever the reason, Taliban fighters who fled Afghanistan took refuge in Pakistan's tribal regions and populated cities like Peshawar and Quetta. In 2005 and 2006, these sanctuaries aided the rise of the insurgency.

In March 2006, I visited President Musharraf in Islamabad. Our meeting followed a stop in India, where Prime Minister Manmohan Singh and I signed an agreement clearing the way for nuclear cooperation between our two countries. The deal was the culmination of our efforts to improve relations between the world's oldest democracy and the world's largest democracy. I believe India, home to roughly a billion people and an educated middle class, has the potential to be one of America's closest partners. The nuclear agreement was a historic step because it signaled the country's new role on the world stage.

The nuclear deal naturally raised concerns in Pakistan. Our ambassador, a remarkable veteran Foreign Service officer named Ryan Crocker, argued strongly that we should spend the night in Islamabad as a sign of respect. No president had done that since Richard Nixon thirty-seven years earlier. The Secret Service was anxious, especially after a bombing near the U.S. consulate in Karachi the day before we arrived. But symbolism matters in diplomacy, and I wanted to signal that I valued our relationship. At the airport, a decoy motorcade drove to the embassy mostly empty. My chief of protocol, Ambassador Don Ensenat, took my place in the presidential limo, while Laura and I flew secretly via Black Hawk helicopter.

In contrast to the rigid security precautions, President Musharraf organized a relaxed and enjoyable visit. He and his wife, Sehba, received us warmly at their version of the White House, known as the Aiwan-e-Sadr. We met with survivors of the previous October's 7.6-magnitude earthquake in northern Pakistan, which killed more than seventy-three thousand people. America had provided $500 million in relief. Our Chinook helicopters became known as "angels of mercy." The experience reinforced a lesson: One of the most effective forms of diplomacy is to show the good heart of America to the world.

Later in the day, I went to the embassy courtyard to watch some cricket, Pakistan's national pastime. There I met national team captain Inzamam-ul-Haq, the Pakistani equivalent of Michael Jordan. To the delight of the schoolchildren on hand, I took a few whacks with the cricket bat. I didn't master the game, but I did pick up some of the lingo. At the elegant state dinner that night, I opened my toast by saying, "I was fooled by a googly,* otherwise I would have been a better batsman."

My meetings with President Musharraf focused on two overriding priorities. One was his insistence on serving as both president and top general, a violation of the Pakistani constitution. I pushed him to shed his military affiliation and govern as a civilian. He promised to do it. But he wasn't in much of a hurry.

I also stressed the importance of the fight against extremists. "We've got to keep these guys from slipping into your country and back into Afghanistan," I said.

"I give you our assurances that we will cooperate with you against terrorism," Musharraf said. "We are totally on board."

The violence continued to grow. As the insurgency worsened, Hamid Karzai became furious with Musharraf. He accused the Pakistani president of destabilizing Afghanistan. Musharraf was insulted by the allegation. By the fall of 2006, the two were barely on speaking terms. I decided to step in with some serious personal diplomacy. I invited Karzai and Musharraf to dinner at the White House in September 2006. When I welcomed them in the Rose Garden, they refused to shake hands or even look at each other. The mood did not improve when we sat down for dinner in the Old Family Dining Room. Dick Cheney, Condi Rice, Steve Hadley, and I watched as Karzai and Musharraf traded barbs. At one point, Karzai accused Musharraf of harboring the Taliban.

"Tell me where they are," Musharraf responded testily.

"You know where they are!" Karzai fired back.

"If I did, I would get them," said Musharraf.

"Go do it!" Karzai persisted.

I started to wonder whether this dinner had been a mistake.

I told Musharraf and Karzai that the stakes were too high for personal bickering. I kept the dinner going for two and a half hours, trying

---

*A spinning pitch that is hard to hit, similar to a screwball in baseball.

to help them find common ground. After a while, the venting stopped and the meeting turned out to be productive. The two leaders agreed to share more intelligence, meet with tribes on both sides of the border to urge peace, and stop bad-mouthing each other in public.

As a way to staunch the flow of Taliban fighters, Musharraf informed us that he had recently struck a series of deals with tribes in the border region. Under the agreements, Pakistani forces would leave the areas alone, while tribal leaders would commit to stopping the Taliban from recruiting operatives or infiltrating into Afghanistan.

While well intentioned, the strategy failed. The tribes did not have the will or the capacity to control the extremists. Some estimates indicated that the flow of Taliban fighters into Afghanistan increased fourfold.

Musharraf had promised Karzai and me—both skeptics of the strategy—that he would send troops back into the tribal areas if the deals failed. But instead of focusing on that problem, Musharraf and the Pakistani military were increasingly distracted by a political crisis. In March 2007, Musharraf suspended the chief justice of the Supreme Court, who he feared would rule that he was violating the law by continuing to serve as both president and army chief of staff. Lawyers and democracy advocates marched in the streets. Musharraf responded by declaring a state of emergency, suspending the constitution, removing more judges, and arresting thousands of political opponents.

Pressure mounted on me to cut ties with Musharraf. I worried that throwing him overboard would add to the chaos. I had a series of frank conversations with him in the fall of 2007. "It looks ugly from here. The image here is that you have lawyers being beaten and thrown into jail," I said. "I am troubled by the fact that there is no apparent way forward." I strongly suggested one: set a date for free elections, resign from the army, and lift the state of emergency.

Musharraf made each of those commitments, and he kept them. When he scheduled parliamentary elections, former Prime Minister Benazir Bhutto returned from exile to compete. She ran on a pro-democracy platform, which made her a target of the extremists. Tragically, she was assassinated on December 27, 2007, at a political rally in Rawalpindi. In February 2008, her followers won the elections soundly. They formed a government, and Musharraf stepped down peacefully. Asif Ali Zardari,

Bhutto's widower, took his place as president. Pakistan's democracy had survived the crisis.

Over time, the Pakistani government learned the lesson of the Bhutto assassination. Pakistani forces returned to the fight in the tribal areas—not just against al Qaeda, but against the Taliban and other extremists as well. Yet more than a year had been lost, as Pakistan's attention was focused on its internal political crisis. The Taliban and other extremists exploited that window of opportunity to increase their tempo of operations in Afghanistan, which drove up the violence and led many Afghans to turn against their government and our coalition. It was essential that we find a way to retake the offensive.

---

By the middle of 2008, I was tired of reading intelligence reports about extremist sanctuaries in Pakistan. I thought back to a meeting I'd had with Special Forces in Afghanistan in 2006.

"Are you guys getting everything you need?" I asked.

One SEAL raised his hand and said, "No, sir."

I wondered what his problem might be.

"Mr. President," he said, "we need permission to go kick some ass inside Pakistan."

I understood the urgency of the threat and wanted to do something about it. But on this issue, Musharraf's judgment had been well-founded. When our forces encountered unexpected resistance, they got into a firefight and made international news. "U.S. Commandos Attack Pakistan Sovereignty," one Pakistani headline said. Islamabad exploded with outrage. Both houses of parliament passed unanimous resolutions condemning our action. No democracy can tolerate violations of its sovereignty.

I looked for other ways to reach into the tribal areas. The Predator, an unmanned aerial vehicle, was capable of conducting video surveillance and firing laser-guided bombs. I authorized the intelligence community to turn up the pressure on the extremists. Many of the details of our actions remain classified. But soon after I gave the order, the press started reporting more Predator strikes. Al Qaeda's number-four man, Khalid al-Habib, turned up dead. So did al Qaeda leaders responsible for pro-paganda, recruitment, religious affairs, and planning attacks overseas. One of the last reports I received described al Qaeda as "embattled and eroding" in the border region.

We also stepped up our support for Pakistan's democratic govern-ment. We provided money, training, and equipment, and proposed joint counterterrorism operations—all aimed at helping increase Pakistani capabilities. When the financial crisis hit in the fall of 2008, we took steps to make sure Pakistan received the assistance it needed to mitigate the effects of the recession and stay focused on fighting the extremists.

One of my national security team's last projects was a review of our strategy in Afghanistan. It was led by Doug Lute, a brainy three-star gen-eral who coordinated day-to-day execution of our operations in Afghan-istan and Iraq. The report called for a more robust counterinsurgency effort, including more troops and civilian resources in Afghanistan and closer cooperation with Pakistan to go after the extremists. We debated whether to announce our findings publicly in the final weeks of my presidency. Steve Hadley checked with his counterpart in the incoming administration, who preferred that we pass along our report quietly. I decided the new strategy would have a better chance of success if we gave the new team an opportunity to revise it as they saw fit and then adopt it as their own.

———

In December 2008, I made a farewell trip to Afghanistan. Air Force One landed at Bagram Air Base around 5:00 a.m., just ahead of the dawn. "I have a message to you, and to all who serve our country," I told a hangar full of troops. "Thanks for making the noble choice to serve and protect your fellow Americans. What you're doing in Afghanistan is important, it is courageous, and it is selfless. It's akin to what American troops did in places like Normandy and Iwo Jima and Korea. Your generation is every bit as great as any that has come before. And the work you do every day is shaping history for generations to come."

I shook hands with the troops and boarded a Black Hawk helicopter for the forty-minute flight to Kabul. Afghanistan is one of those places you have to see to understand. The mountains are gigantic and rugged; the terrain is harsh and bare; the landscape feels desolate and forbidding. Like many Americans, I sometimes wondered how anyone could hide from our military for seven years. When I looked at the topography of Afghanistan, it was easy to understand.

As we got closer to Kabul, I picked up an acrid smell. I realized it was coming from burning tires—sadly, an Afghan way of keeping warm. The air quality was no better on the ground. I was coughing for a week when I got home, a reminder that the country had a long way to go.

When we landed at the presidential palace, President Karzai strode over to meet me in his trademark robe and cap. He introduced me to his cabinet ministers and escorted me to a large sitting room for tea. As usual, he was energetic and exuberant. He beamed with pride as he showed me photos of his young son, Mirwais, his only child. He talked about his plans to increase Afghanistan's agricultural yield and stimulate its business sector in areas like telecommunications. After the meetings, he walked me out into the dusty courtyard. We parted with a handshake and a hug. No doubt he had made mistakes. But despite all the forces working against him, he never lost his determination to lead his country toward a better day. He helped give the Afghan people hope, something they hadn't had in many years. For that, he will always have my gratitude and respect.

As I climbed aboard the chopper, I thought back to the afternoon in October 2001 when I announced the opening of the war from the Treaty Room. A country dominated by one of history's cruelest regimes was now governed by freely elected leaders. Women who had been prisoners in their homes were serving in parliament. While still a danger, al Qaeda had lost the camps it used to train ten thousand terrorists and plan 9/11. The Afghan people had cast their ballots in multiple free elections and had built an increasingly capable army of seventy-nine thousand soldiers. Afghanistan's economy had doubled in size. School enrollment had risen from nine hundred thousand to more than six million, including more than two million girls. Access to health care had gone from 8 percent to 80 percent. In 2010, the Pentagon revealed that geologists had discovered nearly a trillion dollars' worth of mineral deposits in Afghanistan, a potential source of wealth for the Afghan people that the Taliban would never have found.

I also knew I was leaving behind unfinished business. I wanted badly to bring bin Laden to justice. The fact that we did not ranks among my great regrets. It certainly wasn't for lack of effort. For seven years, we kept the pressure on. While we never found the al Qaeda leader, we did force him to change the way he traveled, communicated, and operated. That helped us deny him his greatest wish after 9/11: to see America attacked again.

As I write in 2010, the war in Afghanistan continues. The Taliban remain active, and the Afghan government is struggling to gain full control of its country. From the beginning, I knew it would take time to help the Afghan people build a functioning democracy consistent with its culture and traditions. The task turned out to be even more daunting than I anticipated. Our government was not prepared for nation building. Over time, we adapted our strategy and our capabilities. Still, the poverty in Afghanistan is so deep, and the infrastructure is so lacking, that it will take many years to complete the work.

I strongly believe the mission is worth the cost. Fortunately, I am not the only one. In the fall of 2009, President Obama stood up to critics by deploying more troops, announcing a new commitment to counterinsurgency in Afghanistan, and increasing the pressure on Pakistan to fight the extremists in the tribal areas.

Ultimately, the only way the Taliban and al Qaeda can retake Afghanistan is if America abandons the country. Allowing the extremists to reclaim power would force Afghan women back into subservience, remove girls from school, and betray all the gains of the past nine years. It would also endanger our security. After the Cold War, the United States gave up on Afghanistan. The result was chaos, civil war, the Taliban takeover, sanctuary for al Qaeda, and the nightmare of 9/11. To forget that lesson would be a dreadful mistake.

———

Before I took off from Bagram Air Base for the flight home in December 2008, I returned to the hangar for the final meeting of my last foreign trip as president. Standing in the room was a group of Special Forces. Many had served multiple tours, hunting the terrorists and Taliban in the freezing mountains. They had one of the hardest and most dangerous jobs in the world. I shook their hands and told them how grateful I was for their service.

Then a small group of soldiers from the 75th Ranger Regiment entered the room. Their platoon leader, Captain Ramon Ramos, asked if I would be willing to participate in a brief ceremony. He reached into a pouch, unfurled a large American flag, and raised his right hand. Several of his men stood opposite him and did the same. He delivered an oath, which the men repeated. "I do solemnly swear that I will support and defend the Constitution of the United States against all enemies, foreign and domestic. . . ."

There in that lonely hangar, in the nation where 9/11 was planned, in the eighth year of a war to protect America, these men on the front lines chose to reenlist.

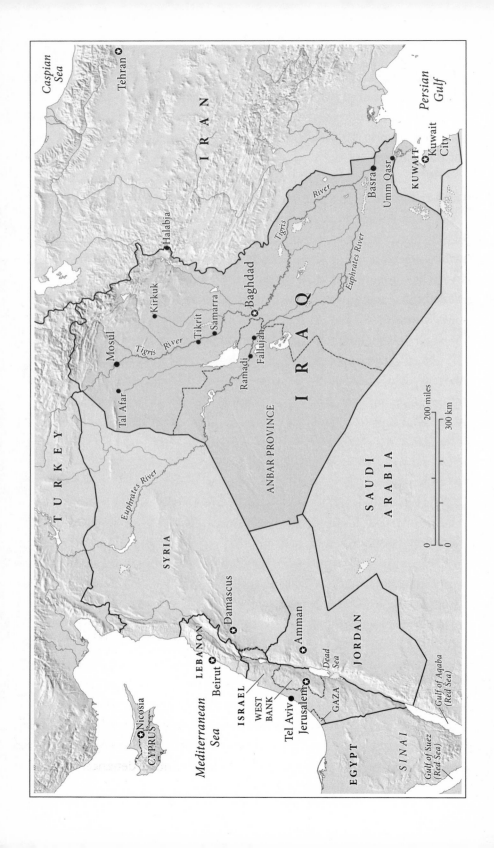

# 8

# IRAQ

On Wednesday, March 19, 2003, I walked into a meeting I had hoped would not be necessary.

The National Security Council had gathered in the White House Situation Room, a nerve center of communications equipment and duty officers on the ground floor of the West Wing. The top center square of the secure video screen showed General Tommy Franks sitting with his senior deputies at Prince Sultan Air Base in Saudi Arabia. In the other five boxes were our lead Army, Navy, Marine, Air Force, and Special Operations commanders. Their counterparts from the British Armed Forces and Australian Defense Forces joined as well.

I asked each man two questions: Do you have everything you need to win? And are you comfortable with the strategy?

Each commander answered affirmatively.

Tommy spoke last. "Mr. President," the commanding general said, "this force is ready."

I turned to Don Rumsfeld. "Mr. Secretary," I said, "for the peace of the world and the benefit and freedom of the Iraqi people, I hereby give the order to execute Operation Iraqi Freedom. May God bless the troops."

Tommy snapped a salute. "Mr. President," he said, "may God bless America."

As I saluted back, the gravity of the moment hit me. For more than a year, I had tried to address the threat from Saddam Hussein without war. We had rallied an international coalition to pressure him to come clean about his weapons of mass destruction programs. We had obtained a unanimous United Nations Security Council resolution making clear there would be serious consequences for continued defiance. We had reached out to Arab nations about taking Saddam into exile. I had given Saddam and his sons a final forty-eight hours to avoid war. The dictator rejected every opportunity. The only logical conclusion was that he had something to hide, something so important that he was willing to go to war for it.

I knew the consequences my order would bring. I had wept with widows of troops lost in Afghanistan. I had hugged children who no longer had a mom or a dad. I did not want to send Americans into combat again. But after the nightmare of 9/11, I had vowed to do what was necessary to protect the country. Letting a sworn enemy of America refuse to account for his weapons of mass destruction was a risk I could not afford to take.

I needed time to absorb the emotions of the moment. I left the Situation Room, walked up the stairs and through the Oval Office, and took a slow, silent lap around the South Lawn. I prayed for our troops, for the safety of the country, and for strength in the days ahead. Spot, our springer spaniel, bounded out of the White House toward me. It was comforting to see a friend. Her happiness contrasted with the heaviness in my heart.

There was one man who understood what I was feeling. I sat down at my desk in the Treaty Room and scrawled out a letter:

*Dear Dad, . . .*

*At around 9:30 a.m., I gave the order to SecDef to execute the war plan for Operation Iraqi Freedom. In spite of the fact that I had decided a few months ago to use force, if need be, to liberate Iraq and rid the country of WMD, the decision was an emotional one. . . .*

*I know I have taken the right action and do pray few will lose life. Iraq will be free, the world will be safer. The emotion of the moment has passed and now I wait word on the covert action that is taking place.*

*I know what you went through.*

*Love,*
*George*

A few hours later, his reply came across the fax:

*Dear George,*

*Your handwritten note, just received, touched my heart. You are doing the right thing. Your decision, just made, is the toughest decision you've had to make up until now. But you made it with strength and with com-passion. It is right to worry about the loss of innocent life be it Iraqi or American. But you have done that which you had to do.*

*Maybe it helps a tiny bit as you face the toughest bunch of problems any President since Lincoln has faced: You carry the burden with strength and grace. . . .*

*Remember Robin's words 'I love you more than tongue can tell.'*
*Well, I do.*

*Devotedly,*
*Dad*

———

The bombs that fell on Baghdad that night marked the opening phase in the liberation of Iraq. But that was not the first airstrike on Iraq to make news during my presidency.

In February 2001, I visited President Vicente Fox in San Cristóbal, Mexico. My first foreign trip as president was designed to highlight our commitment to expanding democracy and trade in Latin America. Un-fortunately, news out of Iraq intruded. As we admired the serene vistas of Vicente's ranch, American bombers struck Iraq's air defense system. It was a relatively routine mission to enforce the no-fly zones that had been created after Saddam massacred thousands of innocent Shia and Kurds following the Gulf War.*

Saddam fired off a barrage that lit up the Baghdad sky and grabbed

---

*The Shia, a Muslim sect, make up about 60 percent of Iraq's population. Kurds, who are mostly Muslim but identify primarily by their ethnic group, comprise about 20 percent. Sunni Arabs, the Muslim sect that enjoyed privileged status under Saddam, account for 15 percent. Christians, Yezidis, Mandaeans, Jews, and others make up the rest.

the attention of CNN. When Vicente and I stepped out of his home for a press conference, a Mexican reporter began, "I have a question for President Bush. . . . Is this the beginning of a new war?"

The flare-up was a reminder of the deteriorating situation America faced in Iraq. More than a decade earlier, in August 1990, Saddam Hussein's tanks blasted across the border into Kuwait. Dad declared that Saddam's unprovoked aggression would not stand and gave him an ultimatum to withdraw from Kuwait. When the dictator defied his demands, Dad rallied a coalition of thirty-four countries—including Arab nations—to enforce it.

The decision to send American troops to Kuwait was agonizing for Dad—and frustrating to implement. The Senate voted to authorize military force by a slim margin, 52 to 47. A group of lawmakers presented Dad with a letter that predicted ten thousand to fifty thousand American deaths. Former President Jimmy Carter urged members of the Security Council to oppose the war. The UN voted to support it anyway.

Operation Desert Storm proved a stunning success. Coalition forces drove the Iraqi army out of Kuwait in fewer than 100 hours. Ultimately, 149 Americans were killed in action. I was proud of Dad's decisiveness. I wondered if he would send troops all the way to Baghdad. He had a chance to rid the world of Saddam once and for all. But he stopped at the liberation of Kuwait. That was how he had defined the mission. That was what Congress had voted for and the coalition had signed up to do. I fully understood his rationale.

———

As a condition for ending hostilities in the Gulf War, UN Resolution 687 required Saddam to destroy his weapons of mass destruction and missiles with a range of more than ninety miles. The resolution banned Iraq from possessing biological, chemical, or nuclear weapons or the means to produce them. To ensure compliance, Saddam was required to submit to a UN monitoring and verification system.

At first, Saddam claimed he had only a limited stockpile of chemical weapons and Scud missiles. Over time, UN inspectors discovered a vast, haunting arsenal. Saddam had filled thousands of bombs, shells, and warheads with chemical agents. He had a nuclear weapons program that was about two years from yielding a bomb, much closer than the CIA's prewar estimate of eight to ten years. When his son-in-law defected in 1995, Saddam acknowledged that the regime had been hiding a biological weapons program that included anthrax and botulinum toxin.

To keep Saddam in check, the UN imposed strict economic sanctions. But as outrage over Iraq's invasion of Kuwait faded, the world's attention drifted. Saddam diverted nearly two billion dollars from the Oil-for-Food program—which the UN had created to provide for the basic humanitarian needs of innocent Iraqis—to enrich his cronies and reconstitute his military strength, including programs related to weapons of mass destruction. As children starved, he launched a propaganda campaign blaming sanctions for the suffering.

By 1998 Saddam had persuaded key trading partners like Russia and France to lobby the UN to loosen the restrictions. Then he forced the UN weapons inspectors to leave the country. The problem was clear: Saddam had never verified that he had destroyed all of his weapons from the Gulf War. With the inspectors gone, the world was blind to whether he had restarted his programs.

The Clinton administration responded by launching Operation Desert Fox—a four-day bombing campaign conducted jointly with Great Britain and aimed at degrading Saddam's WMD capabilities. In a prime-time address from the Oval Office in December 1998, President Clinton explained:

> *The hard fact is that so long as Saddam remains in power, he threatens the well-being of his people, the peace of his region, the security of the world. The best way to end that threat once and for all is with a new Iraqi government—a government ready to live in peace with its neighbors, a government that respects the rights of its people. . . .*
>
> *Heavy as they are, the costs of action must be weighed against the price of inaction. If Saddam defies the world and we fail to respond, we will face a far greater threat in the future. Saddam will strike again at his neighbors. He will make war on his own people. And mark my words, he will develop weapons of mass destruction. He will deploy them, and he will use them.*

The same year, Congress overwhelmingly passed and President Clinton signed the Iraq Liberation Act. The law declared a new official policy of the United States: "To support efforts to remove the regime headed by Saddam Hussein from power in Iraq and to promote the emergence of a democratic government."

———

By early 2001, Saddam Hussein was waging a low-grade war against the United States. In 1999 and 2000, his forces had fired seven hundred times at our pilots patrolling the no-fly zones.

For my first eight months in office, my policy focused on tightening the sanctions—or, as Colin Powell put it, keeping Saddam in his box. Then 9/11 hit, and we had to take a fresh look at every threat in the world. There were state sponsors of terror. There were sworn enemies of America. There were hostile governments that threatened their neighbors. There were nations that violated international demands. There were dictators who repressed their people. And there were regimes that pursued WMD. Iraq combined all those threats.

Saddam Hussein didn't just sympathize with terrorists. He had paid the families of Palestinian suicide bombers and given sanctuary to terrorists like Abu Nidal, who led attacks that killed nineteen people at an Israeli airline's ticket counters in Rome and Vienna, and Abu Abbas, who hijacked the Italian cruise ship *Achille Lauro* and murdered an elderly, wheelchair-bound American.

Saddam Hussein wasn't just a sworn enemy of America. He had fired at our aircraft, issued a statement praising 9/11, and made an assassination attempt on a former president, my father.

Saddam Hussein didn't just threaten his neighbors. He had invaded two of them, Iran in the 1980s and Kuwait in the 1990s.

Saddam Hussein didn't just violate international demands. He had defied sixteen UN resolutions, dating back to the Gulf War.

Saddam Hussein didn't just rule brutally. He and his henchmen had tortured innocent people, raped political opponents in front of their families, scalded dissidents with acid, and dumped tens of thousands of Iraqis into mass graves. In 2000, Saddam's government decreed that people who criticized the president or his family would have their tongues slashed out. Later that year, an Iraqi obstetrician was beheaded on charges of prostitution. The woman's true crime was speaking out about corruption in the Iraqi health ministry.

Saddam Hussein didn't just pursue weapons of mass destruction. He had used them. He deployed mustard gas and nerve agents against the Iranians and massacred more than five thousand innocent civilians in a 1988 chemical attack on the Kurdish village of Halabja. Nobody knew what Saddam had done with his biological and chemical stockpiles, especially after he booted inspectors out of the country. But after reviewing the information, virtually every major intelligence agency in the world had reached the same conclusion: Saddam had WMD in his arsenal and the capacity to produce more. One intelligence report summarized the problem: "Since the end of inspections in 1998, Saddam has maintained the chemical weapons effort, energized the missile program, made a bigger investment in biological weapons, and has begun to try to move forward in the nuclear area."

Before 9/11, Saddam was a problem America might have been able to manage. Through the lens of the post-9/11 world, my view changed. I had just witnessed the damage inflicted by nineteen fanatics armed with box cutters. I could only imagine the destruction possible if an enemy dictator passed his WMD to terrorists. With threats flowing into the Oval Office daily—many of them about chemical, biological, or nuclear weapons—that seemed like a frighteningly real possibility. The stakes were too high to trust the dictator's word against the weight of the evidence and the consensus of the world. The lesson of 9/11 was that if we waited for a danger to fully materialize, we would have waited too long. I reached a decision: We would confront the threat from Iraq, one way or another.

———

My first choice was to use diplomacy. Unfortunately, our track record with Iraq was not encouraging. We maintained a bilateral relationship with Baghdad in the 1980s. We obtained UN Security Council resolutions in the 1990s. Despite our engagement, Saddam grew only more belligerent.

If diplomacy was going to succeed, we needed a fundamentally different approach. We believed Saddam's weakness was that he loved power and would do anything to keep it. If we could convince him we were serious about removing his regime, there was a chance he would give up his WMD, end his support for terror, stop threatening his neighbors, and, over time, respect the human rights of his people. The odds of success were long. But given the alternative, it was worth the effort. The approach was called coercive diplomacy.

Coercive diplomacy with Iraq consisted of two tracks: One was to rally a coalition of nations to make clear that Saddam's defiance of his international obligations was unacceptable. The other was to develop a credible military option that could be used if he failed to comply. These tracks would run parallel at first. As the military option grew more visible and more advanced, the tracks would converge. Our maximum leverage would come just before they intersected. That would be the moment of decision. And ultimately, it would be Saddam Hussein's decision to make.

———

In February 2001, British Prime Minister Tony Blair and his wife, Cherie, came to visit Laura and me at Camp David. Tony was the first foreign leader we invited, a tribute to the special relationship between the United States and Great Britain.

I wasn't sure what to expect from Tony. I knew he was a left-of-center Labour Party prime minister and a close friend of Bill Clinton's. I quickly found he was candid, friendly, and engaging. There was no stuffiness about Tony and Cherie. After dinner, we decided to watch a movie. When they agreed on *Meet the Parents*, a comedy starring Robert De Niro and Ben Stiller, Laura and I knew the Bushes and Blairs would get along.

Tony and I talked through the major issues of the day. He gave me a briefing on the politics of Europe. We discussed our common goals to expand free trade, relieve suffering in Africa, and address the violence in the Holy Land. We didn't spend much time on the social issues. That was left for Cherie and me.

In the summer of 2001, the Blairs invited Laura and me to Chequers, the storied country estate of the British prime minister. Chequers is a large, creaky house filled with rustic, comfortable furniture and portraits of former prime ministers. Rather than throw a formal reception, the Blairs arranged a cozy family dinner with their four children—including little Leo, age fourteen months.

About halfway through the meal, the death penalty came up. Cherie made clear she didn't agree with my position. Tony looked a little uncomfortable. I listened to her views and then defended mine. I told her I believed the death penalty, when properly administered, could save lives by deterring crime. A talented lawyer whom I grew to respect, Cherie rebutted my arguments. At one point, Laura and I overheard Euan, the Blairs' bright seventeen-year-old son, say, "Give the man a break, Mother."

The more time we spent together, the more I respected Tony. Over the years, he grew into my closest partner and best friend on the world stage. He came to the United States for meetings more than thirty times during my presidency. Laura and I visited him in Northern Ireland, Scotland, and London. In November 2003, Tony and Cherie invited us to their home in Trimdon Colliery, an old mining area in the countryside. They served us a cup of tea in their redbrick Victorian and took us to a town pub, the Dun Cow Inn. We ate fish and chips with mushy peas, which I washed down with a nonalcoholic Bitburger lager. After lunch, we dropped by a local school and watched a soccer practice—known as football to our hosts. The people were decent and welcoming, aside from the protester who carried a sign that read "Mad Cowboy Disease."

Tony had a quick laugh and a sharp wit. After our first meeting, a British reporter asked what we had in common. I quipped, "We both use Colgate toothpaste." Tony fired back, "They're going to wonder how you know that, George." When he addressed a Joint Session of Congress in 2003, Tony brought up the War of 1812, when British troops burned the White House. "I know this is kind of late," he said, "but . . . sorry."

Unlike many politicians, Tony was a strategic thinker who could see beyond the immediate horizon. As I would come to learn, he and I were kindred spirits in our faith in the transformative power of liberty. In the final week of my presidency, I was proud to make him one of the few foreign leaders to receive the Presidential Medal of Freedom.*

Above all, Tony Blair had courage. No issue demonstrated it more clearly than Iraq. Like me, Tony considered Saddam a threat the world could not tolerate after 9/11. The British were targets of the extremists. They had extensive intelligence on Saddam. And they understood in a personal way the menace he posed. Saddam was shooting at their pilots, too.

If we had to remove Saddam from power, Tony and I would have an obligation to help the Iraqi people replace Saddam's tyranny with a democracy. The transformation would have an impact beyond Iraq's borders. The Middle East was the center of a global ideological struggle. On one side were decent people who wanted to live in dignity and peace. On the other were extremists who sought to impose their radical views through violence and intimidation. They exploited conditions of hopelessness and repression to recruit and spread their ideology. The best way to protect our countries in the long run was to counter their dark vision with a more compelling alternative.

That alternative was freedom. People who could choose their leaders at the ballot box would be less likely to turn to violence. Young people growing up with hope in the future would not search for meaning in the ideology of terror. Once liberty took root in one society, it could spread to others.

In April 2002, Tony and Cherie visited Laura and me in Crawford. Tony and I talked about coercive diplomacy as a way to address the threat from Iraq. Tony suggested that we seek a UN Security Council resolution that presented Saddam with a clear ultimatum: allow weapons inspectors back into Iraq, or face serious consequences. I didn't have a lot of faith in the UN. The Security Council had passed sixteen resolutions against Saddam to no avail. But I agreed to consider his idea.

———

*At the same ceremony, I presented the Medal of Freedom to Prime Minister John Howard of Australia, who I called a "man of steel," and to President Alvaro Uribe, the courageous leader of Colombia.

I raised Iraq with other world leaders throughout 2002. Many shared my assessment of the threat, including John Howard of Australia, José Maria Aznar of Spain, Junichiro Koizumi of Japan, Jan Peter Balkenende of the Netherlands, Anders Fogh Rasmussen of Denmark, Aleksander Kwasniewski of Poland, and most other leaders in Central and Eastern Europe. It was revealing that some of the strongest advocates for confronting Saddam were those with the freshest memories of tyranny. "In the late 1930s, the Western democracies hesitated in the face of danger," Prime Minister Siim Kallas of Estonia, a former Soviet republic, told me. "As a consequence, we fell under dictatorships and many people lost their lives. Action is sometimes necessary."

Other leaders had a different outlook. Vladimir Putin didn't consider Saddam a threat. It seemed to me that part of the reason was Putin didn't want to jeopardize Russia's lucrative oil contracts. France also had significant economic interests in Iraq. I was not surprised when Jacques Chirac told me he would support intrusive weapons inspections but cautioned against threatening military force. The problem with his logic was that without a credible threat of force, the diplomacy would be toothless once again.

One of the toughest leaders to figure out was Chancellor Gerhard Schroeder of Germany. I met with Gerhard five times in 2001. He was relaxed, affable, and interested in strengthening our bilateral relationship. I appreciated his leadership on Afghanistan, especially his willingness to host the *loya jirga* in Bonn.

I discussed Iraq with Gerhard during his visit to the White House on January 31, 2002. In my State of the Union address two days earlier, I had outlined the threats posed by Iraq, Iran, and North Korea. "States like these, and their terrorist allies, constitute an axis of evil, arming to threaten the peace of the world," I said. The media seized on the phrase "axis of evil." They took the line to mean that the three countries had formed an alliance. That missed the point. The axis I referred to was the link between the governments that pursued WMD and the terrorists who could use those weapons. There was a larger point in the speech that no one could miss: I was serious about dealing with Iraq.

In a small Oval Office meeting, joined by Condi Rice and Andy Card, I told the German chancellor I was determined to make diplomacy work.

I hoped he would help. I also assured him our words would not be empty. The military option was my last choice, but I would use it if necessary.

"What is true of Afghanistan is true of Iraq," he said. "Nations that sponsor terror must face consequences. If you make it fast and make it decisive, I will be with you."

I took that as a statement of support. But when the German elections arrived later that year, Schroeder had a different take. He denounced the possibility of using force against Iraq. His justice minister said, "Bush wants to divert attention from domestic political problems. . . . Hitler also did that." I was shocked and furious. It was hard to think of anything more insulting than being compared to Hitler by a German official. I continued to work with Gerhard Schroeder on areas of mutual interest. But as someone who valued personal diplomacy, I put a high premium on trust. Once that trust was violated, it was hard to have a constructive relationship again.

———

Two months after 9/11, I asked Don Rumsfeld to review the existing battle plans for Iraq. We needed to develop the coercive half of coercive diplomacy.

Don tasked General Tommy Franks with updating the plans. Just after Christmas 2001, Tommy came to Crawford to brief me on Iraq. The plan on the shelf required a six-month buildup and four hundred thousand troops. The experience in Afghanistan was at the forefront of our minds. Thanks to new technology and innovative planning, we had destroyed the Taliban and closed the al Qaeda camps using far fewer troops. We were not viewed as occupiers by the Afghan people.

Tommy told the national security team that he was working to apply the same concept of a light footprint to Iraq. He envisioned a fast invasion from Kuwait in the south, Saudi Arabia and Jordan in the west, and Turkey in the north. "If we have multiple, highly skilled Special Operations Forces identifying targets for precision-guided munitions, we will need fewer conventional ground forces," he said. "That's an important lesson learned from Afghanistan."

I had a lot of concerns. I wanted to know how fast our troops could move and what kind of basing we would need. As in Afghanistan, I was concerned about starvation of the local population and asked what we could do to protect innocent life. I worried about Saddam sabotaging the oil fields or firing missiles at Israel. My biggest fear was that he would use biological or chemical weapons against our troops, our allies, or Iraqi civilians.

I asked the team to keep working on the plan. "We should remain optimistic that diplomacy and international pressure will succeed in disarming the regime," I said at the end of the meeting. "But we cannot allow weapons of mass destruction to fall into the hands of terrorists. I will not allow that to happen."

———

Between December 2001 and August 2002, I met or spoke with Tommy more than a dozen times. The plan was getting better, but I wasn't satisfied. I wanted to make sure we had thought through as many contingencies as possible. I asked Don and Tommy a lot of questions that started with "What if Saddam decides to . . . ?" One scenario I brought up frequently was Saddam consolidating his forces in Baghdad and engaging our troops in bloody urban combat. I remembered the battle in Somalia in 1993 and did not want to see that repeated in Iraq. Tommy and his team didn't have all the answers on the spot, and I didn't expect them to. But they were working hard to refine the plan, and every iteration they brought me was an improvement on the previous version.

The updated plan Tommy presented in the Situation Room on August 5, 2002, resolved several key concerns. We had lined up basing and overflight permission from leaders in the Gulf. Tommy had devised a plan for Special Operations to secure suspected WMD sites, Iraq's southern oil fields, and Scud missile launchers. He had also designed a massive aerial bombardment that would make it costly for Saddam's elite Republican Guard units to remain in the capital, reducing the chances of a Fortress Baghdad scenario. "Mr. President," Tommy said in his Texas drawl, "this is going to be shock and awe."

There were plenty of issues left to resolve. We all worried about the possibility of Saddam launching a biological or chemical attack on our troops, so the military was in the process of procuring hazmat suits. We had gradually increased the level of troops and equipment in Kuwait under the guise of training and other routine exercises, which would make it possible to begin combat operations rapidly if I gave the order to launch. Joint Chiefs Chairman Dick Myers talked about the importance of persuading Turkey to open its territory so we could establish a northern front. George Tenet raised concern about a broader regional war in which Syria attacked Israel, or Iran directed its proxy terrorist group, Hezbollah, to foment instability. Don Rumsfeld pointed out that a war could destabilize Jordan and Saudi Arabia, that America could get stuck in a manhunt for Saddam, and that Iraq could fracture after liberation.

Those potential scenarios were sobering. But so were the briefings we were receiving. A report in July read, "Iraq has managed to preserve and in some cases even enhance the infrastructure and expertise necessary for WMD production." Another briefing warned that Saddam's regime was "almost certainly working to produce the causative agent for anthrax along with botulinum toxin, aflatoxin, and ricin." It continued: "Unmanned aerial vehicles give Baghdad a more lethal means to deliver biological . . . weapons." It went on, ominously, "Experience shows that Saddam produces weapons of mass destruction to use, not just to deter."

In the summer of 2002, I received a startling piece of news. Abu Musab al-Zarqawi, an al Qaeda–affiliated terrorist who had experimented with biological weapons in Afghanistan, was operating a lab in northeastern Iraq. "Suspect facility in this area may be producing poisons and toxins for terrorist use," the briefing read. "Al-Zarqawi is an active terrorist planner who has targeted U.S. and Israeli interests: Sensitive reporting from a [classified] service indicates that al-Zarqawi has been directing efforts to smuggle an unspecified chemical material originating in northern Iraq into the United States."

We couldn't say for sure whether Saddam knew Zarqawi was in Iraq. We did have intelligence indicating that Zarqawi had spent two months in Baghdad receiving medical treatment and that other al Qaeda operatives had moved to Iraq. The CIA had worked with a major Arab intelligence service to get Saddam to find and extradite Zarqawi. He refused.

The question was whether to bomb the poisons lab in the summer of

2002. We held a series of NSC meetings on the topic. General Dick Myers talked through the options: Tomahawk missiles, a B-2 bomber strike, or a covert ground raid. Dick Cheney and Don saw Zarqawi as a clear threat and argued that taking him out would reinforce the doctrine that America would not tolerate safe havens for terror.

Colin and Condi felt a strike on the lab would create an international firestorm and disrupt our efforts to build a coalition to confront Saddam—especially our attempt to recruit Turkey, which was highly sensitive about any activity in northeastern Iraq. "This would be viewed as a unilateral start to the war in Iraq," Colin said.

I faced a dilemma. If America was hit with a biological attack from Iraq, I would be responsible for not having taken out the threat when we had the chance. On the other hand, bombing the camp could undermine diplomacy and trigger a military conflict.

I told the intelligence community to keep a close eye on the facility. For the time being, I decided to continue on the diplomatic track. But one thing was clear to me: Iraq was a serious threat growing more dangerous by the day.

———

I spent much of August 2002 in Crawford, a good place to reflect on the next decision I faced: how to move forward on the diplomatic track.

One option was to seek a UN resolution calling on Saddam to readmit weapons inspectors. The other was to issue an ultimatum demanding that he disarm—and rally a coalition to remove him if he did not comply.

From a legal standpoint, a resolution was unnecessary. Three years earlier, President Clinton and our NATO allies had removed the dictator Slobodan Milosevic from power in Serbia without an explicit UN resolution. Dick and Don argued we didn't need one for Iraq, either. After all, we already had sixteen. They believed that going to the UN would trigger a long bureaucratic process that would leave Saddam even more dangerous.

I shared that concern. On the other hand, almost every ally I consulted—even staunch advocates of confronting Saddam like Prime

Minister John Howard of Australia—told me a UN resolution was essential to win public support in their countries.

Colin agreed. The day before I left for Crawford, I asked him to meet with me privately in the Treaty Room. Colin was more passionate than I had seen him at any NSC meeting. He told me a UN resolution was the only way to get any support from the rest of the world. He went on to say that if we did take out Saddam, the military strike would be the easy part. Then, as Colin put it, America would "own" Iraq. We would be responsible for helping a fractured country rebuild. I listened carefully and shared Colin's concern. It was another reason I hoped that diplomacy would work.

That summer, the possibility of war had become an all-consuming news story in Washington. Reporters asked frequently whether I had a war plan on my desk.

On August 15, I opened the *Wall Street Journal* to find a column by Brent Scowcroft, Dad's national security adviser. It was headlined "Don't Attack Saddam." Brent argued that war with Iraq would distract from the war on terror and could unleash "an Armageddon in the Middle East." His conclusion was that we should "be pressing the United Nations Security Council to insist on an effective no-notice inspection regime for Iraq."

That was a fair recommendation. But I was angry that Brent had chosen to publish his advice in the newspaper instead of sharing it with me. I called Dad. "Son, Brent is a friend," he assured me. That might be true. But I knew critics would later exploit Brent's article if the diplomatic track failed.

Some in Washington speculated that Brent's op-ed was Dad's way of sending me a message on Iraq. That was ridiculous. Of all people, Dad understood the stakes. If he thought I was handling Iraq wrong, he damn sure would have told me himself.

———

On Saturday, September 7, 2002, I convened a meeting of the national security team at Camp David to finalize my decision on the resolution. Fifty-one weeks earlier, we had gathered in Laurel Lodge to plan the war in Afghanistan. Now we sat in the same room trying to find a way to remove the threat in Iraq without war.

I gave everyone on the team a chance to make their arguments. Dick

Cheney recommended that we restate the case against Saddam, give him thirty to sixty days to come clean, and then disarm him by force if he refused to comply. "It is time to act," Dick said. "We can't delay for another year. . . . An inspection regime does not solve our problem."

Colin pushed for the UN resolution. "If we take the case to the UN, we can get allies to join. If not, it will be hard to act unilaterally. We won't have the international support we need to execute the military plan."

After listening to the options one last time, I made a decision: We would seek a resolution. "There's ambiguity in the international community's view of Saddam," I said, "and we need to clear it up. Either he will come clean about his weapons, or there will be war."

I told the team I would deliver that message in a speech to the United Nations the following week. I would remind the UN that Saddam's defiance was a threat to the credibility of the institution. Either the words of the Security Council would be enforced, or the UN would exist only as a useless international body like the League of Nations.

Tony Blair came to dinner that night at Camp David. He was pleased when I told him I was planning to ask the UN for the resolution. "Many opponents wish we would just be unilateral—then they could complain," he said. "But you are calling their bluff."

We both understood what the decision meant. Once we laid out our position at the UN, we had to be willing to follow through with the consequences. If diplomacy failed, there would be only one option left. "I don't want to go to war," I told Tony, "but I will do it."

Tony agreed. After the meeting, I told Alastair Campbell, one of Tony's top aides, "Your man has got *cojones.*" I'm not sure how that translated to the refined ears of 10 Downing Street. But to anyone from Texas, its meaning was clear.

———

"All the world now faces a test," I told UN delegates on September 12, 2002, "and the United Nations a difficult and defining moment. Are Security Council resolutions to be honored and enforced, or cast aside without consequence? Will the United Nations serve the purpose of its founding, or will it be irrelevant?"

Delivering the speech was a surreal experience. The delegates sat silent, almost frozen in place. It was like speaking to a wax museum.

The response outside the chamber was encouraging. Allies thanked me for respecting the UN and accepting their advice to seek a resolution. Many at home appreciated that I had challenged the UN. An editorial in the *Washington Post* read: "If the United Nations remains passive in the face of this long-standing and flagrant violation of its authority in a matter involving weapons of mass destruction, it certainly will risk the irrelevance of which Mr. Bush warned."

———

While the UN debate unfolded, we went to work on another resolution, a congressional war authorization. As part of the debate, leaders on Capitol Hill asked the intelligence community to prepare a National Intelligence Estimate analyzing Saddam's WMD programs. The CIA compiled the NIE using much of the same intelligence it had been showing to me for the past eighteen months. In a summary sentence later declassified, the NIE concluded, "Baghdad has chemical and biological weapons as well as missiles with ranges in excess of UN restrictions; if left unchecked, it probably will have a nuclear weapon during this decade."

The intelligence had an impact on members of Congress. Senator John Kerry said, "When I vote to give the president of the United States the authority to use force, if necessary, to disarm Saddam Hussein, it is because I believe that a deadly arsenal of weapons of mass destruction in his hands is a threat, and a grave threat."

Senator Jay Rockefeller, a respected Democrat on the Intelligence Committee, followed up: "Saddam's existing biological and chemical weapons capabilities pose real threats to America today, tomorrow. . . . He could make these weapons available to many terrorist groups, third parties, which have contact with his government. Those groups, in turn, could bring those weapons into the United States and unleash a devastating attack against our citizens. I fear that greatly."

Senator Chuck Hagel, a Nebraska Republican, supported the resolution. He said, "The risks of inaction are too high. We are elected to solve problems, not just debate them. The time has come to chart a new course in Iraq and in the Middle East."

On October 11, 2002, the Senate passed the resolution 77 to 23. The House passed it 296 to 133. Both margins were larger than those of the votes for the Gulf War. The resolution garnered votes from prominent Democrats, including House Minority Leader Dick Gephardt, Senate Majority Leader Tom Daschle, and Senators Hillary Clinton, Joe Biden, John Kerry, John Edwards, and Harry Reid.

Some members of Congress would later claim they were not voting to authorize war but only to continue diplomacy. They must not have read the resolution. Its language was unmistakable: "The President is authorized to use the Armed Forces of the United States as he determines to be necessary and appropriate in order to defend the national security of the United States against the continuing threat posed by Iraq; and enforce all relevant United Nations Security Council resolutions regarding Iraq."

———

The decisive vote at the UN came on November 8. Colin had been horse-trading on minor issues, but he stayed tough on the provisions holding Saddam to account. The question was whether the resolution would have the votes. We needed nine of the fifteen Security Council members, without a veto from France, Russia, or China. We had been burning up the phone lines, trying to get everyone on board. Shortly after the Security Council vote, the phone in the Oval Office rang. "Hey, Boss," Colin said. "We got it done."

The vote was unanimous, 15 to 0. Not only had France voted for the resolution, but so had Russia, China, and Syria. The world was now on record: Saddam had a "final opportunity to comply" with his obligation to disclose and disarm. If he did not, he would face "serious consequences."

Under the terms of UN Security Council Resolution 1441, Iraq had thirty days to submit a "currently accurate, full, and complete declaration" of all WMD-related programs. The resolution made clear the burden of proof rested with Saddam. The inspectors did not have to prove that he had weapons. He had to prove that he did not.

When the deadline arrived on December 7, Saddam submitted his report. I viewed it as a key test. If he came forward with honest admissions, it would send a signal that he understood the message the world was sending. Instead, he submitted reams of irrelevant paperwork clearly designed to deceive. Hans Blix, the mild-mannered Swedish diplomat who led the UN inspections team, later called it "rich in volume but poor in information." Joe Lieberman was more succinct. He said the declaration was a "twelve-thousand-page, one-hundred-pound lie."

If Saddam continued his pattern of deception, the only way to keep the pressure on Iraq would be to present some of the evidence ourselves. I asked George Tenet and his capable deputy, John McLaughlin, to brief me on what intelligence we could declassify to explain Iraq's WMD programs.

A few days before Christmas, John walked me through their first effort. It was not very convincing. I thought back to CIA briefings I had received, the NIE that concluded Saddam had biological and chemical weapons, and the data the CIA had provided for my UN speech in September. "Surely we can do a better job of explaining the evidence against Saddam," I said. George Tenet agreed.

"It's a slam dunk," he said.

I believed him. I had been receiving intelligence briefings on Iraq for nearly two years. The conclusion that Saddam had WMD was nearly a universal consensus. My predecessor believed it. Republicans and Democrats on Capitol Hill believed it. Intelligence agencies in Germany, France, Great Britain, Russia, China, and Egypt believed it. As the German ambassador to the United States, not a supporter of war, later put it, "I think all of our governments believe that Iraq has produced weapons of mass destruction and that we have to assume that they still have . . . weapons of mass destruction." If anything, we worried that the CIA was underestimating Saddam, as it had before the Gulf War.

In retrospect, of course, we all should have pushed harder on the intelligence and revisited our assumptions. But at the time, the evidence and the logic pointed in the other direction. *If Saddam doesn't actually have WMD*, I asked myself, *why on earth would he subject himself to a war he will almost certainly lose?*

Every Christmas during my presidency, Laura and I invited our extended family to join us at Camp David. We were happy to continue the tradition started by Mother and Dad. We cherished the opportunity to relax with them, Laura's mom, Barbara and Jenna, and my brothers and sister and their families. We loved to watch the children's pageant at the Camp David chapel and to sing carols with military personnel and their families. One of the highlights was an annual Pink Elephant gift exchange, in which my teenage nieces and nephews were not above pilfering the latest iPod or other coveted item from the president of the United States. In later years, we started a tradition of making donations in another family member's name. Jeb and Doro donated books to the library aboard the USS *George H.W. Bush*. Marvin and his wife, Margaret, donated a communion chalice to the Camp David chapel on behalf of Laura and me. We gave a gift to the Dorothy Walker Bush Pavilion at the Southern Maine Medical Center in Mother and Dad's name.

Amid the Christmas celebrations in 2002, Dad and I talked about Iraq. For the most part, I didn't seek Dad's advice on major issues. He and I both understood that I had access to more and better information than he did. Most of our conversations were for me to reassure him that I was doing fine and for him to express his confidence and love.

Iraq was one issue where I wanted to know what he thought. I told Dad I was praying we could deal with Saddam peacefully but was preparing for the alternative. I walked him through the diplomatic strategy—the solid support from Blair, Howard, and Aznar; the uncertainty with Chirac and Schroeder; and my efforts to rally the Saudis, Jordanians, Turks, and others in the Middle East.

He shared my hope that diplomacy would succeed. "You know how tough war is, son, and you've got to try everything you can to avoid war," he said. "But if the man won't comply, you don't have any other choice."

Shortly after New Year's, I sent Barbara and Jenna a letter at college. "I am working hard to keep the peace and avoid a war," I wrote. "I pray that the man in Iraq will disarm in a peaceful way. We are putting pressure on him to do just that and much of the world is with us."

As 2003 began, it became increasingly clear that my prayer would not be answered. On January 27, Hans Blix gave a formal report to the United Nations. His inspections team had discovered warheads that Saddam had failed to declare or destroy, indications of the highly toxic VX nerve agent, and precursor chemicals for mustard gas. In addition, the Iraqi government was defying the inspections process. The regime had violated Resolution 1441 by blocking U-2 flights and hiding three thousand documents in the home of an Iraqi nuclear official. "Iraq appears not to have come to a genuine acceptance, not even today, of the disarmament that was demanded of it," Blix said.

I could see what was happening: Saddam was trying to shift the burden of proof from himself to us. I reminded our partners that the UN resolution clearly stated that it was Saddam's responsibility to comply. As Mohamed ElBaradei, director of the International Atomic Energy Agency, explained in late January, "The ball is entirely in Iraq's court. . . . Iraq now has to prove that it is innocent. . . . They need to go out of their way to prove through whatever possible means that they have no weapons of mass destruction."

In late January, Tony Blair came to Washington for a strategy session. We agreed that Saddam had violated UN Security Council Resolution 1441 by submitting a false declaration. We had ample justification to enforce the "serious consequences." But Tony wanted to go back to the UN for a second resolution clarifying that Iraq had "failed to take the final opportunity afforded to it."

"It's not that we need it," Tony said. "A second resolution gives us military and political protection."

I dreaded the thought of plunging back into the UN. Dick, Don, and Condi were opposed. Colin told me that we didn't need another resolution and probably couldn't get one. But if Tony wanted a second resolution, we would try. "As I see it, the issue of the second resolution is how best to help our friends," I said.

The best way to get a second resolution was to lay out the evidence against Saddam. I asked Colin to make the presentation to the UN. He had credibility as a highly respected diplomat known to be reluctant about the possibility of war. I knew he would do a thorough, careful job. In early February, Colin spent four days and four nights at the CIA personally reviewing the intelligence to ensure he was comfortable with every word in his speech. On February 5, he took the microphone at the Security Council.

"The facts on Iraq's behavior," he said, "demonstrate that Saddam Hussein and his regime have made no effort—no effort—to disarm as required by the international community. Indeed, the facts and Iraq's behavior show that Saddam Hussein and his regime are concealing their efforts to produce more weapons of mass destruction."

Colin's presentation was exhaustive, eloquent, and persuasive. Coming against the backdrop of Saddam's defiance of the weapons inspectors, it had a profound impact on the public debate. Later, many of the assertions in Colin's speech would prove inaccurate. But at the time, his words reflected the considered judgment of intelligence agencies at home and around the world.

"We are both moral men," Jacques Chirac told me after Colin's speech. "But in this case, we see morality differently." I replied politely, but I thought to myself: *If a dictator who tortures and gasses his people is not immoral, then who is?*

Three days later, Chirac stepped in front of the cameras and said, "Nothing today justifies war." He, Gerhard Schroeder, and Vladimir Putin issued a joint statement of opposition. All three of them sat on the Security Council. The odds of a second resolution looked bleak.

Tony urged that we forge ahead. "The stakes are now much higher," he wrote to me on February 19. "It is apparent to me from the EU summit that France wants to make this a crucial test: Is Europe America's partner or competitor?" He reminded me we had support from a strong European coalition, including Spain, Italy, Denmark, the Netherlands, Portugal, and all of Eastern Europe. In a recent NATO vote, fifteen members of the alliance had supported military action in Iraq, with only Belgium and Luxembourg standing with Germany and France. Portuguese Prime Minister José Barroso spoke for many European leaders when he asked, incredulously, "We are faced with the choice of America or Iraq, and we're going to pick Iraq?"

Tony and I agreed on a strategy: We would introduce the second resolution at the UN, joined by the visionary leader of Spain, Prime Minister José Maria Aznar. If we lined up enough yes votes, we might be able to persuade France and Russia to abstain rather than veto. If not, we would pull down the resolution, and it would be clear they had blocked the final diplomatic effort.

The second resolution, which we introduced on February 24, 2003, was important for another reason. Tony was facing intense internal pressure on the issue of Iraq, and it was important for him to show that he had exhausted every possible alternative to military force. Factions of the Labour Party had revolted against him. By early March, it wasn't clear if his government could survive.

I called Tony and expressed my concern. I told him I'd rather have him drop out of the coalition and keep his government than try to stay in and lose it.

"I said I'm with you," Tony answered.

I pressed my point again.

"I understand that, and that's good of you to say," he replied. "I absolutely believe in this. I will take it up to the very last."

I heard an echo of Winston Churchill in my friend's voice. It was a moment of courage that will stay with me forever.

———

At Tony's request, I made one last effort to persuade Mexico and Chile, two wavering Security Council members, to support the second resolution. My first call was to my friend President Vicente Fox. The conversation got off to an inauspicious start. When I told Vicente I was calling about the UN resolution, he asked which one I meant. "If I can give you some advice," I said, "you should not be seen teaming up with the French." He said he would think about it and get back to me. An hour passed. Then Condi heard from the embassy. Vicente had checked into the hospital for back surgery. I never did hear from him on the issue.

My conversation with President Ricardo Lagos of Chile did not go much better. He was a distinguished, scholarly man and an effective leader. We had negotiated a free trade agreement that I hoped Congress would approve soon. But public opinion in Chile ran against a potential war, and Ricardo was reluctant to support the resolution. He talked about giving Saddam an additional two or three weeks. I told him a few more weeks would make no difference. Saddam had already had years to comply. "It is sad it has come down to this," I said. I asked one last time how he planned to vote. He said no.

As the diplomatic process drifted along, the pressure for action had been mounting. In early 2003, Federal Reserve Chairman Alan Greenspan told me the uncertainty was hurting the economy. Prince Bandar of Saudi Arabia, the kingdom's longtime ambassador to Washington and a friend of mine since Dad's presidency, came to the Oval Office and told me our allies in the Middle East wanted a decision.

Whenever I heard someone claim that we had rushed to war, I thought back to this period. It had been more than a decade since the Gulf War resolutions had demanded that Saddam disarm, over four years since he had kicked out the weapons inspectors, six months since I had issued my ultimatum at the UN, four months since Resolution 1441 had given Saddam his "final opportunity," and three months past the deadline to fully disclose his WMD. Diplomacy did not feel rushed. It felt like it was taking forever.

Meanwhile, the threats continued. President Hosni Mubarak of Egypt had told Tommy Franks that Iraq had biological weapons and was certain to use them on our troops. He refused to make the allegation in public for fear of inciting the Arab Street. But the intelligence from a Middle Eastern leader who knew Saddam well had an impact on my thinking. Just as there were risks to action, there were risks to inaction as well: Saddam with a biological weapon was a serious threat to us all.

———

In the winter of 2003, I sought opinions on Iraq from a variety of sources. I asked for advice from scholars, Iraqi dissidents in exile, and others outside the administration. One of the most fascinating people I met with was Elie Wiesel, the author, Holocaust survivor, and deserving Nobel Peace Prize recipient. Elie is a sober and gentle man. But there was passion in his seventy-four-year-old eyes when he compared Saddam Hussein's brutality to the Nazi genocide. "Mr. President," he said, "you have a moral obligation to act against evil." The force of his conviction affected me deeply. Here was a man who had devoted his life to peace urging me to intervene in Iraq. As he later explained in an op-ed: "Though I oppose war, I am in favor of intervention when, as in this case because of Hussein's equivocations and procrastinations, no other option remains."

I've always wondered why many critics of the war did not acknowledge the moral argument made by people like Elie Wiesel. Many of those who demonstrated against military action in Iraq were devoted advocates of human rights. Yet they condemned me for using force to remove the man who had gassed the Kurds, mowed down the Shia by helicopter gunship, massacred the Marsh Arabs, and sent tens of thousands to mass graves. I understood why people might disagree on the threat Saddam Hussein posed to the United States. But I didn't see how anyone could deny that liberating Iraq advanced the cause of human rights.

---

With diplomacy faltering, our military planning sessions had increasingly focused on what would happen after the removal of Saddam. In later years, some critics would charge that we failed to prepare for the postwar period. That sure isn't how I remember it.

Starting in the fall of 2002, a group led by Deputy National Security Adviser Steve Hadley produced in-depth plans for post-Saddam Iraq. Two of our biggest concerns were starvation and refugees. Sixty percent of Iraqis were dependent on the government as a source of food. An estimated two million Iraqis could be displaced from their homes during war.

On January 15, Elliott Abrams, a senior NSC staffer, delivered a detailed briefing on our preparations. We planned to prestation food, blankets, medicine, tents, and other relief supplies. We produced maps of where refugees could be sheltered. We deployed experienced humanitarian relief experts to enter Iraq alongside our troops. We had pinpointed the locations of most of Iraq's fifty-five thousand food distribution points and made arrangements with international organizations—including the World Food Programme—to make sure plenty of food was available.

We also developed plans for long-term reconstruction. We focused on ten areas: education, health, water and sanitation, electricity, shelter, transportation, governance and rule of law, agriculture, communications, and economic policy. For each, we gathered data, formulated a strategy, and set precise goals. For example, USAID determined that Iraq had 250 nonmilitary general hospitals, 20 military hospitals, 5 medical college hospitals, and 995 civilian medical care centers. Our plan called for surging medical supplies into the country, working to recruit Iraqi doctors and nurses living abroad to return home, training new medical personnel, and, ultimately, handing control to a new Iraqi health ministry.

One of the toughest questions was how to plan for a post-Saddam political system. Some in the administration suggested that we turn over power immediately to a group of Iraqi exiles. I didn't like the idea. While the exiles had close connections in Washington, I felt strongly that the Iraqis' first leader should be someone they selected. I was mindful of the British experience in Iraq in the 1920s. Great Britain had installed a non-Iraqi king, Faisal, who was viewed as illegitimate and whose appointment stoked resentment and instability. We were not going to repeat that mistake.

The other major challenge was how to provide security after Saddam. Some intelligence reports predicted that most of Saddam's army and police would switch sides once the regime was gone. The top commanders—those with innocent blood on their hands—would not be invited to rejoin. But we would draw on the rest of the Saddam-era forces to form the foundation of the new Iraqi military and police.

In January 2003, I issued a presidential directive, NSPD 24, creating a new Office of Reconstruction and Humanitarian Assistance. ORHA was charged with turning our conceptual plans into concrete action. We based the office in the Pentagon, so that our civilian efforts in Iraq would run through the same chain of command as our military operations. To lead the office, Don Rumsfeld tapped Jay Garner, a retired general who had coordinated the military's relief effort in northern Iraq in 1991. He recruited a cadre of civilian experts from across the government who would stand by to deploy to Baghdad.

By having our plans and personnel ready before the war, I felt we were well prepared. Yet we were aware of our limitations. Our nation building capabilities were limited, and no one knew for sure what needs would arise. The military had an old adage: "No battle plan survives first contact with the enemy." As we would learn in Iraq, that was doubly true of a plan for the postwar environment.

———

By March 2003, the battle plan was ready. After more than a year of probing and questioning, Tommy Franks and his team had developed an operation that I was confident would overthrow Saddam Hussein swiftly and decisively, while minimizing the loss of American and Iraqi life. The one remaining uncertainty was the role of Turkey. For months, we had been pressing the Turks to give us access to their territory so that we could send fifteen thousand troops from the Fourth Infantry Division to enter Iraq from the north. We promised to provide economic and military aid, help Turkey access key programs from the International Monetary Fund, and maintain our strong support for Turkey's admission to the European Union.

At one point, it looked like we would get permission. Prime Minister Abdullah Gül's cabinet approved our request. But when the Turkish parliament held a final vote on March 1, it came up just short of passage. I was frustrated and disappointed. On one of the most important requests we had ever made, Turkey, our NATO ally, had let America down.

Don and Tommy held the Fourth Infantry Division in the eastern Mediterranean Sea, where it could deploy through Turkey if the government changed its mind or, otherwise, join the invasion from Kuwait. We also planned to deploy a thousand paratroopers from the 173rd Airborne to the Kurdish region of northern Iraq. This wasn't our first choice, but at least we would have a foothold for a northern front.

In the south, we had more than 150,000 American troops on Iraq's border, with some 90,000 more stationed in the Gulf region. I had made it abundantly clear that we would use them if necessary. Coercive diplomacy had brought us to our maximum point of leverage. The military and diplomatic tracks had fully converged. The choice between war and peace belonged to Saddam Hussein alone.

For months, the National Security Council had been meeting almost daily to discuss Iraq. I knew where all my advisers stood. Dick Cheney was concerned about the slow diplomatic process. He warned that Saddam Hussein could be using the time to produce weapons, hide weapons, or plot an attack. At one of our weekly lunches that winter, Dick asked me directly, "Are you going to take care of this guy, or not?" That was his way of saying he thought we had given diplomacy enough time. I appreciated Dick's blunt advice. I told him I wasn't ready to move yet. "Okay, Mr. President, it's your call," he said. Then he deployed one of his favorite lines. "That's why they pay you the big bucks," he said with a gentle smile.

Don Rumsfeld was not as definitive. He assured me the military would be ready if I gave the order. He also warned that we couldn't leave 150,000 troops sitting on Iraq's border forever. The logistical strain of supporting that many forces was immense. At some point, the buildup would lose its coercive value because Saddam would conclude we weren't serious about sending the troops in.

Condi was careful to stay neutral at the NSC meetings, but she gave me her opinion in private. She had been a strong supporter of inspections. But after meeting with Blix and his team, she was convinced Saddam would do nothing but stall. She reluctantly concluded that the only way to enforce the UN resolution would be to use the military option.

Colin had the deepest reservations. In a one-on-one meeting in early 2003, he had told me he believed we could manage the threat of Iraq diplomatically. He also told me he was not fully comfortable with the war plans. That did not surprise me. The operation Tommy Franks had conceived would use about a third as many troops as we had in the Gulf War. It marked a stark departure from the belief that America could win wars only by deploying massive, decisive force—commonly known as the Powell Doctrine.

I was pleased when Colin told me he had shared his concerns about the plan with Tommy. Colin had been chairman of the Joint Chiefs during Desert Storm, and I was confident Tommy would take his input seriously. While I was still hopeful diplomacy would work, I told Colin it was possible that we would reach the point where war was the only option left. Neither of us wanted war, but I asked if he would support military action as a last resort. "If this is what you have to do," he said, "I'm with you, Mr. President."

On Sunday morning, March 16, I boarded Air Force One and winged my way to the Azores Islands, a Portuguese territory about two thirds of the way from Washington to Lisbon. I was headed to a last-minute summit on diplomatic strategy with Tony Blair, José Maria Aznar, and Prime Minister José Barroso of Portugal. With the French, Germans, and Russians opposed to the second UN resolution, and the Mexicans and Chileans unwilling to provide their votes, we all agreed the diplomatic track had reached its end. We planned to withdraw the second UN resolution Monday morning. That evening, I would give Saddam Hussein and his sons forty-eight hours to leave the country, a final opportunity to avoid war.

Tony's critical vote in parliament would come Tuesday. He told me he would resign if the vote failed, meaning that Great Britain would withdraw from the military coalition. I never imagined I would be following a British parliamentary vote so closely, let alone pulling for the Labour Party prime minister. I shook hands with my friend and his team as we left the Azores. "I hope that's not the last time we ever see them," Condi said on the walk to Air Force One.

The flight home was long and quiet. After so much planning and waiting, the moment had arrived. Unless Saddam fled the country, we would be at war in three days. I was deeply disappointed that diplomacy had failed. But I had promised the American people, our allies, and the world that we would enforce the UN resolutions. I was not going to break my word.

For months I had solicited advice, listened to a variety of opinions, and considered the counterarguments. Some believed we could contain Saddam by keeping the inspectors in Iraq. But I didn't see how. If we were to tell Saddam he had another chance—after declaring this was his last chance—we would shatter our credibility and embolden him.

Others suggested that the threat wasn't as serious as we thought. That was easy for them to say. They weren't responsible for protecting the country. I remembered the shattering pain of 9/11, a surprise attack for which we had received no warning. This time we had a warning like a blaring siren. Years of intelligence pointed overwhelmingly to the conclusion that Saddam had WMD. He had used them in the past. He had not met his responsibility to prove their destruction. He had refused to cooperate with the inspectors, even with the threat of an invasion on his doorstep. The only logical conclusion was that he was hiding WMD. And given his support of terror and his sworn hatred of America, there was no way to know where those weapons would end up.

Others alleged that America's real intent was to control Iraq's oil or satisfy Israel. Those theories were false. I was sending our troops into combat to protect the American people.

I knew the cost would be high. But inaction had a cost, too. Given everything we knew, allowing Saddam to stay in power would have amounted to an enormous gamble. I would have had to bet that either every major intelligence agency was wrong or that Saddam would have a change of heart. After seeing the horror of 9/11, that was not a chance I was willing to take. Military action was my last resort. But I believed it was necessary.

The next day, Monday, March 17, 2003, Ambassador John Negroponte withdrew the second resolution at the UN. That night, I addressed the nation from the Cross Hall of the White House. "The United Nations Security Council has not lived up to its responsibilities, so we will rise to ours," I said, ". . . Saddam Hussein and his sons must leave Iraq within forty-eight hours. Their refusal to do so will result in military conflict, commenced at a time of our choosing."

———

The next two days felt like a week. We did get some good news on Tuesday: Tony Blair had won his vote in parliament by a solid margin. Great Britain would be at our side.

George Tenet and Colin Powell kept me updated on the latest developments with Iraq. Our last-ditch hope was that Saddam would agree to go into exile. At one point, an offer from a Middle Eastern government to send Saddam to Belarus with $1 to $2 billion looked like it might gain traction. Instead, in one of his last acts, Saddam ordered the tongue of a dissident slashed out and left the man to bleed to death. The dictator of Iraq had made his decision. He chose war.

On Wednesday morning, I convened the entire National Security Council in the Situation Room, where I gave the order to launch Operation Iraqi Freedom. Six hours later, I got an unexpected call from Don Rumsfeld. He said that he had something major to discuss. He and George Tenet were on their way to the Oval Office.

"What's going on?" I asked when they arrived.

"Mr. President," George said, "we think we have a chance to kill Saddam Hussein."

What followed was one of the most extraordinary meetings of my presidency. With the full national security team gathered in the Oval Office, advisers scrambled in and out providing the latest updates from the field. A network of intelligence sources in Iraq reported that Saddam and some of his family were likely to spend the night at a complex outside Baghdad called Dora Farms. If we bombed the site, we might be able to decapitate the regime.

I was skeptical. If I ordered the airstrike, we would be departing from our well-conceived plan, which called for two days of covert operations before the air war commenced. I pictured all that could go wrong. Two F-117 bombers would have to fly unescorted over a heavily fortified city. My biggest concern was that the intelligence was a trap. What if it was not Saddam headed to Dora Farms, but a busload of kids? The first images of the war would show us killing innocent Iraqi children.

The safest course was to stick with the plan. But one thought kept recurring: By killing the dictator we might be able to end the war before it began, and spare lives. I felt a responsibility to seize this opportunity. General Myers briefed me that the planes were gassed up and the Tomahawk Land Attack Missiles were programmed. I turned to the team gathered in the Oval Office and said, "Let's go." Just after the forty-eight-hour deadline expired, the bombing began.

Condi called early the next morning. A witness had seen a man who resembled Saddam being carried out of the rubble at Dora Farms. But as the days passed, the reports changed. The operation was a harbinger of things to come. Our intent was right. The pilots performed bravely. But the intelligence was wrong.

The day after the opening shot at Dora Farms, a flurry of military activity commenced. From Iraq's southern border with Kuwait, the V Corps and First Marine Expeditionary Force started their parallel charge to Baghdad. Meanwhile, our air forces bombarded the capital. In the initial wave of the strike, more than three hundred cruise missiles—followed by stealth bombers—took out most of Saddam's military command and government headquarters. Unlike the firebombing of Dresden, the nuclear strikes on Hiroshima and Nagasaki, or the use of napalm on Vietnam, our attack spared much of Baghdad's civilian population and infrastructure. It was not only shock and awe, but one of the most precise air raids in history.

In southern Iraq, Marines deployed to protect key oil fields. Polish Special Forces and U.S. Navy SEALs secured offshore oil infrastructure. A British armored division liberated the southern city of Basra and the vital port of Umm Qasr. The oil fires and sabotage we feared never materialized, and we had cleared a path for humanitarian aid to flow into Iraq.

In northern Iraq, paratroopers seized key transit points and helped build an air bridge for supplies and humanitarian aid. With support from Kurdish forces, the Zarqawi camp was destroyed. In western Iraq, American, British, and Australian Special Forces patrolled the desert for Scud missiles and made sure Saddam never had the chance to attack Saudi Arabia, Jordan, Israel, or other allies in the region.

By the end of the second week, our troops had reached the outskirts of Baghdad. They had endured blinding sandstorms, searing heat, and heavy hazmat gear to protect against the biological or chemical attack we feared. They faced fierce resistance from Saddam's most loyal forces, who attacked from civilian vehicles and hid behind human shields. Yet they completed the fastest armored advance in the history of warfare. Along the way, they handed out candy and medicine to children and risked their lives to protect Iraqi civilians.

On April 4, Sergeant Paul Ray Smith and his men were securing a courtyard near the Baghdad airport. Saddam's Republican Guards ambushed them, wounding several of Sergeant Smith's men. Exposed to enemy fire, Sergeant Smith manned a machine gun and kept shooting until he suffered a mortal wound. The Army's after-action report revealed that he had killed fifty enemy soldiers and saved as many as one hundred Americans. For his act of bravery, Paul Ray Smith became the first soldier in the war on terror to earn the Medal of Honor. In April 2005, I presented the medal to his widow, Birgit, and young son at the White House.

The day after Sergeant Smith gave his life to secure the airport, the Third Infantry Division entered Baghdad. The First Marine Division arrived two days later. At the NSC meeting on the morning of April 9, Tommy Franks reported that the Iraqi capital could fall at any moment. My next meeting was with President Rudolf Schuster of Slovakia. His young democracy, one of forty-eight countries that had pledged military or logistical support in Iraq, had deployed a unit trained to manage the impact of a WMD attack. President Schuster had tears in his eyes as he described his nation's pride in helping liberate Iraq. I kept that moment in mind when I heard critics allege that America acted unilaterally. The false charge denigrated our allies and pissed me off.

When the meeting ended, Dan Bartlett told me I ought to take a look at the TV. I didn't keep one in the Oval Office, so I went to the area outside where my personal assistants sat. I watched as a crowd of Iraqis in Baghdad's Firdos Square cheered while a Marine vehicle dragged down a forty-foot-tall statue of Saddam.

For twenty days I had been filled with anxiety. Now I was overwhelmed with relief and pride. I was also mindful of the challenges ahead. Saddam's forces still controlled parts of northern Iraq, including his hometown of Tikrit. There were pockets of resistance from ruthless Baathist fighters called Fedayeen Saddam. And Saddam and his sons were on the run. As I told José Maria Aznar when I called to share the news, "You won't see us doing any victory dances or anything."

———

I should have followed my own advice. Tommy Franks felt it was important to show that a new phase in the war had begun. As a way to do that, I decided to give a speech aboard the USS *Abraham Lincoln*, which was returning home after ten months at sea. The five thousand sailors, airmen, and Marines aboard the carrier had supported operations in both the Afghan and Iraqi theaters.

On May 1, 2003, I climbed into the seat of a military jet for the first time in more than thirty years. Navy pilot Scott Zellem, known by his call sign as Z-Man, briefed us on the safety procedures at Naval Air Station North Island in San Diego.* Commander John "Skip" Lussier, a fine pilot with more than five hundred carrier landings on his résumé, got our S-3B Viking off the ground. At one point, he handed the controls to me, and I flew the jet for a few minutes over the Pacific Ocean. I was rusty, but after a few porpoises I steadied out. The commander wisely took over as we approached the carrier. He guided the plane down to the deck and caught the final arresting wire.

Aboard the *Lincoln*, I visited with the landing crew, marveled at take-offs and landings in the catapult zone, and ate chow with the sailors and Marines. "My fellow Americans," I said in my speech, "Major combat operations in Iraq have ended. . . . The transition from dictatorship to democracy will take time, but it is worth every effort. Our coalition will stay until our work is done. Then we will leave, and we will leave behind a free Iraq."

I hadn't noticed the large banner my staff had placed on the bridge of the ship, positioned for TV. It read "Mission Accomplished." It was intended as a tribute to the folks aboard the *Lincoln*, which had just completed the longest deployment for an aircraft carrier of its class. Instead, it looked like I was doing the victory dance I had warned against. "Mission Accomplished" became a shorthand criticism for all that subsequently went wrong in Iraq. My speech made clear that our work was far from done. But all the explaining in the world could not reverse the perception. Our stagecraft had gone awry. It was a big mistake.

———

With Saddam gone from power, our central objective became helping the Iraqis develop a democracy that could govern itself, sustain itself, defend itself, and serve as an ally in the war on terror. The objective was ambitious, but I was optimistic. Many of the dire contingencies we had planned for and worried about before the war had not come to pass. There had been no Fortress Baghdad, no massive oil field fires, no

---

*Tragically, Lieutenant Commander Zellem died in a training accident in 2004.

widespread starvation, no civilian massacre by Saddam, no WMD attack on our troops, and no terrorist attack on America or our allies.

There was one important contingency for which we had not adequately prepared. In the weeks after liberation, Baghdad descended into a state of lawlessness. I was appalled to see looters carrying precious artifacts out of Iraq's national museum and to read reports of kidnapping, murder, and rape. Part of the explanation was that Saddam had released tens of thousands of criminals shortly before the war. But the problem was deeper than that. Saddam had warped the psychology of Iraqis in a way we didn't fully understand. The suspicion and fear that he had cultivated for decades were rising to the surface.

"What the hell is happening?" I asked during an NSC meeting in late April. "Why isn't anybody stopping these looters?"

The short answer was that there was a manpower shortage in Baghdad. The Iraqi police force had collapsed when the regime fell. The Iraqi army had melted away. Because of Turkey's decision, many of the American troops who liberated Baghdad had been required to continue north to free the rest of the country. The damage done in those early days created problems that would linger for years. The Iraqis were looking for someone to protect them. By failing to secure Baghdad, we missed our first chance to show that we could.

The security vacuum was accompanied by a political vacuum. I decided to name an American administrator to provide order while we worked to develop a legitimate government. The idea grew into the Coalition Provisional Authority, authorized by a United Nations resolution and led by a distinguished foreign service officer and counterterrorism expert, Ambassador L. Paul "Jerry" Bremer.

Jerry impressed me from the start. He was an aggressive leader who shared my conviction that the Iraqis were capable of democracy. He knew it would take time for them to write a constitution and prepare for elections. In one of our first meetings, he told me he'd read a study of previous postwar operations and thought we needed more troops in Iraq.

I raised the question of troop levels with Don Rumsfeld and the military leadership. They assured me we had enough. They anticipated the arrival of more forces from Coalition partners and believed we could train an Iraqi army and police force fairly quickly. They were also concerned about stirring up Iraqi nationalism and inciting violence by appearing to occupy the country.

I accepted Don and the military's judgment. The chaos and violence we witnessed was alarming, but it was still early. The situation reminded me of the difficult first days in Afghanistan. I refused to give up on our plan before it had a chance to work.

Bremer arrived in Iraq on May 12, 2003. One of his first tasks was to assemble an Iraqi Governing Council that would take responsibility for key ministries and prepare for a formal return of sovereignty. Navigating Iraq's tribal, religious, and ethnic politics was highly complicated. But Jerry and his team did a superb job. The Governing Council took office in July, just four months after liberation. It included twenty-five Iraqis from all backgrounds. Iraqis still had a long way to go, but they had taken their first step toward a representative government.

Forming the Governing Council was an important way to demonstrate that Saddam's tyranny was gone forever. With that in mind, Jerry issued two orders shortly after his arrival in Baghdad. One declared that certain members of Saddam's Baath Party would not be eligible to serve in the new government of Iraq. The other formally disbanded the Iraqi army, which had largely disappeared on its own.

In some ways, the orders achieved their objectives. Iraq's Shia and Kurds—the majority of the population—welcomed the clean break from Saddam. But the orders had a psychological impact I did not foresee. Many Sunnis took them as a signal they would have no place in Iraq's future. This was especially dangerous in the case of the army. Thousands of armed men had just been told they were not wanted. Instead of signing up for the new military, many joined the insurgency.

In retrospect, I should have insisted on more debate on Jerry's orders, especially on what message disbanding the army would send and how many Sunnis the de-Baathification would affect. Overseen by longtime exile Ahmed Chalabi, the de-Baathification program turned out to cut much deeper than we expected, including mid-level party members like teachers. It is possible we would have issued the orders anyway. They were tough calls, and any alternative would have created a separate set of problems. Had the Shia concluded that we were not serious about ending the era of the Baath Party, they may have turned against the coalition, rejected the goal of a unified Iraqi democracy, and aligned themselves with Iran. There is no way to know for sure what would have happened, but the discussion would have better prepared us for what followed.

———

The security situation continued to deteriorate over the summer. Iraq was becoming a magnet for extremists—Baathist insurgents, Fedayeen Saddam, foreign terrorists affiliated with al Qaeda, and, later, militant Shia and agents of Iran. These groups had different ideologies, but they shared an immediate goal: to drive America out of Iraq. They knew they could never win a direct fight against our troops, so they deployed roadside bombs and attacked nonmilitary targets such as the Jordanian embassy and the UN complex in Baghdad. Another tactic was to kidnap reconstruction workers and execute them in grisly Internet videos. Their strategy was to present an image of Iraq as hopeless and unwinnable, swinging American public opinion against the war and forcing us to withdraw as we had in Vietnam.

To an extent, they succeeded. It was difficult for the average American to differentiate the twisted terrorists from the millions of ordinary Iraqis who were grateful for liberation. We tried to get the good news out—the relative calm in the Kurdish north and Shia south, the rebuilding of schools and hospitals, and the training of a new Iraqi army. But in the eyes of the media—and, therefore, of the public—none of this quiet progress could compete with the bombings and the beheadings.

In early July, a reporter asked me about attacks on our troops. "There are some who feel like that if they attack us that we may decide to leave prematurely," I said. ". . . My answer is: Bring 'em on."

Anytime I spoke on Iraq, there were multiple audiences listening, each of which had a different perspective. I thought about four in particular.

The first audience was the American people. Their support was essential to funding and fighting the war. I believed that most Americans wanted to win in Iraq. But if the cost seemed too high or victory too distant, they would grow weary. It was important for me to reinforce the importance of the cause and our determination to prevail.

The second audience was our troops. They had volunteered to serve and were risking their lives far from home. They and their families needed to know I believed in them, stood firmly behind their mission, and would not make military decisions based on politics.

The third audience was the Iraqi people. Some wanted us gone, but I was convinced that the vast majority of Iraqis wanted us to stay long enough to help a democratic society emerge. It was important that I communicate my resolve to complete the work we had begun. If Iraqis suspected we were going to abandon them, they would turn to other sources of protection.

The final audience was the enemy. They believed their acts of savagery could affect our decisions. I had to make clear they never would.

My "bring 'em on" comment was intended to show confidence in our troops and signal that the enemy could never shake our will. But the firestorm of criticism showed that I had left a wrong impression with other audiences. I learned from the experience and paid closer attention to how I communicated with each audience in the years ahead.

---

By the fall of 2003, the international coalition in Iraq was comprised of ground forces from thirty countries, including two multinational divisions led by Great Britain and Poland, and logistical support from many others. Coalition forces had discovered torture chambers, rape rooms, and mass graves containing thousands of bodies. They found a facility containing state-of-the-art hazmat suits and syringes with the antidote for VX nerve agent. But they had not found the stockpiles of biological and chemical weapons that virtually every major intelligence agency in the world believed Saddam had.

When Saddam didn't use WMD on our troops, I was relieved. When we didn't discover the stockpile soon after the fall of Baghdad, I was surprised. When the whole summer passed without finding any, I was alarmed. The press corps constantly raised the question, "Where are the WMD?"

I was asking the same thing. The military and intelligence teams assured me they were looking constantly. They examined hidden sites Saddam had used during the Gulf War. They collected intelligence and responded to tips. At one point, the CIA heard that large canisters had been spotted from a bridge over the Euphrates River. Navy frogmen deployed to the scene. They found nothing. A high-ranking official from the United Arab Emirates brought drawings of tunnels he believed Saddam had used to hide weapons. We dug up the ground. Nothing materialized.

George Tenet recruited David Kay, the UN's chief weapons inspector in Iraq in 1991, to lead a new inspections team. Kay conducted a thorough search of Iraq and found irrefutable evidence that Saddam had lied to the world and violated Resolution 1441. "Iraq's WMD programs spanned more than two decades, involved thousands of people, billions of dollars, and were elaborately shielded by security and deception operations that continued even beyond the end of Operation Iraqi Freedom," he told Congress in October 2003. But there was one thing Kay did not find: the WMD stockpiles everyone expected.

The left trotted out a new mantra: "Bush Lied, People Died." The charge was illogical. If I wanted to mislead the country into war, why would I pick an allegation that was certain to be disproven publicly shortly after we invaded the country? The charge was also dishonest. Members of the previous administration, John Kerry, John Edwards, and the vast majority of Congress had all read the same intelligence that I had and concluded Iraq had WMD. So had intelligence agencies around the world. Nobody was lying. We were all wrong. The absence of WMD stockpiles did not change the fact that Saddam was a threat. In January 2004, David Kay said, "It was reasonable to conclude that Iraq posed an imminent threat. . . . What we learned during the inspection made Iraq a more dangerous place potentially than in fact we thought it was even before the war."

Still, I knew the failure to find WMD would transform public perception of the war. While the world was undoubtedly safer with Saddam gone, the reality was that I had sent American troops into combat based in large part on intelligence that proved false. That was a massive blow to our credibility—my credibility—that would shake the confidence of the American people.

No one was more shocked or angry than I was when we didn't find the weapons. I had a sickening feeling every time I thought about it. I still do.

While the fight in Iraq was more difficult than I expected, I remained optimistic. I was inspired by the courage of the one hundred thousand Iraqis who volunteered to join their security forces, by leaders who stepped forward to replace members of the Governing Council who had been assassinated, and by ordinary people who longed for freedom.

Nothing gave me more confidence than our troops. Thanks to them, most of the senior members of Saddam's regime had been captured or killed by the end of 2003. In July, we got an intelligence tip that Saddam's two sons were in the Mosul area of northern Iraq. Joined by Special Forces, troops from the 101st Airborne under the command of General David Petraeus laid siege to the building where Hussein's sons, Uday and Qusay, were hiding. After a six-hour firefight, both were dead. We later received intelligence that Saddam had ordered the killing of Barbara and Jenna in return for the death of his sons.

Two days after the fall of Baghdad, Laura and I visited Walter Reed Army Medical Center in Washington and the National Naval Medical Center in Bethesda. We met with almost a hundred wounded service members and their families. Some were from Afghanistan; many were from Iraq. It was a heart-wrenching experience to look into a hospital bed and see the consequences of sending Americans into combat. One comfort was that I knew they would receive superb medical care from the skilled and compassionate professionals of the military health-care system.

At Walter Reed, I met a member of the Delta Team, one of our elite Special Forces units. For classification reasons, I cannot give his name. He had lost the lower half of his leg. "I appreciate your service," I said as I shook his hand. "I'm sorry you got hurt."

"Don't feel sorry for me, Mr. President," he replied. "Just get me another leg so I can go back in."

At the National Naval Medical Center, I met forty-two-year-old Marine Master Gunnery Sergeant Guadalupe Denogean. He had been wounded a few weeks earlier, when a rocket-propelled grenade struck his vehicle. The explosion blew off part of his skull and his right hand; shrapnel penetrated his upper back and legs, and his eardrums burst.

When asked if he had any requests, Guadalupe said he had two. He asked for a promotion for the corporal who had saved his life. And he wanted to become an American citizen. After 9/11, I had issued an executive order making all foreign nationals serving in the military eligible for immediate citizenship.

Guadalupe had come to the United States from Mexico as a boy. He picked fruit to help his family make a living until he joined the Marines at age seventeen. After serving for twenty-five years—and deploying for two wars with Iraq—he wanted the flag on his uniform to be his own. That day in the hospital, Laura and I attended his naturalization ceremony, conducted by Director Eduardo Aguirre of the Bureau of Citizenship and Immigration Services. Guadalupe raised his right hand, covered in bandages, and swore the oath of citizenship.

A few moments later, he was followed by Marine Lance Corporal O.J. Santamaria, a native of the Philippines. He was twenty-one years old and had suffered a serious wound in Iraq. He was hooked up to an intravenous blood transfusion. About halfway through the ceremony, he broke down in tears. He powered through to the end of the oath. I was proud to respond, "My fellow American."

———

In the fall of 2003, Andy Card came to me with an idea. Was I interested in making a trip to Iraq to thank the troops? You bet I was.

The risk was high. But Deputy Chief of Staff Joe Hagin, working with the Secret Service and White House Military Office, came up with a way to pull it off. The week of Thanksgiving, I would travel to Crawford and tell the press I was staying for the full holiday. Then, on Wednesday night, I would slip out of the ranch and fly to Baghdad.

I told Laura several weeks ahead of the trip. She was reassured when I told her we would abort the trip if news of it leaked. I told Barbara and Jenna about thirty minutes before I left. "I'm scared, Dad," Barbara said. "Be safe. Come home."

Condi and I climbed into an unmarked Suburban, our baseball caps pulled low, and headed for the airport. To maintain secrecy, there was no motorcade. I had nearly forgotten what a traffic jam felt like, but riding on I-35 the day before Thanksgiving brought the memories back. We crept along, passing an occasional car full of counterassault agents, and made it to Air Force One on schedule. Timeliness was important. We needed to land as the sun was setting in Baghdad.

We flew from Texas to Andrews Air Force Base, where we switched to the twin version of Air Force One and took off for Iraq. The plane carried a skeleton crew of staff, military and Secret Service personnel, and a press contingent sworn to secrecy. I slept little on the ten-and-a-half-hour flight. As we neared Baghdad, I showered, shaved, and headed to the cockpit to watch the landing. Colonel Mark Tillman manned the controls. I trusted him completely. As Laura always put it, "That Mark can sure land this plane."

With the sun dropping on the horizon, I could make out the minarets of the Baghdad skyline. The city seemed so serene from above. But we were concerned about surface-to-air missiles on the ground. While Joe Hagin assured us the military had cleared a wide perimeter around Baghdad International Airport, the mood aboard the plane was anxious. As we descended in a corkscrew pattern with the shades drawn, some staffers joined together in a prayer session. At the last moment, Colonel Tillman leveled out the plane and kissed the runway, no sweat.

Waiting for me at the airport were Jerry Bremer and General Ricardo Sanchez, the senior ground commander in Iraq. "Welcome to a free Iraq," Jerry said.

We went to the mess hall, where six hundred troops had gathered for a Thanksgiving meal. Jerry was supposed to be the guest of honor. He told the troops he had a holiday message from the president. "Let's see if we've got anybody more senior here . . . ," he said.

That was my cue. I walked out from behind a curtain and onto the stage of the packed hall. Many of the stunned troops hesitated for a split second, then let out deafening whoops and hooahs. Some had tears running down their faces. I was swept up by the emotion. These were the souls who just eight months earlier had liberated Iraq on my orders. Many had seen combat. Some had seen friends perish. I took a deep breath and said, "I bring a message on behalf of America. We thank you for your service, we're proud of you, and America stands solidly behind you."

After the speech, I had dinner with the troops and moved to a side room to meet with four members of the Governing Council, the mayor of Baghdad, and members of the city council. One woman, the director of a maternity hospital, told me how women had more opportunities now than they had ever dreamed about under Saddam. I knew Iraq still faced big problems, but the trip reinforced my faith that they could be overcome.

The most dangerous part left was the takeoff from Baghdad. We were told to keep all lights out and maintain total telephone silence until we hit ten thousand feet. I was still on an emotional high. But the exhilaration of the moment was replaced by an eerie feeling of uncertainty as we blasted off the ground and climbed silently through the night.

After a few tense minutes, we reached a safe altitude. I called one of the operators on the plane and asked him to connect me with Laura. "Where are you?" she asked. "I am on the way home," I said. "Tell the girls all is well."

She sounded relieved. It turns out she'd had a little mix-up with the timing. She couldn't remember whether I said I would be in the air at 10:00 a.m. or noon. At 10:15, she had called a Secret Service agent at the ranch and asked if he had heard from President Bush. "Let me check," the agent said.

A few seconds passed. "Yes, ma'am," he replied. "They are ninety minutes away."

She realized he was talking about Mother and Dad, who were on their way to spend Thanksgiving with us. "No, I mean my George," she said. The agent paused. "Well, ma'am," he said, "we show he is in the ranch house."

Secrecy was so tight that the agents on the ranch were still unaware that I had slipped away for the most thrilling trip of my presidency.

---

On Saturday, December 13, Don Rumsfeld called. He had just spoken to General John Abizaid, who had replaced Tommy Franks after his retirement in July. John was a cerebral, Lebanese American general who spoke Arabic and understood the Middle East. John believed we had captured

Saddam Hussein. Before we announced it to the world, we had to be 100 percent sure.

The next morning, Condi called back to confirm the report. It was Saddam. His tattoos—three blue dots near his wrist, a symbol of his tribe—provided the telltale evidence. I was elated. Getting Saddam would be a big lift for our troops and for the American people. It would also make a psychological difference for the Iraqis, many of whom feared he would return. Now it was clear: The era of the dictator was over forever.

Several months later, four men came to see me at the White House. They were members of the Delta Team that had captured Saddam. They told me the story of the hunt. Intelligence pointed them to a farm near Saddam's hometown of Tikrit. As the soldiers combed the grounds, one discovered a hole. He climbed in and pulled out a disheveled, angry man.

"My name is Saddam Hussein," the man said. "I am the president of Iraq and I want to negotiate."

"Regards from President Bush," the soldier replied.

Saddam had three weapons with him, including a pistol that the men presented to me in a glass box. I told them I would display the gift in the private study off the Oval Office and one day in my presidential library. The pistol always reminded me that a brutal dictator, responsible for so much death and suffering, had surrendered to our troops while cowering in a hole.

As I record these thoughts more than seven years after American troops liberated Iraq, I strongly believe that removing Saddam from power was the right decision. For all the difficulties that followed, America is safer without a homicidal dictator pursuing WMD and supporting terror at the heart of the Middle East. The region is more hopeful with a young democracy setting an example for others to follow. And the Iraqi people are better off with a government that answers to them instead of torturing and murdering them.

As we hoped, the liberation of Iraq had an impact beyond its borders. Six days after Saddam's capture, Colonel Muammar Qaddafi of Libya—a longtime enemy of America and state sponsor of terror—publicly confessed that he had been developing chemical and nuclear weapons. He pledged to dismantle his WMD programs, along with related missiles, under a system of strict international verification. It's possible the timing was a coincidence. But I don't think so.

The war also led to consequences we did not intend. Over the years, I've spent a great deal of time thinking about what went wrong in Iraq and why. I have concluded that we made two errors that account for many of the setbacks we faced.

The first is that we did not respond more quickly or aggressively when the security situation started to deteriorate after Saddam's regime fell. In the ten months following the invasion, we cut troop levels from 192,000 to 109,000. Many of the remaining troops focused on training the Iraqi army and police, not protecting the Iraqi people. We worried we would create resentment by looking like occupiers. We believed we could train Iraqi security forces to lead the fight. And we thought progress toward a representative democracy, giving Iraqis of all backgrounds a stake in their country, was the best path to lasting security.

While there was logic behind these assumptions, the Iraqi people's desire for security trumped their aversion to occupation. One of the ironies of the war is that we were criticized harshly by the left and some in the international community for wanting to build an empire in Iraq. We never sought that. In fact, we were so averse to anything that looked like an empire that we made our job far more difficult. By reducing our troop presence and focusing on training Iraqis, we inadvertently allowed the insurgency to gain momentum. Then al Qaeda fighters flocked to Iraq seeking a new safe haven, which made our mission both more difficult and more important.

Cutting troop levels too quickly was the most important failure of execution in the war. Ultimately, we adapted our strategy and fixed the problems, despite almost universal pressure to abandon Iraq. It took four painful, costly years to do so. At the time, progress felt excruciatingly slow. But history's perspective is broader. If Iraq is a functioning democracy fifty years from now, those four hard years might look a lot different.

The other error was the intelligence failure on Iraq's WMD. Almost a decade later, it is hard to describe how widespread an assumption it was that Saddam had WMD. Supporters of the war believed it; opponents of the war believed it; even members of Saddam's own regime believed it. We all knew that intelligence is never 100 percent certain; that's the nature of the business. But I believed that the intelligence on Iraq's WMD was solid. If Saddam didn't have WMD, why wouldn't he just prove it to the inspectors? Every psychological profile I had read told me Saddam was a survivor. If he cared so much about staying in power, why would he gamble his regime by pretending to have WMD?

Part of the explanation came after Saddam's capture, when he was debriefed by the FBI. He told agents that he was more worried about looking weak to Iran than being removed by the coalition. He never thought the United States would follow through on our promises to disarm him by force. I'm not sure what more I could have done to show Saddam I meant what I said. I named him part of an axis of evil in my State of the Union address. I spoke to a packed chamber of the United Nations and promised to disarm him by force if diplomacy failed. We presented him with a unanimous Security Council resolution. We sought and received strong bipartisan backing from the U.S. Congress. We deployed 150,000 troops to his border. I gave him a final forty-eight-hours' notice that we were about to invade his country. How much clearer could I have been?

It's true that Saddam was getting mixed signals from France, Germany, and Russia—and from antiwar demonstrators around the world. That didn't help. But the war is not their fault. There was one person with the power to avoid war, and he chose not to use it. For all his deception of the world, the person Saddam ultimately deceived the most was himself.

I decided early on that I would not criticize the hardworking patriots at the CIA for the faulty intelligence on Iraq. I did not want to repeat the nasty finger-pointing investigations that devastated the morale of the intelligence community in the 1970s. But I did want to know why the information I received was wrong and how we could prevent a similar mistake in the future. I appointed a nonpartisan commission co-chaired by Judge Larry Silberman and former Democratic Senator Chuck Robb to study the question. Their investigation produced valuable recommendations—such as increasing coordination between agencies and publishing more dissenting opinions—that will make intelligence more reliable for future presidents, without undermining our intelligence community's ability to do its job.

———

The nature of history is that we know the consequences only of the action we took. But inaction would have had consequences, too. Imagine what the world would look like today with Saddam Hussein still ruling Iraq. He would still be threatening his neighbors, sponsoring terror, and piling bodies into mass graves. The rising price of oil—which jumped from just over $30 a barrel in 2003 to almost $140 five years later—would have left Saddam awash in wealth. The sanctions, already falling apart, almost certainly would have crumbled. Saddam still had the infrastructure and know-how to make WMD. And as the final weapons inspections report by Charles Duelfer concluded, "Saddam wanted to re-create Iraq's WMD capability . . . after sanctions were removed and Iraq's economy stabilized."

Had Saddam followed through on that intention, the world would likely have witnessed a nuclear arms race between Iraq and Iran. Saddam could have turned to Sunni terrorist groups like al Qaeda—a marriage of convenience, not ideology—as surrogates in an attempt to match Iran's use of Shia terrorist groups like Hezbollah. The chance of biological, chemical, or nuclear weapons falling into the hands of terrorists would have increased. The pressure on our friends in the region—especially Israel, Kuwait, Saudi Arabia, and the United Arab Emirates—would have been intense. And the American people would be much less secure today.

Instead, as a result of our actions in Iraq, one of America's most committed and dangerous enemies stopped threatening us forever. The most volatile region in the world lost one of its greatest sources of violence and mayhem. Hostile nations around the world saw the cost of supporting terror and pursuing WMD. And in the space of nine months, twenty-five million Iraqis went from living under a dictatorship of fear to seeing the prospect of a peaceful, functioning democracy. In December 2003, the Iraqis were still a long way from that dream. But they had a chance, and that was a lot more than they'd had before.

The hardest days of the war were still ahead. In January 2004, our troops intercepted a letter from Zarqawi to senior al Qaeda leaders. He wrote about the growing pressure he was feeling and laid out his plan for survival. "We need to bring the Shia into the battle," he wrote, "because it is the only way to prolong the duration of the fight between the infidels and us." He set a new goal for the jihadists in Iraq—igniting "a sectarian war."

# 9

# LEADING

"Tonight in this hall, we resolve to be the party not of repose but of reform. We will write not footnotes but chapters in the American story. We will add the work of our hands to the inheritance of our fathers and mothers and leave this nation greater than we found it. . . . If you give me your trust, I will honor it. Grant me a mandate, I will use it. Give me the opportunity to lead this nation, and I will lead."

I meant the words I spoke at the Republican National Convention in 2000. When I entered politics, I made a decision: I would confront problems, not pass them on to future generations. I admired presidents who used their time in office to enact transformative change. I had studied Theodore Roosevelt, who served in the White House almost exactly a century before me. He had taken on the financial trusts, built a powerful Navy, and launched the conservation movement. I also learned from Ronald Reagan, who combined an optimistic demeanor with the moral clarity and conviction to cut taxes, strengthen the military, and face down the Soviet Union despite withering criticism throughout his presidency.

One of the lessons I took from Roosevelt and Reagan was to lead the public, not chase the opinion polls. I decided to push for sweeping reforms, not tinker with the status quo. As I told my advisers, "I didn't take this job to play small ball."

———

Two weeks after we moved into the White House, Laura and I held our first movie night in the Family Theater. Situated on the ground floor of the White House, the theater features forty-six comfortable chairs and a ninety-three-square-foot projection screen. The Motion Picture Association of America, led for years by a fascinating Texan, Jack Valenti, generously made movies available to the first family. We never had to sit through coming attractions.

For our first screening, Laura and I chose *Thirteen Days*, about President Kennedy's handling of the Cuban Missile Crisis. The movie was a fitting choice for our guest of honor, Senator Ted Kennedy of Massachusetts.

On the surface, Ted and I didn't have a whole lot in common. He was liberal; I was conservative. He grew up on Cape Cod; I was raised in West Texas. He had spent almost forty years on Capitol Hill; I was relatively new to town.

Ted and I did share what Laura called the family business. My grandfather Prescott Bush had represented Connecticut in the Senate at the same time John F. Kennedy had represented Massachusetts. Laura and I enjoyed meeting Ted's wife, Vicki; son Patrick, a congressman from Rhode Island; and niece Kathleen Kennedy Townsend, the lieutenant governor of Maryland, along with her daughter Kate.

Ted was friendly, gracious, and full of life. He had the trademark Kennedy accent and a great Irish glow. His smile came easily and often gave way to a big, warm laugh. I felt a connection to history as we watched a movie about how his brothers had defused a crisis from the West Wing.

The movie hadn't been my only purpose for inviting Ted. He was the ranking Democrat on the Senate committee that drafted education legislation. He had sent signals that he was interested in my school reform proposal, No Child Left Behind.

Ted and I were both appalled by the results coming from our public schools. In the competitive global economy, good jobs demanded knowledge and skills. But American students routinely trailed their peers in key subjects. On an international math test comparing twenty-one countries, America's high school seniors placed ahead of only Cyprus and South Africa.

Part of the problem was that millions of children were shuffled from one grade to the next without anybody asking what they had learned. Many came from poor and minority backgrounds. In 2000, nearly

70 percent of fourth-graders from high-poverty backgrounds couldn't read at grade level. Some 40 percent of minority students failed to finish high school in four years. How could a society that promised equal opportunity for all quit on its neediest citizens? Starting in the 2000 campaign I had called the problem "the soft bigotry of low expectations." I had promised to take on the big issues. This was sure one of them.

In recent years, the national education debate had bogged down in modest proposals like school uniforms and unrealistic calls to abolish the Department of Education. Success was often defined by dollars spent, not results achieved. I had come from a world where accountability was a daily reality. In baseball, any interested party can open the newspaper, analyze your performance in a box score, and demand change. "More pitching, Bush!" was a familiar refrain. Education was a lot more important than baseball, yet most people had no idea how their schools were performing.

As governor, I worked with the legislature to pass a law requiring schools to test students on the basics every year, report the results publicly, and allow parents to transfer their children out of underperforming schools. Between 1994 and 1998, the percentage of third-graders performing at grade level grew from 58 to 76. Minority students showed the largest gains, closing the achievement gap with their white peers.

When I ran for president, I decided to propose federal legislation that set clear goals—every child would learn to read and do math at grade level—and held schools accountable for progress. Under No Child Left Behind, states would test students in reading and math every year between third and eighth grade, and once in high school. Schools would post scores publicly, broken down by ethnicity, income level, and other subcategories. The data would allow parents and concerned citizens to evaluate schools, teachers, and curricula. Schools that scored below standards would receive extra help at first, including money for students to attend after-school tutoring, public or private. But if schools repeatedly failed to make adequate progress, there would be consequences. Parents would have the option to transfer their child to a better-performing public or charter school. The principle was straightforward: You cannot solve a problem until you diagnose it. Accountability would serve as a catalyst for reform.

I highlighted No Child Left Behind at almost every campaign event, including the NAACP convention. I told reporters I hoped to be known as "the education president." I told Ted Kennedy the same thing the night we watched *Thirteen Days*. "I don't know about you, but I like to surprise people," I said. "Let's show them Washington can still get things done."

The next morning, a letter arrived in the Oval Office:

*Dear Mr. President,*

*You and Mrs. Bush couldn't have been more gracious and generous to Vicki and me and the members of our family last night and these past few days. I very much appreciate your thoughtful consideration. Like you, I have every intention of getting things done, particularly in education and health care. We will have a difference or two along the way, but I look forward to some important Rose Garden signings.*

*Warm Regards,*
*Ted Kennedy*

I was excited. No Child Left Behind stood a much better chance of becoming law with support from the Lion of the Senate. It was the beginning of my most unlikely partnership in Washington.

———

Ted Kennedy was not the only legislator I courted. Over my first two weeks in office, I met with more than 150 members of Congress from both parties. I hoped to replicate the productive relationship I'd forged with Bob Bullock, Pete Laney, and other legislators in Texas. One news story began, "If relations between Congress and the White House soon deteriorate into bitterness-as-usual, it won't be for lack of effort to avoid that by President Bush." Another suggested that I was conducting "the biggest charm offensive of any modern chief executive."

Whatever the press called my effort, both houses of Congress soon took up No Child Left Behind. By March, the Senate education committee had completed a bill that included all the key elements of my proposal. The House moved next. Congressman John Boehner of Ohio, the skilled

Republican chairman of the House Education Committee, collaborated on a solid bill with Congressman George Miller of California, one of the chamber's most liberal members. The House passed it by a vote of 384 to 45.

The process of reconciling the House and Senate bills dragged through the summer. When Congress returned from recess in early September, I set out to reenergize the debate with two days of school visits in Florida. Laura agreed to give her first-ever testimony on Capitol Hill. As a teacher and librarian, she had great credibility on education. Her appearance was scheduled for September 11, 2001.

By the end of that morning, it was clear I would not be the education president. I was a war president. Throughout the fall, I urged Congress to finish No Child Left Behind. Ted Kennedy gave a courageous speech defending accountability in front of the National Education Association, a teachers' group that contributed heavily to Democrats and strongly opposed the bill. Senator Judd Gregg and Congressman Boehner, once an advocate of abolishing the Education Department, rallied Republicans who were anxious about the federal role in education. Like me, they argued that if we were going to spend money on schools, we ought to know the results it produced. A week before Christmas, Congress passed No Child Left Behind by a bipartisan landslide.

———

Over the years, No Child Left Behind prompted plenty of controversy. Governors and state education officials complained that the bureaucracy was too rigid and that too many schools were labeled as failing. When Margaret Spellings became education secretary in 2005, she modified bureaucratic restrictions and increased flexibility for states. But we both made clear we would not dilute the accountability measures. The purpose of the law was to reveal the truth, even when it was unpleasant.

Some critics said it was unfair to test students every year. I thought it was unfair not to. Measuring progress was the only way to find out which students needed help. Others complained about what they called "teaching to the test." But if the test was well designed to measure knowledge of a subject, all the schools had to do was teach that subject.

Another common claim was that No Child Left Behind was underfunded. That's hard to believe, given that we raised federal education spending by 39 percent over my eight years in office, with much of the extra money going to the poorest students and schools.*

On a more fundamental level, the critics who complained about the money missed the point of No Child Left Behind. The premise of the law is that success cannot be measured by dollars spent; it has to be judged by results achieved.

By the time I left office, fourth- and eighth-grade math scores had reached their highest levels in history. So had fourth-grade reading scores. Hispanic and African American students set new records in multiple categories. The gap had narrowed in exactly the way we wanted: All students improved, but minority students improved the most.

In January 2008, I visited Horace Greeley Elementary School in Chicago to mark the sixth anniversary of No Child Left Behind. The school, named for the nineteenth-century abolitionist, was 70 percent Hispanic and 92 percent poor. It had outperformed most public schools in Chicago. Student proficiency in reading had risen from 51 percent in 2003 to 76 percent in 2007. Math proficiency had improved from 59 percent to 86 percent.

It was uplifting to see a school full of low-income minority students thrive. A sixth-grader, Yesenia Adame, said she enjoyed taking tests. "Then your teachers can know what you need help on," she explained. At the end of my visit, I told students, parents, and the press what I had long believed: No Child Left Behind is a piece of civil rights legislation.

---

I used to quip that I was a product of a faith-based program. By 1986, faith had changed my heart, and I had quit drinking. Ten years later, my eyes opened to the potential of faith-based programs to transform public policy.

In June 1996, two African American churches in the town of

*The increases in federal education funding were significant, since my budget restrained non-security discretionary spending and eventually held it below the rate of inflation. States continued to contribute the vast majority of education funding—about 92 percent—and that's how it should be.

Greenville, Texas, were burned. Until 1965, a sign on the town's main street had advertised "The Blackest Land, The Whitest People." As governor, I feared we were witnessing a surge in old-time racism.

I traveled to Greenville to condemn the burnings. A mixed-race crowd of about four thousand people turned out in the football stadium. "From time to time, Texans boast that ours is a big state." I said. "But as big as this state is, it has no room for cowardice and hatred and bigotry." Then I gave the microphone to Tony Evans, a dynamic African American pastor from Oak Cliff Bible Fellowship in Dallas. He told a story about a house with a crack in the wall. The owner hired a plasterer to cover the crack. A week later, the crack reappeared. So he hired another plasterer. A week later, the crack was back again. Finally the homeowner called an old painter, who took one look and said, "Son, first fix the foundation and then you can fix the crack in the wall."

The crowd nodded and clapped. Then Tony turned to me. "Governor, I have something to say to you," he said.

*Uh-oh*, I thought. *Where is this headed?*

"We need to fix the foundations," he said, "and your old government programs aren't doing the job." He said he had a better alternative. It was the most effective welfare system in the world. It had buildings on many street corners, a list of willing workers, and regular meetings to study the perfect manual for saving lives.

He was talking about houses of worship. And he was right. Faith-based programs had the potential to change lives in ways secular ones never could. "Government can hand out money," I said, "but it cannot put hope in a person's heart or a sense of purpose in a person's life."

I looked for ways for Texas to partner with faith-based organizations. I met with Chuck Colson, Richard Nixon's White House counsel, who had spent time in a federal penitentiary and found redemption. Chuck had founded an organization devoted to spreading the Gospel behind bars. We agreed to start a faith-based program in one wing of a Texas prison. Chuck's program, the InnerChange Freedom Initiative, would provide instructors for Bible study and a life lessons course. The program would be optional and open to prisoners near the end of their sentences. Each inmate who participated would be connected with a mentor and welcomed into a church congregation upon release.

In October 1997, I visited the Jester II prison near Sugar Land, Texas, where several dozen inmates had enrolled in InnerChange. At the end of the tour, a group of men in white jumpsuits filed into the courtyard. They formed a semicircle and struck up "Amazing Grace." After a few stanzas, I joined the chorus.

The next morning, Karen Hughes brought me the *Houston Chronicle*. There I was on the front page, shoulder to shoulder with the prison choir. The story noted that the man next to me, George Mason, had pled guilty to killing a woman twelve years earlier. That day in the prison yard, he did not seem like a murderer. He had a gentle manner and a kind smile. No question he had become a spirit-filled man.

———

When I ran for president, I decided to make a nationwide faith-based initiative a central part of my campaign. In my first major policy speech, delivered in Indianapolis, I said, "In every instance where my administration sees a responsibility to help people, we will look first to faith-based organizations, to charities, and to community groups."

Nine days after my inauguration, I issued executive orders creating an Office of Faith-Based and Community Initiatives in the White House and in five Cabinet departments. The offices changed regulations and broke down barriers that had prevented faith-based charities from accessing the federal grant-making process. To emphasize the initiative's nonpartisan nature, I appointed Democrats to serve as the first two directors. One was John Dilulio, an innovative professor from the University of Pennsylvania. The other was Jim Towey, a thoroughly decent man who had led Florida's social services department and served as Mother Teresa's lawyer. I used to tell Towey that we sure have a litigious society if Mother Teresa needed a lawyer.

Some said the faith-based initiative blurred the line between church and state. I took that concern seriously. Government should never impose religion. Every citizen has the right to worship as he or she wishes, or not to worship at all. I was always wary of people who used faith as a political weapon, suggesting they were more righteous than their opponents. My favorite Bible verse for politicians is Matthew 7:3—"Why do you see the speck that is in your brother's eye, but do not notice the log that is in your own eye?"

At the same time, government need not fear religion. If social service programs run by people of faith did not proselytize or discriminate against people receiving services, I thought they deserved a chance to compete for taxpayer dollars. The government should ask which organization would deliver the best results, not whether they had a cross, a crescent, or a Star of David on their wall.

The initiative opened up roughly $20 billion a year in federal funding to competition from faith-based groups. Many of these organizations had no experience interfacing with government, so we held forty conferences and more than four hundred grant-writing seminars to help them apply for funding. Ultimately, more than five thousand faith-based and community organizations, mostly small grassroots charities, received federal grants.

In January 2008, I visited the Jericho Program of East Baltimore. Operated by Episcopal Community Services of Maryland and funded by a grant from the Department of Labor, the program provided mentoring, counseling, and job training services to recently released adult male convicts. The nine men from Jericho were quiet when I walked into the room. I detected a fair amount of skepticism. "I drank too much at one point in my life," I said to break the ice, "and I understand how a changed heart can help you deal with addiction."

The men opened up and told their stories. One had been convicted of selling drugs, another of cocaine possession, another of theft. Many had been in and out of prison several times and had abandoned their families. Thanks to the services they received at Jericho, they had begun to find purpose in their lives. One man emotionally explained how thrilled he was to have reunited with his three daughters. "Six months ago, I was broken down," he said. "Now I am shaking hands with the president." Another told me proudly that he had received two job offers. "Drugs have always been a problem in my life, up until now," he said. "Thanks to Jericho," he said, "I got my groove."

The Jericho Program's recidivism rate was 22 percent, less than half of Baltimore's overall rate. The men I met that day were among fifteen thousand who had benefited from the Prisoner Reentry Initiative we launched in 2004. Their recidivism rate was 15 percent, one third of the national average.

My most extraordinary meeting on faith-based initiatives took place right across the hall from the Oval Office. In June 2003, I had convened a roundtable discussion with faith-based leaders. Chuck Colson and several members of InnerChange attended. When I stepped into the Roosevelt Room, I spotted a familiar-looking African American man. I walked over and gave him a big hug. "I'm sure glad you're here," I said.

It was George Mason, the man from the prison choir in Sugar Land. Upon release, he had earned a job as a janitor at his church. He also led a Bible study and served as a mentor for others leaving prison. What a testimony to the redemptive power of Christ: George Mason and George W. Bush together in the West Wing.

---

Created by President Johnson in 1965, Medicare had helped countless seniors enjoy healthier lives. But while medicine had advanced, Medicare had not. Benefits were determined by a government bureaucracy that was wasteful and very slow to change. When private insurers added mammogram coverage to protect against breast cancer, it took Medicare ten years and an act of Congress to catch up.

Medicare's most antiquated feature was that it did not cover prescription drugs. The program would pay $28,000 for ulcer surgery, but not $500 a year for pills that would prevent most ulcers.

I was struck by the stories of older Americans who had to choose between buying groceries and medicine. One sixty-nine-year-old woman I met, Mary Jane Jones of Virginia, had to work twenty hours a week just to afford her nearly $500-a-month bill for prescription drugs and insulin. She told me she sometimes used needles three or four times to save money.

Medicare wasn't just outdated; it was going broke. The combination of rising health costs and the upcoming retirement of the Baby Boom generation had created a $13 trillion unfunded liability. The next generation would get stuck with the bill.

The rising costs bankrupting Medicare affected the whole health-care system. America's health spending had doubled from about 7.5 percent of

GDP in 1972 to more than 15 percent in 2002. Part of the explanation was the cost of new medical technology. Junk lawsuits also played a role. But the primary cause was a fundamental flaw in the system: Most people had no idea what their health care cost.

Seniors and the poor had their bills paid by the government through Medicare and Medicaid. Most working Americans received coverage through their employers and relied on a third party, an insurance company, to negotiate prices and determine payments. Many self-employed Americans couldn't afford health insurance because the tax code disadvantaged them and regulations prohibited small business owners from pooling risk across jurisdictional boundaries.

What the system lacked was market forces. There was no sense of consumerism or ability to shop around for the best deal, no competition for customers' business, and no transparency about quality and price. As a result, there was little incentive for doctors or patients to limit the resources they consumed, which was crucial to holding down costs.

I saw reforming Medicare as a way to solve two problems. First, by adding a prescription drug benefit, we would modernize the program and provide seniors with the quality health care their government had promised. Second, by delivering the drug benefit through private insurance plans that compete for seniors' business, we could inject market forces into the health care system. Reforming the program would also create an opportunity to expand Medicare Plus Choice, later renamed Medicare Advantage, which allowed seniors to obtain all their health care through flexible, affordable private insurance plans.

I knew Medicare reform would be a tough political issue. Introducing market forces into a government health program would upset the left. Adding an expensive prescription drug benefit would be unpopular with the right. But I decided to take on the challenge.

Under our plan, seniors who wanted the new prescription drug benefit would have to choose private plans instead of government-run Medicare. We would change Medicare's funding formula so that the government-run program had to compete with private plans on a level playing field. Both reforms would introduce more market forces and help address the rising costs of health care.

Before announcing my plan publicly, I previewed it with Republican leaders in the House. They told me my proposal didn't stand a chance on Capitol Hill. Democrats would never support a bill that required seniors to give up their government-run Medicare coverage to receive a prescription drug benefit. Some Republicans wouldn't either.

I faced a tough decision. I could fight for a lost cause or make a compromise. I decided to propose a prescription drug benefit that would be administered by private health plans but open to all seniors, including those who wanted to keep government-run Medicare coverage.

My Medicare team* worked closely with Senate Majority Leader Bill Frist and Finance Committee Chairman Chuck Grassley of Iowa. Chuck wisely brought two key Democratic counterparts, Senators Max Baucus of Montana and John Breaux of Louisiana, into the drafting process. They produced a solid bill that garnered support from thirty-five Democrats. The Senate passed the bill in June by a vote of 76 to 21.

In the House, some conservatives balked at the cost of the drug benefit, which we eventually estimated at $634 billion over ten years. But Speaker Denny Hastert, Majority Leader Tom DeLay, and Ways and Means Committee Chairman Bill Thomas built a fragile coalition to pass the bill 216 to 215. Just nine House Democrats voted for a benefit they had demanded for years. The rest voted no. During the debate on the floor of Congress, not a single Democrat criticized the Medicare bill for costing too much. Most wanted to spend more money.

The razor-thin House margin made it essential that the House and Senate bills be combined in a way that retained Republican support. To address cost concerns, we included a so-called trigger provision that would take effect if Medicare spending rose faster than expected. Congress would then be required to make reforms to address the problem.†

We also highlighted health savings accounts, an innovative new health insurance product created by the House bill. Designed to make coverage affordable for small businesses and individuals, HSAs coupled

---

*My team was led by Health and Human Services Secretary Tommy Thompson; Food and Drug Administration Commissioner Mark McClellan; Medicare Administrator Tom Scully; White House staffers Steve Friedman, Keith Hennessey, David Hobbs, and Doug Badger; and OMB expert Jim Capretta.

† Unfortunately, the trigger provision was later repealed by the Democratically controlled Congress.

low-premium, high-deductible insurance against catastrophic illness with a tax-free savings account to pay routine medical expenses. Employers or individuals could contribute to the account, which belonged to the individual and could be taken from job to job. Because HSA owners paid their own health-care expenses and kept any money left over, they had incentives to stay healthy, shop for good deals, and negotiate better prices.

In mid-November, AARP, the influential seniors' advocacy group, endorsed the compromise bill. "This is not a perfect bill, but America cannot wait for the perfect," CEO Bill Novelli said. He was then excoriated by Democratic leaders, labor unions, and liberal editorial pages. But his stand went a long way with wavering members of Congress.

The decisive vote came on November 21, 2003. Laura and I had long been scheduled to spend that day in Great Britain, as part of the first official state visit there by an American president since Woodrow Wilson. Some suggested postponing the trip. I refused. "They have phones in London, you know," I reminded the team.

———

Laura and I enjoyed spending time with Queen Elizabeth II, a gracious, charming woman with a keen sense of humor. In 2007, Her Majesty and Prince Philip came to celebrate the four hundredth anniversary of the Jamestown settlement. In my welcoming remarks before seven thousand people on the South Lawn, I thanked the queen for her long friendship with America. "You helped our nation celebrate its bicentennial in 17 . . ." I caught myself before I could finish the date, 1776, a rough year in U.S.-British relations and an unflattering commentary on the queen's longevity. The eighty-one-year-old monarch glanced at me with a wry smile. "She gave me a look that only a mother could give a child," I said. At a dinner at the British embassy the next night, Her Majesty said, "I wondered whether I should start this toast by saying, 'When I was here in 1776 . . .'"

Queen Elizabeth's hospitality at Buckingham Palace during our 2003 state visit was exquisite. We received a forty-one-gun salute, inspected the royal troops in the courtyard, and slept in the immaculately appointed Belgian Suite. Our room had been occupied by Queen Elizabeth's uncle,

King Edward VIII, before he abdicated the throne in 1936 to marry an American divorcée. It included a three-hundred-year-old mirror, some 10 million British pounds'—$15 million—worth of antiques, and a beautiful view of the palace gardens. At our afternoon tea with Her Majesty and Prince Philip, I asked the queen about her dogs. A few minutes later, a royal footman appeared with her famous corgis. They were friendly and polite. My only hope was that if Barney ever met the queen, he would behave as well as they did—and not bark for Scottish independence.

That evening, Her Majesty and Prince Philip gave an elegant state banquet in our honor. Our places were set with ten pieces of silverware and seven crystal wine goblets. Evidently, word hadn't reached the royal pantry that I had quit drinking. Before I stood to make my toast in white tie and tails, I looked over at Laura in her beautiful burgundy gown. I wondered if she was thinking what I was: *We've come a long way from that backyard barbecue in Midland.*

———

The stateliness of Buckingham Palace marked a stark contrast to what awaited on the flight home. As Air Force One took off, legislative director David Hobbs called me with a list of about a dozen wavering House members, mostly conservatives. I started dialing for votes over the Atlantic. Several congressmen were unavailable to take my call. One junior member did answer. "I didn't come to Washington to increase the size of government," he told me.

"You know what, I didn't, either," I answered. "I came to make sure the government works. If we're going to have a Medicare program, it ought to be modern, not broken."

"This is just another entitlement that will keep growing forever," he said.

"So are you for abolishing Medicare?" I responded. "This is an opportunity to introduce competition into the system and hold down costs. Just so you know, this is a helluva lot better deal than you're going to get from any other president."

He wasn't persuaded. When I landed in Washington, I made another round of calls. We were making some headway, but it was going to be tight. When the House voted at 3:00 a.m., the initial count came up short. Speaker Denny Hastert took the rare step of holding the vote open in the hope he could persuade a few congressmen to change their votes. Just before 5:00 a.m., David Hobbs woke me up with a call from the Capitol. "We need two more votes," he said. "Can you talk to a few more members?"

He passed his cell phone around to several Republicans who might be persuaded to change their minds. I argued the case as best I could, given my jet lag. David called back a little while later. Miracle of miracles, the House had passed the bill, 220 to 215. The Senate followed a few days later. I signed the Medicare Modernization Act of 2003 on December 8, 2003, at Constitution Hall. Behind me on the stage was a group of seniors who would benefit from the new law. One was Mary Jane Jones, the woman from Virginia who had to reuse her needles to afford insulin. The prescription drug benefit would save her an estimated $2,700 a year.

The new law called for the prescription drug benefit to take effect on January 1, 2006. Skeptics said that seniors would have trouble picking from all the competing private options. I disagreed. I believed that seniors were plenty capable of making decisions about their lives, and that the government ought to trust them to do so.

My effective secretary of health and human services, Mike Leavitt, worked with Medicare Administrator Mark McClellan and his team on a massive public outreach campaign. It paid off. More than 22 million seniors signed up for a prescription drug benefit during the initial five-month enrollment period. In a 2008 survey, 90 percent of Medicare prescription drug recipients—and 95 percent of low-income beneficiaries—said they were satisfied with the program.

Ultimately, Medicare modernization was a tradeoff. We created a needed new benefit but spent more money than I wanted. We introduced market-based competition among private drug plans, but we were unable to use the new benefit as leverage to move more seniors from government-run Medicare to private Medicare Advantage plans. We created health savings accounts, but we could not convince Congress to require government-run Medicare to compete on a level playing field with private plans.

By the time I left office, more than 90 percent of Medicare beneficiaries had coverage for prescription drugs. Ten million were enrolled in private-sector health-care plans through Medicare Advantage. Almost seven million Americans owned health savings accounts, more than a third of whom had not previously owned health insurance.

Thanks to competition between private-sector plans, the average monthly premium for prescription drug coverage dropped from an initial estimate of $35 to $23 the first year. By 2008, the initial estimate of $634 billion had dropped below $400 billion. The Medicare prescription drug benefit became one of the few government programs ever to come in well under budget. Market forces had worked. And we had moved America's health care system in the right direction: away from government control and toward the choices and competition of a private market system, which is the best way to control costs in the long run.

———

"I'm optimistic," I told Dad as we hunted quail in South Texas on New Year's Day, 2004. "This election is going to come down to who knows how to lead, who will take on the big issues, and who can keep America safe."

Dad was concerned. For months, he had watched the Democratic presidential candidates take swings at me every day. The poundings were having an impact. My approval ratings had topped 90 percent after 9/11 and 75 percent after the liberation of Iraq. By the end of 2003, I had dropped to the fifties in some polls. Dad had seen the pattern before. His approval rating had skyrocketed in 1991, then crashed before the 1992 election.

I assured him that our mutual friend Karl Rove had developed a solid campaign strategy. "If we do this right, it will come out just fine," I said. "Especially if they nominate Howard Dean."

I knew the Democratic front-runner, the former governor of Vermont, from events we had attended in the 1990s. Dean was loud, shrill, and undisciplined. I was pulling hard for him to get the nomination.

Unfortunately, Dean's lead evaporated before he won a single delegate. Senator John Kerry of Massachusetts claimed an upset victory in Iowa, won the New Hampshire primary, and cruised to the nomination. A Vietnam veteran and four-term senator, Kerry was a hard worker, a polished debater, and a tough campaigner. I considered him a formidable opponent.

Kerry also had weaknesses. He had the process-oriented mindset of a longtime legislator and a voting record that qualified as the most liberal in the Senate. In the fall of 2003, he had voted against an $87 billion bill to fund troops in Iraq and Afghanistan. Shortly after he clinched the nomination, my campaign ran an ad highlighting his position. Kerry responded, "I actually did vote for the $87 billion before I voted against it."

I spoke to Karl the moment I heard the sound bite. "There's our opening," I said. "The American people expect their president to take a clear stand and defend it, especially when it comes to supporting troops in combat." We grabbed the "flip-flop" theme and ran with it for the rest of the campaign.

———

On March 10, 2004, I received a letter from Jenna, who was in her senior year at the University of Texas. In 2000, neither Jenna nor Barbara had attended a single campaign event. They had made it clear they wanted nothing to do with politics. So it was quite a surprise to read Jenna's words:

*Dear Dad,*

*I had a vivid dream last night, a dream so vivid I woke in tears. Although I am not yet as spiritual as you, I have taken this dream as a sign. You have worked your entire life to give Barbara and me everything we have ever wanted or needed. You have given us love, support; and I know you have included us in every decision you have ever made.*

*You and Mom have taught us the meaning of unconditional love. I watched as Mom selflessly, gently gave herself to Pa as he suffered. And I watched you give a year of your life to Gampy; I watched your shared pain on election night. At age twenty-two, I finally have learned what that selfless pain must have felt like.*

*I hate hearing lies about you. I hate when people criticize you. I hate that everybody can't see the person I love and respect, the person that I hope I someday will be like.*

*It is because of all of these reasons that I have decided that if you want me to I would love to work full-time for you in the fall. Please think about it, talk to Mom about it, and get back to me. For now I have stopped ap-*

*plying for jobs in New York. I know I may be a little rough around the*
*edges, but with the proper training I could get people to see the Dad I love.*

*This may seem like a rushed, impulsive decision, but I have been*
*thinking about it constantly. I want to try to give you something for the*
*twenty-two years you have given me.*

*In my dream, I didn't help you. And I watched somebody win who*
*isn't supposed to. And I cried, I cried for you, for our country, and for my*
*guilt. I don't want my dream to become reality, so if I can help in any way*
*please let me. We can talk more about it during Easter.*

*I love you and am so proud of you,*

> *Love,*
> *Jenna*

I still choke up when I read her sweet words, which also reflected Barbara's sentiments. I was thrilled they wanted to join the campaign. My last campaign would be their first.

The first event Barbara and I attended together was a rally in front of eleven thousand people in Marquette, Michigan, an Upper Peninsula town that hadn't seen a visit from a sitting president since William Howard Taft. Just before I gave my speech, Barbara took her seat in the front row behind the podium.

The announcer introduced me, and the audience roared. As I stepped up to the microphone, I turned to look at Barbara. She had tears streaming down her face. After four years on a college campus, she was surprised and touched to see such enthusiastic support for her dad. It reminded me of the feeling I had when I first heard a crowd cheer for my father. The circle was complete.

———

In some ways, the 2004 campaign was easier than 2000. I benefited from the trappings of the presidency, especially Air Force One and Marine One. In another way, 2004 was tougher. I was both candidate and president. I had to strike a balance between the two.

I drew energy from the people around me, especially Laura and the girls. I loved our bus tours through the Midwest, where thousands of citizens lined the main streets of small towns. One day in Wisconsin we rolled through the hometown of Dick Tubb, the multitalented Air Force doctor who traveled everywhere with me. I saw a handpainted sign that read "Welcome Home, Dr. Tubb!" Underneath, in smaller print, the person had added, "You Too, George W."

Nothing buoyed my spirits like our supporters on the campaign trail. I was energized by their intensity, and their dedication inspired me to work harder so that I would not let them down. In the 16,500-person town of Poplar Bluff, Missouri, 23,000 people turned out for a speech. In the township of West Chester, Ohio, 41,000 people packed Voice of America Park. As I outlined John Kerry's shifting positions, a sea of arms swayed left and right amid a chant of "Flip-Flop, Flip-Flop." Some people came dressed as human-size flip-flops. I encountered new groups, including Barristers for Bush, Buckeyes for Bush, and Barbara and Jenna's favorite, Twins for Bush.

I was especially encouraged by signs that read "God Bless You." As I shook hands and posed for photos on the rope line, I was amazed by the number who said the same four words: "I pray for you." I told them their prayers were a wonderful gift. They gave me strength. Seeing those voters also gave me hope that some Bush supporters who stayed home after the DUI revelation in 2000 would come back to the polls in 2004.

———

John Kerry had intense supporters of his own. Hollywood filmmaker Michael Moore came out with a so-called documentary that was nothing more than campaign propaganda. In return, Kerry said that Hollywood entertainers conveyed "the heart and soul of our country." Wealthy donors like investment mogul George Soros gave Kerry huge amounts of money through 527s, fundraising organizations that circumvented the campaign finance laws so many Democrats had championed.* Renegade staffers at the CIA leaked information intended to embarrass the admin-

*Republicans used 527s, too, but Democrats outraised us three to one, $186.8 million to $61.5 million.

istration. The assault culminated in Dan Rather's false report, based on forged documents, that I had not fulfilled my duties in the Texas Air National Guard.

While the media was eager to scrutinize my military service, their appetite was noticeably less ravenous when Kerry's came into question. In February 2004, I sat down for an hour-long, one-on-one interview with Tim Russert. After grilling me mainly on Iraq, he pushed me on whether I would make all my military records available to the public. I promised I would. Soon after, I instructed the Defense Department to release every document related to my Guard service.

"You did yourself some good today, Mr. President," Tim said after the cameras went dark.

"Thanks, Tim," I said. "By the way, I sure hope you will be as tough on John Kerry about his military records as you were on me."

"Oh, believe me," he said, "we will."

Tim interviewed John Kerry two months later, and he did ask about the military records. Kerry promised to release them to the public during the campaign, but he never did.

At the Democratic National Convention in Boston, Kerry invited former shipmates and accepted the nomination with a salute. "I'm John Kerry, and I'm reporting for duty," he declared in his opening line. His speech called for "telling the truth to the American people" and promised he would "be a commander in chief who will never mislead us into war."

Kerry's argument that I had misled the country on Iraq didn't pass the commonsense test. As a member of the Senate in 2002, he had access to the same intelligence I did and decided to cast his vote in support of the war resolution.

Kerry had trapped himself in a contradiction. "My opponent hasn't answered the question of whether, knowing what we know now, he would have supported going into Iraq," I said at a campaign stop in New Hampshire. A few days later, standing on the rim of the Grand Canyon, Kerry took the bait. "Yes," he said, "I would have voted for the authority."

It was a stunning admission. After using the grand stage of his convention to charge that I had misled America into war—one of the most serious allegations anyone can level at a commander in chief—John Kerry said he would vote to authorize the war again if he had the chance.

Making the case against Kerry was important, but it was even more important to show voters that I would continue to lead on the big issues. I had seen incumbents like Ann Richards run backward-looking campaigns, and I vowed not to repeat their mistake. "The only reason to look back in a campaign is to determine who best to lead us forward," I said. "Even though we've done a lot, I'm here to tell you there's more to do."

At the Republican National Convention in New York, and in speeches across the country, I laid out an ambitious second-term agenda. I pledged to modernize Social Security, reform the immigration system, and overhaul the tax code, while continuing No Child Left Behind and the faith-based initiative, implementing Medicare reform, and above all, fighting the war on terror.

I crisscrossed the country throughout the fall, with interruptions for each of the three debates. The first was held at the University of Miami. Debating was a strong suit for John Kerry. Like a prizefighter, he charged out of his corner and punched furiously after every question. It was an effective technique. I spent too much time trying to sort through which of his many attacks to answer.

I did land one roundhouse. When Kerry suggested that American military action should be subject to a "global test," I countered, "I'm not exactly sure what you mean, 'passes the global test' . . . My attitude is you take preemptive action in order to protect the American people."

On the car ride to the post-debate rally, I received a phone call from Karen Hughes. She told me the networks had broadcast split-screen images showing my facial expressions while Kerry was speaking. Apparently I hadn't done a very good job of disguising my opinion of his answers. Just as Al Gore's sighs dominated the coverage of the first debate in 2000, my scowls became the story in 2004. I thought it was unfair both times.

An even stranger story unfolded a few days later, when a photograph from the debate surfaced. It showed a wrinkle down the back of my suit. Somebody came up with the idea that the crease was actually a hidden radio connected to Karl Rove. The rumor flew around the Internet and became a sensation among conspiracy theorists. It was an early taste of a twenty-first-century phenomenon: the political bloggers. In retrospect, it's too bad I didn't have a radio, so Karl could have told me to quit grimacing.

The second and third debates went better. My face was calm, my suit was pressed, and I was better prepared to counter Kerry's jabs. But as is usually the case in presidential debates, the most damaging blow was self-inflicted. At our final debate in Tempe, moderator Bob Schieffer raised the topic of same-sex marriage and asked, "Do you believe homosexuality is a choice?"

"I just don't know," I said. "I do know that we have a choice to make in America, and that is to treat people with tolerance and respect and dignity." I then expressed my conviction that marriage is between a man and a woman, and said the law should reflect that time-honored truth.

Kerry, who also opposed same-sex marriage, began his answer, "We're all God's children, Bob, and I think if you were to talk to Dick Cheney's daughter, who is a lesbian, she would tell you that she's being who she was, she's being who she was born as."

I glanced at Laura, Barbara, and Jenna in the front row. I could see the shock on their faces. Karen Hughes later told me she heard audible gasps. There is an unwritten rule in American politics that a candidate's children are off-limits. For John Kerry to raise my running mate's daughter's sexuality in a nationally televised debate was appalling.

It was not unprecedented. In the vice presidential debate a week earlier, Kerry's running mate, North Carolina Senator John Edwards, also found a way to bring up the issue. One reference might have been an accident. Two was a plot. Kerry and Edwards were hoping to peel off conservative voters who objected to Dick's daughter's orientation. Instead, they came across looking cynical and mean. Lynne Cheney spoke for a lot of us when she called it a "cheap and tawdry political trick."

———

In 2000, our October Surprise had come in the form of the DUI revelation. In 2004, it came from Osama bin Laden. On October 29, the al Qaeda leader released a videotape threatening Americans with "another Manhattan" and mocking my response to 9/11 in the Florida classroom. It sounded like he was plagiarizing Michael Moore. "Americans will not be intimidated or influenced by an enemy of our country," I said. John Kerry made a similar statement of resolve.

The final election day of my political career, November 2, 2004, began aboard Marine One, on a midnight flight from Dallas to the ranch. We had just finished an emotional rally with eight thousand supporters at Southern Methodist University, Laura's alma mater—my seventh stop on a daylong, 2,500-mile blitz across the country.

Laura, Barbara, Jenna, and I were up at dawn the next day. We eagerly cast our ballots at the Crawford firehouse, four solid votes in the Bush-Cheney column. "I trust the judgment of the American people," I told the assembled reporters. "My hope, of course, is that this election ends tonight."

I checked in with brother Jeb. "Florida is looking good, George," the governor said.

Then I spoke to Karl. He was a little worried about Ohio, so off we went for my twentieth campaign stop in the Buckeye State. After thanking the volunteers and working a phone bank in Columbus, we loaded up for the flight to D.C.

As the plane descended toward Andrews Air Force Base, Karl came to the front cabin. The first round of exit polls had arrived.

"They're dreadful," he said.

I felt like he had just punched me in the stomach. I was down more than twenty points in the battleground state of Pennsylvania. Rock-solid Republican states like Mississippi and South Carolina were too close to call. If the numbers were right, I would suffer a landslide defeat.

I walked from the airplane to Marine One in a daze. The ten-minute flight to the White House felt like hours. Finally the wheels of the chopper hit the South Lawn. The press corps swarmed to get a good shot for the evening news. Karen Hughes had good advice: "Everybody smile!"

I went upstairs to the residence and moped around the Treaty Room. I just couldn't believe it. After all the hard work of the past four years, and all the grueling months on the campaign trail, I was going to be voted out of office decisively. I knew life would go on, as it had for Dad. But the rejection was going to sting.

Before long, Karl called. He had been crunching the numbers and was convinced that the methodology was flawed. I felt relieved and angry at the same time. I worried that the bogus numbers would demoralize our supporters and depress turnout in time zones where the polling places were still open. We were thinking the same thing: *Here we go again.*

At 8:00 p.m., the polls in Florida closed. As Jeb predicted that morning, the early returns looked promising. The exit poll results in South Carolina and Mississippi were quickly contradicted by solid victories in both states. The rest of the East Coast came in as expected. The outcome would turn on four states: Iowa, New Mexico, Nevada, and Ohio. Ken Mehlman, my brilliant campaign manager who had organized a historic effort to turn out the vote, was confident we had won all four states. Each had been called in our favor by at least one news network. But after the fiasco of 2000, no network wanted to be the first to put me over the top.

The focus was Ohio, with its 20 electoral votes. I held a solid lead of more than 120,000 votes. The clock struck midnight, one o'clock, two o'clock. At around 2:45, I took a phone call from Tony Blair. He told me he had gone to bed in London thinking I had lost and was prepared to deal with President Kerry. "Not only did you win, George," he said, "you got more votes than any president in history."

"If only the Kerry campaign would recognize that," I replied. "I haven't been up this late since college!"

At around four o'clock, we started hearing rumors that Kerry and Edwards planned to file a lawsuit contesting the vote in Ohio. In another replay of 2000, several advisers urged me to declare victory even though the networks hadn't called the race and my opponent had not conceded. Four years earlier, it was Jeb who wisely advised me against giving my speech in Austin. This time it was Laura. "George, you can't go out there," she said. "Wait until you've been declared the winner."

At around the same time, Dan Bartlett picked up a useful piece of intelligence. Nicolle Wallace, my campaign's communications director, had connected Dan with Kerry aide Mike McCurry. McCurry told him the senator would make the right decision if we gave him time. "Don't press the guy," Dan advised.

Once again, a disappointed crowd waited for a candidate who never arrived. I so wanted to give my supporters the victory party we had been denied in 2000. But it wasn't to be. Just after 5:00 a.m., I sent Andy Card in my place. "President Bush decided to give Senator Kerry the respect of more time to reflect on the results of this election," he said. "We are convinced that President Bush has won reelection with at least 286 electoral votes."

———

At 11:02 the next morning, my personal assistant, Ashley Kavanaugh, opened the door to the Oval Office. "Mr. President," she said, "I have Senator Kerry on the line."

John was gracious. I told him he was a worthy opponent who had run a spirited campaign. I called Laura and hugged the small group of senior aides gathered in the Oval Office. I walked down the hallway to Dick's office, where I gave him a hearty handshake. Dick isn't really the hugging type.

Eventually I reached Mother and Dad on the phone. After staying up most of the night, they had slipped out of the White House early that morning and flown back to Houston without knowing the results. "Congratulations, son," Dad said. He said it more with relief than joy. We hadn't talked about it, but 2000 was not the only election that had been on our minds. We both remembered the pain of 1992. I could tell he was very happy I would not have to go through what he had.

After its bleak start, election night 2004 had turned into a big victory. I became the first president to win a majority of the popular vote since Dad in 1988. As in 2002, Republicans gained ground in both the House and Senate.

The day after Kerry conceded, I held a morning press conference. One of the reporters asked if I felt "more free."

I thought about the ambitious agenda I had outlined over the past year. "Let me put it to you this way," I said. "I earned capital in the campaign, political capital, and now I intend to spend it."

———

For as long as I can remember, Social Security has been the third rail of American politics. Grab ahold of it, and you're toast.

In 2005, I did more than touch the third rail. I hugged it. I did so for one reason: It is unfair to make a generation of young people pay into a system that is going broke.

Created by Franklin Roosevelt in 1935, Social Security is a pay-as-you-go system. The checks collected by retirees are financed by payroll taxes paid by today's workers. The system worked fine when there were forty workers for every beneficiary, as there were in 1935. But over time, demographics changed. Life expectancy rose. The birthrate fell. As a result, by 2005 there were only three workers paying into the Social Security system for every beneficiary taking money out. By the time a young person starting work in the first decade of the twenty-first century retires, the ratio will be two to one.

To compound the problem, Congress had set Social Security benefits to rise faster than inflation. Starting in 2018, Social Security was projected to take in less money than it paid out. The shortfall would increase every year, until the system hit bankruptcy in 2042. The year 2042 sounded a long way off, until I did the math. That was when my daughters, born in 1981, would be approaching retirement.

For someone looking to take on big issues, it didn't get much bigger than reforming Social Security. I decided there was no better time to launch the effort than when I was fresh off reelection.

I started by setting three principles for reform. First, nothing would change for seniors or people near retirement. Second, I would seek to make Social Security solvent without raising payroll taxes, which had already expanded from about 2 percent to 12 percent. Third, younger workers should have the option of earning a better return by investing part of their Social Security taxes in a personal retirement account.

Personal retirement accounts would be new to Social Security, but most Americans were familiar with the concept. Like 401(k) accounts, they could be invested in a safe mix of stock and bond funds, which would grow over time and benefit from the power of compound interest. The accounts would be managed by reputable financial institutions charging low fees, and there would be prohibitions against withdrawing the money before retirement. Even at a conservative rate of return of 3 percent, an account holder's money would double every twenty-four years. By contrast, Social Security's return of 1.2 percent would take sixty

years to double. Unlike Social Security benefits, personal retirement accounts would be an asset owned by individual workers, not the government, and could be passed from one generation to the next.

In early 2005, I sat down with Republican congressional leaders to
talk through our legislative strategy. I told them modernizing Social Security would be my first priority. The reaction was lukewarm, at best.

"Mr. President," one leader said, "this is not a popular issue. Taking
on Social Security will cost us seats."

"No," I shot back, "failing to tackle this issue will cost us seats."

It was clear they were thinking about the two-year election cycle of
Capitol Hill. I was thinking about the responsibility of a president to lead
on issues affecting the long-term prospects of the country. I reminded
them that I had campaigned on this issue twice, and the problem was
only going to get worse. By solving it, we would do the country a great
service. And ultimately, good policy makes for good politics.

"If you lead, we'll be behind you," one House leader said, "but we'll
be way behind you."

———

The meeting with congressional Republicans showed what an uphill climb
I had on Social Security. I decided to press ahead anyway. When I looked
back on my presidency, I didn't want to say I had dodged a big issue.

"Social Security was a great moral success of the twentieth century,
and we must honor its great purposes in this new century," I said in my
2005 State of the Union address. "The system, however, on its current
path, is headed toward bankruptcy. And so we must join together to
strengthen and save Social Security."

The next day, I embarked on a series of trips to raise awareness about
Social Security's problems and rally the American people to insist on
change. I gave speeches, convened town halls, and even held an event
with my favorite Social Security beneficiary, Mother. "I'm here because
I'm worried about our seventeen grandchildren, and so is my husband,"
she said. "They will get no Social Security."

One of my most memorable trips was to a Nissan auto-manufacturing plant in Canton, Mississippi. Many in the audience were African American workers. I asked how many had money invested in a 401(k). Almost every hand in the room shot up. I loved the idea of people who had not traditionally owned assets having a nest egg they could call their own. I also thought about how much more was possible. Social Security was especially unfair to African Americans. Because their life expectancy was shorter, black workers who spent a lifetime paying into Social Security received an average of $21,000 less in benefits than whites of comparable income levels. Personal accounts, which could be passed along to the next generation, would go a long way toward reducing that disparity.

On April 28, I called a primetime press conference to lay out a specific proposal. The plan I embraced was the brainchild of a Democrat, Robert Pozen. His proposal, known as progressive indexing, set benefits to grow fastest for the poorest Americans and slowest for the wealthiest. There would be a sliding scale for everyone in between. By changing the benefit growth formula, the plan would wipe out the vast majority of the Social Security shortfall. In addition, all Americans would have the opportunity to earn higher returns through personal retirement accounts.

I hoped both sides would embrace the proposal. Republicans would be pleased that we could vastly improve the budget outlook without raising taxes. Democrats should have been pleased by a reform that saved Social Security, the crown jewel of the New Deal, by offering the greatest benefits to the poor, minorities, and the working class—the constituents they claimed to represent.

My legislative team* pushed the plan hard, but it received virtually no support. Democratic leaders in the House and Senate alleged I wanted to "privatize" Social Security. That was obviously poll-tested language designed to scare people. It wasn't true. My plan saved Social Security, modernized Social Security, and gave Americans the opportunity to own a piece of their Social Security. It did not privatize Social Security. I sensed there was something broader behind the Democrats' opposition. National Economic Council Director Al Hubbard told me about

*The Social Security team was led by Treasury Secretary John Snow and White House advisers Andy Card, Karl Rove, Al Hubbard, Keith Hennessey, and Chuck Blahous.

a meeting he'd had on Capitol Hill. "I'd like to be helpful on this," one senior Democratic senator told him, "but our leaders have made clear we're not supposed to cooperate."

The rigid Democratic opposition on Social Security came in stark contrast to the bipartisanship I had been able to forge on No Child Left Behind and during my years in Texas. I was disappointed by the change, and I've often thought about why it occurred. I think there were some on the other side of the aisle who never got over the 2000 election and were determined not to cooperate with me. Others resented that I had campaigned against Democratic incumbents in 2002 and 2004, helping Republican candidates unseat Democratic icons like Senator Max Cleland of Georgia and Senate Majority Leader Tom Daschle.

No doubt I bear some of the responsibility as well. I don't regret campaigning for fellow Republicans. I had always made clear that I intended to increase our party's strength in Washington. While I was willing to fine-tune legislation in response to Democratic concerns, I would not compromise my principles, which was what some seemed to expect in return for cooperation. On Social Security, I may have misread the electoral mandate by pushing for an issue on which there had been little bipartisan agreement in the first place. Whatever the cause, the breakdown in bipartisanship was bad for my administration and bad for the country, too.

With no Democrats on board, I needed strong Republican backing to get a Social Security bill through Congress. I didn't have it. Many younger Republicans, such as Congressman Paul Ryan of Wisconsin, supported reform. But few in Congress were willing to address such a contentious issue.

The collapse of Social Security reform is one of the greatest disappointments of my presidency. Despite our efforts, the government ended up doing exactly what I had warned against: We kicked the problem down the road to the next generation. In retrospect, I'm not sure what I could have done differently.

I made the case for reform as widely and persuasively as I could. I tried hard to reach across the aisle and made a Democratic economist's proposal the crux of my plan. The failure of Social Security reform shows the limits of the president's power. If Congress is determined not to act, there is only so much a president can do.

Inaction had a cost. In the five years since I proposed reform, the Social Security crisis has grown more acute. The projected bankruptcy date has moved from 2042 to 2037. The shortfall in Social Security—the cost of fixing the problem—has grown more than $2 trillion since I raised the issue in 2005. That is more than we spent on the war in Iraq, Medicare modernization, and the Troubled Asset Relief Program combined. For anyone concerned about the deficits facing future generations, the failure to reform Social Security ranks among the most expensive missed opportunities of modern times.

———

She was standing on the doorstep, alone in the rain. She looked tired and scared. A few days earlier, Paula Rendón had said goodbye to her family in Mexico and boarded a bus bound for Houston. She arrived with no money and no friends. All she had was an address, 5525 Briar Drive, and the names of her new employers, George and Barbara Bush.

I was thirteen years old when I opened the door that evening in 1959. Before long, Paula became like a second mother to my younger brothers and sister and me. She worked hard, taking care of our family in Texas and her own in Mexico. Eventually she bought a home and moved her family to Houston. She always says the proudest day of her life came when she saw her grandson graduate from college. As governor and president, I had Paula in mind when I spoke about immigration reform. "Family values don't stop at the Rio Grande," I said.

Like Paula, most who left Mexico for the United States came to put food on the table for their families. Many worked backbreaking jobs, picking crops in the field or laying tar on roofs under the Texas sun. Some, like Paula, received permanent work visas. Others came as temporary workers through the Bracero Program. Some crossed the border illegally.

Over the next four decades, the size of America's economy expanded from under $3 trillion to more than $10 trillion. The need for workers skyrocketed. Yet immigration and employment laws were slow to change. The Bracero Program expired in 1964 and was not replaced. The supply of permanent work visas did not rise anywhere near as fast as the demand for labor. With no practical way to enter the country lawfully, increasing numbers of immigrants came illegally.

An underground industry of document forgers and smugglers, known as coyotes, sprang up along the border. They stuffed people in the trunks of cars or left them to walk miles across the searing desert. The number of deaths was appalling. Yet immigrants, many of them determined to feed their families, kept coming.

By the time I ran for president, illegal immigration was a serious problem and getting worse. Our economy needed workers, but our laws were being undermined and human rights were being violated. In my 2000 campaign, I decided to take on the issue. I was confident we could find a rational solution that served our national interests and upheld our values.

My first partner on immigration reform was President Vicente Fox of Mexico. Vicente and his wife, Marta, were our guests at the first state dinner Laura and I held, on September 5, 2001. I discussed the possibility of creating a temporary worker program that would allow Mexicans to enter the United States lawfully to work a specific job for a fixed period of time. Vicente supported the idea, but he wanted more. He hoped America would legalize all Mexicans in the United States, a policy he called regularization. I made clear that would not happen. I believed amnesty—making illegal immigrants automatic citizens—would undercut the rule of law and encourage further illegal immigration.

Then 9/11 hit, and my most serious concern was that terrorists would slip into our country undetected. I put the idea of a temporary worker program on hold and concentrated on border security. In the four years after 9/11, we worked with Congress to increase funding for border protection by 60 percent, hired more than nineteen hundred new Border Patrol agents, and installed new technology, such as infrared cameras.

In October 2005, I signed a homeland security bill providing an additional $7.5 billion for border enforcement. The bill deepened our investment in technology and intelligence infrastructure at the border. It also funded an increase in bed space at federal detention facilities near the border, which allowed officials to stop letting the illegal immigrants they arrested return to society—a frustrating practice known as catch and release.

I hoped our focus on security would reassure the American people that we were serious about stopping illegal immigrants from entering the country. But defensive measures alone would not solve the problem. America's economy was a magnet for the poor and the hopeful. The longest and tallest fence in the world would not stop those determined to provide for their families. A temporary worker program was the solution. If immigrants coming to work could enter the country lawfully, they would not have to sneak across the border. The economy would have a reliable supply of labor. The coyotes and human rights abusers would lose their market. And Border Patrol agents could focus on stopping the criminals, drug dealers, and terrorists.

On May 15, 2006, I gave the first-ever primetime presidential address on immigration. "We're a nation of laws, and we must enforce our laws," I said. "We're also a nation of immigrants, and we must uphold that tradition, which has strengthened our country in so many ways."

I then laid out a five-part plan to reform the immigration system. The first component was a major new investment in border security, including a pledge to double the size of the Border Patrol by the end of 2008 and temporarily deploy six thousand National Guard troops to support the Border Patrol. The second part was the temporary worker program, which would include a tamper-proof identification card. The third was stricter immigration enforcement at businesses, which would reduce exploitation and help slow demand for illegal workers. Fourth was to promote assimilation by requiring immigrants to learn English. Finally, I took on the thorniest question in the debate: What to do with the approximately twelve million illegal immigrants in the country?

"Some in this country argue that the solution is to deport every illegal immigrant, and that any proposal short of this amounts to amnesty," I said. "I disagree. . . . There is a rational middle ground between granting an automatic path to citizenship for every illegal immigrant and a program of mass deportation."

I went on to differentiate between illegal immigrants who crossed the border recently and those who had worked in America for many years and put down roots as responsible members of the community. I proposed that illegal immigrants in the latter category be allowed to apply for citizenship after meeting a stringent set of criteria, including paying a fine, making good on back taxes, learning English, and waiting in line behind those who had followed the law.

Ten days after the speech, the Senate passed a bill sponsored by Senators Chuck Hagel of Nebraska and Mel Martinez of Florida that conformed to my outline. But the House, which had been focused on border security alone, couldn't get a comprehensive bill done before the midterm elections in November 2006. Then the Democrats took control of Congress.

———

Shortly after the 2006 elections, I invited a group of senior lawmakers to the Oval Office. Afterward, I pulled Ted Kennedy aside. Unfortunately, our relationship had deteriorated since the days of No Child Left Behind. I knew Ted disagreed with my decision to remove Saddam Hussein. But I was disappointed by his vitriolic speeches, in which he claimed I had "broken the basic bond of trust with the American people," compared me to Richard Nixon, and called Iraq "George Bush's Vietnam."

His harsh words were such a contrast to the affable, polite man I'd come to know. I was particularly surprised given that Ted had been on the receiving end of so many nasty political attacks over the years. One of my regrets is that I never sat down with Ted for a talk about the war. I wouldn't have changed his mind, but he was a decent man, and our discussion might have persuaded him to tone down his rhetoric.

I hoped immigration reform would provide a chance to rekindle our cooperation. "I think this is something we can get done," I told him at our meeting after the elections. "Let's prove the skeptics wrong again." He agreed.

In the spring of 2007, Ted collaborated with Arizona's Republican senators, John McCain and Jon Kyl, on a bill that strengthened border security, created the temporary worker program, and set up a tough but fair path to citizenship for law-abiding immigrants who had been in America for a number of years.

I traveled the country touting the bill, especially its emphasis on border security and assimilation. Passions ran high on both sides of the issue. As immigrants took jobs across the country, they put pressure on local schools and hospitals. Residents worried about their communities changing. Talk radio hosts and TV commentators warned of a "third world invasion and conquest of America." Meanwhile, a huge crowd of legalization supporters marched through major cities waving Mexican flags, an in-your-face display that offended many Americans.

The mood on the airwaves affected the attitude in Washington. Congressmen pledged, "We will not surrender America," and suggested that supporters of reform "wear a scarlet letter A for 'amnesty.'" On the other side, the chairman of the Democratic Party compared the temporary worker program to "indentured servitude." The head of America's largest labor union labeled the reform bill "anti-family and anti-worker."

At the height of the frenzy, I got a call from Ted Kennedy after I'd finished delivering a speech at the Naval War College in Newport, Rhode Island. "Mr. President," he said, "you need to call Harry Reid and tell him to keep the Senate in session over the weekend." We believed we were within a vote or two of getting the comprehensive reform bill passed, but the Senate was scheduled to break for its Fourth of July recess. Given the importance of the legislation, I thought it would be worthwhile to allow them a little extra time for the bill to pass. Apparently, Harry Reid did not.

If Ted Kennedy couldn't persuade the majority leader of his own party, my odds were not good. I made my pitch, but it was too late. Harry had made his decision. He called a cloture vote, which failed, and then adjourned the Senate. Senators went home and listened to angry constituents stirred up by the loud voices on radio and TV. By the time they came back to Washington, immigration reform was dead. As a result, the coyotes are still in business, immigrants continue to cross the border illegally, and a divisive political issue remains unresolved.

———

While I am disappointed I didn't sign bills into law, I do not regret taking on Social Security and immigration reform. Our efforts raised public awareness about problems that are not going away. One lesson of history is that it sometimes takes more than one president, even more than one generation, to accomplish a major legislative objective. Lyndon Johnson built on Harry Truman's efforts to create Medicare. I hope our work on Social Security and immigration will provide a foundation for a future president to reform both. At the minimum, I was able to take some of the shock out of the third rail.

If I had it to do over again, I would have pushed for immigration reform, rather than Social Security, as the first major initiative of my second term. Unlike Social Security, immigration reform had bipartisan support. The wildfire of opposition that erupted against immigration reform in 2006 and 2007 might not have raged as hot in 2005. We also would not have had to overcome the tensions caused by escalating violence in Iraq and Hurricane Katrina. Once a successful immigration bill was passed, it could have created a sense of momentum that would have made Social Security easier to tackle. Instead, the reverse happened. When Social Security failed, it widened the partisan divide and made immigration reform tougher.

The failure of immigration reform points out larger concerns about the direction of our politics. The blend of isolationism, protectionism, and nativism that affected the immigration debate also led Congress to block free trade agreements with Colombia, Panama, and South Korea. I recognize the genuine anxiety that people feel about foreign competition. But our economy, our security, and our culture would all be weakened by an attempt to wall ourselves off from the world. Americans should never fear competition. Our country has always thrived when we've engaged the world with confidence in our values and ourselves. The same will be true in the twenty-first century.

One way to reduce the influence of the ideological extremes is to change the way we elect our members of Congress. In 2006, only about 45 of 435 House races were seriously contested. Since members in so-called safe districts do not have to worry about challenges from the opposite party, their biggest vulnerability is getting outflanked in their own party. This is especially true in the era of bloggers, who make national targets out of politicians they deem ideologically impure. The result is that members of Congress from both parties tend to drift toward the extremes as insurance against primary challengers.

Our government would be more productive—and our politics more civilized—if congressional districts were drawn by panels of nonpartisan elders instead of partisan state legislatures. This would make for more competitive general elections and a less polarized Congress. Making the change would require politicians to give up some of their power, never an easy task. But for future presidents looking to tackle a big problem, this would be a worthy one to take on.

———

One of the most interesting aspects of my time in office was seeing how my philosophy was interpreted differently by different audiences. It was amusing to read newspapers labeling me the most conservative president in history while people on the right denounced me as a conservative apostate. Often they were discussing the same issue. I was an archconservative ideologue for injecting market forces into Medicare and a big-government liberal for creating a prescription drug benefit. I was a heartless conservative for exposing failing schools and a bleeding-heart liberal for spending more money on poor students. It all depended on whom you asked.

I am proud to have signed No Child Left Behind and Medicare modernization, two pieces of legislation that improved life for our citizens and showed that conservative principles of accountability and market-based competition are effective ways to get results. I am pleased that the faith-based initiative continues. I am confident Social Security and immigration reform will be a reality some day. No matter what, I am satisfied that we led on the issues that mattered most—and never played small ball.

# 10

# KATRINA

"Who's in charge of security in New Orleans?" I asked. My question silenced the raucous discussion in the Air Force One conference room on Friday, September 2, 2005. "The governor is in charge," Mayor Ray Nagin said, pointing across the dark wood table at Governor Kathleen Blanco.

Every head pivoted in her direction. The Louisiana governor froze. She looked agitated and exhausted. "I think it's the mayor," she said noncommittally.

Four days had passed since Hurricane Katrina smashed into the Gulf Coast. Winds above 120 miles per hour had flattened the Mississippi coastline and driven a wall of water through the levees of New Orleans. Eighty percent of the city, home to more than 450,000 people, had flooded. Reports of looting and violence filled the news.

By law, state and local authorities lead the response to natural disasters, with the federal government playing a supporting role. That approach had worked during the eight hurricanes, nine tropical storms, and more than two hundred tornadoes, floods, wildfires, and other emergencies we had faced since 2001. State and local first responders were in command of the Katrina response in Alabama and Mississippi, where I had visited earlier in the day. But after four days of chaos, it was clear the authorities in Louisiana could not lead.

The initial plan had been for me to land at the New Orleans airport, pick up Governor Blanco and Mayor Nagin, and survey the damage on an aerial tour. But on the Marine One flight from Mississippi, we received word that the governor, mayor, and a Louisiana congressional delegation were demanding a private meeting on Air Force One first.

The tone started out tense and got worse. The governor and mayor bickered. Everyone blasted the Federal Emergency Management Agency for failing to meet their needs. Congressman Bobby Jindal pointed out that FEMA had asked people to email their requests, despite the lack of electricity in the city. I shook my head. "We'll fix it," I said, looking at FEMA Director Mike Brown. Senator Mary Landrieu interrupted with unproductive emotional outbursts. "Would you please be quiet?" I had to say to her at one point.

I asked to speak to Governor Blanco privately. We walked out of the conference room, through a narrow passageway, and into the small cabin at the front tip of Air Force One. I told her it was clear the state and local response forces had been overwhelmed. "Governor," I pressed, "you need to authorize the federal government to take charge of the response."

She told me she needed twenty-four hours to think it over.

"We don't have twenty-four hours," I snapped. "We've waited too long already."

The governor refused to give an answer.

Next I asked to meet privately with Mayor Nagin. He had spent four days since Katrina holed up in a downtown hotel. He hadn't bathed or eaten a hot meal until he used my shower and ate breakfast on Air Force One. In a radio interview the previous evening, he had vented his frustrations with the federal government. "Get off your asses and do something," he said, "and let's fix the biggest goddamn crisis in the history of this country." Then he broke down in tears. When I met him on the plane, Ray whispered an apology for his outburst and explained that he was exhausted.

I asked the mayor what he thought about federalizing the response. He supported it. "Nobody's in charge," he said. "We need a clear chain of command." But only the governor could request that the federal government assume control of the emergency.

———

By the time the damage had been tallied, Hurricane Katrina ranked as the costliest natural disaster in American history. In truth, it was not a single disaster, but three—a storm that wiped away miles of the Gulf Coast, a flood caused by breaches in the New Orleans levees, and an outbreak of violence and lawlessness in the city.

On one level, the tragedy showed the helplessness of man against the fury of nature. Katrina was an enormously powerful hurricane that struck a part of the country that lies largely below sea level. Even a flawless response would not have prevented catastrophic damage.

The response was not only flawed but, as I said at the time, unacceptable. While there were inspiring acts of selflessness and heroism during and after the storm, Katrina conjures impressions of disorder, incompetence, and the sense that government let down its citizens. Serious mistakes came at all levels, from the failure to order a timely evacuation of New Orleans to the disintegration of local security forces to the dreadful communications and coordination. As the leader of the federal government, I should have recognized the deficiencies sooner and intervened faster. I prided myself on my ability to make crisp and effective decisions. Yet in the days after Katrina, that didn't happen. The problem was not that I made the wrong decisions. It was that I took too long to decide.

I made an additional mistake by failing to adequately communicate my concern for the victims of Katrina. This was a problem of perception, not reality. My heart broke at the sight of helpless people trapped on their rooftops waiting to be rescued. I was outraged by the fact that the most powerful country in the world could not deliver water to mothers holding their dehydrated babies under the baking sun. In my thirteen visits to New Orleans after the storm, I conveyed my sincere sympathy for the suffering and my determination to help residents rebuild. Yet many of our citizens, particularly in the African American community, came away convinced their president didn't care about them.

Just as Katrina was more than a hurricane, its impact was more than physical destruction. It eroded citizens' trust in their government. It exacerbated divisions in our society and politics. And it cast a cloud over my second term.

Soon after the storm, many made up their minds about what had happened and who was responsible. Now that time has passed and passions have cooled, our country can make a sober assessment of the causes of the devastation, the successes and failures of the response, and, most important, the lessons to be learned.

———

I replayed the scene in my mind: The storm damage was extensive. The governor bashed Washington for being slow and bureaucratic. The media fixed blame on the White House. Politicians claimed the federal government was out of touch.

The year was 1992, and I watched as Dad endured our family's first bout with natural disaster politics. With the presidential election approaching, Hurricane Andrew had pounded the Florida coast. Governor Lawton Chiles, a Democrat, and Bill Clinton's campaign exploited the devastation to claim the federal government had not performed. Their criticism was unfair. Dad had ordered a swift response to the storm. He sent Andy Card, then transportation secretary, to live in Florida to oversee the recovery. But once the public had formed a perception that Dad was disengaged, it was hard to reverse it.

As governor of Texas, I managed numerous natural disasters, from fires in Parker County to floods in the Hill Country and Houston to a tornado that tore through the small city of Jarrell. There was never any doubt about the division of labor. Under the Stafford Act, passed by Congress in 1988, state and local officials were responsible for leading the initial response. The federal government arrived later, at the state's request. As a governor, that was exactly the way I wanted it.

As president, I became responsible for the other side of the state-federal partnership. I appointed Joe Allbaugh, my chief of staff in the governor's office, to lead FEMA. After 9/11, he sent twenty-five search-and-rescue teams to New York and the Pentagon, the largest such deployment in history. Joe worked effectively with Rudy Giuliani and George Pataki to remove debris, support local fire and police, and deliver billions of dollars to help New York recover.

When I worked with Congress to reorganize the government in 2002, FEMA, an independent agency since 1979, became part of the new Department of Homeland Security. I thought it was logical for officials tasked with preventing a terrorist attack to work alongside those preparing to respond. But the move meant a loss of autonomy for FEMA. I don't know if it was the reorganization or his desire to move to the private sector, but Joe Allbaugh decided to leave. He recommended his deputy, Michael Brown, to succeed him. I took his advice.

The first major test of the new emergency response structure came during the 2004 hurricane season. In the space of six weeks, four major hurricanes—Charley, Frances, Ivan, and Jeanne—battered Florida. It was the first time in almost 120 years that one state had faced that many storms. I made four trips to the state, where I visited residents who had lost their homes in Pensacola, citrus growers in Lake Wales whose crops had been wiped out, and relief workers delivering supplies in Port St. Lucie.

Overall, the four hurricanes caused more than $20 billion in damages, knocked out power to more than 2.3 million residents, and took 128 lives. The toll was immense, yet the loss of life could have been far worse. Florida's governor was a strong chief executive who understood the need for state and local officials to take the lead in disaster response. My brother Jeb declared a state of emergency, established clear lines of communication, and made specific requests to the federal government.

FEMA responded by deploying 11,000 workers across Florida and other affected states, the largest operation in its history. In Florida, FEMA sent 14 million meals, 10.8 million gallons of water, and nearly 163 million pounds of ice. The agency then helped deliver $13.6 billion in emergency relief to suffering people. Mike Brown earned my trust with his performance, and I wasn't the only one. A tough critic, Jeb later told me Mike had done a fine job.

The effective management of the 2004 hurricanes saved lives and helped victims to rebuild. Having tested our model against four consecutive major hurricanes, we were convinced we could handle anything.

———

On Tuesday, August 23, 2005, the National Weather Service detected a storm forming over the Bahamas. Initially dubbed Tropical Depression Twelve, it strengthened into a tropical storm and earned a name, Katrina.

By August 25, Katrina was a Category One hurricane headed toward South Florida. At 6:30 p.m., Katrina ripped off rooftops with eighty-mile-per-hour winds and dropped more than a foot of rain. Despite orders to evacuate, some people unwisely chose to ride out the storm. Fourteen people lost their lives.

I received regular updates in Crawford, where Laura and I spent much of August. The press called my time away from Washington a vacation. Not exactly. I received my daily intelligence briefings at the secure trailer across the street, checked in regularly with advisers, and used the ranch as a base for meetings and travel. The responsibilities of the presidency followed me wherever I went. We had just moved the West Wing twelve hundred miles farther west.

After pummeling South Florida, Katrina charged across the Gulf of Mexico toward Alabama, Mississippi, and Louisiana. My senior aide in Crawford, Deputy Chief of Staff Joe Hagin, kept me updated on the developments. By Saturday, August 27, Katrina was a Category Three. On Sunday, it strengthened into a Category Four and then a Category Five, the most dangerous rating. The National Hurricane Center had also revised its projection of the storm's direction. As of Saturday morning, Katrina was headed for New Orleans.

I knew the city well. New Orleans was about a six-hour drive from Houston, and I had made the trek often in my younger days. I loved the food, culture, and vibrant people of The Big Easy. I was also aware of the city's lurking fear. The locals called it The Big One, the pray-it-never-happens storm that could drown their city.

Anyone who has visited New Orleans can understand their anxiety. The low-lying city is shaped like a crescent bowl. A system of levees and canals—the rim of the bowl—provides the city's primary flood protection. Built by the Army Corps of Engineers, the levees had a troubled history. When I was governor, I read John Barry's fascinating book *Rising Tide*, about the Great Mississippi Flood of 1927. After huge rains drove up the height of the river, New Orleans officials persuaded the Louisiana governor to dynamite a levee to the south in hopes of sparing the city. The move devastated two rural parishes, Plaquemines and St. Bernard. Over time, the levees were strengthened, especially after Hurricane Betsy hit in 1965. They held through seven hurricanes over the next forty years.

One lesson of the 2004 Florida hurricanes was that solid preparation before a storm is essential to a successful response. When we learned that Katrina was headed for New Orleans, I put FEMA on its highest level of alert. The government prestaged more than 3.7 million liters of water, 4.6 million pounds of ice, 1.86 million meals ready to eat, and 33 medical teams. Taken together, this marked the largest prepositioning of relief supplies in FEMA's history.

The military moved assets into place as well. Admiral Tim Keating—the head of the new Northern Command, which we created after 9/11 to protect the homeland—deployed disaster-response teams to the Gulf Coast. The Coast Guard put its choppers on alert. More than five thousand National Guard personnel in the affected states stood ready. Guard forces from other states were prepared to answer calls for assistance. Contrary to later claims, there was never a shortage of Guardsmen available, either because of Iraq or any other reason.

All of this federal activity was intended to support state and local officials. My team, led by Secretary of Homeland Security Mike Chertoff—a brilliant lawyer and decent man who had resigned his lifetime appointment as a federal judge to take the job—stayed in close touch with the governors of Louisiana, Mississippi, Alabama, and Florida. Governor Blanco requested an emergency declaration allowing Louisiana to use federal resources to pay for and support her state's disaster-response preparations. Only once in recent history—before Hurricane Floyd in 1999—had a president issued an emergency declaration before a storm made landfall. I signed it Saturday night, along with similar declarations for Mississippi and Alabama the next day.

———

On Sunday morning, the National Hurricane Center described Katrina as "not only extremely intense but also exceptionally large." Mayor Nagin had given instructions for a voluntary evacuation. I knew New Orleans well enough to understand that wouldn't work. People had heard apocalyptic storm warnings for years. Some used them as an excuse to party on Bourbon Street in defiance of the hurricane gods. Others didn't have the means to evacuate. The evacuation needed to be mandatory, with special arrangements for people who needed help, such as buses to transport those without cars—a step the city never took, leading to the heartbreaking scene of empty New Orleans school buses submerged in an abandoned parking lot.

I called Governor Blanco at 9:14 a.m.

"What's going on in New Orleans?" I asked. "Has Nagin given the mandatory order?"

She said he had not, despite the dire warnings they had received the previous night from Max Mayfield, the director of the National Hurricane Center. Max later said it was only the second time in his thirty-six-year career he had been anxious enough to call elected officials personally.

"The mayor's got to order people to leave. That's the only way they'll listen," I told Governor Blanco. "Call him and tell him. My people tell me this is going to be a terrible storm."

"They're not going to be able to get everyone out in time," she said. Unfortunately, I knew she was right. But it was better to start now than wait any longer.

"What else do you need from the federal government?" I asked the governor.

She assured me she had been working closely with my team and had what she needed.

"Are you sure?" I asked.

"Yes, Mr. President, we've got it under control," she said.

"Okay, hang in there," I said, "and call Ray and get him to evacuate, now."

An hour later, Mayor Nagin announced the first mandatory evacuation in New Orleans history. "This is a threat that we've never faced before," he said. Katrina's landfall was less than twenty-four hours away.

I also called Governor Haley Barbour of Mississippi, Governor Bob Riley of Alabama, and my brother Jeb in Florida. I told them they could count on strong support from the federal government.

A little before 11:00 a.m., I joined a FEMA videoconference with officials from the states in Katrina's projected path. It was rare for a president to attend a staff-level briefing like this. I saw some surprised looks on the screen when my face appeared. But I wanted to convey to the entire government how seriously I took this storm.

There was a discussion of potential flooding along the coastline and the possibility that water might spill over the top of the New Orleans levees. But no one predicted the levees would break—a different and much more severe problem than overtopping.

"The current track and forecast we have now suggests that there will be minimal flooding in the city of New Orleans itself," Max Mayfield said. "But we've always said that the storm surge model is only accurate within about twenty percent."

A few minutes later, I stepped out in front of the cameras. "Hurricane Katrina is now designated a Category Five hurricane," I said. "We cannot stress enough the danger this hurricane poses to Gulf Coast communities. I urge all citizens to put their own safety and the safety of their families first by moving to safe ground. Please listen carefully to instructions provided by state and local officials."

———

At 6:10 a.m. Central Time on Monday, August 29, Hurricane Katrina made landfall in Louisiana. The eye of the storm passed over Plaquemines Parish, at the far southeastern tip of the state, and plowed north across the Louisiana-Mississippi border, about forty miles east of New Orleans. "The worst weather in this system is indeed going to bypass downtown New Orleans and go to our east," NBC News's Brian Williams reported. He said New Orleans was experiencing "the best of the worst-case scenarios." Several journalists on the scene said the city had "dodged a bullet." Governor Blanco confirmed that while some water had spilled over the tops of the levees, they had detected no breaches. My staff and I went to bed thinking the levees had held.

In Mississippi, there was no uncertainty about the damage. Eighty miles of coastline had been obliterated. Downtown Gulfport sat under ten feet of water. Casinos, barges, and bridges were ruined. US-90, a major highway running across southern Mississippi, was shut down. In the city of Waveland, 95 percent of structures were severely damaged or destroyed.

———

Early Tuesday morning, Day Two of Katrina, I learned that the first reports were wrong. The levees in New Orleans had been breached. Water from Lake Pontchartrain began to pour into the city, filling the bowl. An estimated 80 to 90 percent of residents had evacuated, but tens of thousands had not, including many of the poor and vulnerable in low-lying areas like the Lower Ninth Ward.

While it was important to get relief supplies into the city, our first priority had to be saving lives. Coast Guard helicopters took the lead in the effort. As pilots dodged power lines and trees, rescuers rappelled down dangling ropes in midair to pluck residents from rooftops. When I heard critics say the federal response to Katrina was slow, I thought about those brave Coast Guardsmen who mounted one of the most rapid and effective rescue operations in American history.

"This morning our hearts and prayers are with our fellow citizens along the Gulf Coast who have suffered so much from Hurricane Katrina," I said in San Diego, where I had come to commemorate the sixtieth anniversary of America's victory in the Pacific theater of World War II. ". . . The good folks in Louisiana and Mississippi and Alabama and other affected areas are going to need the help and compassion and prayers of our fellow citizens."

After the speech, I decided to head back to Crawford, pack up for the capital, and return to Washington on Wednesday morning. Joe Hagin had reached out to Governors Blanco and Barbour to discuss the possibility of a visit. Both felt it was too early. A presidential arrival would have required dozens of law enforcement officials to provide security at the airport, an ambulance and medical personnel on standby, and numerous other resources. Neither governor wanted to divert rescue assets to prepare for my arrival. I agreed.

Aboard Air Force One, I was told that our flight path would take us over some of the areas hit by Katrina. We could fly low over the Gulf Coast to give me a closer look. If I wasn't going to land in the disaster zone, I figured the next best thing was to get a sense of the devastation from above.

What I saw took my breath away. New Orleans was almost totally submerged. In some neighborhoods, all I could see were rooftops peeking out from the water. The Superdome roof had peeled off. The I-10 bridge connecting New Orleans with Slidell had collapsed into Lake Pontchartrain. Cars floated down rivers that used to be streets. The landscape looked like something out of a horror movie.

The devastation in Mississippi was even more brutal. For miles and miles along the shore, every standing structure had been reduced to timber. Pine trees were strewn across the coast like matchsticks. Huge casinos that sat on barges in the Gulf were destroyed and washed ashore in pieces. The bridge over Bay St. Louis was gone. *This must be what it looks like when a nuclear bomb explodes*, I thought.

Staring out the window, all I could think about was what the people on the ground were enduring. What goes through your mind when your entire community is destroyed? Do you take a mental inventory of everything you left behind? I worried most about the people stranded. I imagined the desperation they must be feeling as they scrambled to their rooftops to outrace the rising water. I said a silent prayer for their safety.

At some point, our press team ushered photographers into the cabin. I barely noticed them at the time; I couldn't take my eyes off the devastation below. But when the pictures were released, I realized I had made a serious mistake. The photo of me hovering over the damage suggested I was detached from the suffering on the ground. That wasn't how I felt. But once the public impression was formed, I couldn't change it. For all my efforts to avoid the perception problem Dad faced during Hurricane Andrew, I ended up repeating it.

I've often reflected on what I should have done differently that day. I believe the decision not to land in New Orleans was correct. Emergency responders would have been called away from the rescue efforts, and that would have been wrong. A better option would have been to stop at the airport in Baton Rouge, the state capital. Eighty miles north of the flood zone, I could have strategized with the governor and assured Katrina victims that their country stood with them.

Landing in Baton Rouge would not have saved any lives. Its benefit would have been good public relations. But public relations matter when you are president, particularly when people are hurting. When Hurricane Betsy devastated New Orleans in 1965, Lyndon Johnson flew in from Washington to visit late at night. He made his way to a shelter in the

Ninth Ward by flashlight. "This is your president!" he called out when he arrived in the dark and crowded space. "I'm here to help you!" Unfortunately, I did not follow his example.

———

When I landed at the White House Wednesday afternoon, I convened an emergency meeting in the Cabinet Room to discuss the response. "Every agency needs to step forward," I told the team. "Look at your resources and find a way to do more."

I gave a statement in the Rose Garden outlining the federal response. The Transportation Department had sent trucks to deliver supplies. Health and Human Services provided medical teams and mortuary units. Energy opened the Strategic Petroleum Reserve to protect against a major spike in gasoline prices. The Defense Department deployed the USS *Bataan* to conduct search-and-rescue and the USNS *Comfort*, a hospital ship, to provide medical care. FEMA surged supplies into the disaster region and set up shelters for evacuees. We later learned there were major problems with organization and tracking, leading many deliveries to be delayed or never completed.

These logistical measures were necessary, but they seemed inadequate compared to the images of desperation Americans saw on their television screens. There were victims begging for water, families stranded on overpasses, and people standing on rooftops holding signs that read "Help Me!" More than one person interviewed said the same thing: "I can't believe this is happening in the United States of America."

On top of the hurricane and flood, we were now facing the third disaster: chaos and violence in New Orleans. Looters smashed windows to steal guns, clothing, and jewelry. Helicopters couldn't land because of gunfire. Downtown buildings were aflame.

The police force was powerless to restore order. While many officers carried out their duty honorably, some abandoned their posts to deal with their own personal emergencies. Others joined the criminals. I was enraged to see footage of police officers walking out of a store carrying big-screen TVs. I felt like I was watching a reverse of what had happened

four years earlier in Manhattan. Instead of charging into burning buildings to save lives, some first responders in New Orleans were breaking
into stores to steal electronics.

A horrific scene was developing at the Superdome, where tens of
thousands of people had gathered to take shelter. After three days, the
roof was leaking, the air-conditioning had stopped working, and sanitation facilities had broken down. The media issued reports of sadistic
behavior, including rape and murder. Between the chaos and the poor
communications, the government never knew for sure what was happening. It took us several days to learn that thousands of other people had
gathered with no food or water at the New Orleans Convention Center.

With the police unable to stop the lawlessness, the only solution was
a stronger troop presence. As of Wednesday afternoon, New Orleans had
about four thousand National Guard forces, with reinforcements on the
way. But the Guard, under the command of the governor, seemed overwhelmed. One option was to deploy active-duty troops and put both them
and Guard forces in Louisiana under the unified command of the federal
government.

Forces from the 82nd Airborne Division awaited orders to deploy,
and I was prepared to give them. But we had a problem. The Posse Comitatus Act of 1878 prohibited active-duty military from conducting law
enforcement within the United States. Don Rumsfeld, speaking for many
in the military, opposed sending the 82nd Airborne.

There was one exception to Posse Comitatus. If I declared New
Orleans to be in a state of insurrection, I could deploy federal troops
equipped with full law enforcement powers. The last time the Insurrection Act had been invoked was 1992, when Dad sent the military to
suppress the Los Angeles riots. In that case, Governor Pete Wilson of
California had requested the federal deployment. The Insurrection Act
could be invoked over a governor's objections. In the most famous example, President Dwight Eisenhower defied Governor Orval Faubus by
deploying the 101st Airborne to enforce the Supreme Court's decision
desegregating Central High School in Little Rock, Arkansas.

On Thursday morning, Day Four, Andy Card formally raised the
prospect of federalizing the response with Governor Blanco and her
team. The governor did not want to give up authority to the federal gov-

ernment. That left me in a tough position. If I invoked the Insurrection Act against her wishes, the world would see a male Republican president usurping the authority of a female Democratic governor by declaring an insurrection in a largely African American city. That would arouse controversy anywhere. To do so in the Deep South, where there had been centuries of states' rights tension, could unleash holy hell. I had to persuade the governor to change her mind. I decided to make my case in person the next day.

I was as frustrated as I had been at any point in my presidency. All my instincts told me we needed to get federal troops into New Orleans to stop the violence and speed the recovery. But I was stuck with a resistant governor, a reluctant Pentagon, and an antiquated law. I wanted to overrule them all. But at the time, I worried that the consequence could be a constitutional crisis, and possibly a political insurrection as well.

———

On Friday morning, Day Five, I convened a seven o'clock meeting in the Situation Room with the government-wide Katrina response team. "I know you all are trying hard as you can," I said. "But it's not cutting it. We have to establish order in New Orleans as soon as possible. Having this situation spiral out of control is unacceptable."

As Mike Chertoff and I walked out to Marine One for the trip to the Gulf Coast, I delivered the same message to the press pool. "The results are not acceptable," I said. "I'm headed down there right now."

We took Air Force One into Mobile, Alabama, where I was met by Governors Bob Riley and Haley Barbour. Both were impressive leaders who had carried out effective evacuation plans, worked closely with local authorities, and launched recovery operations rapidly.

I asked Bob and Haley if they were getting the federal support they needed. Both told me they were. "That Mike Brown is doing a heck of a job," Bob said. I knew Mike was under pressure, and I wanted to boost his morale. When I spoke to the press a few minutes later, I repeated the praise.

"Brownie," I said, "you're doing a heck of a job."

I never imagined those words would become an infamous entry in the political lexicon. As complaints about Mike Brown's performance mounted, especially in New Orleans, critics turned my words of encouragement into a club to bludgeon me.

Our next stop was Biloxi, Mississippi. I had flown over the area two days earlier, but nothing prepared me for the destruction I witnessed on the ground. I walked through a wasteland. There were uprooted trees and debris strewn everywhere. Virtually no structures were standing. One man was sitting on a block of concrete, with two smaller slabs in front. I realized it was the foundation of a house. The two slabs used to be his front steps. Nearby was a mangled appliance that looked like it might have been his dishwasher.

I sat next to him and asked how he was holding up. I expected him to tell me that everything he owned had been ruined. Instead he said, "I'm doing fine. . . . I'm alive, and my mother is alive."

I was struck by his spirit and sense of perspective. I found the same outlook in many others. One of the most impressive people I met was Mayor A.J. Holloway of Biloxi. "All the Way Holloway" had been a running back for the 1960 National Champion Ole Miss football team. While Katrina destroyed more than six thousand homes and businesses in Biloxi, there wasn't an ounce of self-pity in the mayor. He resolved to rebuild the city better than before. Governor Barbour put the spirit of the state into words when he said people were "hitching up their britches and rebuilding Mississippi."

———

Our final stop was New Orleans, where I made my appeal to Governor Blanco on Air Force One. Despite my repeated urging, she made clear she wasn't going to give me an answer on federalizing the response. There was nothing to gain by pushing her harder; the governor was dug in.

After a helicopter tour of the flooded city, we touched down at a Coast Guard station near the breached Seventeenth Street levee. On one side of the levee sat the town of Metairie, relatively dry. On the other was Orleans Parish, deep underwater for as far as I could see. I stared into the three-hundred-foot breach, a gateway for a destructive cascade of water. Unlike 1927, no levee had been dynamited in 2005. But the horrific impact on the people in the flood's path was the same.

When I got back to the White House that evening, Andy Card met me in the Oval Office. He and White House Counsel Harriet Miers had spent the day—and the previous night—working with the lawyers and the Pentagon on a way to get federal troops into Louisiana. They had come up with an interesting proposal: A three-star general would command all military forces in Louisiana. On matters concerning the active-duty forces, he would report to me. On matters concerning the Guard, he would report to Governor Blanco. This dual-hat structure gave the federal government what we needed—a clear chain of command and active-duty troops to secure the city—while accommodating the governor's concerns. Andy faxed her a letter outlining the arrangement just before midnight.

The next morning, Day Six, a call from Baton Rouge came in to the White House. The governor had declined.

I was exasperated. I had spent three days trying to persuade the governor. It had been a waste of time. At 10:00 a.m., I stepped into the Rose Garden to announce the deployment of more than seven thousand active-duty troops to New Orleans—without law enforcement powers. I was anxious about the situation. If they got caught in a crossfire, it would be my fault. But I decided that sending troops with diminished authority was better than not sending them at all.

The commander of Joint Task Force Katrina was a six-foot-two, no-nonsense general known as the Ragin' Cajun. A descendant of Creole ancestors from southern Louisiana, General Russ Honoré had lived through many hurricanes and knew the people of the Gulf Coast well.

General Honoré brought exactly what the situation required: common sense, good communication skills, and an ability to make decisions. He quickly earned the trust of elected officials, National Guard commanders, and local police chiefs. When a unit of Guard and police forces tried to enter the Convention Center to make a food delivery with their guns drawn, Honoré was caught on camera yelling, "Weapons down, damn it!" The general came up with a perfect motto to describe his approach: "Don't get stuck on stupid."

While we couldn't federalize the response by law, General Honoré effectively did so with his strong will and force of personality. Mayor Nagin summed him up as a "John Wayne dude . . . who came off the doggone chopper, and he started cussing and people started moving."

Had I known he could be so effective without the authority I assumed he needed, I would have cut off the legal debate and sent troops in without law enforcement powers several days sooner.

———

On Monday, September 5, Day Eight, I made my second trip to the Gulf Coast. General Honoré met me in Baton Rouge and briefed me on the response. Search-and-rescue operations were almost complete. The Superdome and Convention Center had been evacuated. Water was being pumped out of the city. Most important, our troops had restored order without firing a shot.

Laura and I visited an evacuee center run by a church called the Bethany World Prayer Center. Hundreds of people, including many from the Superdome, were spread across a gymnasium floor on mats. Most looked dazed and exhausted. One girl cried as she said, "I can't find my mother." My friend T.D. Jakes, a Dallas pastor who had joined us for the visit, prayed for their comfort and well-being. T.D. is the kind of man who puts his faith into action. He told me members of his church had welcomed twenty victims of Katrina into their homes.

There were similar examples of compassion across the Gulf Coast. For all the depressing aspects of the Katrina aftermath, these stories stand out as shining examples of the American character. Southern Baptists set up a mobile kitchen to feed tens of thousands of hungry people. New York City firefighters drove down in a truck the New Orleans Fire Department had loaned them after 9/11. Volunteers from the American Red Cross and Salvation Army set up twenty-four-hour-a-day centers to help disaster victims get assistance. Every state in the country took in evacuees. The city of Houston alone welcomed two hundred fifty thousand. The evacuation went down as the largest movement of Americans since the Dust Bowl of the 1930s.

To lead private-sector fundraising for Katrina victims, I had tapped an unlikely duo: Dad and Bill Clinton. Katrina was actually their encore performance. After a massive tsunami struck Southeast Asia in December 2004, they had teamed up at my request and raised more than $1 billion for the victims. As they traveled the world together, the former presidents—41 and 42, as I called them—developed a bond. Dad rose above the disappointment of 1992 and embraced his former rival. I appreciated that Bill treated Dad with deference and respect, and I grew to like him. When I asked them to lead another fundraising drive after Katrina, they agreed immediately. Mother called me afterward. "I see you've reunited your father and your stepbrother," she quipped.

Unfortunately, the spirit of generosity did not carry over to everyone. At an NBC telethon to raise money for Katrina victims, rapper Kanye West told a primetime TV audience, "George Bush doesn't care about black people." Jesse Jackson later compared the New Orleans Convention Center to the "hull of a slave ship." A member of the Congressional Black Caucus claimed that if the storm victims had been "white, middle-class Americans" they would have received more help.

Five years later, I can barely write those words without feeling disgusted. I am deeply insulted by the suggestion that we allowed American citizens to suffer because they were black. As I told the press at the time, "The storm didn't discriminate, and neither will the recovery effort. When those Coast Guard choppers, many of whom were first on the scene, were pulling people off roofs, they didn't check the color of a person's skin."

The more I thought about it, the angrier I felt. I was raised to believe that racism was one of the greatest evils in society. I admired Dad's courage when he defied near-universal opposition from his constituents to vote for the Open Housing Bill of 1968. I was proud to have earned more black votes than any Republican governor in Texas history. I had appointed African Americans to top government positions, including the first black woman national security adviser and the first two black secretaries of state. It broke my heart to see minority children shuffled through the school system, so I had based my signature domestic policy initiative, the No Child Left Behind Act, on ending the soft bigotry of low expectations. I had launched a $15 billion program to combat HIV/AIDS in Africa. As part of the response to Katrina, my administration worked with Congress to provide historically black colleges and universities in the Gulf Coast with more than $400 million in loans to restore their campuses and renew their recruiting efforts.

I faced a lot of criticism as president. I didn't like hearing people claim I had lied about Iraq's weapons of mass destruction or cut taxes to benefit the rich. But the suggestion that I was a racist because of the response to Katrina represented an all-time low. I told Laura at the time that it was the worst moment of my presidency. I feel the same way today.

———

During Week Two of the Katrina response, Mike Chertoff recommended that we make a personnel change. State and local officials had been complaining about the slowness of FEMA, and Chertoff told me he had lost confidence in Director Mike Brown. He felt the FEMA director had frozen under the pressure and become insubordinate. I accepted Chertoff's recommendation to bring in Vice Admiral Thad Allen—the chief of staff of the Coast Guard who had done a brilliant job leading the search-and-rescue efforts—as the principal federal officer coordinating operations in the Gulf Coast.

On Sunday of that week, Day Fourteen, I made my third visit to the Gulf Coast. I choppered onto the USS *Iwo Jima*, which had docked in the Mississippi River. Two years earlier, I had deployed the *Iwo Jima* to free Liberia from the dictator Charles Taylor. It was surreal to be standing aboard an amphibious assault ship overlooking a major American city suffering the wounds of a violent storm.

The next morning, we boarded ten-ton military trucks for a tour through New Orleans. The Secret Service was anxious. The drive was one of very few times a president had traveled through a major metropolitan city in an open-top vehicle since the Kennedy assassination in 1963. We had to dodge dangling power lines and drive through deep pools of standing water. Virtually all the houses were still abandoned. Some of their walls were spray-painted with the date they had been searched and the number of bodies discovered inside. I saw a few people wandering around in a daze. Nearby was a pack of mangy dogs scavenging for food, many with bite marks on their bodies. It was a vivid display of the survival-of-the-fittest climate that had overtaken the city.

On September 15, Day Eighteen, I returned to New Orleans to deliver a primetime address to the nation. I decided to give the speech from Jackson Square, named for General Andrew Jackson, who defended New Orleans against the British at the end of the War of 1812. The famous French Quarter landmark had suffered minimal damage during the storm.

I viewed the speech as my opportunity to explain what had gone wrong, promise to fix the problems, and lay out a vision to move the Gulf Coast and the country forward. Abandoned New Orleans was the eeriest setting from which I had ever given a speech. Except for generators, the power was still out in the city. In one of the world's most vibrant cities, the only people around were a handful of government officials and the soldiers from the 82nd Airborne.

With St. Louis Cathedral bathed in blue light behind me, I began:

> Good evening. I'm speaking to you from the city of New Orleans—nearly empty, still partly under water, and waiting for life and hope to return. . . .
>
> Tonight I . . . offer this pledge of the American people: Throughout the area hit by the hurricane, we will do what it takes, we will stay as long as it takes, to help citizens rebuild their communities and their lives. And all who question the future of the Crescent City need to know there is no way to imagine America without New Orleans, and this great city will rise again.

I laid out a series of specific commitments: to ensure victims received the financial assistance they needed; to help people move out of hotels and shelters and into longer-term housing; to devote federal assets to cleaning up debris and rebuilding roads, bridges, and schools; to provide tax incentives for the return of businesses and the hiring of local workers; and to strengthen New Orleans's levees to withstand the next big storm. I continued:

> Four years after the frightening experience of September the 11th, Americans have every right to expect a more effective response in a time of emergency. When the federal government fails to meet such an obligation, I, as president, am responsible for the problem, and for the solution. So I've ordered every Cabinet Secretary to participate in a comprehensive review of the government response to the hurricane. This government will learn the lessons of Hurricane Katrina.

I took those promises seriously. Over the coming months, I worked with Congress to secure $126 billion in rebuilding funds, by far the most for any natural disaster in American history. I decided to create a new position to ensure that one person was accountable for coordinating the rebuilding and ensuring the money was spent wisely. Thad Allen held the role at first. When I nominated him to be commandant of the Coast Guard, I asked Don Powell, a fellow Texan and former chairman of the Federal Deposit Insurance Commission, to take his place.

I told Chief of Staff Andy Card—and later Josh Bolten—that I expected regular progress reports on our initiatives in the Gulf Coast. Top government officials gathered routinely in the Roosevelt Room for detailed briefings on issues such as how many victims had received disaster benefits checks, the number of Gulf Coast schools reopened, and the cubic yardage of debris cleared.

I wanted the people of the Gulf Coast to see firsthand that I was committed to rebuilding, so I made seventeen trips between August 2005 and August 2008. Laura made twenty-four visits in all. We both came away impressed by the determination and spirit of the people we met.

In March 2006, I visited the Industrial Canal levee, which had ruptured and flooded the Lower Ninth Ward. We saw huge piles of debris and trash as we drove to the site, a reminder of how far the neighborhood still had to go. Mayor Nagin and I grabbed our hard hats, climbed to the top of the levee, and watched pile drivers pound pillars seventy feet underground—a solid foundation designed to withstand a Katrina-size storm. Nothing was more important to reassuring New Orleans's exiled residents that it was safe to return to the city they loved.

On the second anniversary of the storm, Laura and I visited the Dr. Martin Luther King, Jr., Charter School for Science and Technology. Two years earlier, the school had been submerged under fifteen feet of water. Thanks in large part to a determined local principal, Doris Hicks, MLK became the first school in the Lower Ninth Ward to reopen. As a former librarian, Laura had been saddened by the number of books destroyed in the storm. She started a private fundraising campaign to help New Orleans schools rebuild their collections. Over the years, her leadership and the generosity of the American people helped send tens of thousands of books to schools across the Gulf Coast.

The story in Mississippi was just as uplifting. In August 2006, I went back to Biloxi, where I visited four days after the storm. Beaches that had been covered with debris a year earlier had been returned to their shimmering white-sand beauty. Seven casinos, supporting hundreds of jobs, had reopened. Church congregations that had been separated were back together again. Few people's lives had changed more than Lynn Patterson's. When I met him a year earlier, he was digging cars out of the muck in a neighborhood where all the houses were gone. When I came back to Biloxi, he gave Laura and me a tour of his new home, which had been rebuilt with the help of taxpayer dollars.

---

In the wake of Katrina, I asked Fran Townsend—a talented former New York City prosecutor who served as my top homeland security adviser in the White House—to study how we could better respond to future disasters. Her report reaffirmed the longstanding principle that state and local officials are best positioned to lead an effective emergency response. It also recommended changes in the federal government's approach. We devised new ways to help state and local authorities conduct early evacuations, developed backup communications systems, established a National Operations Center to distribute timely situation reports, and set up an orderly process for deploying federal resources—including active-duty troops—in cases where state and local first responders had become overwhelmed.*

The new emergency response system was tested in August 2008, when Hurricane Gustav barreled across the Gulf of Mexico toward New Orleans. I held regular videoconferences with federal, state, and local officials in the days leading up to the storm. Mike Chertoff and the new FEMA director, former Miami-Dade fire chief Dave Paulison, relocated

---

*In the fall of 2006, Congress amended the Insurrection Act to allow the president to deploy federal troops with law enforcement powers during natural disasters. Then, in 2008, they repealed the amendment.

to Baton Rouge to oversee preparations. Shelters were ready and well stocked. Louisiana Governor Bobby Jindal, the talented Republican elected in 2007, worked closely with Mayor Nagin to order a mandatory evacuation. "You need to be scared and you need to get your butts out of New Orleans right now," the mayor said.

When Gustav made landfall, the first reports were that New Orleans had dodged a direct hit. I had heard that before. This time, though, the levees held and damages in New Orleans were minimal. A few weeks later, Hurricane Ike smashed into Galveston, Texas. Property damage was extensive—only Andrew and Katrina were costlier—but thanks to good preparation at the state level, many lives were spared. For all the devastation Katrina caused, part of the storm's lasting impact is that it improved the federal government's ability to support state and local governments in responding to major disasters.

—

Even when the neighborhoods of New Orleans are restored and the homes of Mississippi are rebuilt, no one who endured Katrina will ever fully recover. That is especially true for the tens of thousands who lost their homes and possessions, and—worst of all—the families of the more than eighteen hundred Americans who died.

In a different way, it is true of me, too. In a national catastrophe, the easiest person to blame is the president. Katrina presented a political opportunity that some critics exploited for years. The aftermath of Katrina—combined with the collapse of Social Security reform and the drumbeat of violence in Iraq—made the fall of 2005 a damaging period in my presidency. Just a year earlier, I had won reelection with more votes than any candidate in history. By the end of 2005, much of my political capital was gone. With my approval ratings plummeting, many Democrats—and some Republicans—concluded they would be better off opposing me than working together. We managed to get important things done, including reauthorizing the AIDS initiative, fully funding our troops, confirming Sam Alito to the Supreme Court, and responding to the financial crisis. But the legacy of fall 2005 lingered for the rest of my time in office.

This is not to suggest that I didn't make mistakes during Katrina. I should have urged Governor Blanco and Mayor Nagin to evacuate New Orleans sooner. I should have come straight back to Washington from California on Day Two or stopped in Baton Rouge on Day Three. I should have done more to signal my sympathy for the victims and my determination to help, the way I did in the days after 9/11.

My biggest substantive mistake was waiting too long to deploy active-duty troops. By Day Three, it was clear that federal troops were needed to restore order. If I had it to do over again, I would have sent the 82nd Airborne immediately, without law enforcement authority. I hesitated at the time because I didn't want to leave our troops powerless to stop sniper attacks and the other shocking acts of violence we were hearing about on TV. We later learned these accounts were wildly overstated, the result of overzealous correspondents under pressure to fill every second of the twenty-four-hour cable news cycle.

Ultimately, the story of Katrina is that it was the storm of the century. It devastated an area the size of Great Britain, produced almost nine times more debris than any previously recorded hurricane, and killed more people than any storm in seventy-five years. The economic toll—three hundred thousand homes destroyed and $96 billion in property damage—outstripped that of every previous hurricane on record.

Yet destruction and death did not have the final word for the people of the Gulf Coast. In August 2008, I visited Gulfport, Mississippi, and Jackson Barracks in New Orleans, the home of the Louisiana National Guard, which had flooded during Katrina. It was striking to see how much had changed in three years.

In Mississippi, workers had cleared forty-six million cubic yards of storm debris, double the amount Hurricane Andrew left behind. More than forty-three thousand residents had repaired or rebuilt their homes. Traffic flowed over new bridges spanning Biloxi Bay and Bay St. Louis. Tourists and employees had returned to revitalized casinos and beachfront hotels. And in an inspiring sign, every school damaged by Katrina had reopened.

While many predicted New Orleans would never be a major city again, 87 percent of the population before Katrina had returned. The I-10 bridge connecting New Orleans and Slidell had reopened. The number of restaurants in the city had exceeded the pre-Katrina figure. More than seventy thousand citizens had repaired or rebuilt their homes. The flood-walls and levees around New Orleans had been strengthened, and the Army Corps of Engineers had begun a massive project to provide "100-year flood protection." The Superdome that once housed thousands of Katrina victims became the proud home of the Super Bowl champion New Orleans Saints.

The most uplifting change of all has come in education. Public schools that were decaying before the storm have reopened as modern facilities, with new teachers and leaders committed to reform and results. Doz-ens of charter schools have sprouted up across the city, offering parents more choices and greater flexibility. The Catholic archdiocese, led by Archbishop Alfred Hughes, continued its long tradition of educational excellence by reopening its schools quickly. The year after Katrina, New Orleans students improved their test scores. They improved more the next year, and even more the year after that.

When I gave my Farewell Address from the East Room of the White House in January 2009, one of the guests I invited was Dr. Tony Recas-ner, principal of Samuel J. Green Charter School in New Orleans. Tony started at the school in July 2005, after it had underperformed so severely that it was taken over by the state. Then Katrina hit.

When I visited in 2007, Tony told me about his innovative teach-ing methods, such as having students focus on one subject at a time for several weeks. He also told me about the results. Despite the enormous disadvantages facing his students, the percentage of those reading and doing math at grade level had more than tripled. "This school, which did not serve the community well in the past, is now really going to be a beacon of light," Tony said.

The spirit of renewal at S.J. Green Charter School is present all across the Gulf Coast. With leadership from people like Tony, a new generation can build a better life than the one they inherited. And the true legacy of Katrina will be one of hope.

# 11

# LAZARUS EFFECT

On July 30, 2008, Mohamad Kalyesubula sat in the front row of the East Room. He was a tall, trim African man. He had a big, bright smile. And he was supposed to be dead.

Five years earlier, Laura and I had met Mohamad in Entebbe, Uganda, at a clinic run by The AIDS Support Organization, TASO. Located in a simple one-story brick building, the TASO clinic served thousands of AIDS patients. Like most suffering the advanced stages of the disease, Mohamad was wasting away. He ate little. He battled constant fevers. He had been confined to a bed for almost a year.

I expected TASO to be a place of abject hopelessness. But it was not. A handpainted sign over the door read "Living Positively with HIV/AIDS." A choir of children, many of them orphans who had lost parents to AIDS, sang hymns that proclaimed their faith and hope. They ended with a sweet rendition of "America the Beautiful." "I have a dream," Mohamad told me from his hospital bed. "One day, I will come to the United States."

I left the clinic inspired. The patients reaffirmed my conviction that every life has dignity and value, because every person bears the mark of Almighty God. I saw their suffering as a challenge to the words of the Gospel: "To whom much is given, much is required."

America had been given a lot, and I resolved that we would answer the call. Earlier that year I had proposed, and Congress had passed, a $15 billion initiative to fight HIV/AIDS in Africa. The President's Emergency Plan for AIDS Relief, PEPFAR, constituted the largest international health initiative to combat a specific disease. I hoped it would serve as a medical version of the Marshall Plan. "This is my country's pledge to the people of Africa and the people of Uganda," I said at the TASO clinic. "You are not alone in this fight. America has decided to act."

Three months later, Mohamad received his first antiretroviral drugs. The medicine renewed his strength. Eventually he was able to get out of bed. He took a job at the TASO clinic and earned enough money to support his six children. In the summer of 2008, we invited Mohamad to the White House to watch me sign a bill more than doubling our worldwide commitment to fight HIV/AIDS. I hardly recognized him. His shriveled body had grown robust and strong. He had returned to life.

He was not the only one. In five years, the number of Africans receiving AIDS medicine had risen from fifty thousand to nearly three million—more than two million of them supported by PEPFAR. People who had been given up for dead were restored to healthy and productive lives. Calling to mind the story of Jesus raising his friend from the dead, Africans came up with a phrase to describe the transformation. They called it the Lazarus Effect.

———

In 1990, Dad asked me to lead a delegation to Gambia to celebrate its twenty-fifth anniversary of independence. A small West African nation with a population of about nine hundred thousand, Gambia was best known in America as the home of the forebears of Alex Haley, the author of *Roots*. Laura and I had read the Pulitzer Prize–winning book in which Haley traces his lineage back to an African man taken by slave traders in the 1700s.

Sadly, Gambia did not seem to have developed much since then. Laura and I were driven around the capital, Banjul, in an old Chevrolet provided by the embassy. The main road was paved. The rest were dirt. Most people we saw traveled by foot, often with heavy loads on their backs. The highlight of the trip was the ceremony celebrating Gambian independence. It took place in the national stadium, where the paint was peeling and concrete was chipped away. I remember thinking that high school stadiums in West Texas were a lot more modern than Gambia's showcase.

Gambia was in the back of my mind eight years later when I started thinking about running for president. Condi Rice and I spent long hours discussing foreign policy on the back porch of the Governor's Mansion. One day our conversation turned to Africa. Condi had strong feelings on the subject. She felt Africa had great potential, but had too often been neglected. We agreed that Africa would be a serious part of my foreign policy.

I considered America a generous nation with a moral responsibility to do our part to help relieve poverty and despair. The question was how to do it effectively. Our foreign assistance programs in Africa had a lousy track record. Most were designed during the Cold War to support anti-communist governments. While our aid helped keep friendly regimes in power, it didn't do much to improve the lives of ordinary people. In 2001, Africa received $14 billion in foreign aid, more than any other continent. Yet economic growth per capita was flat, even worse than it had been in the 1970s.

Another problem was that the traditional model of foreign aid was paternalistic: A wealthy donor nation wrote a check and told the recipient how to spend it. I decided to take a new approach in Africa and elsewhere in the developing world. We would base our relationships on partnership, not paternalism. We would trust developing countries to design their own strategies for using American taxpayer dollars. In return, they would measure their performance and be held accountable. The result would be that countries felt invested in their own success, while American taxpayers could see the impact of their generosity.

As Condi made clear in our first discussion, one problem in Africa stood out above all others: the humanitarian crisis of HIV/AIDS. The statistics were horrifying. Some ten million people in sub-Sarahan Africa had died. In some countries, one out of every four adults carried HIV. The total number infected was expected to exceed one hundred million by 2010. The United Nations projected that AIDS could be the worst epidemic since the bubonic plague of the Middle Ages.

When I took office, the United States was spending a little over $500 million a year to fight global AIDS. That was more than any other country. Yet it was paltry compared with the scope of the pandemic. The money was spread haphazardly across six different agencies. Much of their work was duplicative, a sign there was no clear strategy.

American taxpayers deserved—and conscience demanded—a plan that was more effective than this disjointed effort. I decided to make confronting the scourge of AIDS in Africa a key element of my foreign policy.

In March 2001, I met with United Nations Secretary-General Kofi Annan, a soft-spoken diplomat from Ghana. Kofi and I didn't agree on every issue, but we found common ground in our determination to deal with the AIDS pandemic. He suggested creating a new Global Fund to Fight HIV/AIDS, Tuberculosis, and Malaria that would marshal resources from around the world.

I listened but made no commitment. I considered the UN to be cumbersome, bureaucratic, and inefficient. I was concerned that a fund composed of contributions from different countries with different interests would not spend taxpayer money in a focused or effective way.

Nevertheless, Secretary of State Colin Powell and Health and Human Services Secretary Tommy Thompson recommended that I support the Global Fund with an initial pledge of $200 million. They felt it would send a good signal for America to be the first contributor. Their persistence overcame my skepticism. I announced our commitment on May 11, 2001, with Kofi and President Olusegun Obasanjo of Nigeria in the Rose Garden. "I thank you, on behalf of all AIDS sufferers in the world, but particularly on behalf of all AIDS sufferers in Africa," President Obasanjo said.

"This morning, we have made a good beginning," I said in my speech. I didn't add that I had plans to do more.

Four months to the day after we announced our pledge to the Global Fund, the terrorists struck America. Before 9/11, I had considered alleviating disease and poverty a humanitarian mission. After the attacks, it became clear to me that this was more than a mission of conscience. Our national security was tied directly to human suffering. Societies mired in poverty and disease foster hopelessness. And hopelessness leaves people ripe for recruitment by terrorists and extremists. By confronting suffering in places like Africa, America would strengthen its security and collective soul.

By early 2002, I had concluded that the Global Fund was not a sufficient response to the AIDS crisis. While America had increased our contribution to $500 million, the Fund was short on money and slow to act. Meanwhile, the AIDS epidemic was sending more Africans to their graves. The majority were between ages fifteen and forty-nine, the key demographic for productive nations. Left unchecked, the disease was projected to kill sixty-eight million people by 2020, more than had died in World War II.

I couldn't stand the idea of innocent people dying while the international community delayed. I decided it was time for America to launch a global AIDS initiative of our own. We would control the funds. We would move fast. And we would insist on results.

Josh Bolten assembled a team* to develop recommendations. In June, they came to me with a proposal to focus on one particularly devastating part of the AIDS crisis: its impact on women and children. At the time, 17.6 million women and 2.7 million children were living with HIV/AIDS. Every forty-five seconds, another baby in Africa was born with the virus.

Recently, scientists had discovered new medicines, particularly a drug called Nevirapine, that could reduce the rate of mother-to-child transmission by 50 percent. But it was not widely available in Africa or other parts of the developing world. The team proposed spending $500 million over five years to purchase medicine and train local health-care workers in the most heavily affected African and Caribbean countries.

"Let's get it started right now," I said. The plan was tailored to a specific part of the crisis in the neediest parts of the world. It put local officials in the lead. And it had an ambitious but realistic goal: to treat one million mothers and save one hundred fifty thousand babies every year after five years.

On June 19, 2002, I announced the International Mother and Child

---

*The team included Dr. Tony Fauci, the longtime director of the National Institute of Allergy and Infectious Diseases, and his assistant director, Dr. Mark Dybul; Gary Edson, my deputy national security adviser and top staffer on international development; Jay Lefkowitz, my deputy domestic policy director; Robin Cleveland from the Office of Management and Budget; Kristen Silverberg, one of Josh's deputies; and, later, Dr. Joe O'Neill, the director of national AIDS policy.

HIV Prevention Initiative in the Rose Garden. In seventeen months, we had doubled America's commitment to fighting global AIDS.

———

The morning I unveiled the mother and child program, I called Josh Bolten into the Oval Office. "This is a good start, but it's not enough," I told him. "Go back to the drawing board and think even bigger."

A few months later, he and the team recommended a large-scale program focused on AIDS treatment, prevention, and care—the strategy that would ultimately become PEPFAR.

The first part of the proposal, treatment, was the most revolutionary. Across Africa, it was estimated that four million AIDS patients required antiretroviral drugs to stay alive. Fewer than fifty thousand were receiving them. Thanks to advances in drug technology, AIDS treatment regimens that used to require thirty pills a day could be taken as a twice-a-day cocktail drug. Soon, only one pill was required. The new medicine was more potent and less toxic to patients. And the price had declined from $12,000 a year to under $300. For $25 a month, America could extend an AIDS patient's life for years.

"We need to take advantage of the breakthrough," I told the team, "but how will we get the drugs to the people?"

Tony Fauci described a program in Uganda led by Dr. Peter Mugyenyi, an innovative doctor who operated an advanced clinic and was one of the first people to bring antiretroviral drugs to Africa. At one Oval Office meeting, Tony showed me photos of Ugandan health workers from TASO climbing aboard motorcycles to bring antiretroviral drugs door-to-door to homebound patients. While only partially complete, the Mugyenyi and TASO programs showed what could be possible with more support.

In addition to treatment, Uganda employed an aggressive prevention campaign known as ABC: Abstinence, Be faithful, or else use a Condom. The approach was successful. According to estimates, Uganda's infection rate had dropped from 15 percent in 1991 to 5 percent in 2001.

PEPFAR would include one additional element: caring for victims of AIDS, especially orphans. It broke my heart that fourteen million children had lost parents to AIDS. It also worried me. A generation of rootless, desperate young people would be vulnerable to recruitment by extremists.

I pressed for specifics on the plan. "What are our goals?" I asked. "What can we accomplish?"

We set three objectives: treat two million AIDS patients, prevent seven million new infections, and care for ten million HIV-affected people. We would partner with the government and people of countries committed to battling the disease. Local leaders would develop the strategies to meet specific goals, and we would support them.

The next question was which countries to include. I decided to focus on the poorest and sickest nations, twelve in sub-Saharan Africa and two in the Caribbean.* These fourteen countries accounted for 50 percent of the world's HIV infections. If we could stop the spread of the disease at its epicenter, we could create a model for other countries and the Global Fund to follow.

The final decision was how much money we should spend. Josh's group had recommended a stunning $15 billion over five years. My budget team expressed concern. In late 2002, the U.S. economy was struggling. The American people might not understand why we were spending so much money overseas when our own citizens were suffering.

I was willing to take on that objection. I was confident I could explain how saving lives in Africa served our strategic and moral interests. Healthier societies would be less likely to breed terror or genocide. They would be more prosperous and better able to afford our goods and services. People uncertain of America's motives would see our generosity and compassion. And I believed the American people would be more supportive if we could show that their tax dollars were saving lives.

Critics would later claim that I started PEPFAR to appease the religious right or divert attention from Iraq. Those charges are preposterous.

---

*Botswana, Côte d'Ivoire, Ethiopia, Guyana, Haiti, Kenya, Mozambique, Namibia, Nigeria, Rwanda, South Africa, Tanzania, Uganda, and Zambia. At Congress's request, we later added one Asian nation to PEPFAR, Vietnam.

I proposed the AIDS initiative to save lives. Mike Gerson, my chief speechwriter and trusted adviser, put it best in a November 2002 meeting. "If we can do this and we don't," he said, "it will be a source of shame."

I made the decision to move forward with PEPFAR in December 2002. Only a few people knew about the plan. I instructed the team to keep it that way. If word leaked out, there would be a turf war among government agencies for control of the money. Members of Congress would be tempted to dilute the program's focus by redirecting funds for their own purposes. I didn't want PEPFAR to end up hamstrung by bureaucracy and competing interests.

"Seldom has history offered a greater opportunity to do so much for so many," I said in my State of the Union address on January 28, 2003. ". . . Tonight I propose the Emergency Plan for AIDS Relief—a work of mercy beyond all current international efforts to help the people of Africa."

Members of both parties rose to support the plan. Standing next to Laura in the First Lady's box was a man whose program and country had served as an inspiration for PEPFAR, Dr. Peter Mugyenyi of Uganda.

———

I had intended the announcement to make a big impact, and it did. President Clinton's top AIDS official called it "inspiring and clearly heartfelt." The *Chicago Tribune* summarized the reaction of many newspapers when it editorialized, "'Astonishing' is not too strong a word for President Bush's announcement."

As expected, there were some objections. The biggest came in response to the ABC prevention strategy. Critics on the left denounced the abstinence component as an ideological "war on condoms" that would prove unrealistic and ineffective. I pointed out that abstinence worked every time. Some on the right objected to distributing condoms, which they felt would encourage promiscuity. At least members of Congress were smart enough not to criticize the B, being faithful within marriage.

Ironically, both sides charged that we were imposing our values— religious fundamentalism if you asked one camp, sexual permissiveness if you asked the other. Neither argument made much sense to me, since

On the South Lawn after ordering troops into Iraq.
*White House/Eric Draper*

Sitting in the cockpit of Air Force One on the approach to Baghdad on Thanksgiving Day 2003.
*White House/Tina Hager*

When he was wounded in Iraq, Master Gunnery Sergeant Guadalupe Denogean had two requests: a promotion for the Marine who saved his life, and to become an American citizen. *White House/Eric Draper*

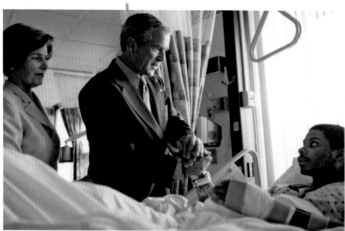

Visiting the wounded was both the toughest and most inspiring part of my job. Here, with Sergeant Patrick Hagood at Walter Reed Army Medical Center. *White House/Paul Morse*

In the Oval Office, an Iraqi man used his new prosthetic hand to write a "prayer for God to bless America." *White House/Eric Draper*

At the NATO summit in Turkey, Don Rumsfeld passes me Condi's note informing me of the successful transfer of Iraqi sovereignty, which I celebrated with Tony Blair. *White House/Eric Draper*

With Senator Ted Kennedy in early 2001. We worked together on education and immigration reform even though we disagreed on the war.
*White House/Eric Draper*

At Horace Greeley Elementary School in Chicago, a 92 percent low-income school where reading and math proficiency improved under No Child Left Behind. *White House/Joyce Boghosian*

I drew strength from the crowds on the 2004 campaign trail. Speaking here in Troy, Ohio.
*White House/Paul Morse*

Exiting Marine One on Election Day 2004. We'd just received exit polls showing I would lose badly. *White House/Paul Morse*

In the White House residence on Election Night 2004, waiting for the decision.
*White House/Eric Draper*

The haunting view of New Orleans from Air Force One two days after Katrina. I should have landed in Baton Rouge, where I could have expressed my concern without disrupting rescue efforts.

*White House/Paul Morse*

Comforting victims of Katrina four days after landfall. The allegation that racism played a role in the government's response was one of the worst moments of my presidency. *White House/Eric Draper*

Sitting with a Biloxi, Mississippi, man on what used to be his front steps. *White House/Eric Draper*

Aboard Air Force One at the New Orleans airport, I urged Louisiana officials to federalize the response to Katrina, but Governor Blanco refused (*clockwise at table*: Mayor Ray Nagin, Senator Mary Landrieu, Senator David Vitter, Homeland Security Secretary Mike Chertoff, Representative Bobby Jindal, Representative William Jefferson, and Governor Kathleen Blanco). *White House/Eric Draper*

Governor Haley Barbour of Mississippi showed superb leadership. "People are hitching up their britches and rebuilding Mississippi," he said.
*White House/Eric Draper*

Holding Baron Tantoh from Cape Town, South Africa, who was born HIV-free thanks to the mother and child initiative. *White House/Eric Draper*

Five years after I met Moha-mad Kalyesubula at the TASO Clinic in Uganda, he came to the East Room to watch me sign a bill doubling our PEPFAR commitment. *White House/Joyce Boghosian*

With Irish rock star Bono. "Used to be married to Cher, didn't he?" I asked Josh Bolten before our first meeting. *White House/Paul Morse*

Passing out bed nets to mothers in Arusha, Tanzania, as part of our malaria initiative. *White House/Eric Draper*

An interesting fashion statement in Dar es Salaam, Tanzania. For some reason these didn't catch on back home. *White House/Chris Greenberg*

Iraqis defied the terrorists by voting three times in 2005. Here with absentee voters in the Oval Office. *White House/Paul Morse*

At Brooke Army Medical Center, Staff Sergeant Christian Bagge told me he wanted to run again. "When you're ready, just call me," I said. Six months later, he showed up for a jog around the South Lawn. *White House/Eric Draper*

Visiting with troops in Anbar in 2007. My greatest honor as president was serving as commander in chief. *White House/ Eric Draper*

In Anbar Province, with the Sunni sheikhs who rallied their tribes against al Qaeda. "If you need us, my men and I will go to Afghanistan!" one said. *White House/Eric Draper*

At the 2007 retirement ceremony of Joint Chiefs Chairman Pete Pace (*left*). Next to us are his successor, Admiral Mike Mullen (*right*), and Secretary of Defense Bob Gates. *White House/David Bohrer*

After flying secretly to Baghdad in June 2006, I met with Prime Minister Nouri al Maliki (*right*) and convened a joint U.S.–Iraqi national security meeting via secure videoconference. U.S. Ambassador Zal Khalilzad is to the left of me. *White House/Eric Draper*

The toughest decision of the presidency was ordering the surge. I sent 30,000 additional troops under a new counterinsurgency strategy implemented by General David Petraeus (*right*) and Ambassador Ryan Crocker. *White House/Eric Draper*

Walking Jenna down the aisle at her wedding in Crawford in May 2008.
*White House/Shealah Craighead*

At a White House reception for Jenna and her husband, Henry Hager. *White House/Eric Draper*

The extended Bush family celebrating Mother and Dad's sixtieth wedding anniversary in 2005. No president and first lady have been married longer than them. *White House/Eric Draper*

Congratulating Romania on its admission into NATO. Just before I spoke, a full-spectrum rainbow appeared. "God is smiling on us today," I said. *White House/Paul Morse*

My father had fought his father in World War II, but Prime Minister Junichiro Koizumi of Japan and I worked to spread democracy—and even visited the home of his childhood idol, Elvis Presley. *White House/Eric Draper*

On a ride around the ranch with Crown Prince Abdullah of Saudi Arabia. When a lone hen turkey appeared in the road, he grabbed my arm. "My brother," he said, "it is a sign from Allah." *White House/Eric Draper*

With Israeli Prime Minister Ariel Sharon (*left*) and Palestinian Prime Minister Mahmoud Abbas in Aqaba, Jordan, where they agreed to work toward a democratic Palestinian state.
*White House/Eric Draper*

With Jacques Chirac of France (*left*) and Vladimir Putin of Russia.
*White House/Eric Draper*

Announcing TARP with Federal Reserve Chairman Ben Bernanke (*left*) and Treasury Secretary Hank Paulson.
*White House/Eric Draper*

With John McCain after he sealed the
Republican nomination in 2008.
*White House/Eric Draper*

With President-elect Barack
Obama and his wife, Michelle, in
the Blue Room on Inauguration
Day, 2009. *White House/Eric Draper*

Conferring with Counselor
Ed Gillespie (*left*) and Chief of
Staff Josh Bolten, two trusted
aides and good friends, in the
trying final months of the
administration.
*White House/ Eric Draper*

Leaving the Oval Office for the last time. *White House/Eric Draper*

At a welcome-home rally in Midland. "Laura and I may have left Texas," I said, "but Texas never left us." *Eric Draper*

the ABC strategy had been developed in Africa, implemented in Africa, and successful in Africa.

In the spring of 2003, the House of Representatives took up PEPFAR legislation. The bill was sponsored by Republican Congressman Henry Hyde of Illinois and Democratic Congressman Tom Lantos of California, two principled supporters of human rights. In a fine example of bipartisan cooperation, they helped steer the bill through the House with a vote of 375 to 41.

The bill then moved to the Senate, where it received strong backing from Majority Leader Bill Frist, a doctor who took annual medical missionary trips to Africa, and Senator Dick Lugar of Indiana, the thoughtful chairman of the Foreign Relations Committee. Bill and Dick rallied support among a wide range of lawmakers, from conservatives like Jesse Helms of North Carolina to liberals like Joe Biden of Delaware and John Kerry of Massachusetts. I told Bill I hoped to sign a bill before I left for the 2003 G-8 summit in Evian, France, so that I would have more leverage to persuade our allies to join us. Bill worked tirelessly to meet the deadline. Three days before I left the country, I signed PEPFAR into law.

———

Two months later, Laura and I touched down in sub-Saharan Africa. Our first stop was Senegal. After a morning meeting at the presidential palace, President Abdoulaye Wade and his wife, Viviane, escorted us to one of the most haunting places I visited as president, Gorée Island.

Our tour began in a pink stucco structure, the Slave House. The museum curator showed Laura and me through the small, hot rooms. One had contained scales to weigh the slaves. Another was divided into cells to separate men, women, and children. We walked through a narrow passageway to the Door of No Return, the starting point for the horrific Middle Passage. I could only imagine the fear of those hopeless souls who were stolen from their families and shoved onto ships bound for an unfamiliar land. I put my arm around Laura as we peered out at the blue ocean.

Standing behind us were Colin Powell and Condi Rice. I thought

about the contrast between what their ancestors had endured and what
Colin and Condi had accomplished. After the tour, I gave a speech from
the island:

> *At this place, liberty and life were stolen and sold. Human beings were*
> *delivered and sorted, and weighed, and branded with the marks of com-*
> *mercial enterprises, and loaded as cargo on a voyage without return. One*
> *of the largest migrations of history was also one of the greatest crimes of*
> *history. . . .*
>
> *For two hundred fifty years the captives endured an assault on their*
> *culture and their dignity. The spirit of Africans in America did not break.*
> *Yet the spirit of their captors was corrupted. . . . A republic founded on*
> *equality for all became a prison for millions. And yet in the words of the*
> *African proverb, "No fist is big enough to hide the sky." All the generations*
> *of oppression under the laws of man could not crush the hope of freedom*
> *and defeat the purposes of God. . . .*
>
> *In the struggle of the centuries, America learned that freedom is not*
> *the possession of one race. We know with equal certainty that freedom is*
> *not the possession of one nation. This belief in the natural rights of man,*
> *this conviction that justice should reach wherever the sun passes, leads*
> *America into the world. With the power and resources given to us, the*
> *United States seeks to bring peace where there is conflict, hope where there*
> *is suffering, and liberty where there is tyranny.*

PEPFAR was a new chapter in Africa's unfolding story of freedom,
dignity, and hope. In every country I visited, I promised that America
would meet our commitments. In South Africa, where nearly five million lived with HIV, I urged a reluctant President Thabo Mbeki to confront the disease openly and directly. In Botswana, a relatively wealthy
country where 38 percent of the adult population was infected, President
Festus Mogae pledged to use PEPFAR funds to continue the impressive
effort he had begun to fight the disease. At the national hospital in Abuja,
Nigeria, I visited with women who had benefited from the mother and
child initiative. They beamed with joy as they showed me their healthy
children. But for every infant born infection-free, many more began life
facing the burden of HIV.

The most memorable part of the trip was our visit to the TASO clinic in Uganda, where I met Mohamad Kalyesubula. Escorted by President Yoweri Museveni and his wife Janet, Laura and I went around the room and hugged the patients. Many opened up to us. They shared their hopes and fears. One nurse named Agnes told me her husband had died of AIDS in 1992. When she got tested, she found out that she, too, had HIV. She was one of the lucky few who had been able to get antiretroviral drugs. She urged me to send more medicine, as soon as possible. When the drugs supported by PEPFAR reached Uganda, Agnes helped nurse many of TASO's patients back to health. One was Mohamad. When he came to the White House in 2008, Agnes came too.

The director of TASO, a doctor named Alex Coutinho, later said I was the first world leader he had seen hug an African with AIDS. I was surprised. I remembered that Mother had made international news when she hugged an HIV-infected baby in 1989. Her act dispelled the myth that the disease could be transmitted by incidental human contact. I was proud to carry on her legacy by reducing the stigma associated with AIDS. I hoped in some small way to restore the dignity of suffering people. Above all, I wanted to show that the American people cared.

———

One highlight of our Africa trip was that our daughter Barbara joined us. In Botswana, she, Laura, and I went on safari in the Mokolodi Nature Reserve. We were hoping to relax, get some fresh air, and see some wild animals. To feed the appetite of the traveling press, the White House staff decided we should have a photo op.

As always, the preparations were meticulous. A press truck full of cameras and reporters was prestationed in a clearing. As our vehicle rounded the corner, the press was lined up for a perfect shot of us observing several elephants. Apparently, the elephants were not given the script. Shortly after we arrived, a randy male elephant mounted one of his female counterparts on live international TV. Our advance team turned pale under the hot African sun. Laura, Barbara, and I burst out laughing.

The trip was Barbara's first to Africa, and it touched her deeply. After graduating from college and volunteering on my 2004 campaign, she went to work for a pediatric AIDS clinic at the Red Cross War Memorial Hospital in Cape Town, South Africa. Inspired by her experience, she later founded a nonprofit, Global Health Corps. Based on a model similar to Teach for America, her organization sends recent college graduates to clinics in three African countries and two American inner cities. They support care for patients with AIDS and other diseases, strengthening the health infrastructure and helping people live with dignity and hope.

Jenna also discovered a passion for working with AIDS patients. She volunteered for UNICEF in several Latin American countries. When she got home, she wrote a wonderful book, a bestseller called *Ana's Story*, about a girl who was born with HIV.

Laura and I are very proud of our daughters. They have become professional women serving a cause greater than themselves. They are part of a larger movement of Americans who devote their time and money to helping the less fortunate. These good souls are part of what I call the armies of compassion. Many come from faith-based organizations and seek no compensation. They receive payment in another form.

———

One of the most important early decisions on PEPFAR was who should run it. I wanted a proven manager who knew how to structure an organization that would focus on results. I found the right man in an experienced Indiana businessman, former Eli Lilly CEO Randall Tobias.

Randy's first reports were discouraging. A year after I signed PEPFAR, fewer than one hundred thousand patients were receiving antiretroviral drugs. "That's it?" I snapped. "We're a long way from two million."

Randy assured me PEPFAR was on track. The most important tasks during the first year were to get partner countries to devise their strategies, mobilize manpower, and start establishing infrastructure. Once we had this foundation in place, the number of people receiving drugs would ramp up dramatically.

By the fall of 2005, our African partners were fully engaged. Faith-based and other groups supported by PEPFAR, both African and American, helped staff clinics and spread prevention messages to millions across the continent. Orphans and the dying were receiving compassionate care. Some four hundred thousand people were taking antiretroviral drugs. We were on pace to reach our goal.

———

Unfortunately, AIDS wasn't the only disease ravaging Africa. By 2005, malaria was killing approximately one million Africans a year, the majority of them children under the age of five. Transmitted by a mosquito bite, malaria accounted for 9 percent of all deaths in Africa, even more than AIDS. Economists estimated that the disease cost Africa $12 billion a year in medical expenses and lost productivity, a crippling blow to already fragile economies.

Every one of those deaths was unnecessary. Malaria is treatable and preventable. The United States had eradicated malaria in the 1950s, and there was a well-established strategy for battling the disease. It called for a combination of insecticide sprays, bed nets, and medicine for infected patients. The remedies were not particularly expensive. Bed nets cost $10 each, including delivery.

In June 2005, I announced a five-year, $1.2 billion program that would fund malaria-eradication efforts in fifteen countries. Like PEPFAR, the President's Malaria Initiative would empower Africans to design strategies to meet their needs. We would work toward a measurable goal: cutting malaria mortality rates by 50 percent over the next five years.

I named Rear Admiral Tim Ziemer, a retired Navy pilot with experience in international relief efforts, to lead the Malaria Initiative. In its first two years, the initiative reached eleven million Africans. It also generated a passionate response from the American people. Boys and Girls Clubs, scout troops, and school classes donated money in ten-dollar increments to buy bed nets for African children. Faith-based organizations and major corporations, especially those doing business in Africa, gave generously to the cause.

With support from the Malaria Initiative, infection rates in the targeted countries began to decline. The most dramatic turnaround was in Zanzibar. Health officials adopted an aggressive campaign of spraying, bed net distribution, and medicine for malaria victims and pregnant women. On one Zanzibar island, the number of malaria cases dropped more than 90 percent in a single year.

On April 25, 2007, Laura and I hosted America's first-ever Malaria Awareness Day in the Rose Garden. It was an opportunity to herald progress and show our citizens the results of their generosity.

At the end of my remarks, the KanKouran West African Dance Company performed a lively song. Caught up in the celebratory mood, I joined the dancers onstage. My moves were replayed on the national news and became a minor sensation on YouTube. The girls took great delight in teasing me: "I don't think you should audition for *Dancing with the Stars*, Dad."

"I told you my goal was to raise awareness," I replied.

———

In 2006, Mark Dybul succeeded Randy Tobias as the coordinator of PEP-FAR. As a medical doctor and respected figure in the AIDS community, Mark brought great credibility to PEPFAR. After one of his trips to Africa, he told me many on the continent were anxious about what would happen after PEPFAR's five-year authorization expired in 2008. Governments were counting on our continued support, and so were the people. Mark told me he had asked a health clinic official in Ethiopia if anyone knew what the acronym PEPFAR stood for. "Yes," the man said. "PEP-FAR means the American people care about us."

Mark believed we had a responsibility to continue the program—and an opportunity to build on our progress. By doubling PEPFAR's initial funding level, we could treat 2.5 million people, prevent 12 million infections, and support care for 12 million people over the next five years.

Doubling funding would be a big commitment. But the AIDS initiative was working, and I decided to keep the momentum going. On May 30, 2007, I stepped into the Rose Garden and called for Congress to reauthorize the initiative with a new commitment of $30 billion over the next five years.

To highlight the progress, I invited a South African woman named Kunene Tantoh. Laura had met her two years earlier and shared her inspiring story with me. Kunene was HIV-positive, but thanks to medicine she received through the mother and child initiative, she had given birth to an HIV-free boy. After the speech I held four-year-old Baron in my arms and smiled at the thought that his precious life had been saved by the American taxpayers. He demonstrated his energy and good health by wiggling around and waving to the cameras. Then he gave me the international look for "Enough is enough. Put me down."

The next step was to get other nations to join us. In the summer of 2007, Laura and I flew to Germany for the G-8 summit, hosted by Chancellor Angela Merkel. One key mission was to persuade my fellow G-8 leaders to match America's pledges on HIV/AIDS and malaria.

Angela told me the summit's primary topic would be global warming. I was willing to be constructive on the issue. In my 2006 State of the Union address, I had said that America was "addicted to oil"—a line that didn't go over so well with some friends back in Texas. I had worked with Congress to promote alternatives to oil, including biofuels, hybrid and hydrogen vehicles, natural gas, clean coal, and nuclear power. I also proposed an international process that, unlike the flawed Kyoto Protocol, brought together all major emitters—including China and India—and relied on clean energy technologies to cut greenhouse gas emissions without stifling the economic growth necessary to solve the problem.

I worried that the intense focus on climate change would cause nations to overlook the desperate immediate needs in the developing world. "If world leaders are going to sit around talking about something that might be a problem fifty years from now," I told Angela, "we'd better do something about the people dying from AIDS and malaria right now."

With Angela's help, the other G-8 leaders agreed to match the AIDS-relief goals America had set. Together, we would provide treatment for five million people, prevent twenty-four million more infections, and support care for twenty-four million additional people over the next five years. They also agreed to match the goals of our Malaria Initiative. Those historic commitments can make an enormous difference in the lives of people in Africa and around the world. It will be up to future administrations to ensure that nations follow through on their pledges.

The principles of accountability and partnership that guided PEPFAR were also behind the centerpiece of our new approach to economic development, the Millennium Challenge Account. To be eligible for MCA funds, countries had to meet three clearly defined criteria: govern free of corruption, pursue market-based economic policies, and invest in the health and education of their people. The change in approach was dramatic. Economic aid would be treated like an investment instead of a handout. Success would be measured by results produced, not money spent.

MCA drew support from some unexpected sources. One was Bono, the Irish lead singer of U2. Josh and Condi had gotten to know Bono and told me the star wanted to visit me in the Oval Office. I was skeptical of celebrities who seemed to adopt the cause of the moment as a way to advance their careers. But they assured me Bono was the real deal.

His visit was scheduled for the morning I announced MCA, March 14, 2002. Josh gave me a quick briefing on the issues likely to come up. Ever meticulous, he had one last question before showing our guest into the Oval Office. "Mr. President, you do know who Bono is, right?"

"Of course," I said. "He's a rock star." Josh nodded and turned toward the door. "Used to be married to Cher, didn't he?" I said. Josh wheeled around in disbelief. I kept a straight face for as long as I could.

Bono bounded into the Oval Office with his high-voltage personality and signature shades. He quickly dispelled the notion that he was a self-promoter. He knew our budgets, understood the facts, and had well-informed views about the challenges in Africa. He brought me a thoughtful gift, an old Irish Bible.

"Do you know that 2,003 verses of Scripture pertain directly to the world's poor?" he asked. "People are quick to point out the obvious sins like marital infidelity," he continued. "But sometimes we ignore the most serious ones. The only place the Bible speaks directly of judgment is in Matthew 25: 'Whatever you did for one of the least of these brothers of mine, you did for me.'"

"You're right," I said. "The sin of omission is just as serious as the others." I was pleased when he expressed his strong support for MCA, which he believed would revolutionize the way the world pursued development.

I listened carefully as he urged me to do more on HIV/AIDS. "With a few pills you can save millions of lives. It would be the best possible advertisement for the United States. You ought to paint the things red, white, and blue."

After our meeting, Bono joined me and Cardinal Theodore McCarrick, a gentle, spirit-filled man, for the limo ride to the speech at the Inter-American Development Bank. Bono participated in the event and praised our policy. I later learned that one of his major funders, ultra-liberal investor George Soros, had excoriated Bono for joining me at the MCA event without getting more in return. "You've sold out for a plate of lentils," Soros told Bono.

My respect for Bono grew over time. He was warm to Laura and the girls. He frequently sent notes of thanks. He is a man of genuine faith. Bono could be edgy, but never in a cynical or political way. When PEPFAR got off to a slow start, he came to see me in the Oval Office. "You're the measurable results guy," he said, "so where are the results?" I would have told him, but he wouldn't let me get a word in edgewise. Once the program was up and running, he came back. "I'm sorry I doubted you," he said. "By the way, do you know the U.S. government is now the world's largest purchaser of condoms?"

I laughed. Bono had a big heart and a sharp needle. His only motive was his passion for the cause we shared. Laura, Barbara, Jenna, and I consider him a friend.

———

Not everybody agreed with Bono. Three months after I announced the MCA, I went to the G-8 summit in Kananaskis, Canada. Prime Minister Jean Chrétien raised the topic of foreign aid. I was one of the first to speak. I talked about the results-oriented principles of MCA, a stark departure from the G-8's tradition of measuring generosity by the percentage of GDP a nation spent on foreign aid.

When I finished, Jacques Chirac leaned over and patted my arm. "George, you are so unilateralist," he said. Then he unleashed. "How can America insist on tying aid to anti-corruption? After all, the free world created corruption!" He made it clear he thought I didn't understand the African culture.

It was my first Chirac drive-by. I was not amused. He seemed to be willing to condemn people in the developing world to the status quo of corruption, poverty, and bad governance all because he felt guilty about what nations like France had done in the colonial era.

When the lecture concluded, I raised my hand. Chrétien shook his head. He wanted to give other leaders a chance to speak. But I couldn't let Chirac's statement stand. I butted back in: "America did not colonize African nations. America did not create corruption. And America is tired of seeing good money stolen while people continue to suffer. Yes, we are changing our policy, whether you like it or not."

Chirac had vented. So had I. Most of the other leaders looked shocked. My friend Prime Minister Koizumi of Japan flashed a slight smile and gave me a subtle nod of approval.

Over the next six years, the MCA invested $6.7 billion of seed money with thirty-five partner countries. Lesotho used its MCA compact to upgrade its water supply. Burkina Faso created a reliable system of property rights. Projects like these were catalysts for countries to develop markets that foster private-sector growth, attract foreign capital, and facilitate trade, which was another cornerstone of my development agenda. Free and fair trade benefits the United States by creating new buyers for our products, along with more choices and better prices for our consumers. Trade is also the surest way to help people in the developing world grow their economies and lift themselves out of poverty. According to one study, the benefits of trade are forty times more effective in reducing poverty than foreign aid.

When I took office, America had free trade agreements in place with three countries: Canada, Mexico, and Israel. By the time I left, we had agreements with seventeen, including developing countries such as Jordan, Morocco, Oman, and the young democracies of Central America. To further boost African economies, we worked with G-8 partners to cancel more than $34 billion in debt from poor African countries. The initiative built on the substantial debt relief President Clinton had secured. A report by Bono's DATA organization concluded that debt relief has allowed African nations to send forty-two million more children to school.

One vital economic initiative was the African Growth and Opportunity Act, which eliminated tariffs on most African exports to the United States. President Clinton signed AGOA; I worked with Congress to expand it. And I saw its impact firsthand when I met entrepreneurs in Ghana who exported their products to the United States. One woman had started a business called Global Mamas. She specialized in helping women artisans find new markets to sell goods such as soaps, baskets, and jewelry. In five years, her company had grown from seven employees to about three hundred. A dressmaker named Esther told me, "I'm helping other women, and I'm helping my family, too."

———

In February 2008, Laura and I returned to sub-Saharan Africa. The trip was my second and her fifth. We viewed the visit as a chance to showcase some of Africa's best leaders, who were serving their people with integrity and tackling problems like poverty, corruption, and disease. Their good example stood in stark contrast to the African leader dominating the headlines, Robert Mugabe of Zimbabwe. Mugabe had stifled democracy, subjected his people to hyperinflation, and turned the country from a net food exporter to a net importer. His disgraceful record was proof that one man could ruin a country. I wanted to show the world that good leadership could help a country reach its potential.

Laura and I made five stops on the trip.* At each, we saw inspiring examples of our new partnerships with Africa. I met schoolchildren in Benin and Liberia who had textbooks, thanks to our Africa Education Initiative. In Rwanda, I signed a bilateral investment treaty that would increase access to financing for Rwandan entrepreneurs. In Ghana, I announced a new initiative to fight neglected tropical diseases like hookworm and snail fever.

Our longest visit was to Tanzania, a nation of forty-two million people on Africa's east coast. Under the leadership of President Jakaya Kikwete, Tanzania participated in PEPFAR, the Malaria Initiative, and

*We visited Benin, led by Yayi Boni; Tanzania, led by Jakaya Kikwete; Rwanda, led by Paul Kagame; Ghana, led by John Kufuor; and Liberia, led by Ellen Johnson Sirleaf.

MCA. As Air Force One descended toward Dar es Salaam, I was told I might see a group of Tanzanian women wearing dresses with my photo printed on the cloth. As I walked down the steps of the plane, a cluster of women danced to the festive beat of drums and horns. As one rotated to the music, I saw my photo stretched across her backside.

Like many sub-Saharan African countries, Tanzania's economy was weakened by the AIDS crisis. President Kikwete was passionate about the fight against disease. He and his wife, Salma, had taken an AIDS test on national television to set a good example for the Tanzanian people. Even more impressive, the Kikwetes adopted an orphan whose parents had died of AIDS.

President Kikwete took us to an HIV/AIDS clinic at the Amana District Hospital, which had opened in 2004 with support from PEPFAR. As the director of the hospital showed us around, Laura and I saw a girl sitting on a bench in the courtyard with her grandmother. She was nine years old and HIV-positive. She had received the virus from her mother, who had died. AIDS had taken her father, too. Yet the little girl was smiling. Her grandmother explained that Catholic Relief Services had been paying for the girl to receive treatment at the PEPFAR clinic. "As a Muslim," the elderly woman said, "I never imagined that a Catholic group would help me like that. I am so grateful to the American people."

At a news conference, I reiterated my call for Congress to reauthorize and expand PEPFAR. President Kikwete jumped in: "If this program is discontinued or disrupted, there would be so many people who will lose hope; certainly there will be death. My passionate appeal is for PEPFAR to continue." An American reporter asked him if Tanzanians were excited about the prospect of Barack Obama becoming president. Kikwete's reply warmed my heart. "For us," he said, "the most important thing is, let him be as good a friend of Africa as President Bush has been."

---

As we were flying back to Washington, Laura and I agreed the trip had been the best of the presidency. There was a new and palpable sense of energy and hope across Africa. The outpouring of love for America was overwhelming. Every time I hear an American politician or commentator talk about our country's poor image in the world, I think about the tens of thousands of Africans who lined the roadsides to wave at our motorcade and express their gratitude to the United States.

By the time I left office in January 2009, PEPFAR had supported treatment for 2.1 million people and care for more than 10 million people. American taxpayer dollars had helped protect mothers and babies during more than 16 million pregnancies. More than 57 million people had benefited from AIDS testing and counseling sessions.

The results of the Malaria Initiative were equally encouraging. Through the distribution of insecticide-treated bed nets, indoor spraying, and the delivery of medicine for infected and pregnant mothers, the Malaria Initiative helped protect twenty-five million people from unnecessary death. Several countries, including Ethiopia, Rwanda, Tanzania, and Zambia, were ahead of schedule in meeting the goal of cutting malaria infection rates by more than 50 percent.

Africa's needs remain tremendous. There are still more than twenty-two million people living with AIDS. Some who need antiretroviral drugs still go without. While malaria is in retreat, there are still children dying needlessly from mosquito bites. Poverty remains rampant. Infrastructure is lacking. And there are pockets of terrorism and brutality.

While these challenges are daunting, the African people have strong partners at their side. The United States, the G-8, the UN, the faith-based community, and the private sector are all far more engaged than ever before. The health infrastructure put in place as part of PEPFAR and the Malaria Initiative will bring wide-ranging benefits in other areas of African life.

Perhaps the most important change in recent years is in the way Africans see themselves. Just as AIDS is no longer viewed as a death sentence, the African people have newfound optimism that they can overcome their problems, reclaim their dignity, and go forward with hope.

On our trip to Rwanda in 2008, Laura and I visited a school where teenagers—many of them orphans—were taught about HIV/AIDS prevention. One lesson focused on showing girls how to reject the advances of older men, part of the abstinence component of PEPFAR.

As I walked by a cluster of students, I said, "God is good." They shouted back in unison, "All the time!"

Here in Rwanda, a country that had lost hundreds of thousands to genocide and AIDS, these children felt blessed. Surely those of us in comfortable places like America could learn a lesson. I decided to say it again.

"God is good."

The chorus responded even louder, "All the time!"

12

---

# SURGE

In September 2006, with the midterm elections approaching, my friend Mitch McConnell came to the Oval Office. The senior senator from Kentucky and Republican whip had asked to see me alone. Mitch has a sharp political nose, and he smelled trouble.

"Mr. President," he said, "your unpopularity is going to cost us control of the Congress."

Mitch had a point. Many Americans were tired of my presidency. But that wasn't the only reason our party was in trouble. I flashed back to the Republican congressmen sent to jail for taking bribes, disgraced by sex scandals, or implicated in lobbying investigations. Then there was the wasteful spending, the earmarks for pork-barrel projects, and our failure to reform Social Security despite majorities in both houses of Congress.

"Well, Mitch," I asked, "what do you want me to do about it?"

"Mr. President," he said, "bring some troops home from Iraq."

He was not alone. As violence in Iraq escalated, members of both parties had called for a pullout.

"Mitch," I said, "I believe our presence in Iraq is necessary to protect America, and I will not withdraw troops unless military conditions warrant." I made it clear I would set troop levels to achieve victory in Iraq, not victory at the polls.

What I did not tell him was that I was seriously considering the opposite of his recommendation. Rather than pull troops out, I was on the verge of making the toughest and most unpopular decision of my presidency: deploying tens of thousands more troops into Iraq with a new strategy, a new commander, and a mission to protect the Iraqi people and help enable the rise of a democracy in the heart of the Middle East.

The pessimism of September 2006 came in contrast to the hope so many felt after the liberation of Iraq. In the year after our troops entered the country, we toppled Saddam's regime, captured the dictator, rebuilt schools and health clinics, and formed a Governing Council representing all major ethnic and sectarian groups. While the lawlessness and violence exceeded our expectations, most Iraqis seemed determined to build a free society. On March 8, 2004, the Governing Council reached agreement on the Transitional Administrative Law. This landmark document called for a return of sovereignty in June, followed by elections for a national assembly, the drafting of a constitution, and another round of elections to choose a democratic government.

For almost three years, this road map guided our strategy. We believed that helping the Iraqis meet those milestones was the best way to show Shia, Sunnis, and Kurds they had a stake in a free and peaceful country. Once Iraqis were invested in the democratic process, we hoped they would resolve disputes at the ballot box, thereby marginalizing the enemies of a free Iraq. In short, we believed political progress was the path to security—and, ultimately, the path home.

Our military strategy focused on pursuing the extremists while training the Iraqi security forces. Over time, we would move toward a smaller military footprint, countering the perception that we were occupiers and boosting the legitimacy of Iraq's leaders. I summed up the strategy: "As the Iraqis stand up, we will stand down." Don Rumsfeld had a more memorable analogy: "We have to take our hand off the bicycle seat."

I had studied the histories of postwar Germany, Japan, and South Korea. Each had required many years—and a U.S. troop presence—to complete the transition from the devastation of war to stable democracies. But once they did, their transformative impact proved worth the costs. West Germany emerged as the engine of European prosperity and a vital beacon of freedom during the Cold War. Japan grew into the world's second-largest economy and the lynchpin of security in the Pacific. South Korea became one of our largest trading partners and a strategic bulwark against its neighbor to the north.

All three countries benefited from relatively homogenous populations and peaceful postwar environments. In Iraq, the journey would be more difficult. Iraq had been plagued by ethnic and sectarian tensions ever since the British created the country from the vestiges of the Ottoman Empire. The fear and distrust bred by Saddam Hussein made it hard for Iraqis to reconcile. So did the brutal attacks carried out by extremists.

Despite the violence, there was hope. Iraq had a young, educated population, a vibrant culture, and functioning government institutions. It had strong economic potential thanks in part to its natural resources. And its citizens were making sacrifices to overcome the insurgents and live in freedom. With time and steadfast American support, I had confidence that democracy in Iraq would succeed.

———

That confidence was tested daily. Every morning, I received an overnight summary from the Situation Room printed on a blue sheet of paper. One section of the report listed the number, place, and cause of American casualties in Afghanistan and Iraq.

The toll mounted over time. America lost 52 troops in Iraq in March 2004. We lost 135 in April, 80 in May, 42 in June, 54 in July, 66 in August, 80 in September, 64 in October, and 137 in November, when our troops launched a major assault on insurgents in Fallujah.

The growing number of deaths filled me with anguish. When I received a blue sheet, I would circle the casualty figure with my pen, pause, and reflect on each individual loss. I comforted family members of the fallen as often as I could. In August 2005, I flew to Idaho for an event honoring the contributions of the National Guard and Reserves. Afterward, I met with Dawn Rowe, who had lost her husband, Alan, in September 2004. Dawn introduced me to her children, six-year-old Blake and four-year-old Caitlin. Even though it had been almost a year since Alan's death, their grief was overwhelming. "My husband loved being a Marine," Dawn told me. "If he had to do it all again, knowing he would die, he would." I made her a promise: Alan's sacrifice would not be in vain.

Over the course of my presidency I met roughly 550 families of the fallen. The meetings were both the most painful and most uplifting part of serving as commander in chief. The vast majority of those I met were like the Rowes: devastated by their loss, but proud of their family member's service. A few families lashed out. When I visited Fort Lewis in Washington State in June 2004, I met a mother who had lost her son in Iraq. She was visibly upset. I tried to put her at ease.

"You are as big a terrorist as Osama bin Laden," she said.

There wasn't much to say in response. She had lost her son; she had the right to speak her mind to the man who had sent him into battle. I was sorry her grief had created such bitterness. If expressing her anger helped ease her pain, that was fine with me.

That same day, I met Patrick and Cindy Sheehan of Vacaville, California. Their fallen son, Specialist Casey Sheehan, had volunteered for his final mission, a courageous attempt to rescue a team of fellow soldiers pinned down in Sadr City. After the meeting, Cindy shared her impressions of me with a Vacaville newspaper: "I now know he's sincere about wanting freedom for the Iraqis. . . . I know he's sorry and feels some pain for our loss. And I know he's a man of faith."

By the following summer, Cindy Sheehan had become an antiwar activist. Over time, her rhetoric grew harsher and more extreme. She became the spokesperson for the antiwar organization Code Pink, spoke out against Israel, advocated for anti-American dictator Hugo Chavez of Venezuela, and eventually ran for Congress against Speaker Nancy Pelosi. I feel sympathy for Cindy Sheehan. She is a mother who clearly loved her son. The grief caused by his loss was so profound that it consumed her life. My hope is that one day she and all the families of our fallen troops will be comforted to see a free Iraq and a more peaceful world as a fitting memorial to the sacrifice of their loved ones.

———

When al Qaeda lost its safe haven in Afghanistan, the terrorists went searching for a new one. After we removed Saddam in 2003, bin Laden exhorted his fighters to support the jihad in Iraq. In many ways, Iraq was more desirable for them than Afghanistan. It had oil riches and Arab roots. Over time, the number of extremists affiliated with al Qaeda in

Afghanistan declined to the low hundreds, while the estimated number in Iraq topped ten thousand.

There were other extremists in Iraq: former Baathists, Sunni insurgents, and Shia extremists backed by Iran. But none were more ruthless than al Qaeda. Critics argued the al Qaeda presence proved we had stirred up terrorists by liberating Iraq. I never accepted that logic. Al Qaeda was plenty stirred up on 9/11, when there wasn't a single American soldier in Iraq. Did anyone really believe that the men sawing off the heads of innocent captives or blowing themselves up in markets would have been peaceful citizens if only we had left Saddam Hussein alone? If these fanatics had not been trying to kill Americans in Iraq, they would have been trying to do it elsewhere. And if we were to let them drive us out of Iraq, they would not have been satisfied to stop there. They would have followed us home.

For all the lives they stole, our enemies failed to stop us from achieving a single one of our strategic objectives in Iraq. In spring 2004, the terrorist Zarqawi—whom Osama bin Laden later designated "the prince of al Qaeda in Iraq"—threatened to disrupt the transfer of sovereignty, scheduled for June 30. In May, a suicide bomber assassinated the president of the Governing Council, Izzedine Salim. A few weeks later, coordinated attacks on Iraqi police and government buildings killed more than one hundred, including three American troops. To disrupt plans for more major attacks, we decided to execute the handover two days ahead of schedule.

I was at the NATO Summit in Istanbul on June 28 when I felt Don Rumsfeld's hand reach over my shoulder. He slipped me a scrap of paper with Condi's handwriting: "Mr. President, Iraq is sovereign. Letter was passed from Bremer at 10:26 a.m., Iraqi time."

I scrawled on the note, "Let freedom reign!" Then I shook hands with the leader on my right. In a fitting twist of history, I shared the moment with a man who had never wavered in his commitment to a free Iraq, Tony Blair.

———

Seven months later, in January 2005, Iraqis reached the next milestone: elections to choose an interim national assembly. Again, the terrorists mounted a campaign to stop the progress. Zarqawi declared "an all-out war on this evil principle of democracy" and pledged to kill any Iraqi involved in the election.

Back home, pressure mounted. One op-ed in the *Los Angeles Times* called the election a "sham" and proposed postponing it. I believed delay would embolden the enemy and cause the Iraqis to question our commitment to democracy. Holding the vote would show faith in the Iraqis and expose the insurgents as enemies of freedom. "The elections have to go forward," I told the national security team. "This will be a moment of clarity for the world."

At 5:51 a.m. on January 30, 2005, I called the duty officer in the Situation Room to get the first readout. He told me our embassy in Baghdad was reporting a large turnout—despite a boycott by many Sunnis. While terrorists pulled off some attacks, broadcasts around the world showed Iraqis waving their ink-stained fingers* in the air with joy. One reporter witnessed a ninety-year-old woman being pushed to the polls in a wheelbarrow. Another news account described a voter who had lost a leg in a terrorist attack. "I would have crawled here if I had to," he said. "Today I am voting for peace."

The elections produced a national assembly, which named a committee to draft the constitution. In August, the Iraqis reached agreement on the most progressive constitution in the Arab world—a document that guaranteed equal rights for all and protected the freedoms of religion, assembly, and expression. When the voters went to the polls on October 15, the turnout was even larger than it was in January. Violence was lower. More Sunnis voted. The constitution was ratified 79 percent to 21 percent.

The third election of the year, held in December, was to replace the interim assembly with a permanent legislature. Once again, Iraqis defied terrorist threats. Nearly twelve million people—a turnout of more than 70 percent—cast their ballots. This time Sunnis participated in overwhelming numbers. One voter stuck his ink-stained finger in the air and shouted, "This is a thorn in the eyes of the terrorists."

I was proud of our troops and thrilled for the Iraqis. With the three

*To prevent fraud, election officials had each voter dip a finger in purple ink.

elections of 2005, they had accomplished a major milestone on the path to democracy. I was hopeful the political progress would isolate the insurgents and allow our troops to pick off al Qaeda fighters one by one. After all the sadness and sacrifice, there was genuine reason for optimism.

——

The Askariya shrine at the Golden Mosque of Samarra is considered one of the holiest sites in Shia Islam. It contains the tombs of two revered imams who were father and grandfather to the hidden imam, a savior the Shia believe will restore justice to humanity.

On February 22, 2006, two massive bombs destroyed the mosque. The attack was an enormous provocation to the Shia, akin to an attack on St. Peter's Basilica or the Western Wall. "This is the equivalent of your 9/11," the influential Shia leader Abdul Aziz al Hakim told me.

I thought back to the letter Zarqawi had written to al Qaeda leaders in 2004, in which he proposed to incite a war between Iraqi Shia and Sunnis. While there were some immediate reprisal attacks, the violence did not seem to be spiraling out of control. I was relieved. The Shia had shown restraint, and I encouraged them to continue. In a speech on March 13, I said the Iraqis had "looked into the abyss and did not like what they saw."

I was wrong. By early April, sectarian violence had exploded. Roving bands of Shia gunmen kidnapped and murdered innocent Sunnis. Sunnis responded with suicide bombings in Shia areas. The crisis was exacerbated by the lack of a strong Iraqi government. Parties had been jockeying for position since the December election. That was a natural part of democracy, but with the violence escalating, Iraq needed a strong leader. I directed Condi and Ambassador Zal Khalilzad—who had moved from Kabul to Baghdad—to lean hard on the Iraqis to select a prime minister. Four months after the election, they made a surprise choice: Nouri al Maliki.

A dissident who had been sentenced to death by Saddam, Maliki had lived in exile in Syria. I called him the day he was selected. Since he had no secure phone, he was at the U.S. embassy. "Mr. President, here's the new prime minister," Zal said.

"Thanks," I said, "but stay on the phone a little longer so the prime minister will know how close you and I are."

"Congratulations, Mr. Prime Minister," I said when Maliki got on. "I want you to know the United States is fully committed to democracy in Iraq. We will work together to defeat the terrorists and support the Iraqi people. Lead with confidence."

Maliki was friendly and sincere, but he was a political novice. I made clear I wanted a close personal relationship. So did he. In the months ahead, we spoke frequently by phone and videoconference. I was careful not to bully him or appear heavy-handed. I wanted him to consider me a partner, maybe a mentor. He would get plenty of pressure from others. From me he would get advice and understanding. Once I had earned his trust, I would be in a better position to help him make the tough decisions.

———

I hoped the formation of the Maliki government would provide a break in the violence. It didn't. The reports of sectarian killings grew more gruesome. Death squads conducted brazen kidnappings. Iran supplied militants with funding, training, and highly sophisticated Explosively Formed Projectiles (EFPs) to kill our troops. Iraqis retreated into their sectarian foxholes, looking for protection wherever they could find it.

Our ground commander in Iraq was General George Casey, an experienced four-star general who had commanded troops in Bosnia and served as vice chief of staff of the Army. Don Rumsfeld had recommended him for the Iraq command when General Ricardo Sanchez stepped down in the summer of 2004.

Before George deployed to Baghdad, Laura and I invited him and his wife, Sheila, to dinner at the White House. We were joined by Ambassador to Iraq John Negroponte*—an experienced and skilled diplomat who had volunteered for the job—and his wife, Diana. George gave me a biography of legendary football coach Vince Lombardi. George had

---

*John answered the call to serve four times in my administration—as ambassador to the United Nations, ambassador to Iraq, director of national intelligence, and deputy secretary of state.

worked as an equipment manager for the Washington Redskins during Lombardi's final season. The gift was telling. Like the coach he admired, George was not flashy or glamorous. He was a solid, straightforward commander—a "block of granite," as Lombardi was once known.

General Casey—like General Abizaid and Don Rumsfeld—was convinced our troop presence created a sense of occupation, which inflamed violence and fueled the insurgency. For two and a half years, I had supported the strategy of withdrawing our forces as the Iraqis stepped forward. But in the months after the Samarra bombing, I had started to question whether our approach matched the reality on the ground. The sectarian violence had not erupted because our footprint was too big. It had happened because al Qaeda had provoked it. And with the Iraqis struggling to stand up, it didn't seem possible for us to stand down.

---

Everyone on the national security team shared my concerns about the deteriorating conditions. But it was my national security adviser, Steve Hadley, who was first to help me find a solution.

Steve came to my attention during the 2000 campaign, when he was part of the foreign policy advisory group assembled by Condi. Steve was a reluctant public figure. Yet when he was placed before the camera, his scholarly demeanor and logical presentation carried great credibility. Behind the scenes, he was thoughtful and steady. He listened, synthesized, and pondered without brooding. He articulated options clearly. Once I had reached a decision, he knew how to work with the team to implement it.

Steve is a formal person. He would board the airplane for long overseas flights in his tie, sleep in his tie, and emerge with a crisp knot still in place. He once volunteered for cedar chopping at the ranch. His job was to pile up cut branches. He performed the task meticulously, effectively, and in his brogan shoes. Behind the formality, Steve is a kind, selfless, humorous man. I spent many weekends at Camp David with him and his wife, Ann. The two have a great love affair. Both are cerebral. Both are hikers. And both are great parents to their two lovely girls.

I met with Steve almost every morning of my second term. After a particularly rough day in the spring of 2006, we reviewed the blue sheet at the Resolute desk. I shook my head and glanced up. Steve was shaking his head, too.

"This is not working," I said. "We need to take another look at the whole strategy. I need to see some new options."

"Mr. President," he responded, "I'm afraid you're right."

Steve went to work organizing a detailed review. Every night, the Iraq team on the NSC staff produced a memo detailing the military and political developments of the past twenty-four hours. The picture they painted was not pretty. One day in the late spring, I asked Meghan O'Sullivan, a Ph.D. who had spent a year working for Jerry Bremer in Iraq, to stay behind after a meeting. She maintained contacts with many senior officials in the Iraqi government. I asked what she was hearing from Baghdad. "It's hell, Mr. President," she said.

In mid-June, Steve arranged to have a group of outside experts brief me at Camp David. Fred Kagan, a military scholar at the American Enterprise Institute, questioned whether we had enough troops to control the violence. Robert Kaplan, a distinguished journalist, recommended adopting a more aggressive counterinsurgency strategy. Michael Vickers, a former CIA operative who helped arm the Afghan Mujahideen in the 1980s, suggested a greater role for Special Operations. Eliot Cohen, the author of *Supreme Command*, a book about the relationship between presidents and their generals that I had read at Steve's suggestion, told me I needed to hold my commanders accountable for results.

To provide another perspective, Steve brought me articles from colonels and one-star generals who had commanded troops in Iraq. A dichotomy emerged: While Generals Casey and Abizaid supported the train-and-withdraw strategy, many of those closest to the fight thought we needed more troops.

One who intrigued me was Colonel H.R. McMaster. I had read his book on Vietnam, *Dereliction of Duty*, which charged the military leadership with not doing enough to correct the strategy adopted by President Johnson and Defense Secretary Bob McNamara. In 2005, Colonel McMaster commanded a regiment in the northern Iraqi city of Tal Afar. He had applied a counterinsurgency strategy, using his troops to clear out insurgents, hold the newly taken territory, and help build the local economy and political institutions. This doctrine of clear, hold, and build had turned Tal Afar from an insurgent stronghold to a relatively peaceful, functioning city.

Another practitioner of counterinsurgency was General David Petraeus. I first met him at Fort Campbell in 2004. He had a reputation as one of the smartest and most dynamic young generals in the Army. He had graduated near the top of his class at West Point and earned a Ph.D. from Princeton. In 1991, he was accidentally shot in the chest during a training exercise. He endured a sixty-mile helicopter flight to Vanderbilt University Medical Center, where his life was saved by Dr. Bill Frist, later the Republican leader of the Senate.

Early in the war, General Petraeus had commanded the 101st Airborne Division in Mosul. He sent his troops to live alongside Iraqi residents and patrol the streets on foot. Their presence reassured residents that we were there to protect them. Petraeus then held local elections to form a provincial council, spent reconstruction funds to revive economic activity, and reopened the border with Syria to facilitate trade. His approach was textbook counterinsurgency. To defeat the enemy, he was trying to win over the people.

It worked. While violence in much of Iraq increased, Mosul remained relatively calm. But when we reduced troops in Mosul, violence returned. The same would happen in Tal Afar.

After overseeing training of the Iraqi security forces, General Petraeus was assigned to Fort Leavenworth, Kansas, to rewrite the Army's counterinsurgency manual. The premise of counterinsurgency is that basic security is required before political gains can follow. That was the reverse of our existing strategy. I decided to keep a close eye on General Petraeus's work—and on him.

———

Amid all the bad news of 2006, we did have one bright spot. In early June, Special Forces under the command of the highly effective General Stanley McChrystal tracked down and killed Zarqawi, al Qaeda's leader in Iraq. For the first time since the December elections, we were able to show the public a dramatic sign of progress.

A week later, I quietly slipped out of Camp David after a day of NSC meetings. I hopped on an Army transport helicopter with a small group of aides, flew to Andrews Air Force Base, and boarded Air Force One. Eleven hours later, we landed in Baghdad.

Unlike my Thanksgiving trip in 2003, when my meetings took place at the airport, I decided to meet Maliki in the Green Zone, the fortified complex in central Baghdad. Army helicopters flew us over the city fast and low, shooting off an occasional flare as a protection against a heat-seeking missile. The prime minister was waiting for me when I got to the embassy. Ever since his selection in April, I had wanted to see Maliki face to face. In our phone calls, he had said the right things. But I wondered if his assurances were real.

"Your decisions and actions will determine success," I told him. "It will not be easy, but no matter how hard it is, we'll help you."

Maliki thanked America for liberating the country and affirmed his desire for a close friendship. "We will achieve victory over terror, which is a victory for democracy," he said. "There are a lot of dark people who fear our success. They are right to be worried, because our success will unseat them from their thrones."

The prime minister had a gentle manner and a quiet voice, but I sensed an inner toughness. Saddam Hussein had executed multiple members of Maliki's family, yet he had refused to renounce his role in the opposition party. His personal courage was a seed that I hoped to nurture, so he could grow into the strong leader the Iraqis needed.

The prime minister took me into a conference room to meet his cabinet, which included Shia, Sunni, and Kurdish leaders. I introduced him to my team via videoconference. My advisers, who did not know that I had left Camp David, were stunned to see me in Baghdad. The Iraqis were thrilled to address their counterparts for the first-ever joint national security meeting between the United States and Iraq.

The other pivotal meeting of the trip was with George Casey. The hardworking general had been in Iraq for two years, extending his tour at my request. He told me that 80 percent of the sectarian violence occurred within thirty miles of Baghdad. Controlling the capital was vital to calming the rest of the country.

General Casey was planning a new effort to secure Baghdad. The offensive, Operation Together Forward, would attempt to apply the clear, hold, and build approach that had once succeeded in Tal Afar and Mosul.

I saw a contradiction. The "clear, hold, and build" strategy was troop-intensive. But our generals wanted to reduce our footprint. He picked up on my doubts. "I need to do a better job explaining it to you," General Casey said.

"You do," I replied.

———

The summer of 2006 was the worst period of my presidency. I thought about the war constantly. While I was heartened by the determination of the Maliki government and the death of Zarqawi, I was deeply concerned that the violence was overtaking all else. An average of 120 Iraqis a day were dying. The war had stretched to more than three years and we had lost more than 2,500 Americans. By a margin of almost two to one, Americans said they disapproved of the way I was handling Iraq.

For the first time, I worried we might not succeed. If Iraq split along sectarian lines, our mission would be doomed. We could be looking at a repeat of Vietnam—a humiliating loss for the country, a shattering blow to the military, and a dramatic setback for our interests. If anything, the consequences of defeat in Iraq would be even worse than in Vietnam. We would leave al Qaeda with a safe haven in a country with vast oil reserves. We would embolden a hostile Iran in its pursuit of nuclear weapons. We would shatter the hopes of people taking risks for freedom across the Middle East. Ultimately, our enemies could use their sanctuary to attack our homeland. We had to stop that from happening.

I made a conscious decision to show resolve, not doubt, in public. I wanted the American people to understand that I believed wholeheartedly in our cause. The Iraqis needed to know we would not abandon them. Our enemies needed to know we were determined to defeat them. Most of all, I thought about our troops. I tried to imagine how it would feel to be a twenty-year-old on the front lines, or a military mom worrying about her son or daughter. The last thing they needed to hear was the commander in chief whining about how conflicted he felt. If I had concerns about the direction of the war, I needed to make changes in the policy, not wallow in public.

I drew strength from family, friends, and faith. When we visited Camp David, Laura and I loved to worship with military families at the base's chapel. The chaplain in 2006, forty-eight-year-old Navy Lieutenant Commander Stan Fornea, was one of the best preachers I've ever heard. "Evil is real, biblical, and prevalent," he said in one sermon. "Some say ignore it, some say it doesn't exist. But evil must not be ignored, it must be restrained." He quoted Sir Edmund Burke, the eighteenth-century British leader: "The only thing needed for the triumph of evil is for good men to do nothing."

Stan believed that the answer to evil was freedom. He also knew there would be a cost. "There has never been a noble cause devoid of sacrifice," he said in one sermon. "If freedom is worthy of defense only to the point it costs us nothing then we are in desperate need as a nation."

Above all, Stan was an optimist, and his sense of hope lifted my spirits. "The Scriptures put great premiums on faithfulness, perseverance, and overcoming," he said. "We do not quit or give up. We always believe there is no such thing as a hopeless situation."

I also found solace in history. In August, I read *Lincoln: A Life of Purpose and Power,* by Richard Carwardine, one of fourteen Lincoln biographies I read during my presidency. They brought to life the devastation Lincoln felt as he read telegrams describing Union defeats at places like Chancellorsville, where the Union suffered seventeen thousand casualties, or Chickamauga, where sixteen thousand were wounded or killed.

The casualties were not his only struggle. Lincoln had to cycle through one commander after another until he found one who would fight. He watched his son Willie die in the White House and his wife, Mary Todd, sink into depression. Yet thanks to his faith in God and his deep belief that he was waging war for a just cause, Lincoln persisted.

One hallmark of Lincoln's leadership was that he established an affectionate bond with rank-and-file soldiers. In the darkest days of the war, he spent long hours with the wounded at the Soldiers' Home in Washington. His empathy taught a powerful lesson and served as a model for other war presidents to follow.

One of the most moving parts of my presidency was reading letters from the families of fallen service members. I received hundreds, and they spanned the full spectrum of reactions. Many of the letters expressed a common sentiment: Finish the job. The parents of a fallen soldier from Georgia wrote, "Our greatest heartache would be to see the mission in Iraq abandoned." A grieving grandmother in Arizona emailed, "We need to finish what we started before pulling out."

In December 2005, I received a letter from a man in Pensacola, Florida:

*Dear President Bush,*

*My name is Bud Clay. My son, SSgt Daniel Clay [United States Marine Corps] was killed last week 12/01/05 in Iraq. He was one of the ten Marines killed by the IED in Falluja.*

*Dan was a Christian—he knew Jesus as Lord and Savior—so we know where he is. In his final letter (one left with me for the family—to be read in case of his death) he says, "If you are reading this, it means my race is over." He's home now—his and our real home.*

*I am writing to you to tell you how proud we (his parents and family) are of you and what you are trying to do to protect us all. This was Dan's second tour in Iraq—he knew and said that his being there was to protect us. Many do not see it that way.*

*I want to encourage you. I hear in your speeches about "staying the course." I also know that many are against you in this "war on Terror" and that you must get weary in the fight to do what is right. We and many others are praying for you to see this through—as Lincoln said "that these might not have died in vain."*

*You have a heavy load—we are praying for you.*

*God bless you,*
*Bud Clay*

I invited Bud; his wife, Sara Jo; and Daniel's widow, Lisa, to my State of the Union address the next month. Before the speech, I met the Clays in the Oval Office. We hugged, and they reiterated that I was in their prayers. I was inspired by their strength. God had worked an amazing deed, turning their hearts from grief to compassion. Their faith was so evident and real that it reconfirmed my own. I was hoping to lift the Clays' spirits, but they lifted mine.

They weren't the only ones. On New Year's Day 2006, Laura and I traveled to Brooke Army Medical Center in San Antonio. We visited fifty-one wounded service members and their families. In one room, we met Staff Sergeant Christian Bagge of the Oregon National Guard, along with his wife, Melissa. Christian had been on patrol in Iraq when his Humvee hit a roadside bomb. He was pinned in the vehicle for forty-five minutes and lost both legs.

Christian told me he used to be a runner and planned to run again someday. That was hard to imagine. I hoped to buoy his spirits. "When you're ready, just call me," I said. "I will run with you."

On June 27, 2006, I met Christian on the South Lawn. He had two prosthetic legs made of carbon fiber. We took a couple of laps around the jogging track Bill Clinton had installed. I marveled at Christian's strength and spirit. I could barely believe this was the same man who had been confined to a hospital bed less than six months earlier. He did not look at himself as a victim. He was proud of what he had done in Iraq, and he hoped his example might inspire others.

I thought about Christian a lot that summer, and in the years that followed. Our country owed him our gratitude and support. I owed him something more: I couldn't let Iraq fail.

On August 17, I convened the national security team in the Roosevelt Room, with General Casey, General Abizaid, and Ambassador Khalilzad on the video screen. The results of Operation Together Forward were not promising. Our troops had driven terrorists and death squads out of Baghdad neighborhoods. But Iraqi forces couldn't maintain control. We could clear but not hold.

"The situation seems to be deteriorating," I said. "I want to be able to say that I have a plan to punch back. Can America succeed? If so, how? How do our commanders answer that?"

General Casey told me we could succeed by transferring responsibility to the Iraqis faster. We needed to "help them help themselves," Don Rumsfeld said. That was another way of saying that we needed to take our hand off the bicycle seat. I wanted to send a message to the team that I was thinking differently. "We must succeed," I said. "If they can't do it, we will. If the bicycle teeters, we're going to put the hand back on. We have to make damn sure we do not fail."

Chief of Staff Josh Bolten, who knew where I was headed, added the exclamation point. "If it gets worse," he said near the end of the meeting, "what radical measures can the team recommend?"

I left the meeting convinced we would have to develop those measures ourselves. I authorized Steve Hadley to formalize the review the NSC Iraq team* had been conducting. I wanted them to challenge every assumption behind our strategy and generate new options. I soon came to view them as my personal band of warriors.

By the fall, my Iraq briefing charts showed an average of almost a thousand attacks per week. I read accounts of sectarian extremists torturing civilians with power drills, kidnapping patients from hospitals, and blowing up worshippers during Friday prayers. General Casey had launched a second major operation to restore security in Baghdad, this time with more Iraqi forces to hold territory. Once again, it failed.

I decided a change in strategy was needed. To be credible to the American people, it would have to be accompanied by changes in personnel. Don Rumsfeld had suggested that I might need fresh eyes on Iraq. He was right. I also needed new commanders. Both George Casey and John Abizaid had served extended tours and were scheduled to return home. It was time for fresh eyes in their posts as well.

With the 2006 midterm elections approaching, the rhetoric on Iraq was hot. "The idea that we're going to win this war is an idea that unfortunately is just plain wrong," DNC Chairman Howard Dean proclaimed. "We are causing the problem," said Congressman John Murtha of Pennsylvania, one of the first prominent Democrats to call for an immediate withdrawal. Senator Joe Biden, the ranking member of the Foreign

---

*It included J. D. Crouch, Steve's deputy and a former ambassador to Romania; Meghan O'Sullivan; Bill Luti, a retired Navy captain; Brett McGurk, a former law clerk to Chief Justice William Rehnquist; Peter Feaver, a Duke political science professor who had taken leave to join the administration; and two-star general Kevin Bergner.

Relations Committee, recommended partitioning Iraq into three separate entities. Republicans were anxious, too, as Mitch McConnell made clear with his Oval Office request for a troop reduction.

I decided to wait until after the elections to announce any policy or personnel changes. I didn't want the American people or our military to think I was making national security decisions for political reasons.

The weekend before the midterms, I met with Bob Gates in Crawford to ask him to become secretary of defense. Bob had served on the Baker-Hamilton Commission, a panel chartered by Congress to study the situation in Iraq. He told me he had supported a troop surge as one of the group's recommendations. I told Bob I was looking for a new commander in Iraq. He would review the candidates and offer his advice. But I suggested that he take a close look at David Petraeus.

After two election cycles in which Republicans increased their numbers in Congress, we took a pounding in 2006. We lost majorities in both the House and Senate. The new speaker of the House, Nancy Pelosi, declared, "The American people have spoken. . . . We must begin the responsible redeployment of our troops outside of Iraq."

———

As our review of the Iraq strategy intensified, we focused on three primary options. The first called for us to accelerate the existing strategy of training Iraqi forces while withdrawing our own. The Iraqis would assume increasing responsibility for dealing with the violence, while we would focus on more limited missions, including hunting al Qaeda.

The second option was to pull our troops back from Baghdad until the sectarian violence burned out. In October, Condi had traveled to Iraq and come back discouraged with Maliki and the other leaders. If they were determined to fight a sectarian war, she argued, why should we leave our troops in the middle of their blood feud?

The third option was to double down. We would deploy tens of thousands more troops—a surge—to conduct a full-scale counterinsurgency campaign in Baghdad. Rather than pull out of the cities, our troops would move in, live among the people, and secure the civilian population.

The fundamental question was whether the Iraqis had the will to succeed. I believed most Iraqis supported democracy. I was convinced that Iraqi mothers, like all mothers, wanted their children to grow up with hope for the future. I had met Iraqi exchange students, doctors, women's activists, and journalists who were determined to live in freedom and peace. A year after the liberation of Iraq, I met a group of small business owners who had manufactured items like watches and textiles during the Saddam era. To buy materials, they traded Iraqi dinars for foreign currency. When the dinar declined in value, Saddam searched for scapegoats and ordered the men's right hands cut off. Documentary producer Don North and Houston TV journalist Marvin Zindler heard the story and brought the Iraqis to Texas, where each was fitted for a prosthetic hand by Dr. Joe Agris, free of charge.

When the Iraqis arrived in the Oval Office, they were still learning to use their right hands. All were grateful to the American people for freeing them from the brutality of Saddam. And all had hope for their country. One Iraqi picked up a pen in his month-old hand and painstakingly scrawled some Arabic words on a piece of paper: "A prayer for God to bless America."

I marveled at the contrast between a regime so brutal that it would hack off men's hands and a society so compassionate that it would help restore their dignity. I believed the Iraqi man who wrote those words spoke for millions of his fellow citizens. They were grateful to America for their liberation. They wanted to live in freedom. And I would not give up on them.

———

In late October, I sent Steve Hadley to meet privately with Prime Minister Maliki in Baghdad. Steve's assessment was that Maliki was "either ignorant of what is going on, misrepresenting his intentions, or that his capabilities are not yet sufficient to turn his good intentions into action." Before I made a decision on the way forward, I needed to determine which of these was true.

On November 29, 2006, I flew to meet Maliki in Amman, Jordan. The Iraqi prime minister's leadership had frustrated us at times. He had not always deployed Iraqi troops when he said he would. Some in his government had suspicious ties to Iran. He hadn't done enough to go after Shia extremists. General Casey was rightly upset that sectarian officials close to Maliki had blocked our troops from going into Shia neighborhoods.

Yet over his six months in power, Maliki had matured as a leader. He had endured death threats, potential coups, and numerous congressional delegations traveling to Iraq to berate him. A few days before our scheduled summit in Jordan, radical Shia leader Moqtada al Sadr threatened to withdraw his supporters from the government if the prime minister met with me. Maliki came anyway.

"Here is my plan," he said proudly as he handed me a document with the new seal of the Iraqi government on the cover. Inside was an ambitious proposal to retake Baghdad with Iraqi forces. I knew his army and police were not ready for such a major undertaking. What mattered was that Maliki recognized the problem of sectarian violence and was showing a willingness to lead.

"Americans want to know whether your plan allows us to go against both Sunni and Shia killers," I asked.

"We don't distinguish by ethnicity," he replied.

I asked to meet with the prime minister alone. Maliki seemed ready to confront the violence. I decided to test his commitment by raising the prospect of a surge.

"The political pressure to abandon Iraq is enormous," I said, "but I am willing to resist that pressure if you are willing to make the hard choices."

I continued: "I'm willing to commit tens of thousands of additional American troops to help you retake Baghdad. But you need to give me certain assurances."

I ran through the list: He had to commit more Iraqi forces, and they had to show up. There could be no political interference in our joint military operations—no more forbidding us from going into Shia neighborhoods. He would have to confront the Shia militias, including Sadr's army. And as security improved, he had to make progress on political reconciliation among Shia, Sunnis, and Kurds.

On every point, Maliki gave me his word that he would follow through.

On the flight home from Jordan, I thought about the options for a new strategy. Accelerating the handover to the Iraqis was not a viable approach. That sounded a lot like our current strategy, which was failing.

I didn't think it was practical to withdraw from the cities and let the violence burn out. I couldn't ask our troops to stand back and watch innocent people being slaughtered by extremists. I worried Iraq could be broken so badly that it would be impossible to put back together.

The surge option brought risks of its own. Increasing our troop levels would be deeply unpopular at home. The fighting would be tough, and casualties could be high. If Maliki let us down, we might not be able to stem the violence.

After seeing Maliki, I believed we could count on his support. The surge was our best chance, maybe our last chance, to accomplish our objectives in Iraq.

---

Over weeks of intense discussion in November and December, most of the national security team came to support the surge. Dick Cheney, Bob Gates, Josh Bolten, and Steve Hadley and his NSC warriors were behind the new approach. Condi would be, too, so long as the plan didn't send more troops under the same old strategy.

On a decision this controversial and important, it was essential to have unity. Congress and the press would probe for any rift within the administration. If they found one, they would exploit it to justify their opposition and block the plan. To reach that consensus, one more group needed to be on board, the Joint Chiefs of Staff.

Established by the National Security Act of 1947, the Joint Chiefs included the heads of each service branch, plus a chairman and vice-chairman. The chiefs are not part of the chain of command, so they have no direct responsibility for military operations. A key part of their role is to advocate the health and strength of our armed forces. By law, the chairman of the Joint Chiefs is the president's principal military adviser.

The chairman of the Joint Chiefs in 2006 was General Pete Pace. Pete was the first Marine to serve as chairman and one of the great officers of his generation. As a young lieutenant in Vietnam, Pete led a platoon that endured heavy fighting. For the rest of his career, he carried the photos of the Marines who gave their lives under his command. When he took office as chairman, he made a point of telling me their names. He never forgot them, or the cost of war.

Pete had launched a strategy review within the Joint Chiefs, and I asked Steve Hadley to make sure the surge concept had a place in their discussions. I decided to go see the chiefs at the Pentagon to listen to their thoughts in person.

Two days before the meeting, Pete came to the Oval Office. He told me I would hear a number of concerns from the chiefs, but they were prepared to support the surge. He also gave Steve an estimate on how many troops might be needed to make a difference: five brigades, about twenty thousand Americans.

On December 13, 2006, I walked into the Tank, the Joint Chiefs' secure wood-paneled conference room at the Pentagon. Coming to their territory was a way to show my respect. I opened by telling them I was there to hear their opinions and ask their advice.

I went around the table one by one. The chiefs laid out their concerns. They worried about Maliki's level of commitment. They felt other agencies of the government needed to contribute more in Iraq. They questioned whether the demands of a surge would leave us unprepared for other contingencies, such as a flare-up on the Korean Peninsula.

Their overriding worry was that a troop increase would "break the military" by putting too much strain on service members and their families. Many of our troops in Iraq were serving their second or third tours in the country. To make the surge possible, we would have to extend some tours from twelve to fifteen months. The effect on recruitment, morale, training, preparedness, and military families could be profound.

Army Chief of Staff Pete Schoomaker and Marine Commandant James Conway recommended an increase in the size of their services. They believed an expansion would ease the stress on our forces and help ensure we were ready for potential conflicts elsewhere in the world. I liked the idea and promised to consider it.

At the end of the meeting, I summarized my thinking. "I share your concern about breaking the military," I said. "The surest way to break the military would be to lose in Iraq."

My initial plan was to announce the new Iraq strategy a week or two before Christmas. But as the date approached, I concluded we needed more time. I wanted Bob Gates, who was sworn in as secretary of defense on December 18, to visit Iraq.

Two days before Christmas, Bob came to see me at Camp David. He told me he had visited with Maliki, who had refined his plan for an Iraqi surge to match ours. Maliki would declare martial law, deploy three additional Iraqi brigades to Baghdad, appoint a military governor, and name two deputy commanders with free rein to go after extremists of any sectarian background. Bob had also decided on his recommendation for a new commander. It would be General David Petraeus. We agreed to nominate General Casey for a promotion to Army chief of staff. George had a long and distinguished record of service, and his experience would benefit the Army. I also wanted to make clear that I did not blame him for the problems in Iraq.

The final question to resolve was the size of the surge. Some in the military proposed that we commit two additional brigades initially—a mini-surge of about ten thousand troops—with the possibility of sending up to three more brigades later. Pete Pace reported that General Petraeus and General Ray Odierno, the number-two commander in Iraq, wanted all five brigades committed up front.

If our commanders on the ground wanted the full force, they would get it. I decided to send five brigades to Baghdad, plus two additional Marine battalions to Anbar Province. We would embed our troops in Iraqi formations, so that we could mentor the Iraqis on the battlefield and prepare the Iraqis to take more responsibility after the surge. Finally, I would accept three key recommendations from the Joint Chiefs. Condi would lead a surge in civilian resources. I would obtain public assurances from Prime Minister Maliki about our troops' freedom to maneuver. And I would call on Congress to increase the size of the Army and Marine Corps by ninety thousand forces.

On January 4, 2007, I held a secure videoconference with Maliki. "A lot of people here don't think we can succeed. I do," I told him. "I'll put my neck out if you put out yours." Two days later, he addressed the Iraqi people and signaled his commitment to the surge. "The Baghdad security plan will not provide a safe haven for any outlaws, regardless of sectarian or political affiliation," he said.

The decision had been tough, but I was confident that I had made it the right way. I had gathered facts and opinions from people inside and outside the administration. I had challenged assumptions and weighed all the options carefully. I knew the surge would be unpopular in the short term. But while many in Washington had given up on the prospect of victory in Iraq, I had not.

At nine o'clock on the evening of January 10, 2007, I stepped before the cameras in the White House Library. "The situation in Iraq is unacceptable to the American people—and it is unacceptable to me," I said. "Our troops in Iraq have fought bravely. They have done everything we have asked them to do. Where mistakes have been made, the responsibility rests with me.

"It is clear that we need to change our strategy in Iraq. . . . So I've committed more than twenty thousand additional American troops to Iraq. The vast majority of them—five brigades—will be deployed to Baghdad."

———

The reaction was swift and one-sided. "I don't believe an expansion of twenty thousand troops in Iraq will solve the problems," one senator said. "I do not believe that sending more troops to Iraq is the answer," said another. A third pronounced it "the most dangerous foreign policy blunder in this country since Vietnam." And those were just the Republicans.

The left was even more outspoken. One freshman senator predicted that the surge would not "solve the sectarian violence there. In fact, I think it will do the reverse." Capturing the view of most of his colleagues, a *Washington Post* columnist called it "a fantasy-based escalation of the war in Iraq, which could only make sense in some parallel universe where pigs fly and fish commute on bicycles."

Condi, Bob Gates, and Pete Pace testified on Capitol Hill the day after I announced the surge. The questioning was brutal from both sides of the aisle. "This is the craziest, dumbest plan I've ever seen or heard of in my life," one Democratic congressman told General Pace. "I've gone along with the president on this, and I bought into his dream," a Republican senator told Condi. "At this stage of the game, I just don't think it's going to happen." Afterward Condi came to see me in the Oval Office. "We've got a tough sell on this, Mr. President," she said.

Amid the near-universal skepticism, a few brave souls defended the surge. Foremost among them were Senator Joe Lieberman of Connecticut, a lifelong Democrat who had been cast aside by his party for supporting the war; Senator Lindsey Graham of South Carolina, a member of the Air Force Reserves; and Senator John McCain of Arizona.

McCain and I had a complex relationship. We had competed against each other in 2000, and we had disagreed on issues from tax cuts to Medicare reform to terrorist interrogation. Yet he had campaigned hard for me in 2004, and I knew he planned to run for president in 2008. The surge gave him a chance to create distance between us, but he didn't take it. He had been a longtime advocate of more troops in Iraq, and he supported the new strategy wholeheartedly. "I cannot guarantee success," he said. "But I can guarantee failure if we don't adopt this new strategy."

The most persuasive advocate of the surge was General Petraeus. As the author of the Army's counterinsurgency manual, he was the undisputed authority on the strategy he would lead. His intellect, competitiveness, and work ethic were well known. On one of his visits home, I invited the general to mountain bike with me at Fort Belvoir, Virginia. He was mainly a runner, but he had enough confidence to accept the challenge. He held his own with the experienced riders of the presidential peloton.

After the ride, I stepped inside a building at Fort Belvoir to take a call from the prime minister of Japan. I heard a noise in the background. I peeked out the door and saw Petraeus leading the peloton through a series of post-ride push-ups and crunches.

Petraeus's rise had attracted some resentment. I had heard gossip from several people warning that he had an outsize ego. Back in 2004, when Petraeus was leading the effort to train Iraqi security forces, Newsweek had run a cover with a close-up photo of him above the headline "Can this man save Iraq?" When I raised the topic with him, he smiled and said, "My classmates from West Point are never going to let me live that

down." I appreciated his self-deprecating remark. It was a good comple-
ment to his drive.

Petraeus's confirmation hearings came late in January. "I think that
at this point in Baghdad the population just wants to be secure," he
said. "And truthfully, they don't care who does it." When John McCain
pressed him on whether the mission could succeed without more troops,
General Petraeus answered, "No, sir." The Senate confirmed him, 81 to 0.

I called the general to the Oval Office to congratulate him on the vote.
Dick Cheney, Bob Gates, Pete Pace, and other members of the national
security team were there to wish him well. "I'd like a moment alone with
my commander," I said.

As the team filed out, I assured General Petraeus that I had confidence in him and that he could have my ear anytime. At the end of the
meeting I said, "This is it. We're doubling down."

As he walked out the door, he replied, "Mr. President, I think it's more
like all in."

On February 10, 2007, David Petraeus took command in Baghdad. His
task was as daunting as any American commander had faced in decades.
As he told his troops on his first day, "The situation in Iraq is exceedingly
challenging, the stakes are very high, the way ahead will be hard and
there undoubtedly will be many tough days." He continued: "However,
hard is not hopeless. These tasks are achievable; this mission is doable."

As our surge troops flowed into Iraq, Generals Petraeus and Odierno
relocated our forces from bases on the outskirts of Baghdad to small outposts inside the city. Our troops lived alongside Iraqi security forces and
patrolled the city on foot, instead of inside armored Humvees. As they
entered enemy strongholds for the first time, the extremists fought back.
We lost 81 troops in February, 81 in March, 104 in April, 126 in May,
and 101 in June—the first time in the war we had faced triple-digit losses
three months in a row. The casualties were agonizing. But something felt
different in 2007: America was on offense again.

General Petraeus drew my attention to an interesting metric of progress: the number of intelligence tips from Iraqi residents. In the past,

Iraqis had feared retribution from insurgents or death squads for co-operating with our forces. But as security improved, the number of tips grew from about 12,500 in February to almost 25,000 in May. Our troops and intelligence operators used the tips to take insurgents and weapons off the street. The counterinsurgency strategy was working: We were winning over the people by providing what they needed most, security.

We followed up the clearing and holding with building, thanks in large part to the civilian surge led by Ambassador Ryan Crocker. I first met Ryan in Pakistan, where he was serving as ambassador, during my visit in 2006. He came across as a patient, unassuming diplomat. But beneath his calm exterior was a fearless man widely regarded as the best Foreign Service officer of his generation. Fluent in Arabic, Ryan had served all over the Middle East, including several tours in Iraq. He had survived the 1983 terrorist attack on our embassy in Lebanon and escaped an angry mob plundering his residence in Syria. When I announced the new strategy in Iraq, I decided we should change ambassadors, too. I nominated Zal Khalilzad, who had done a fine job in Baghdad, to be our permanent representative to the UN. Condi didn't take long to recommend a replacement for him. She said Ryan was the only man for the job.

Ryan gained my respect quickly. He had a knack for detecting problems and heading them off. He spoke bluntly about challenges but had a wry sense of humor and liked to laugh. "What have you got for me today, Sunshine?" I asked him during one particularly rough stretch. He started his briefing with a big grin. He worked seamlessly with General Petraeus. And he earned the trust of Iraqis from all factions.

The heart of the civilian surge was doubling the number of Provincial Reconstruction Teams, which paired civilian experts with military personnel. I held several videoconferences and meetings with PRT team leaders deployed across Iraq. They were an impressive group. Several were grizzled combat veterans. Another was a female Foreign Service officer whose son served as a Marine in Iraq. They described their projects, which ranged from supporting a local newspaper in Baghdad to helping set up courts in Ninewa to creating a soil-testing laboratory to improve agriculture in Diyala. It wasn't always glamorous work, but it was critical to the counterinsurgency strategy we were carrying out.

I spoke to General Petraeus and Ambassador Crocker by secure video-conference at least once a week, sometimes more often. I believed a close personal relationship and frequent contact were critical to making the new strategy succeed. The conversations gave me a chance to hear first-hand reports on conditions in Iraq. They allowed Petraeus and Crocker to share frustrations and push for decisions directly from the com-mander in chief.

The situation was improving, but we all worried about the possibility of another Samarra-like bombing, a game-changer that would reignite sectarian violence. Petraeus pinpointed another problem. "The Wash-ington clock is ticking a lot faster than the Baghdad clock," he said.

He was right. Less than one week after General Petraeus arrived in Iraq, the new Democratic majority in the House of Representatives had passed a nonbinding resolution that declared, "Congress disapproves of the decision of President George W. Bush announced on January 10, 2007, to deploy more than 20,000 additional United States combat troops to Iraq."

After a day of heavy violence in April, Senator Harry Reid of Nevada declared, "This war is lost, the surge is not accomplishing anything." The majority leader of the U.S. Senate had just used his platform to tell 145,000 American troops and their families that they were fighting for a lost cause. He had written off the surge as a failure before all of the ad-ditional troops had even arrived. It was one of the most irresponsible acts I witnessed in my eight years in Washington.

On May 1, Congress sent me a war-funding bill mandating a troop withdrawal deadline later in the year. Setting an arbitrary pullout date would allow our enemies to wait us out and would undermine our ability to win over the local leaders who were critical to our success. I vetoed the bill. Led by Senate Minority Leader Mitch McConnell—who supported the surge after I announced it and graciously later admitted to me that he had been wrong to suggest a withdrawal—and House Minority Leader John Boehner, Republicans on Capitol Hill stood firm. Democrats didn't have the votes to override the veto. On May 25, I signed a bill fully fund-ing our troops with no timetable for withdrawal.

They called it "The Awakening."

Anbar is Iraq's largest province, a sprawling expanse of desert that extends from the western boundary of Baghdad to the borders of Syria, Jordan, and Saudi Arabia. At fifty-three thousand square miles, Anbar covers nearly the same amount of land as New York State. Its population is mostly Sunni. For almost four years, it served as a stronghold for insurgents—and a sanctuary for al Qaeda.

Al Qaeda took over Anbar's principal cities, infiltrated the security forces, and imposed their ideology on the population. Like the Taliban, they forbade women from leaving their homes without a male escort and banned sports and other leisure activities. They attacked American troops, Iraqi security forces, and anyone else who resisted them. By 2006, Anbar was home to an average of forty-one attacks per day.

Our troops discovered an al Qaeda document laying out an elaborate governing structure for Anbar, including an Education Department, a Social Services Department, and an "Execution Unit." Our intelligence community believed Anbar was to be al Qaeda's base for planning attacks on the United States. In August 2006, a senior Marine Corps intelligence officer in Anbar wrote a widely publicized report concluding that the province was lost.

Then everything changed. The people of Anbar had a look at life under al Qaeda, and they didn't like what they saw. Starting in mid-2006, tribal sheikhs banded together to take their province back from the extremists. The Awakening drew thousands of recruits.

As part of the surge, we deployed four thousand additional Marines to Anbar, where they reinforced the tribal sheikhs and boosted their confidence. Many of the al Qaeda jihadists fled into the desert. Violence in the province plummeted by more than 90 percent. Within months, the brave people of Anbar—with support from our troops—had retaken their province. An al Qaeda safe haven had become the site of its greatest ideological defeat.

On Labor Day 2007, I made a surprise visit to Anbar. Air Force One flew over what looked like a giant sand dune and touched down at Al Asad Air Base, a patch of black asphalt amid miles of brown. We walked down the stairs into the searing heat and quickly moved to an air-conditioned room at the base. I listened to several briefings and then met with a group of tribal sheikhs who had started the Anbar uprising. They were a rough-hewn, earthy bunch. Their friendly, animated mannerisms reminded me of local officials in West Texas. But instead of jeans and boots, they were wearing full-length robes and colorful headdresses.

The sheikhs beamed with pride as they described what they had accomplished. Violence was down dramatically; mayors' offices and city councils were functioning; judges were hearing cases and meting out justice. With the help of our civilian surge, the provincial council in Ramadi had reopened, with thirty-five members present for the inaugural session.

Prime Minister Maliki and President Jalal Talabani joined the meeting. It was extraordinary to watch Maliki, a Shia; Talabani, a Kurd; and a roomful of Sunni sheikhs discuss the future of their country. When the prime minister asked what they needed, they had a long list of requests: more money, more equipment, and more infrastructure. Maliki complained that there wasn't enough in the budget for everything they asked for. Talabani helped referee the disputes. I sat back and enjoyed the scene. Democracy was at work in Iraq.

I thanked the sheikhs for their hospitality and their bravery in the war on terror. "If you need us," one sheikh jubilantly told me, "my men and I will go to Afghanistan!"

---

Washington was abuzz when Petraeus and Crocker arrived on September 10 to testify before Congress and make recommendations on the way forward in Iraq. For months, Democrats had pledged to use their testimony to cut off funding for the war. In July, the New York Times declared the cause in Iraq "lost" and called for an all-out withdrawal, despite the likelihood that an immediate pullout could result in "further ethnic cleansing, even genocide" and "a new stronghold from which terrorist activity could proliferate." It was stunning to see the Times, which rightly championed human rights, advocate a policy it admitted could lead to genocide.

The morning of the hearings, the left-wing group MoveOn.org ran a full-page newspaper ad that read, "General Petraeus or General Betray Us? Cooking the Books for the White House." It was an astonishing character attack on a four-star general. It was also a political mistake. Democrats in Congress tried to avoid endorsing the ad while supporting the antiwar sentiment behind it. One New York senator denounced the ad but said Petraeus's report required "the willing suspension of disbelief."

For their part, Petraeus and Crocker were stoic, resilient, and highly credible. They reported the facts. Iraqi civilian deaths had declined 70 percent in Baghdad and 45 percent across the country. Deaths from sectarian violence had plunged 80 percent in Baghdad and 55 percent across the country. IED attacks had dropped by a third, and car bombings and suicide attacks had declined almost 50 percent. The Awakening movement we had witnessed in Anbar had spread to Diyala Province and the Sunni neighborhoods of Baghdad. The picture was unmistakable: The surge was working.

Two nights after the testimony, I spoke to the nation. "Because of this success, General Petraeus believes we have now reached the point where we can maintain our security gains with fewer American forces," I said. ". . . The principle guiding my decisions on troop levels in Iraq is 'return on success.' The more successful we are, the more American troops can return home."

The most quoted phrase in the speech was "return on success." The clever play on words was suggested by Ed Gillespie, a smart and valued friend who agreed to lead my communications team when Dan Bartlett returned home to Texas. But in my mind, the most important message was that we were keeping as many troops in Iraq as our commanders needed, for as long as they needed them.

The day of my speech, I heard that General Petraeus's friend, retired General Jack Keane, was meeting with Dick Cheney. I liked and respected Jack. He had provided valuable advice during the decision-making process and supported the surge publicly. I asked Jack to convey a personal message from me to General Petraeus: "I waited over three years for a successful strategy. And I'm not giving up on it prematurely. I am not reducing further unless you are convinced that we should reduce further."

—

Three weeks after the much-awaited testimony, I rode to the military parade grounds at Fort Myer, Virginia, to say farewell to a friend.

Shortly after I announced the surge, Bob Gates had recommended that I not renominate General Pete Pace to a second term as chairman of the Joint Chiefs. The environment on Capitol Hill was hostile, and Bob had heard from several senators—especially Carl Levin, the new chairman of the Senate Armed Services Committee—that Pete's confirmation hearing would be contentious. The concern was that senators would use him as a punching bag for all their frustrations with Iraq.

I admired Pete. I had benefited from his advice for six years. I knew how much our troops loved him. I wanted to end the presidency with my friend as chairman. But I pictured the spectacle of the hearing— protestors yelling and senators preening for the cameras, all ending with a negative vote that would humiliate Pete. I reluctantly agreed with Bob's judgment. I nominated Mike Mullen, a fine Navy admiral, to be the next chairman.

Pete never complained. He served nobly to the end. After turning over his duties, he removed the four stars from his uniform, pinned them to a note card, and left it at the foot of the Vietnam Memorial near the name of a Marine lost four decades earlier. He brought no cameras or press. Later, the card was found at the foot of the wall. It read, "To Guido Farinaro, USMC, These [stars] are yours, not mine! With love and respect, Your platoon leader, Pete Pace."

I ached for Pete and his family. When I presented him with a well-deserved Presidential Medal of Freedom in 2008, it only partly assuaged my regret.

———

The momentum of the surge continued into 2008. By spring more than ninety thousand Iraqis, both Sunni and Shia, had joined Concerned Local Citizens groups like those that had started in Anbar. Many of these forces, now known as Sons of Iraq, integrated into the increasingly effective army and police force, which had grown to more than 475,000. They drove the remaining hard-core insurgents and al Qaeda from their strongholds. The terrorists resorted to using children and the mentally handicapped as suicide bombers, revealing both their moral depravity and their inability to recruit.

Just as counterinsurgency experts predicted, the security gains of 2007 translated into political progress in 2008. Free from the nightmare of sectarian violence, the Iraqis passed a flurry of major legislation, including a law resolving the status of former Baath Party members, a national budget, and legislation paving the way for provincial elections. While the government still had work to do on some key measures, including an oil-revenue-sharing law, the Iraqis' political performance was a remarkable feat given all that they had endured.

The biggest concern in the spring of 2008 was the presence of Shia extremists. While security in most of Iraq improved during the surge, Shia extremists, many with close ties to Iran, had taken over large parts of Basra, Iraq's second-largest city.

On March 25, 2008, Iraqi forces attacked the extremists in Basra. Prime Minister Maliki traveled to the south to oversee the operation. Most of my national security team was somewhere between anxious and petrified. The military worried that Maliki did not have a well-defined plan. Some in the embassy questioned whether he had enough support within the Iraqi government. The CIA gave Maliki's assault a bleak prognosis.

I felt differently. Maliki was leading. For almost two years, I had urged him to show his evenhandedness. "A Shia murderer is as guilty as a Sunni murderer," I said many times. Now he had followed through in a highly public way. When Steve Hadley and Brett McGurk came to the Oval Office the morning after Maliki launched the attack, I said, "Don't tell me this is a bad thing. Maliki said he would do this and now he's doing it. This is a defining moment. We just need to help him succeed."

The assault was far from textbook, but it worked. The Iraqi forces brought security to Basra. Their success stunned Shia radicals like Moqtada al Sadr and their backers in Iran. Above all, the Basra operation established Maliki as a strong leader. The prime minister had reached a major decision point of his own, and he had made the right call.

A few weeks after the Iraqi government's offensive in Basra, Petraeus and Crocker returned to Washington to testify in April. This time, there

were no antiwar ads in the newspapers and no prolonged battle for funding. NBC News, which in November 2006 had officially pronounced Iraq
in a state of civil war, stopped using the term. There was no grand announcement of the retraction.

Calling our gains in Iraq "fragile and reversible," General Petraeus
recommended that we continue withdrawing troops until we hit pre-
surge levels, and then pause for further assessment. As Ryan Crocker
put it, "In the end, how we leave [Iraq] and what we leave behind will be
more important than how we came. Our current course is hard, but it is
working. . . . We need to stay with it." I agreed.

———

It was a measure of the surge's success that one of the biggest military
controversies of early 2008 did not involve Iraq. In March, Admiral Fox
Fallon—who had succeeded John Abizaid as commander of CENTCOM—
gave a magazine interview suggesting he was the only person standing
between me and war with Iran. That was ridiculous. I asked Joint Chiefs
Chairman Mike Mullen and Vice Chairman Hoss Cartwright what they
would do if they were in Fallon's position. Both said they would resign.
Soon after, Fox submitted his resignation. To his credit, he never brought
up the issue again. At our last meeting, I thanked him for his service and
told him I was proud of his fine career.

I had to find a new commander to lead CENTCOM. There was only
one person I wanted: David Petraeus. He had spent three of the past four
years in Iraq, and I knew he was hoping to assume the coveted NATO
command in Europe. But we needed him at CENTCOM. "If the twenty-
two-year-old kids can stay in the fight," he said, "I can, too."

I asked General Petraeus who should replace him in Iraq. Without
hesitation, he named his former deputy commander, General Ray Odierno. I first met Ray years earlier when I toured Fort Hood as governor of
Texas. Six foot five with a clean-shaven head, the general is an imposing
man. He was an early proponent of the surge, and he helped the strategy
succeed by positioning the additional troops wisely throughout Baghdad.

For General Odierno, winning in Iraq was more than his duty as a soldier. It was personal. When Ray was home on leave in December 2004, I welcomed his family to the Oval Office, including his son, Lieutenant Anthony Odierno, a West Point graduate who had lost his left arm in Iraq. His father stood silently, beaming with pride, as his son raised his right arm to salute me. Even though Ray had just left for a top position back home at the Pentagon, he accepted the call to return as commander in Baghdad.

It gave me solace to know that the next president would be able to rely on the advice of these two wise, battle-tested generals. In our own way, we had continued one of the great traditions of American history. Lincoln discovered Generals Grant and Sherman. Roosevelt had Eisenhower and Bradley. I found David Petraeus and Ray Odierno.

———

By the time the surge ended in the summer of 2008, violence in Iraq had dropped to the lowest level since the first year of the war. The sectarian killing that had almost ripped the country apart in 2006 was down more than 95 percent. Prime Minister Maliki, once the object of near-universal blame and scorn, had emerged as a confident leader. Al Qaeda in Iraq had been severely weakened and marginalized. Iran's malign influence had been reduced. Iraqi forces were preparing to take responsibility for security in a majority of provinces. American deaths, which routinely hit one hundred a month in the worst stretch of the war, never again topped twenty-five, and dropped to single digits by the end of my presidency. Nevertheless, every death was a painful reminder of the costs of war.

My last major goal was to put Iraq policy onto a stable footing for my successors. In late 2007, we started work on two agreements. One, called a Status of Forces Agreement (SOFA), laid the legal predicate for keeping American troops in Iraq after the United Nations mandate expired at the end of 2008. The other, called a Strategic Framework Agreement (SFA), pledged long-term diplomatic, economic, and security cooperation between our countries.

Hammering out the agreements took months. Maliki had to deal with serious opposition from factions of his government, especially those with suspected ties to Iran. In the middle of a presidential campaign, Demo-cratic candidates denounced the SOFA as a scheme to keep our troops in Iraq forever. The CIA doubted that Maliki would sign the agreement. I asked the prime minister about it directly. He assured me he wanted the SOFA. He had kept his word in the past, and I believed he would again.

Maliki proved a tough negotiator. He would obtain a concession from our side* and then come back asking for more. On one level, the end-less horse trading was frustrating. But on another level, I was inspired to see the Iraqis conducting themselves like representatives of a sovereign democracy.

As time passed without agreement, I started to get anxious. In one of our weekly videoconferences, I said, "Mr. Prime Minister, I only have a few months left in office. I need to know whether you want these agree-ments. If not, I have better things to do." I could tell he was a little taken aback. This was my signal that it was time to stop asking for more. "We will finish these agreements," he said. "You have my word."

By November, the agreements were almost done. The final conten-tious issue was what the SOFA would say about America's withdrawal from Iraq. Maliki told us it would help him if the agreement included a promise to pull out our troops by a certain date. Our negotiators settled on a commitment to withdraw our forces by the end of 2011.

For years, I had refused to set an arbitrary timetable for leaving Iraq. I was still hesitant to commit to a date, but this was not arbitrary. The agreement had been negotiated between two sovereign governments, and it had the blessing of Generals Petraeus and Odierno, who would oversee its implementation. If conditions changed and Iraqis requested a continued American presence, we could amend the SOFA and keep troops in the country.

Maliki's political instincts proved wise. The SOFA and SFA, initially seen as documents focused on our staying in Iraq, ended up being viewed as agreements paving the way for our departure. The blowback we ini-tially feared from Capitol Hill and the Iraqi parliament never material-ized. As I write in 2010, the SOFA continues to guide our presence in Iraq.

---

*Led by Condi, Ryan Crocker, Brett McGurk, and State Department adviser David Sat-terfield.

On December 13, 2008, I boarded Air Force One for my fourth trip to Iraq, where I would sign the SOFA and SFA with Prime Minister Maliki. On the flight over, I thought about my previous trips to the country. They traced the arc of the war. There was the joy of the first visit on Thanksgiving Day 2003, which came months after liberation and a few weeks before the capture of Saddam. There was the uncertainty of the trip to meet Maliki in June 2006, when sectarian violence was rising and our strategy was failing. There was the cautious optimism of Anbar in September 2007, when the surge appeared to be working but still faced serious opposition. Now there was this final journey. Even though much of America seemed to have tuned out the war, our troops and the Iraqis had created the prospect of lasting success.

We landed in Baghdad and choppered to Salam Palace, which six years earlier had belonged to Saddam and his brutal regime. As president, I had attended many arrival ceremonies. None was more moving than standing in the courtyard of that liberated palace, next to President Jalal Talabani, watching the flags of the United States and a free Iraq fly side by side as a military band played our national anthems.

From there we drove to the prime minister's complex, where Maliki and I signed the SOFA and the SFA and held a final press conference. The room was packed tight, and the audience was closer than at a normal event. A handful of Iraqi journalists sat in front of me on the left. To my right was the traveling press pool and a few reporters based in Iraq. As Maliki called for the first question, a man in the Iraqi press rose abruptly. He let out what sounded like a loud bark, something in Arabic that sure wasn't a question. Then he wound up and threw something in my direction. What was it? A shoe?

The scene went into slow motion. I felt like Ted Williams, who said he could see the stitching of a baseball on an incoming pitch. The wingtip was helicoptering toward me. I ducked. The guy had a pretty live arm. A split second later, he threw another one. This one was not flying as fast. I flicked my head slightly and it drifted over me. I wish I had caught the damn thing.

Chaos erupted. People screamed, and security agents scrambled. I

had the same thought I'd had in the Florida classroom on 9/11. I knew
my reaction would be broadcast around the world. The bigger the frenzy,
the better for the attacker.

I waved off Don White, my lead Secret Service agent. I did not want
footage of me being hustled out of the room. I glanced at Maliki, who
looked stricken. The Iraqi reporters were humiliated and angry. One
man was shaking his head sadly, mouthing apologies. I held up my hands
and urged everyone to settle down.

"If you want the facts, it's a size-ten shoe that he threw," I said. I hoped
that by trivializing the moment, I could keep the shoe thrower from accomplishing his goal of ruining the event.

After the press conference, Maliki and I went to a dinner upstairs
with our delegations. He was still shaken and apologized profusely. I took
him aside privately with Gamal Helal, our Arabic interpreter, and told
him to stop worrying. The prime minister gathered himself and asked to
speak before the dinner. He gave an emotional toast about how the shoe
thrower did not represent his people, and how grateful his nation was
to America. He talked about how we had given them two chances to be
free, first by liberating them from Saddam Hussein and again by helping
them liberate themselves from the sectarian violence and terrorists.

Having a shoe thrown at me by a journalist ranked as one of my more
unusual experiences. But what if someone had said eight years earlier
that the president of the United States would be dining in Baghdad with
the prime minister of a free Iraq? Nothing—not even flying footwear at a
press conference—would have seemed more unlikely than that.

———

Years from now, historians may look back and see the surge as a forgone
conclusion, an inevitable bridge between the years of violence that followed liberation and the democracy that emerged. Nothing about the
surge felt inevitable at the time. Public opinion ran strongly against it.
Congress tried to block it. The enemy fought relentlessly to break our
will.

Yet thanks to the skill and courage of our troops, the new counterinsurgency strategy we adopted, the superb coordination between our ci-

vilian and military efforts, and the strong support we provided for Iraq's political leaders, a war widely written off as a failure has a chance to end in success. By the time I left office, the violence had declined dramatically. Economic and political activity had resumed. Al Qaeda had suffered a significant military and ideological defeat. In March 2010, Iraqis went to the polls again. In a headline unimaginable three years earlier, *Newsweek* ran a cover story titled "Victory at Last: The Emergence of a Democratic Iraq."

Iraq still faces challenges, and no one can know with certainty what the fate of the country will be. But we do know this: Because the United States liberated Iraq and then refused to abandon it, the people of that country have a chance to be free. Having come this far, I hope America will continue to support Iraq's young democracy. If Iraqis request a continued troop presence, we should provide it. A free and peaceful Iraq is in our vital strategic interest. It can be a valuable ally at the heart of the Middle East, a source of stability in the region, and a beacon of hope to political reformers in its neighborhood and around the world. Like the democracies we helped build in Germany, Japan, and South Korea, a free Iraq will make us safer for generations to come.

I have often reflected on whether I should have ordered the surge earlier. For three years, our premise in Iraq was that political progress was the measure of success. The Iraqis hit all their milestones on time. It looked like our strategy was working. Only after the sectarian violence erupted in 2006 did it become clear that more security was needed before political progress could continue. After that, I moved forward with the surge in a way that unified our government. If I had acted sooner it could have created a rift that would have been exploited by war critics in Congress to cut off funding and prevent the surge from succeeding.

From the beginning of the war in Iraq, my conviction was that freedom is universal—and democracy in the Middle East would make the region more peaceful. There were times when that seemed unlikely. But I never lost faith that it was true.

I never lost faith in our troops, either. I was constantly amazed by their willingness to volunteer in the face of danger. In August 2007, I traveled to Reno, Nevada, to speak to the American Legion. Afterward, I met Bill and Christine Krissoff from Truckee, California. Their son, twenty-five-year-old Marine Nathan Krissoff, had given his life in Iraq. His brother, Austin, also a Marine, was at the meeting. Austin and Christine told me how much Nathan loved his job. Then Bill spoke up.

"Mr. President, I'm an orthopedic surgeon," he said. "I want to join the Navy Medical Corps in Nathan's honor."

I was moved and surprised. "How old are you?" I asked.

"I'm sixty, sir," he replied.

I was sixty-one, so sixty didn't sound that old to me. I looked at his wife. She nodded. Bill explained that he was willing to retire from his orthopedic practice in California, but he needed a special age waiver to qualify for the Navy.

"I'll see what I can do," I said.

When I got back to Washington, I told Pete Pace the story after a morning briefing. Before long, Dr. Krissoff's waiver came through. He underwent extensive training in battlefield medicine. Shortly after I left office, he deployed to Iraq, where he served alongside Austin and treated wounded Marines.

"I like to think that Austin and I are completing Nate's unfinished task here in Iraq," he wrote. "We honor his memory by our work here." In 2010, I learned that Dr. Krissoff had returned home from Iraq—and then shipped off to Afghanistan.

Nathan Krissoff is one of the 4,229 American service members who gave their lives in Iraq during my presidency. More than 30,000 suffered wounds of war. I will always carry with me the grief their families feel. I will never forget the pride they took in their work, the inspiration they brought to others, and the difference they made in the world. Every American who served in Iraq helped to make our nation safer, gave twenty-five million people the chance to live in freedom, and changed the direction of the Middle East for generations to come. There are things we got wrong in Iraq, but that cause is eternally right.

# 13

## FREEDOM AGENDA

Just before noon on January 20, 2005, I stepped onto the Inaugural platform. From the west front of the Capitol, I looked out on the crowd of four hundred thousand that stretched back across the National Mall. Behind them I could see the Washington Monument, the Lincoln Memorial, and Arlington National Cemetery on the other side of the Potomac.

The 2005 Inauguration marked the third time I had admired that view. In 1989, I was a proud son watching his dad get sworn in. In 2001, I took the presidential oath under freezing rain and the clouds of a disputed election. I had to concentrate on each step down the Capitol stairs, which were a lot narrower than I'd expected. It took time for my senses to adjust to the flurry of sounds and sights. I stared out at the huge huddled mass of black and gray overcoats. I wondered if the sleet would make it hard to see the TelePrompTer when I gave my Inaugural Address.

Four years later, the sky was sunny and clear. The colors seemed more vibrant. And the election results had been decisive. As I walked down the blue-carpeted steps toward the stage, I was able to pick out individual faces in the crowd. I saw Joe and Jan O'Neill, along with a large contingent from Midland. I smiled at the dear friends who had introduced me to the wonderful woman at my side. One thing was for sure: As we enjoyed our burgers that night in 1977, none of us expected this.

I took my seat in the row ahead of Laura, Barbara, and Jenna. Mother and Dad, Laura's mom, and my brothers and sister sat nearby. Senator Trent Lott, the chairman of the Inaugural Committee, called Chief Justice William Rehnquist to the podium. I stepped forward with Laura, Barbara, and Jenna. Laura held the Bible, which both Dad and I had used to take the oath. It was open to Isaiah 40:31, "But those who hope in the Lord will renew their strength. They will soar on wings like eagles; they will run and not grow weary, they will walk and not be faint."

I put my left hand on the Bible and raised my right as the ailing chief justice administered the thirty-five-word oath. When I closed with "So help me God," the cannons boomed a twenty-one-gun salute. I hugged Laura and the girls, stepped back, and soaked in the moment.

Then it was time for the speech:

> At this second gathering, our duties are defined not by the words I use, but by the history we have seen together. For a half century, America defended our own freedom by standing watch on distant borders. After the shipwreck of communism came years of relative quiet, years of repose, years of sabbatical—and then there came a day of fire.
>
> We have seen our vulnerability—and we have seen its deepest source. For as long as whole regions of the world simmer in resentment and tyranny—prone to ideologies that feed hatred and excuse murder—violence will gather, and multiply in destructive power, and cross the most defended borders, and raise a mortal threat. There is only one force of history that can break the reign of hatred and resentment, and expose the pretensions of tyrants, and reward the hopes of the decent and tolerant, and that is the force of human freedom.
>
> We are led, by events and common sense, to one conclusion: The survival of liberty in our land increasingly depends on the success of liberty in other lands. The best hope for peace in our world is the expansion of freedom in all the world. . . . So it is the policy of the United States to seek and support the growth of democratic movements and institutions in every nation and culture, with the ultimate goal of ending tyranny in our world.

After 9/11, I developed a strategy to protect the country that came to be known as the Bush Doctrine: First, make no distinction between the terrorists and the nations that harbor them—and hold both to account. Second, take the fight to the enemy overseas before they can attack us again here at home. Third, confront threats before they fully materialize.

And fourth, advance liberty and hope as an alternative to the enemy's ideology of repression and fear.

The freedom agenda, as I called the fourth prong, was both idealistic and realistic. It was idealistic in that freedom is a universal gift from Almighty God. It was realistic because freedom is the most practical way to protect our country in the long run. As I said in my Second Inaugural Address, "America's vital interests and our deepest beliefs are now one."

The transformative power of freedom had been proven in places like South Korea, Germany, and Eastern Europe. For me, the most vivid example of freedom's power was my relationship with Prime Minister Junichiro Koizumi of Japan. Koizumi was one of the first world leaders to offer his support after 9/11. How ironic. Sixty years earlier, my father had fought the Japanese as a Navy pilot. Koizumi's father had served in the government of Imperial Japan. Now their sons were working together to keep the peace. Something big had changed since World War II: By adopting a Japanese-style democracy, an enemy had become an ally.

---

Announcing the freedom agenda was one step. Implementing it was another. In some places, such as Afghanistan and Iraq, we had a unique responsibility to give the people we liberated a chance to build free societies. But these examples were the exception, not the rule. I made clear that the freedom agenda was "not primarily the task of arms." We would advance freedom by supporting fledgling democratic governments in places like the Palestinian Territories, Lebanon, Georgia, and Ukraine. We would encourage dissidents and democratic reformers suffering under repressive regimes in Iran, Syria, North Korea, and Venezuela. And we would advocate for freedom while maintaining strategic relationships with nations like Saudi Arabia, Egypt, Russia, and China.

Critics charged that the freedom agenda was a way for America to impose our values on others. But freedom is not an American value; it is a universal value. Freedom cannot be imposed; it must be chosen. And when people are given the choice, they choose freedom. At the end of World War II, there were about two dozen democracies in the world. When I took office in January 2001, there were 120.

Shortly after the 2004 election, I read *The Case for Democracy* by Natan Sharansky, a dissident who spent nine years in the Soviet gulags. In the book Sharansky describes how he and his fellow prisoners were inspired by hearing leaders like Ronald Reagan speak with moral clarity and call for their freedom.

In one memorable passage, Sharansky describes a fellow Soviet dissident who likened a tyrannical state to a soldier who constantly points a gun at a prisoner. Eventually, his arms tire and the prisoner escapes. I considered it America's responsibility to put pressure on the arms of the world's tyrants. Making that goal a central part of our foreign policy was one of my most consequential decisions as president.

———

The great tide of freedom that swept much of the world during the second half of the twentieth century had largely bypassed one region: the Middle East.

The UN's Arab Human Development Report, released in 2002, revealed the bleak state of the region: One in three people was illiterate. Unemployment averaged 15 percent. Less than 1 percent of the population had access to the Internet. Maternal mortality rates rivaled those of the least developed countries in the world. Economic output per capita was minuscule.

The authors of the UN report, a group of respected Arab scholars, attributed the depressing results to three deficits: a deficit in knowledge, a deficit in women's empowerment, and, most important, a deficit in freedom.

For most of the Cold War, America's priority in the Middle East was stability. Our alliances were based on anticommunism, a strategy that made sense at the time. But under the surface, resentment and anger built. Many people turned to radical clerics and mosques as a release. Amid these conditions, terrorists found fertile recruiting ground. Then nineteen terrorists born in the Middle East turned up on planes in the United States. After 9/11, I decided that the stability we had been promoting was a mirage. The focus of the freedom agenda would be the Middle East.

———

Six months before I took office, the Camp David peace talks between the Israelis and Palestinians fell apart. President Clinton had worked tirelessly to bring together Israeli Prime Minister Ehud Barak and Palestinian leader Yasser Arafat. Barak made a generous offer to turn over most of the West Bank and Gaza, two territories with majority Palestinian populations that were occupied by Israeli forces and dotted with Israeli settlements. Arafat turned him down.

Two months later, in September 2000, frustration over the failed peace accord—along with prominent Israeli leader Ariel Sharon's provocative visit to Jerusalem's Temple Mount—led to the Second Intifada. Palestinian extremists, many affiliated with the terrorist group Hamas, launched a wave of terrorist attacks against innocent civilians in Israel.

I didn't blame President Clinton for the failure at Camp David or the violence that followed. I blamed Arafat. America, Europe, and the United Nations had flooded the Palestinian Territories with development aid. A good portion of it was diverted to Arafat's bank account. He made the *Forbes* list of the world's wealthiest "kings, queens, and despots." Yet his people remained trapped in poverty, hopelessness, and extremism. For a Nobel Peace Prize recipient, he sure didn't seem very interested in peace.

The Israeli people responded to the violent onslaught the way any democracy would: They elected a leader who promised to protect them, Ariel Sharon. I first met Sharon in 1998, when Laura and I went to Israel with three fellow governors* on a trip sponsored by the Republican Jewish Coalition.

The visit was my first to the Holy Land. The most striking memory of the trip came when Ariel Sharon, then a minister in the cabinet of Prime Minister Benjamin Netanyahu, gave us a helicopter tour of the country. Sharon was a bull of a man, a seventy-year-old former tank commander who had served in all of Israel's wars. Shortly after the chopper lifted off, he pointed to a patch of ground below. "I fought there," he said with pride in his gruff voice. When the helicopter turned toward the West Bank, he gestured at an isolated cluster of homes. "I built that settlement," he said.

---

*Governor Mike Leavitt of Utah, who became my Environmental Protection Agency director and Health and Human Services secretary; Governor Paul Cellucci of Massachusetts, who served as my ambassador to Canada; and Governor Marc Racicot of Montana, who led the Republican National Committee from 2002 to 2003.

Sharon subscribed to the Greater Israel policy, which rejected territorial concessions. He knew every inch of the land, and it didn't sound like he intended to give any of it back.

"Here our country was only nine miles wide," Sharon said at another point, referring to the distance between the 1967 borders and the sea. "We have driveways longer than that in Texas," I later joked. I was struck by Israel's vulnerability in a hostile neighborhood. Ever since President Harry Truman defied his secretary of state by recognizing Israel in 1948, America had been the Jewish state's best friend. I came away convinced that we had a responsibility to keep the relationship strong.

A little over two years later, I called Ariel Sharon from the Oval Office to congratulate him on his election as prime minister. "Maybe, after so many years and wars in which I have participated," he said, "we will have peace in the region."

On June 1, 2001, a suicide bomber killed twenty-one Israelis at the Dolphinarium nightclub in Tel Aviv. Other attacks struck Israeli buses, train stations, and shopping malls. Israeli Defense Forces targeted operations at Hamas strongholds, but innocent Palestinians—including five boys walking to school one day—were killed during the operations.

I was appalled by the violence and loss of life on both sides. But I refused to accept the moral equivalence between Palestinian suicide attacks on innocent civilians and Israeli military actions intended to protect their people. My views came into sharper focus after 9/11. If the United States had the right to defend itself and prevent future attacks, other democracies had those rights, too.

I spoke to Yasser Arafat three times in my first year as president. He was courteous, and I was polite in return. But I made clear we expected him to crack down on extremism. "I know these are difficult issues for you and your people," I told him in February 2001, "but the best way to settle this and start resolving the situation is to stop the violence in the region."

In January 2002, the Israeli navy intercepted a ship called the *Karine A* in the Red Sea. Aboard was an arsenal of deadly weapons. The Israelis believed the ship was headed from Iran to the Palestinian city of Gaza. Arafat sent a letter pleading his innocence. "The smuggling of arms is in total contradiction of the Palestinian Authority's commitment to the peace process," he wrote. But we and the Israelis had evidence that disproved the Palestinian leader's claim. Arafat had lied to me. I never trusted him again. In fact, I never spoke to him again. By the spring of 2002, I had concluded that peace would not be possible with Arafat in power.

———

"When will the pig leave Ramallah?" Crown Prince Abdullah* asked me. It was April 25, 2002. Clearly the Saudi ruler was not happy with Ariel Sharon.

Ever since President Franklin Roosevelt met with Saudi Arabia's founder, King Abdul Aziz, aboard the USS *Quincy* in 1945, America's relationship with the kingdom had been one of our most critical. The Sunni Arab nation sits on a fifth of the world's oil and has tremendous influence among Muslims as the guardian of the holy mosques at Mecca and Medina.

I had invited Crown Prince Abdullah—one of Abdul Aziz's thirty-six sons—to our ranch in Crawford as a way to strengthen our personal relationship. In anticipation of the March 2002 Arab League summit in Beirut, the crown prince showed strong leadership by announcing a new peace plan. Under his vision, Israel would return territory to the Palestinians, who would create an independent state that rejected terror and recognized Israel's right to exist. There were many details to negotiate, but the concept was one I could support.

The evening of the Arab League summit, a Hamas suicide bomber walked into a hotel dining room filled with people celebrating Passover in the Israeli city of Netanya. "Suddenly it was hell," one guest said. "There was the smell of smoke and dust in my mouth and a ringing in my ears." One of the bloodiest attacks of the Second Intifada, the bombing killed 30 Israelis and wounded 140.

In response, Prime Minister Sharon ordered a sweeping Israeli offensive into the West Bank. Israeli forces quickly picked up hundreds of suspected militants and surrounded Yasser Arafat in his Ramallah

---

*Abdullah had ruled Saudi Arabia as regent since his half-brother, King Fahd, suffered an incapacitating stroke in 1995.

office. Sharon announced he would build a security barrier separating Israeli communities from the Palestinians in the West Bank. The fence was widely condemned. I hoped it would provide the security Israelis needed to make hard choices for peace.

I urged Sharon privately to end the offensive, which had become counterproductive. Arafat held a TV interview by candlelight and was looking like a martyr. Sharon forged ahead. I gave a Rose Garden speech publicly calling on him to begin a withdrawal. "Enough is enough," I said. Still, Sharon wouldn't budge.

By the time Crown Prince Abdullah arrived at our ranch, his peace plan had been shelved. He was angered by the violence, furious with Sharon, and—I soon learned—frustrated with me.

The crown prince is a gentle, modest, almost shy man. He speaks softly, doesn't drink alcohol, and prays five times a day. In eight years, I never saw him without his traditional robes.

After a brief discussion, Abdullah asked for time alone with his foreign minister and ambassador. A few minutes later, State Department interpreter Gamal Helal came to me with a stricken look on his face. "Mr. President," he said, "I think the Saudis are getting ready to leave."

I was surprised. I thought the meeting had been going fine. But Gamal explained that the Saudis had expected me to persuade Sharon to withdraw from Ramallah before the crown prince arrived. Now they were insisting that I call the Israeli prime minister on the spot. I wasn't going to conduct diplomacy that way. I sent Colin into the living room to see what was going on. He confirmed that our guests were headed for the door. America's pivotal relationship with Saudi Arabia was about to be seriously ruptured.

I walked into the living room with Gamal and asked for a moment alone with the crown prince. I had read two interesting things about him in a background briefing. One was that he was a devout religious believer. The other was that he loved his farm.

"Your Royal Highness," I said. "I would like to discuss religion with you." I talked about my belief in Christianity and the role religion played in my life. I hoped he would reciprocate by talking about his faith. He wasn't in a sharing mood.

In a last-gasp effort, I said, "Before you leave, may I show you my ranch?" He nodded. A few minutes later, the crown prince, flowing robes and all, was climbing into a Ford F-250 pickup. Then he, Gamal, and I took off for a tour of the property. I pointed out the different kinds of hardwood trees, the native prairie grasses that Laura had planted, and the grazing cattle. The crown prince sat silently. I wasn't making much headway.

Then we reached a remote part of the property. A lone hen turkey was standing in the road. I stopped the truck. The bird stayed put.

"What is that?" the crown prince asked.

I told him it was a turkey. "Benjamin Franklin loved the turkey so much he wanted it to be America's national bird," I said.

Suddenly I felt the crown prince's hand grab my arm. "My brother," he said, "it is a sign from Allah. This is a good omen."

I've never fully understood the significance of the bird, but I felt the tension begin to melt. When we got back to the house, our aides were surprised to hear us say we were ready for lunch. The next day, I got a call from Mother and Dad. The crown prince had stopped in Houston to visit them. Mother said he had tears in his eyes as he recounted his time in Crawford and talked about what we could achieve together. For the rest of my presidency, my relationship with the crown prince—soon to be king—was extremely close. I had never seen a hen turkey on that part of the property before, and I haven't seen one since.

———

As I thought more about the turmoil in the Middle East, I concluded that the fundamental problem was the lack of freedom in the Palestinian Territories. With no state, Palestinians lacked their rightful place in the world. With no voice in their future, Palestinians were ripe for recruiting by extremists. And with no legitimately elected Palestinian leader committed to fighting terror, the Israelis had no reliable partner for peace. I believed the solution was a democratic Palestinian state, led by elected officials who would answer to their people, reject terror, and pursue peace with Israel.

As violence in the Holy Land escalated in the spring of 2002, I decided we needed a game-changer. I planned to outline my commitment to a Palestinian democracy with a major speech in the Rose Garden. I would be the first president to publicly call for a Palestinian state as a matter of policy. I hoped setting forward a bold vision would help both sides make the hard choices necessary for peace.

The idea sparked controversy, starting in my administration. While Condi and Steve Hadley supported it, Dick Cheney, Don Rumsfeld, and Colin Powell all told me I shouldn't give the speech. Dick and Don were concerned that supporting a Palestinian state in the midst of an intifada would look like rewarding terrorism. Colin worried that calling for new Palestinian leadership would embarrass Arafat and reduce the chance for a negotiated settlement.

I understood the risks, but I was convinced that a democratic Palestinian state and a new Palestinian leadership were the only way to forge a lasting peace. "My vision is two states, living side by side in peace and security," I said in the Rose Garden on June 24, 2002. "There is simply no way to achieve that peace until all parties fight terror. I call on the Palestinian people to elect new leaders, leaders not compromised by terror. I call upon them to build a practicing democracy, based on tolerance and liberty. If the Palestinian people actively pursue these goals, America and the world will actively support their efforts."

My support for a Palestinian state was overwhelmed by my call for new leadership. "Bush Demands Arafat's Ouster," one headline read. Shortly after the speech, Mother called. "How's the first Jewish president doing?" she asked. I had a funny feeling she disagreed with my policy. That meant Dad probably did as well. I wasn't surprised. While I considered Arafat a failed leader, many in the foreign policy world accepted the view that Arafat represented the best hope for peace. I laughed off Mother's wisecrack, but I took her message to heart: I was in for some serious opposition.

The day after the speech, I flew to Kananaskis, Canada, for the annual G-8 meeting. The summit was supposed to focus on foreign aid, but my speech on the Middle East was on everyone's mind. I ran into Tony Blair in the gym the morning before the first meeting. "You've really kicked up quite a storm, George," he said with a smile.

Others were less accepting. Jacques Chirac, European Commission President Romano Prodi, and Canadian Prime Minister Jean Chrétien clearly disapproved. By rejecting Arafat, the heralded Nobel Peace Prize winner, I had upended their worldview. I told them I was convinced Arafat would never prove a reliable partner for peace.

Colin took the lead in hammering out a detailed plan to move from my speech to a Palestinian state. Called the Roadmap, it included three phases: First, Palestinians would stop terrorist attacks, fight corruption, reform their political system, and hold democratic elections. In return, Israel would withdraw from unauthorized settlements. In the second phase, the two sides would begin direct negotiations, leading to the creation of a provisional Palestinian state. In the third phase, the Palestinians and Israelis would resolve the most complicated issues, including the status of Jerusalem, the rights of Palestinian refugees, and permanent borders. Arab nations would support the negotiations and establish normal relations with Israel.

With Tony Blair's encouragement, I decided to announce the Roadmap in the spring of 2003, shortly after we removed Saddam Hussein from Iraq. Both the Israelis and Palestinians supported the plan. In early June, I met with Arab leaders in Sharm el Sheikh, Egypt, to stress my commitment to peace and urge them to stay engaged in the process. Then I traveled to Aqaba, Jordan, for a session with Palestinian and Israeli representatives.

Given all the recent bloodshed, I expected a tense session. To my surprise, the mood was friendly and relaxed. It was clear many leaders knew one another from previous peace efforts. But I knew there was a lot of history to overcome. Mohammad Dahlan, the Palestinian security chief, liked to remind people where he had learned to speak fluent Hebrew: in the Israeli jails.

The Palestinians had taken an important step by naming a prime minister to represent them at the summit, Mahmoud Abbas. Abbas was a friendly man who seemed to genuinely want peace. He was a little unsure of himself, partly because he hadn't been elected and partly because he was trying to emerge from Arafat's shadow. He said he was willing to confront the terrorists. But before he could turn his words into action, he needed money and reliable security forces.

After the formal meetings, I invited Sharon and Abbas to take a walk

on the lawn. Under the palm trees, I told them we had a historic opportunity for peace. Ariel Sharon made clear—at Aqaba and later in his
landmark Herzliya speech—that he had abandoned the Greater Israel
policy, an enormous breakthrough. "It is in Israel's interest not to govern
the Palestinians, but for the Palestinians to govern themselves in their
own state," he said at Aqaba. Abbas declared, "The armed intifada must
end and we must use and resort to peaceful means in our quest to end the
occupation and the suffering of Palestinians and Israelis." We had a long
way to go, but it was a hopeful moment in the Middle East.

In April 2004, Ariel Sharon came to Washington to brief me on a historic
decision: He planned to withdraw from Israel's settlements in Gaza and
parts of the northern West Bank. As a father of the settlement movement,
it would be agonizing for him to tell Israeli families they had to leave their
homes. But his bold move achieved two important goals: It extricated Israel from the costly occupation of Gaza. And by returning territory to
Palestinian control, it served as a down payment on a future state.

I was hopeful that Abbas would match Sharon's tough decision with
a positive step. But in September 2003, Prime Minister Abbas resigned
after Arafat undermined him at every turn. Just over a year later, Arafat
died. In January 2005, Palestinian voters went to the polls for the first
time in a decade. Abbas campaigned on a platform to halt violence and
resume progress toward a Palestinian state. He was elected in a landslide. He set to work developing the institutions of a democratic state and
called for legislative elections.

Abbas's party, Fatah, was still tainted with the corruption of the Arafat era. The main alternative was Hamas, a terrorist organization that
also had a well-organized political apparatus. The prospect of a Hamas
victory understandably unnerved the Israelis.

I supported the elections. America could not be in the position of endorsing elections only when we liked the projected outcome. I knew the
election would be just one step on the journey to democracy. Whoever
won would inherit the responsibilities of governing—building roads and
schools, enforcing the rule of law, and developing the institutions of a

civil society. If they performed well, they would be reelected. If not, the people would have a chance to change their minds. Whatever the outcome, free and fair elections reveal the truth.

On January 25, 2006, the truth was that Palestinians were tired of Fatah's corruption. Hamas won 74 of 132 seats. Some interpreted the results as a setback for peace. I wasn't so sure. Hamas had run on a platform of clean government and efficient public services, not war with Israel.

Hamas also benefited from Fatah's poorly run campaign. Fatah often ran multiple candidates for the same seat, which split the party vote. The election made clear that Fatah had to modernize its party. It also forced a decision within Hamas: Would it fulfill its promise to govern as a legitimate party, or would it revert to violence?

In March 2006, voters went to the polls for another election. This one was in Israel. Two months earlier, Ariel Sharon had suffered a debilitating stroke. I've always wondered what might have been possible if Ariel had continued to serve. He had established his credibility on security, he had the trust of the Israeli people, and I believe he could have been part of a historic peace.

The vote for a new prime minister would be a test of Israeli commitment to the two-state solution. Deputy Prime Minister Ehud Olmert campaigned hard in support of it. I had met Ehud on my 1998 trip to Israel, when he was mayor of Jerusalem. He was easygoing and confident, with a gregarious manner and a ready laugh. "The only solution now is two states—one Jewish, one Palestinian," he said during the campaign. At one point, he suggested he would create a Palestinian state unilaterally if necessary. Israeli voters rewarded him at the polls.

Olmert and Abbas, who retained the presidency despite Hamas's victory in the legislative elections, quickly developed a working relationship. They found agreement on issues such as security checkpoints and the release of some prisoners. Then, in June 2007, the militant wing of Hamas intervened. In a familiar pattern in the ideological struggle, the extremists responded to the advance of freedom with violence. Hamas terrorists backed by Iran and Syria mounted a coup and seized control of Gaza. Fighters in black masks ransacked Fatah headquarters, threw party leaders off rooftops, and targeted moderate members of Hamas's political wing.

President Abbas responded by expelling Hamas from his cabinet and consolidating his authority on the West Bank. "It's basically a coup d'etat against democracy itself," Abbas told me on the phone. "Syria and Iran are trying to set the Middle East ablaze." We redirected our economic and security assistance to Abbas's government in the West Bank and supported an Israeli naval blockade of Gaza. While we sent humanitarian aid to prevent starvation, the people of Gaza would see a vivid contrast between their living conditions under Hamas and those under the democratic leader, Abbas. Over time, I was confident they would demand change.

Condi and I talked about a way to restart momentum for a democratic Palestinian state. She suggested an international conference to lay the groundwork for negotiations between Abbas's government and the Israelis. At first I was skeptical. The aftermath of a terrorist coup didn't seem the most opportune time for a peace summit. But I came to like the idea. If wavering Palestinians could see that a state was a realistic possibility, they would have an incentive to reject violence and support reform.

We scheduled the conference for November 2007 at the U.S. Naval Academy in Annapolis, Maryland. Condi and I persuaded fifteen Arab nations to send delegations, including Saudi Arabia. Investing Arab partners in the process early would boost Palestinians' confidence and make it harder for them to later reject a peace deal, as Arafat had at Camp David.

The key test of the conference was whether Abbas and Olmert could agree on a joint statement pledging to open negotiations. When we boarded the helicopter for the flight to Annapolis, I asked Condi for the statement. She said they had made a lot of progress but hadn't finished. "You're going to have to deliver this one yourself," she said.

I pulled Abbas and Olmert aside individually. I told them the summit would be viewed as a failure and embolden the extremists if we couldn't agree on a statement. They instructed their negotiators to work with Condi. A few minutes before we were due in front of the cameras, she brought me the document. There was no time to enlarge the font, so I pulled out my reading glasses and read from the page: "We agree to immediately launch good-faith bilateral negotiations in order to conclude a peace treaty . . . and shall make every effort to conclude an agreement before the end of 2008."

The room broke into applause. Abbas and Olmert delivered speeches of their own. "Freedom is the single word that stands for the future of the Palestinians," President Abbas said. "I believe that there is no path other than peace. . . . I believe it is time. We are ready," Prime Minister Olmert said.

It was a historic moment to see the foreign minister of Saudi Arabia listen respectfully to the prime minister of Israel and applaud his words. The Annapolis conference was hailed as a surprise success. "The cynicism about the Annapolis talks shouldn't overshadow the hope that came out of the effort," the *Los Angeles Times* wrote.

Shortly after Annapolis, the two sides opened negotiations on a peace agreement, with Ahmed Qurei representing the Palestinians and Foreign Minister Tzipi Livni representing the Israelis. Palestinian Prime Minister Salam Fayyad, an economist with a Ph.D. from the University of Texas, began carrying out long-needed reforms in the Palestinian economy and security forces. We sent financial assistance and deployed a high-ranking general to help train the Palestinian security forces. The day he left Downing Street, Tony Blair accepted a post as special envoy to help the Palestinians build the institutions of a democratic state. It wasn't glamorous work, but it was necessary. "If I win the Nobel Peace Prize," Tony joked, "you will know I have failed."

The negotiations resolved some important issues, but it was clear that striking an agreement would require more involvement from the leaders. With my approval, Condi quietly oversaw a separate channel of talks directly between Abbas and Olmert. The dialogue culminated in a secret proposal from Olmert to Abbas. His offer would have returned the vast majority of the territory in the West Bank and Gaza to the Palestinians, accepted the construction of a tunnel connecting the two Palestinian territories, allowed a limited number of Palestinian refugees to return to Israel, established Jerusalem as a joint capital of both Israel and Palestine, and entrusted control of the holy sites to a panel of nonpolitical elders.

We devised a process to turn the private offer into a public agreement. Olmert would travel to Washington and deposit his proposal with me.

Abbas would announce that the plan was in line with Palestinian interests. I would call the leaders together to finalize the deal.

The development represented a realistic hope for peace. But once again, an outside event intervened. Olmert had been under investigation for his financial dealings when he was mayor of Jerusalem. By late summer, his political opponents had enough ammunition to bring him down. He was forced to announce his resignation in September.

Abbas didn't want to make an agreement with a prime minister on his way out of office. The talks broke off in the final weeks of my administration, after Israeli forces launched an offensive in Gaza in response to Hamas rocket attacks.

While I was disappointed that the Israelis and Palestinians could not finalize an agreement, I was pleased with the progress we had made. Eight years earlier, I had taken office during a raging intifada, with Yasser Arafat running the Palestinian Authority, Israeli leaders committed to a Greater Israel policy, and Arab nations complaining from the sidelines. By the time I left, the Palestinians had a president and prime minister who rejected terrorism. The Israelis had withdrawn from some settlements and supported a two-state solution. And Arab nations were playing an active role in the peace process.

The struggle in the Holy Land is no longer Palestinian versus Israeli, or Muslim versus Jew. It is between those who seek peace and extremists who promote terror. And there is consensus that democracy is the foundation on which to build a just and lasting peace. Realizing that vision will require courageous leadership from both sides and from the United States.

---

Jacques Chirac and I didn't agree on much. The French president opposed removing Saddam Hussein. He called Yasser Arafat a "man of courage." At one meeting, he told me, "Ukraine is part of Russia."

So it came as quite a surprise when Jacques and I found an area of agreement at our meeting in Paris in early June 2004. Chirac brought up democracy in the Middle East, and I braced myself for another lecture. But he continued: "In this region, there are just two democracies. One is strong, Israel. The other is fragile, Lebanon." I didn't mention that he'd left out a new democracy, Iraq.

He described Lebanon's suffering under the occupation of Syria, which had tens of thousands of troops in the country, siphoned money from the economy, and strangled attempts to expand democracy. He suggested that we work together to stop Syria from dominating Lebanon. I immediately agreed. We decided to look for an opportunity to introduce a UN resolution.

In August 2004, Lebanese President Emile Lahoud, a Syrian puppet, gave us our opening. He announced he would extend his term in office, a violation of the Lebanese constitution. Chirac and I cosponsored UN Resolution 1559, which protested Lahoud's decision and demanded that Syria withdraw its forces. It passed on September 2, 2004.

For six months, Syria responded with defiance. Then, on February 14, 2005, a huge car bomb in Beirut destroyed the motorcade of Rafiq Hariri, Lebanon's pro-independence former prime minister. All the evidence pointed to a Syrian plot. We recalled our ambassador from Damascus and supported a UN investigation.

A week after Hariri's murder, Chirac and I had dinner in Brussels. We issued a joint statement calling the car bombing a "terrorist act" and reiterated our support for a "sovereign, independent, and democratic Lebanon." Chirac and I rallied Arab nations to pressure Syrian President Basher Assad to comply with the UN resolution. On the one-month anniversary of Hariri's murder, nearly a million Lebanese people—a quarter of the nation's population—turned out at Martyrs' Square in Beirut to protest Syria's occupation. People began to speak of a Cedar Revolution, named for the tree in the middle of Lebanon's flag.

The Syrians got the message. Under the combined pressure of the international community and the Lebanese people, Syrian occupation troops began to withdraw in late March. By the end of April, they were gone. "People used to be afraid to say anything here," one Lebanese citizen told a reporter. "People seemed to be opening up more today, and feeling more comfortable to speak their mind."

That spring, the anti-Syrian March 14 Movement won a majority of seats in the parliament. Fouad Siniora, a close adviser to the slain Hariri, was named prime minister.

The Cedar Revolution marked one of the most important successes of the freedom agenda. It took place in a multi-religious country with a Muslim majority. It happened with strong diplomatic pressure from the free world and with no American military involvement. The people of Lebanon achieved their independence for the simplest of reasons: They wanted to be free.

The triumph of democracy in Lebanon came two months after the free elections in Iraq and the election of President Abbas in the Palestinian Territories. Never before had three Arab societies made so much progress toward democracy. Lebanon, Iraq, and Palestine had the potential to serve as the foundation of a free and peaceful region.

"It's strange for me to say it, but this process of change has started because of the American invasion of Iraq," Lebanese political leader Walid Jumblatt said. "I was cynical about Iraq. But when I saw the Iraqi people voting three weeks ago, eight million of them, it was the start of a new Arab world. The Syrian people, the Egyptian people, all say that something is changing. The Berlin Wall has fallen. We can see it."

He wasn't the only one who observed the trend or recognized its consequences. The rising tide of democracy in the Middle East in 2005 jolted the extremists. In 2006, they fought back.

———

On July 12, 2006, Laura and I stopped in Germany on our way to the G-8 summit in St. Petersburg, Russia. German Chancellor Angela Merkel and her husband, Professor Joachim Sauer, had invited us to the town of Stralsund, which was in Angela's home district. Laura and I were fascinated by Angela's description of growing up in communist East Germany. She told us her childhood was happy, but her mother constantly warned her not to mention their family discussions in public. The secret police, the Stasi, were everywhere. Laura and I thought of Angela at Camp David when we watched *The Lives of Others*, a movie depicting life under the Stasi. It was hard to believe that less than twenty years had passed since tens of millions of Europeans lived like that. It was a reminder of how dramatically freedom could change a society.

In addition to serving as a staunch advocate for freedom, Angela was trustworthy, engaging, and warm. She quickly became one of my closest friends on the world stage.

While we were on our way to Germany, Hezbollah terrorists in southern Lebanon launched a raid across the Israeli border, kidnapped two Israeli soldiers, and touched off another foreign policy crisis. Israel responded by attacking Hezbollah targets in southern Lebanon and bombing the Beirut Airport, a transit point for weapons. Hezbollah retaliated by lobbing rockets at Israeli towns, killing or wounding hundreds of civilians.

Like Hamas, Hezbollah had a legitimate political party and a terrorist wing armed and funded by Iran and supported by Syria. Hezbollah was behind the bombing of the American Marine barracks in Lebanon in 1983, the murder of a U.S. Navy diver aboard a hijacked TWA flight in 1985, the attacks on the Israeli embassy and a Jewish community center in Argentina in 1992 and 1994, and the bombing of the Khobar Towers housing complex in Saudi Arabia in 1996.

Now Hezbollah was taking on Israel directly. All the G-8 leaders at the summit had the same initial reaction: Hezbollah had instigated the conflict, and Israel had a right to defend itself. We issued a joint statement that read, "These extremist elements and those that support them cannot be allowed to plunge the Middle East into chaos and provoke a wider conflict."

The Israelis had a chance to deliver a major blow against Hezbollah and their sponsors in Iran and Syria. Unfortunately, they mishandled their opportunity. The Israeli bombing campaign struck targets of questionable military value, including sites in northern Lebanon far from Hezbollah's base. The damage was broadcast on television for all to see. To compound matters, Prime Minister Olmert announced that Syria would not be a target. I thought it was a mistake. Removing the threat of retaliation let Syria off the hook and emboldened them to continue their support for Hezbollah.

As the violence continued into its second week, many of the G-8 leaders who started out supportive of Israel called for a ceasefire. I didn't join. A ceasefire might provide short-term relief, but it wouldn't resolve the root cause of the conflict. If a well-armed Hezbollah continued to threaten Israel from southern Lebanon, it would be only a matter of time before the fighting flared again. I wanted to buy time for Israel to weaken Hezbollah's forces. I also wanted to send a message to Iran and Syria: They would not be allowed to use terrorist organizations as proxy armies to attack democracies with impunity.

Unfortunately, Israel made matters worse. In the third week of the conflict, Israeli bombers destroyed an apartment complex in the Lebanese city of Qana. Twenty-eight civilians were killed, more than half of them children. Prime Minister Siniora was furious. Arab leaders viciously condemned the bombing, the carnage of which played around the clock on Middle Eastern TV. I started to worry that Israel's offensive might topple Prime Minister Siniora's democratic government.

I called a National Security Council meeting to discuss our strategy. The disagreement within the team was heated. "We need to let the Israelis finish off Hezbollah," Dick Cheney said. "If you do that," Condi replied, "America will be dead in the Middle East." She recommended we seek a UN resolution calling for a ceasefire and deploying a multinational peacekeeping force.

Neither choice was ideal. In the short run, I wanted to see Hezbollah and their backers badly damaged. In the long run, our strategy was to isolate Iran and Syria as a way to reduce their influence and encourage change from within. If America continued to back the Israeli offensive, we would have to veto one UN resolution after the next. Ultimately, instead of isolating Iran and Syria, we would isolate ourselves.

I decided that the long-run benefits of keeping the pressure on Syria and Iran outweighed the short-run gains of striking further blows against Hezbollah. I sent Condi to the UN, where she negotiated Resolution 1701, which called for an immediate end to the violence, the disarmament of Hezbollah and other militias in Lebanon, an embargo on weapons shipments, and the deployment of a robust international security force to southern Lebanon. The Lebanese government, Hezbollah, and Israel all accepted the resolution. The ceasefire took effect on the morning of August 14.

Israel's war against Hezbollah in Lebanon was another defining moment in the ideological struggle. While it remains fragile and still faces pressure from Syria, Lebanon's young democracy emerged stronger for having endured the test. The result for Israel was mixed. Its military campaign weakened Hezbollah and helped secure its border. At the same time, the Israelis' shaky military performance cost them international credibility.

As the instigators of the conflict, Hezbollah—along with Syria and Iran—bore responsibility for the bloodshed. The Lebanese people knew it. In the most telling analysis of the war, Hezbollah chief Hassan Nasrallah apologized to the Lebanese people two weeks after the ceasefire. "Had we known that the capture of the soldiers would have led to this," he said, "we would definitely not have done it."

———

When Condi took her first trip to Europe as secretary of state in early 2005, she told me she expected our disagreements over Iraq to be the main issue. A week later, she reported back with a surprising message from the allies she'd met. "They're not talking about Iraq," she said. "They're all worried about Iran."

By the time I took office, the theocratic regime in Iran had presented a challenge to American presidents for more than twenty years. Governed by radical clerics who seized power in the 1979 revolution, Iran was one of the world's leading state sponsors of terror. At the same time, Iran was a relatively modern society with a budding freedom movement.

In August 2002, an Iranian opposition group came forward with evidence that the regime was building a covert uranium-enrichment facility in Natanz, along with a secret heavy water production plant in Arak—two telltale signs of a nuclear weapons program. The Iranians acknowledged the enrichment but claimed it was for electricity production only. If that was true, why was the regime hiding it? And why did Iran need to enrich uranium when it didn't have an operable nuclear power plant? All of a sudden, there weren't so many complaints about including Iran in the axis of evil.

In October 2003, seven months after we removed Saddam Hussein from power, Iran pledged to suspend all uranium enrichment and reprocessing. In return, the United Kingdom, Germany, and France agreed to provide financial and diplomatic benefits, such as technology and trade cooperation. The Europeans had done their part, and we had done ours.

The agreement was a positive step toward our ultimate goal of stopping Iranian enrichment and preventing a nuclear arms race in the Middle East.

In June 2005, everything changed. Iran held a presidential election. The process was suspicious, to say the least. The Council of Guardians, a handful of senior Islamic clerics, decided who was on the ballot. The clerics used the Basij Corps, a militia-like unit of the Iranian Revolutionary Guard Corps, to manage turnout and influence the vote. Tehran Mayor Mahmoud Ahmadinejad was declared the winner. Not surprisingly, he had strong support from the Basij.

Ahmadinejad steered Iran in an aggressive new direction. The regime became more repressive at home, more belligerent in Iraq, and more proactive in destabilizing Lebanon, the Palestinian Territories, and Afghanistan. Ahmadinejad called Israel "a stinking corpse" that should be "wiped off the map." He dismissed the Holocaust as a "myth." He used a United Nations speech to predict that the hidden imam would reappear to save the world. I started to worry we were dealing with more than just a dangerous leader. This guy could be nuts.

As one of his first acts, Ahmadinejad announced that Iran would resume uranium conversion. He claimed it was part of Iran's civilian nuclear power program, but the world recognized the move as a step toward enrichment for a weapon. Vladimir Putin—with my support—offered to provide fuel enriched in Russia for Iran's civilian reactors, once it built some, so that Iran would not need its own enrichment facilities. Ahmadinejad rejected the proposal. The Europeans also offered to support an Iranian civilian nuclear program in exchange for halting its suspect nuclear activities. Ahmadinejad rejected that, too. There was only one logical explanation: Iran was enriching uranium to use in a bomb.

I faced a major decision point. America could not allow Iran to have a nuclear weapon. The theocratic regime would be able to dominate the Middle East, blackmail the world, pass nuclear weapons technology to its terrorist proxies, or use the bomb against Israel. I thought about the problem in terms of two ticking clocks. One measured Iran's progress toward the bomb; the other tracked the ability of the reformers to instigate change. My objective was to slow the first clock and speed the second.

I had three options to consider. Some in Washington suggested that America should negotiate directly with Iran. I believed talking to Ahmadinejad would legitimize him and his views and dispirit Iran's freedom movement, slowing the change clock. I also doubted that America could make much progress in one-on-one talks with the regime. Bilateral negotiations with a tyrant rarely turn out well for a democracy. Because they are subjected to little accountability, totalitarian regimes face no pressure to honor their word. They are free to break agreements and then make new demands. A democracy has a choice: give in or provoke a confrontation.

The second option was multilateral diplomacy conducted with both carrots and sticks. We could join the Europeans in offering Iran a package of incentives in return for abandoning its suspect nuclear activities. If the regime refused to cooperate, the coalition would then impose tough sanctions on Iran individually and through the UN. The sanctions would make it harder for Iran to obtain technology needed for a weapon, slowing the bomb clock. They would also make it harder for Ahmadinejad to fulfill his economic promises, which would strengthen the country's reform movement.

The final option was a military strike on Iran's nuclear facilities. This goal would be to stop the bomb clock, at least temporarily. It was uncertain what the impact on the reform clock would be. Some thought destroying the regime's prized project would embolden the opposition; others worried that a foreign military operation would stir up Iranian nationalism and unite the people against us. I directed the Pentagon to study what would be necessary for a strike. Military action would always be on the table, but it would be my last resort.

I discussed the options with the national security team extensively in the spring of 2006. I consulted closely with Vladimir Putin, Angela Merkel, and Tony Blair. They assured me they would support strong sanctions if Iran did not change its behavior. In May, Condi announced that we would join the Europeans in negotiating with Iran, but only if the regime verifiably suspended its enrichment. She then worked with the UN Security Council to set a deadline for Iran's response: August 31. The summer passed, and the answer never came.

The next challenge was to develop effective sanctions. There wasn't much America could do on our own. We had sanctioned Iran heavily for decades. I directed the Treasury Department to work with its European counterparts to make it harder for Iranian banks and businesses to move money. We also designated the Quds Force of Iran's Revolutionary Guard Corps as a terrorist organization, which allowed us to freeze their assets. Our partners in the diplomatic coalition imposed new sanctions of their own. And we worked with the UN Security Council to pass Resolutions 1737 and 1747, which banned Iranian arms exports, froze key Iranian assets, and prohibited any country from providing Iran with nuclear weapons–related equipment.

Persuading the Europeans, Russians, and Chinese to agree on the sanctions was a diplomatic achievement. But every member faced the temptation to split off and take commercial advantage. I frequently reminded our partners about the dangers of a nuclear-armed Iran. In October 2007, a reporter asked me about Iran at a press conference. "I've told people that if you're interested in avoiding World War Three," I said, "it seems like you ought to be interested in preventing them from having the knowledge necessary to make a nuclear weapon."

My reference to World War III produced near hysteria. Protestors showed up outside my speeches with signs that read, "Keep Us Out of Iran." Journalists authored breathless, gossip-laden stories portraying America on the brink of war. They all missed the point. I wasn't looking to start a war. I was trying to hold our coalition together to avoid one.

In November 2007, the intelligence community produced a National Intelligence Estimate on Iran's nuclear program. It confirmed that, as we suspected, Iran had operated a secret nuclear weapons program in defiance of its treaty obligations. It also reported that, in 2003, Iran had suspended its covert effort to design a warhead—considered by some to be the least challenging part of building a weapon. Despite the fact that Iran was testing missiles that could be used as a delivery system and had announced its resumption of uranium enrichment, the NIE opened with an eye-popping declaration: "We judge with high confidence that in fall 2003, Tehran halted its nuclear weapons program."

The NIE's conclusion was so stunning that I felt certain it would immediately leak to the press. As much as I disliked the idea, I decided to declassify the key findings so that we could shape the news stories with the facts. The backlash was immediate. Ahmadinejad hailed the NIE as "a great victory." Momentum for new sanctions faded among the Europeans, Russians, and Chinese. As *New York Times* journalist David Sanger rightly put it, "The new intelligence estimate relieved the international pressure on Iran—the same pressure that the document itself claimed had successfully forced the country to suspend its weapons ambitions."

In January 2008, I took a trip to the Middle East, where I tried to reassure leaders that we remained committed to dealing with Iran. Israel and our Arab allies found themselves in a rare moment of unity. Both were deeply concerned about Iran and furious with the United States over the NIE. In Saudi Arabia, I met with King Abdullah and members of the Sudairi Seven, the influential full brothers of the late King Fahd.

"Your Majesty, may I begin the meeting?" I asked. "I'm confident every one of you believes I wrote the NIE as a way to avoid taking action against Iran."

No one said a word. The Saudis were too polite to confirm their suspicion aloud.

"You have to understand our system," I said. "The NIE was produced independently by our intelligence community. I am as angry about it as you are."

The NIE didn't just undermine diplomacy. It also tied my hands on the military side. There were many reasons I was concerned about undertaking a military strike on Iran, including its uncertain effectiveness and the serious problems it would create for Iraq's fragile young democracy. But after the NIE, how could I possibly explain using the military to destroy the nuclear facilities of a country the intelligence community said had no active nuclear weapons program?

I don't know why the NIE was written the way it was. I wondered if the intelligence community was trying so hard to avoid repeating its mistake on Iraq that it had underestimated the threat from Iran. I certainly hoped intelligence analysts weren't trying to influence policy. Whatever the explanation, the NIE had a big impact—and not a good one.

I spent much of 2008 working to rebuild the diplomatic coalition against Iran. In March, we were able to get another round of UN sanctions, which banned countries from trading with Iran in dual-use technologies that could be employed in a nuclear weapons program. We also expanded our missile defense shield, including a new system based in Poland and the Czech Republic to protect Europe from an Iranian launch.

At the same time, I worked to speed the reform clock by meeting with Iranian dissidents, calling for the release of political prisoners, funding Iranian civil-society activists, and using radio and Internet technology to broadcast pro-freedom messages into Iran. We also explored a wide variety of intelligence programs and financial measures that could slow the pace or increase the cost of Iran's nuclear weapons program.

I regret that I ended my presidency with the Iranian issue unresolved. I did hand my successor an Iranian regime more isolated from the world and more heavily sanctioned than it had ever been. I was confident that the success of the surge and the emergence of a free Iraq on Iran's border would inspire Iranian dissidents and help catalyze change. I was pleased to see the Iranian freedom movement express itself in nationwide demonstrations after Ahmadinejad's fraudulent reelection in June 2009. In the faces of those brave protesters, I believe we saw the future of Iran. If America and the world stand with them while keeping the pressure on the Iranian regime, I am hopeful the government and its policies will change. But one thing is for certain: The United States should never allow Iran to threaten the world with a nuclear bomb.

———

Iran was not the only nation endangering the freedom agenda by seeking nuclear weapons. In the spring of 2007, I received a highly classified report from a foreign intelligence partner. We pored over photographs of a suspicious, well-hidden building in the eastern desert of Syria.

The structure bore a striking resemblance to the nuclear facility at Yongbyon, North Korea. We concluded that the structure contained a gas-cooled, graphite-moderated reactor capable of producing weapons-grade plutonium. Since North Korea was the only country that had built a reactor of that model in the past thirty-five years, our strong suspicion was that we had just caught Syria red-handed trying to develop a nuclear weapons capability with North Korean help.

That was certainly the conclusion of Prime Minister Olmert. "George, I'm asking you to bomb the compound," he said in a phone call shortly after I received the report.

"Thank you for raising this matter," I told the prime minister. "Give me some time to look at the intelligence and I'll give you an answer."

I convened the national security team for a series of intense discussions. As a military matter, the bombing mission would be straightforward. The Air Force could destroy the target, no sweat. But bombing a sovereign country with no warning or announced justification would create severe blowback.

A second option would be a covert raid. We studied the idea seriously, but the CIA and the military concluded that it would be too risky to slip a team into and out of Syria with enough explosives to blow up the facility.

The third option was to brief our allies on the intelligence, jointly expose the facility, and demand that Syria shutter and dismantle it under the supervision of the IAEA. With the regime's duplicity exposed, we could use our leverage to press Syria to end its support for terror and meddling in Lebanon and Iraq. If Syria refused to dismantle the facility, we would have a clear public rationale for military action.

Before I made a decision, I asked CIA Director Mike Hayden to conduct an intelligence assessment.

He explained that the analysts had high confidence that the plant housed a nuclear reactor. But because they could not confirm the location of the facilities necessary to turn the plutonium into a weapon, they had only low confidence of a Syrian nuclear weapons program.

Mike's report clarified my decision. "I cannot justify an attack on a sovereign nation unless my intelligence agencies stand up and say it's a weapons program," I said to Olmert. I told him I had decided on the diplomatic option backed by the threat of force. "I believe the strategy protects your interests and your state, and makes it more likely we can achieve our interests as well."

The prime minister was disappointed. "This is something that hits at the very serious nerves of this country," he said. He told me the threat of a nuclear weapons program in Syria was an "existential" issue for Israel, and he worried diplomacy would bog down and fail. "I must be honest and sincere with you. Your strategy is very disturbing to me." That was the end of the call.

On September 6, 2007, the facility was destroyed.

The experience was revealing on multiple fronts. It confirmed Syria's intention to develop nuclear weapons. It also provided another reminder that intelligence is not an exact science. While I was told that our analysts had only low confidence that the facility was part of a nuclear weapons program, surveillance after the bombing showed Syrian officials meticulously covering up the remains of the building. If the facility was really just an innocent research lab, Syrian President Assad would have been screaming at the Israelis on the floor of the United Nations. That was one judgment I could make with high confidence.

Prime Minister Olmert's execution of the strike made up for the confidence I had lost in the Israelis during the Lebanon war. I suggested to Ehud that we let some time go by and then reveal the operation as a way to isolate the Syrian regime. Olmert told me he wanted total secrecy. He wanted to avoid anything that might back Syria into a corner and force Assad to retaliate. This was his operation, and I felt an obligation to respect his wishes. I kept quiet, even though I thought we were missing an opportunity.

Finally, the bombing demonstrated Israel's willingness to act alone. Prime Minister Olmert hadn't asked for a green light, and I hadn't given one. He had done what he believed was necessary to protect Israel.

———

One of the most influential books I read during my presidency was *Aquariums of Pyongyang* by the North Korean dissident Kang Chol-hwan. The memoir, recommended by my friend Henry Kissinger, tells the story of Kang's ten-year detention and abuse in a North Korean gulag. I invited Kang to the Oval Office, where he recounted the wrenching suffering in his homeland, including terrible famines and persecution.

Kang's story stirred up my deep disgust for the tyrant who had destroyed so many lives, Kim Jong-il. Early in the administration, Don Rumsfeld showed me satellite photos of the Korean Peninsula at night.

The south was alive with lights, while the north was pure black. I read intelligence reports that malnutrition had left the average North Korean three inches shorter than the average South Korean. When I took office in 2001, an estimated one million North Koreans had died of starvation in the preceding six years.

Meanwhile, Kim Jong-il cultivated his appetite for fine cognac, luxury Mercedes, and foreign films. He built a cult of personality that required North Koreans to worship him as a godlike leader. His propaganda machine claimed that he could control the weather, had written six renowned operas, and had scored five holes in one during his first round of golf.

Kim also maintained a nuclear weapons program and a ballistic missile capability that threatened two U.S. allies—South Korea and Japan—and could potentially reach America's West Coast. Proliferation was a serious concern, as the Syrian reactor incident suggested. In a country desperate for hard currency, nuclear materials and weapons systems made for attractive exports.

Our approach to North Korea was the topic of one of my first National Security Council meetings, the day before a visit by President Kim Dae-jung of South Korea. The previous administration had negotiated the Agreed Framework, which gave Kim Jong-il economic benefits in exchange for freezing his nuclear weapons program. Evidently, he wasn't satisfied. In 1998, the regime fired a Taepodong missile over Japan. In 1999, its ships fired on South Korean vessels in the Yellow Sea. A month after I took office, the regime threatened to restart long-range missile tests if we did not continue negotiations on normalizing relations.

I told my national security team that dealing with Kim Jong-il reminded me of raising children. When Barbara and Jenna were little and wanted attention, they would throw their food on the floor. Laura and I would rush over and pick it up. The next time they wanted attention, they'd throw the food again. "The United States is through picking up his food," I said.

The next year, intelligence reports indicated that North Korea was likely operating a secret highly enriched uranium program—a second path to a nuclear bomb. It was a startling revelation. Kim had cheated on the Agreed Framework. I made a decision: The United States was done negotiating with North Korea on a bilateral basis. Instead, we would rally China, South Korea, Russia, and Japan to present a united front against the regime.

The key to multilateral diplomacy with North Korea was China, which had close ties to its fellow communist nation. The challenge was that China and the United States had different interests on the Korean Peninsula. The Chinese wanted stability; we wanted freedom. They were worried about refugees flowing across the border; we were worried about starvation and human rights. But there was one area where we agreed: It was not in either of our interests to let Kim Jong-il have a nuclear weapon.

In October 2002, I invited President Jiang Zemin of China to the ranch in Crawford. I brought up North Korea. "This is a threat not only to the United States, but also to China," I said. I urged him to join us in confronting Kim diplomatically. "The United States and China have different kinds of influence over North Korea. Ours is mostly negative, while yours is positive. If we combine together, we would make an impressive team."

President Jiang was respectful, but he told me North Korea was my problem, not his. "Exercising influence over North Korea is very complicated," he said.

After a few months with no progress, I tried a different argument. In January 2003, I told President Jiang that if North Korea's nuclear weapons program continued, I would not be able to stop Japan—China's historic rival in Asia—from developing its own nuclear weapons. "You and I are in a position to work together to make certain that a nuclear arms race does not begin," I said. In February, I went one step further. I told President Jiang that if we could not solve the problem diplomatically, I would have to consider a military strike against North Korea.

The first meeting of the Six-Party Talks took place six months later in Beijing. For the first time, North Korean officials sat down at the table and saw representatives of China, Japan, Russia, South Korea, and the United States looking back at them. Progress was gradual. I spent hours on the phone with our partners, reminding them of the stakes and the need to maintain a united front.

In September 2005, our patience was rewarded. The North Koreans agreed to abandon all nuclear weapons and return to their commitments under the Nuclear Nonproliferation Treaty. I was skeptical. Kim Jong-il had violated his commitments in the past. If he did so again, he would be breaking his word not just to the United States, but to all his neighbors, including China.

———

On the Fourth of July 2006, Kim Jong-il threw his food on the floor. He fired a barrage of missiles into the Sea of Japan. The test was a military failure, but the provocation was real. My theory was that Kim saw the world focused on Iran and was craving attention. He also wanted to test the coalition to see how much he could get away with.

I called President Hu Jintao of China, told him Kim Jong-il had insulted China, and urged him to condemn the launch publicly. He released a statement reiterating his commitment to "peace and stability" and opposing "any actions that might intensify the situation." His words were mild, but they were a step in the right direction.

Three months later, North Korea defied the world again by carrying out its first full-fledged nuclear test. President Hu's reaction was firmer this time. "The Chinese government strongly opposes this," he said. "We engaged in conversations to appeal to the North Koreans for restraint. However, our neighbor turned a deaf ear to our advice."

With support from all partners in the Six-Party Talks, the UN Security Council unanimously adopted Resolution 1718. The resolution imposed the toughest sanctions on North Korea since the end of the Korean War. The United States also tightened our sanctions on the North Korean banking system and sought to deny Kim Jong-il his precious luxury goods.

The pressure worked. In February 2007, North Korea agreed to shut down its main nuclear reactor and allow UN inspectors back into the country to verify its actions. In exchange, we and our Six-Party partners provided energy aid, and the United States agreed to remove North Korea from our list of state sponsors of terror. In June 2008, North Korea blew up the cooling tower at Yongbyon on international television. In this case, no further verification was necessary.

The problem was not solved, however. The people of North Korea were still starving and suffering. Intelligence reports provided increased evidence that North Korea was continuing its highly enriched uranium program, even as it claimed to be shutting down its plutonium reprocessing.

In the short run, I believe the Six-Party Talks represented the best chance to maintain leverage on Kim Jong-il and rid the Korean Peninsula of nuclear weapons. In the long run, I am convinced the only path to meaningful change is for the North Korean people to be free.

———

The freedom agenda was a sensitive subject with China. My policy was to engage the Chinese in areas where we agreed, and use this cooperation to build the trust and credibility we needed to speak plainly about our differences.

I worked to develop close relations with China's leaders, Jiang Zemin and Hu Jintao. President Jiang and I got off to a rough start. On April 1, 2001, an American surveillance plane known as an EP-3 collided with a Chinese aircraft and made an emergency landing on Hainan Island. The Chinese pilot ejected from the cockpit and died. Our twenty-four-person crew was held at a military barracks on the island and interrogated. The Iranian hostage crisis was at the forefront of my mind. This was not the way I wanted to start my relationship with China.

After several agonizing days of trying to reach the Chinese, I connected with President Jiang, who was in Chile. The Chinese soon agreed to release the EP-3 crew. In return, I wrote a letter expressing regret over the death of their pilot and our landing on Hainan without verbal clearance. I later learned that China's handling of the EP-3 crisis was based on the government's belief that the Chinese people had perceived weakness in the response to America's accidental bombing of the Chinese embassy in Belgrade in 1999. After the EP-3 incident, the Chinese sent us a $1 million bill for the American crew's food and lodging. We offered them $34,000.

In February 2002, Laura and I made our first trip to Beijing. President Jiang was a cordial and welcoming host. After a banquet in our honor at the Great Hall of the People, he entertained the crowd with a rendition of "O Sole Mio," accompanied by two beautiful Chinese women clad in military uniforms. His serenade was a big change from the previous year, when I couldn't get him on the phone. It was a sign we were developing trust.

That trust was strengthened by an understanding on Taiwan, the island democracy that had been governed separately from the mainland since Chiang Kai-shek clashed with Mao Zedong during the Chinese Civil War in 1949. Every time I met with Chinese leaders, I confirmed that America's longstanding "one China" policy would not change. I also made clear that I opposed any unilateral change to the status quo, including a declaration of independence by Taiwan or military action by China.

When Hu Jintao took office, I was determined to forge a close relationship with him as well. Sixteen years younger than his predecessor, President Hu had an unexcitable demeanor and a keen analytical mind. Like many in the new generation of Chinese leaders, he was trained as an engineer. During a lunch in the East Room, I turned to him with a question that I liked to ask fellow world leaders: "What keeps you up at night?"

I told him I stayed awake worrying about another terrorist attack on America. He quickly replied that his biggest concern was creating twenty-five million new jobs a year. I found his answer fascinating. It was honest. It showed he was worried about the impact of disaffected, unemployed masses. It explained his government's policies in resource-rich places like Iran and Africa. And it was a signal that he was a practical leader focused inward, not an ideologue likely to stir up trouble abroad.

I worked with President Hu to find common ground on issues from North Korea to climate change to trade. Expanding American access to China's one billion potential consumers was a high priority for me, just as access to the U.S. market was essential for the Chinese. I also saw trade as a tool to promote the freedom agenda. I believed that, over time, the freedom inherent in the market would lead people to demand liberty in the public square. One of my first decisions was to continue President Clinton's support for China's entry into the World Trade Organization. To solidify our economic relationship, I asked Treasury Secretary Hank Paulson and Condi to create the Strategic Economic Dialogue.

One area of disagreement with the Chinese leadership was human rights. My focus was on religious liberty, because I believe that allowing people to worship as they choose is a cornerstone of the freedom agenda. In one of our first meetings, I explained to President Jiang that faith was a vital part of my life and that I studied the Word every day. I told him I planned to raise freedom of worship in our conversations. "I read the Bible," he replied, "but I don't trust what it says."

I told both Jiang and Hu that religious believers would be peaceful and productive citizens, the kind of people who would make their country stronger. I told them that for China to reach its full potential, they needed to trust their people with greater freedom. I didn't hector or lecture them; I let my actions send the message. Laura and I attended church in Beijing, met with religious leaders like Cardinal Joseph Zen of Hong Kong, and spoke out for the rights of Chinese underground preachers and worshippers, bloggers, dissidents, and political prisoners.

At the 2007 APEC Summit in Sydney, I told President Hu I planned to attend a ceremony where the Dalai Lama would receive the Congressional Gold Medal. The Buddhist leader was a source of distress for the Chinese government, which accused him of stirring up separatists in Tibet. I met with the Dalai Lama five times during my presidency, and I found him to be a charming, peaceful man. I told China's leaders they should not fear him. "This is not meant as a slap at China," I said, "but as a measure of my respect for the Dalai Lama and for the U.S. Congress. You know my strong belief in religious freedom."

"This is a politically sensitive issue in China," President Hu replied. ". . . It will draw a very strong reaction from the Chinese people." What he meant was that it would draw a strong reaction from the government, which did not want me to be the first American president to appear with the Dalai Lama in public.

"I'm afraid that I have to go to that ceremony," I said.

I also had some good news to share. "How is your Olympic planning coming?" I asked, referring to the 2008 Summer Games, which China had been chosen to host.

He gave me an update on the construction process. I told him I was coming to the Games. I knew I would face pressure not to, and many would try to politicize the Olympics, but I promised he could count on me to attend. "I've got my hotel reservations already," I joked. He looked relieved.

The Beijing Olympics were one of the highlights of my final year in office. I flew over on Air Force One with Laura and Barbara, my brother Marvin, my sister-in-law Margaret, and our friends Roland and Lois Betts and Brad Freeman. Mother, Dad, and Doro met us in China. Dad and I joined Ambassador Sandy Randt, who served in Beijing all eight years, to open a huge new American embassy. It was quite a change from the small diplomatic post Dad led thirty-three years earlier. In an extraordinary gesture of generosity, President Hu hosted a lunch for us all at the government's Zhongnanhai Compound, a Bush family reunion like none before or since.

The Beijing Olympics turned out to be a phenomenal success—and a lot of fun. We were at the Water Cube when the men's swimming team staged a dramatic comeback to edge out France for the gold medal in the freestyle relay. I dropped by to watch the impressive team of Misty May-Treanor and Kerri Walsh practice for their beach volleyball match. I made international news by giving Misty a playful slap on the back—a little north of the traditional target. We visited the locker room before Team USA and China squared off in the most-watched basketball game in history. The players couldn't have been more gracious or impressive. "Hey, Pops!" LeBron James called out when Dad entered the room.

The Olympics gave the world a chance to see the beauty and creativity of China. My hope is that the Games also gave the Chinese people a glimpse of the wider world, including the possibility of an independent press, open Internet, and free speech. Time will tell what the long-term impact of the Beijing Olympics will be. But history shows that once people get a taste of freedom, they eventually want more.

———

November 23, 2002, was a rainy, gray day in Bucharest. Yet tens of thousands had turned out in Revolution Square to mark Romania's admission to NATO, a landmark development for a country that just fifteen years earlier was a Soviet satellite state and a member of the Warsaw Pact. As

I approached the stage, I noticed a brightly lit balcony. "What is that?" I asked the advance man. He told me it was where Nicolai Ceausescu, the communist dictator of Romania, had given his last speech before he was overthrown in 1989.

As President Ion Iliescu introduced me, the rain stopped and a full-spectrum rainbow appeared. It stretched across the sky and ended right behind the balcony that was lit as a memorial to freedom. It was a stunning moment. I ad-libbed: "God is smiling on us today."

Romania was not the only young democracy celebrating that day. I had also cast America's vote to admit Bulgaria, Estonia, Latvia, Lithuania, Slovakia, and Slovenia into NATO. I viewed NATO expansion as a powerful tool to advance the freedom agenda. Because NATO requires nations to meet high standards for economic and political openness, the possibility of membership acts as an incentive for reform.

A year after my speech in Bucharest, a charismatic young democrat named Mikheil Saakashvili burst into the opening session of parliament in the former Soviet republic of Georgia. Speaking for thousands of Georgian demonstrators, he denounced the assembly as the illegitimate result of a corrupt election. President Eduard Shevardnadze felt the groundswell and resigned. The bloodless coup became known as the Rose Revolution. Six weeks later, the Georgian people went to the polls and chose Saakashvili to be their president.

In November 2004, a similar wave of protests broke out after a fraudulent presidential election in Ukraine. Hundreds of thousands braved freezing temperatures to demonstrate for opposition candidate Viktor Yushchenko. At one point during the campaign, Yushchenko suffered a mysterious poisoning that disfigured his face. Yet he refused to drop out of the race. His supporters turned out every day clad in orange scarves and ribbons until the Ukrainian Supreme Court ordered a rerun of the tainted election. Yushchenko won and was sworn in on January 23, 2005, completing the Orange Revolution.

At the 2008 NATO summit in Bucharest, both Georgia and Ukraine applied for Membership Action Plans, MAPs, the final step before consideration for full membership. I was a strong supporter of their applications. But approval required unanimity, and both Angela Merkel and Nicolas Sarkozy, the new president of France, were skeptical. They knew

Georgia and Ukraine had tense relationships with Moscow, and they worried NATO could get drawn into a war with Russia. They were also concerned about corruption.

I thought the threat from Russia strengthened the case for extending MAPs to Georgia and Ukraine. Russia would be less likely to engage in aggression if these countries were on a path into NATO. As for the governance issues, a step toward membership would encourage them to clean up corruption. We agreed on a compromise: We would not grant Georgia and Ukraine MAPs in Bucharest, but we would issue a statement announcing that they were destined for future membership in NATO. At the end of the debate, Prime Minister Gordon Brown of Great Britain leaned over to me and said, "We didn't give them MAPs, but we may have just made them members!"

———

The NATO debate over Georgia and Ukraine highlighted the influence of Russia. In my first meeting with Vladimir Putin in the spring of 2001, he complained that Russia was burdened by Soviet-era debt. At that point, oil was selling for $26 per barrel. By the time I saw Putin at the APEC summit in Sydney in September 2007, oil had reached $71—on its way to $137 in the summer of 2008. He leaned back in his chair and asked how were Russia's mortgage-backed securities doing.

The comment was vintage Putin. He was sometimes cocky, sometimes charming, always tough. Over my eight years as president, I met face to face with Vladimir more than forty times. Laura and I had wonderful visits with him and his wife, Lyudmilla, at our home in Crawford and his dacha outside Moscow, where he showed me his private chapel and let me drive his classic 1956 Volga. He took us on a beautiful boat ride through St. Petersburg during the White Nights Festival. I invited him to Kennebunkport, where we went fishing with Dad. I'll never forget Putin's reaction the first time he came into the Oval Office. It was early in the morning, and the light was streaming through the south windows. As he stepped through the door, he blurted out, "My God . . . This is beautiful!" It was quite a response for a former KGB agent from the atheist Soviet Union.

Through all the ups and downs, Putin and I were candid with each other. We cooperated in some important areas, including fighting terrorism, removing the Taliban from Afghanistan, and securing nuclear materials.

One of the biggest achievements emerged from our first meeting, in Slovenia in 2001. I told Vladimir I planned to give him the required six months' notice that America would withdraw from the Anti-Ballistic Missile Treaty, so that we could both develop effective missile defense systems. He made clear that this wouldn't make me popular in Europe. I told him I had campaigned on the issue and the American people expected me to follow through. "The Cold War is over," I told Putin. "We are no longer enemies."

I also informed him that America would unilaterally cut our arsenal of strategic nuclear warheads by two thirds. Putin agreed to match our reductions. Less than a year later, we signed the Moscow Treaty, which pledged our nations to shrink our number of deployed warheads from 6,600 weapons to between 1,700 and 2,200 by 2012. The treaty amounted to one of the largest nuclear weapons cuts in history, and it happened without the endless negotiations that usually come with arms-control agreements.

Over the course of eight years, Russia's newfound wealth affected Putin. He became aggressive abroad and more defensive about his record at home. In our first one-on-one meeting of my second term, in Bratislava, I raised my concerns about Russia's lack of progress on democracy. I was especially worried about his arrests of Russian businessmen and his crackdown on the free press. "Don't lecture me about the free press," he said, "not after you fired that reporter."

It dawned on me what he was referring to. "Vladimir, are you talking about Dan Rather?" I asked. He said he was. I said, "I strongly suggest you not say that in public. The American people will think you don't understand our system."

At a joint press conference after the meeting, I called on two American reporters and Vladimir called on two Russian journalists. The last question came from Alexei Meshkov of the Interfax news agency. It was addressed to Putin. "President Bush recently stated that the press in Russia is not free," he said. "What is this lack of freedom all about? . . .

Why don't you talk a lot about violations of the rights of journalists in the United States, about the fact that some journalists have been fired?" What a coincidence. The so-called free press of Russia was parroting Vladimir's line.

Putin and I both loved physical fitness. Vladimir worked out hard, swam regularly, and practiced judo. We were both competitive people. On his visit to Camp David, I introduced Putin to our Scottish terrier, Barney. He wasn't very impressed. On my next trip to Russia, Vladimir asked if I wanted to meet his dog, Koni. Sure, I said. As we walked the birch-lined grounds of his dacha, a big black Labrador came charging across the lawn. With a twinkle in his eye, Vladimir said, "Bigger, stronger, and faster than Barney." I later told the story to my friend, Prime Minister Stephen Harper of Canada. "You're lucky he only showed you his dog," he replied.

The Barney story was instructive. Putin was a proud man who loved his country. He wanted Russia to have the stature of a great power again and was driven to expand Russia's spheres of influence. He intimidated democracies on his borders and used energy as an economic weapon by cutting off natural gas to parts of Eastern Europe.

Putin was wily. As a quid pro quo for supporting Jacques Chirac and Gerhard Schroeder in their efforts to counterbalance American influence, Putin convinced them to defend his consolidation of power in Russia. At a G-8 dinner in St. Petersburg, most of the leaders challenged Putin on his democratic record. Jacques Chirac did not. He announced that Putin was doing a fine job running Russia, and it was none of our business how he did it. That was nothing compared to what Gerhard Schroeder did. Shortly after the German chancellor stepped down from office, he became chairman of a company owned by Gazprom, Russia's state-owned energy giant.

Putin liked power, and the Russian people liked him. Huge oil-fed budget surpluses didn't hurt. He used his stature to handpick his successor, Dmitry Medvedev. Then he got himself appointed prime minister.

The low point in our relationship came in August 2008, when Russia sent tanks across the border into Georgia to occupy South Ossetia and Abkhazia, two provinces that were part of Georgia but had close ties to Russia. I was in Beijing for the Opening Ceremony of the Olympic Games.

Laura and I were standing in line to greet President Hu Jintao when Jim Jeffrey, my deputy national security adviser, whispered the news about Russia's offensive. I looked a few places ahead of me in line. There was Vladimir. I decided the receiving line was not the appropriate place for heated diplomacy.

I also thought it was important that I direct my concerns to President Medvedev. I didn't know Medvedev well. In April 2008, just before the change of power, Vladimir had invited Medvedev to visit with us in Sochi, Russia's equivalent of Camp David. The mood was festive. Putin hosted a nice dinner, followed by folk dancing. At one point, members of my delegation, including me, were plucked from our seats to take the stage. The dance felt like a combination of square dancing and the jitterbug. I'm sure I would have been more fluid if I'd had a little vodka in my system. Curiously enough, I rarely saw vodka on my trips to Russia, unlike in the old days of communism.

I appreciated the chance to spend time with Medvedev, Russia's first noncommunist leader since the Bolshevik Revolution in 1917. He had given an impressive speech outlining his commitment to the rule of law, liberalizing the Russian economy, and reducing corruption. I told him I was looking forward to dealing with him president to president. The big question, of course, was whether he would actually run the country. As a way of testing, I asked Vladimir if he would still use the Sochi compound after Medvedev assumed office. "No," he said without hesitation, "this is the summer palace of the president."

I called Medvedev when I got back to my hotel in Beijing. He was hot. So was I. "My strong advice is to start deescalating this thing now," I said. "The disproportionality of your actions is going to turn the world against you. We're going to be with them."

Medvedev told me Saakashvili was like Saddam Hussein. He claimed Saakashvili had launched an unprovoked "barbarian" attack that had killed more than fifteen hundred civilians.

"I hope you're not saying you're going to kill fifteen hundred people in response," I shot back. "You've made your point loud and clear," I said. "I hope you consider what I've asked very seriously."

My biggest concern was that the Russians would storm all the way to Tbilisi and overthrow the democratically elected Saakashvili. It was clear the Russians couldn't stand a democratic Georgia with a pro-Western president. I wondered if they would have been as aggressive if NATO had approved Georgia's MAP application.

I called Saakashvili next. He was understandably shaken. He described the Russian assault and urged me not to abandon Georgia. "I hear you," I said. "We do not want Georgia to collapse." In the coming days, I spoke out in defense of Georgia's territorial integrity, worked with President Sarkozy—who was serving as president of the European Union—to rally nations to call on Russia to withdraw, dispatched relief supplies to Georgia aboard U.S. military aircraft, and promised to help rebuild the Georgian military.

At the Opening Ceremony of the Olympics, Laura and I were seated in the same row as Vladimir and his interpreter. This was the chance to have the conversation I had put off in the Great Hall. Laura and the man next to her, the king of Cambodia, shifted down a few seats. Putin slid in next to me.

I knew the TV cameras would be on us, so I tried not to get overly animated. I told him he'd made a serious mistake and that Russia would isolate itself if it didn't get out of Georgia. He said Saakashvili was a war criminal—the same term Medvedev had used—who had provoked Russia.

"I've been warning you Saakashvili is hot-blooded," I told Putin.

"I'm hot-blooded, too," Putin retorted.

I stared back at him. "No, Vladimir," I said. "You're cold-blooded."

———

After a few weeks of intense diplomacy, Russia had withdrawn most of its invading troops, but they maintained an unlawful military presence in South Ossetia and Abkhazia. Vladimir Putin called me during my last week in office to wish me well, which was a thoughtful gesture. Still, given what I'd hoped Putin and I could accomplish in moving past the Cold War, Russia stands out as a disappointment in the freedom agenda.

Russia was not the only one. I was hopeful that Egypt would be a leader for freedom and reform in the Arab world, just as it had been a leader for peace under Anwar Sadat a generation before. Unfortunately, after a promising presidential election in 2005 that included opposition candidates, the government cracked down during the legislative elections later that year, jailing dissidents and bloggers who advocated a democratic alternative.

Venezuela also slid back from democracy. President Hugo Chavez polluted the airwaves with hard-core anti-American sermons while spreading a version of phony populism that he termed the Bolivarian Revolution. Sadly, he squandered the Venezuelan people's money and is ruining their country. He is becoming the Robert Mugabe of South America. Regrettably, the leaders of Nicaragua, Bolivia, and Ecuador have followed his example.

There are other isolated outposts of tyranny—places like Belarus, Burma, Cuba, and Sudan. My hope is that America will continue to stand with the dissidents and freedom advocates there. I met with more than a hundred dissidents over the course of my presidency. Their plight can look bleak, but it is not hopeless. As I said in my Second Inaugural Address, the freedom agenda demands "the concentrated work of generations." Once change arrives, it often moves quickly, as the world saw in the European revolutions of 1989 and the rapid transformation of East Asia after World War II. When the people are finally set free, it is often the dissidents and the prisoners—people like Václav Havel and Nelson Mandela—who emerge as the leaders of their free countries.

———

Despite the setbacks for the freedom agenda, there were many more examples of hope and progress. Georgians and Ukrainians joined the ranks of free peoples, Kosovo became an independent nation, and NATO expanded from nineteen members to twenty-six. Under the courageous leadership of President Alvaro Uribe, Colombia's democracy reclaimed its sovereign territory from narcoterrorists. With support from the United States, multiethnic democracies from India and Indonesia to Brazil and Chile became leaders in their regions and models for developing free societies around the world.

The most dramatic advances for freedom came in the Middle East. In 2001, the region saw terrorism on the rise, raging violence between

Palestinians and Israelis, the destabilizing influence of Saddam Hussein, Libya developing weapons of mass destruction, tens of thousands of Syrian troops occupying Lebanon, Iran pressing ahead unopposed with a nuclear weapons program, widespread economic stagnation, and little progress toward political reform.

By 2009, nations across the Middle East were actively fighting terrorism instead of looking the other way. Iraq was a multi-religious, multi-ethnic democracy and an ally of the United States. Libya had renounced its weapons of mass destruction and resumed normal relations with the world. The Lebanese people had kicked out Syrian troops and restored democracy. The Palestinian people had an increasingly peaceful government on the West Bank and momentum toward a democratic state that would live side by side with Israel in peace. And Iran's freedom movement was active after the summer 2009 presidential election.

Throughout the region, economic reform and political openness were beginning to advance. Kuwait held its first election in which women were allowed to vote and hold office. In 2009, women won several seats. Women also held government positions in Oman, Qatar, the United Arab Emirates, and Yemen. Bahrain named a Jewish female ambassador to the United States. Jordan, Morocco, and Bahrain held competitive parliamentary elections. While it remains a highly ordered monarchy, Saudi Arabia held its first municipal elections, and King Abdullah founded the kingdom's first university open to both Saudi women and men. Across the region, trade and investment expanded. Internet use rose sharply. And conversations about democracy and reform grew louder—especially among women, who I am confident will lead the freedom movement throughout the Middle East.

In January 2008, I traveled to Abu Dhabi and Dubai, two Arab emirates that had embraced free trade and open societies. Their downtown centers boasted glittering skyscrapers filled with entrepreneurs and business professionals, men and women alike. In Dubai, I visited with university students studying in fields as diverse as business, science, and history.

On the last night of my visit, the forward-looking crown prince of Abu Dhabi, my friend Sheikh Mohammed bin Zayed, invited me to his desert retreat for a traditional dinner. He told me a number of government officials would join us. I expected middle-aged men. But I was wrong. The crown prince's government included young, smart Muslim women. They spoke about their determination to continue reform and progress— and to deepen their friendship with the United States.

The sands of Abu Dhabi were a long way from the Inaugural platform that I stood atop in January 2005. But in the desert that night, I saw the future of the Middle East—a region that honors its ancient culture while embracing the modern world. It will take decades for the changes set in motion in recent years to be fully realized. There will be setbacks along the way. But I am confident in the destination: The people of the Middle East will be free, and America will be more secure as a result.

# 14

# FINANCIAL CRISIS

"**M**r. President, we are witnessing a financial panic."

Those were troubling words coming from Ben Bernanke, the mild-mannered chairman of the Federal Reserve, who was seated across from me in the Roosevelt Room. Over the previous two weeks, the government had seized Fannie Mae and Freddie Mac, two giant housing entities. Lehman Brothers had filed the largest bankruptcy in American history. Merrill Lynch had been sold under duress. The Fed had granted an $85 billion loan to save AIG. Now Wachovia and Washington Mutual were teetering on the brink of collapse.

With so much turbulence in financial institutions, credit markets had seized up. Consumers couldn't get loans for homes or cars. Small businesses couldn't borrow to finance their operations. The stock market had taken its steepest plunge since the first day of trading after 9/11.

As we sat beneath the oil painting of Teddy Roosevelt charging on horseback, we all knew America was facing its most dire economic challenge in decades.

I turned to the Rough Rider of my financial team, Secretary of the Treasury Hank Paulson, a natural leader with decades of experience in international finance.

"The situation is extraordinarily serious," Hank said. He and the team briefed me on three measures to stem the crisis. First, the Treasury would guarantee all $3.5 trillion in money market mutual funds, which were facing depositor runs. Second, the Fed would launch a program to unfreeze the market for commercial paper, a key source of financing for businesses across the country. Third, the Securities and Exchange Commission would issue a rule temporarily preventing the short-selling of financial stocks. "These are dramatic steps," Hank said, "but America's financial system is at stake."

He outlined an even bolder proposal. "We need broad authority to buy mortgage-backed securities," he said. Those complex financial assets had lost value when the housing bubble burst, imperiling the balance sheets of financial firms around the world. Hank recommended that we ask Congress for hundreds of billions to buy up these toxic assets and restore confidence in the banking system.

"Is this the worst crisis since the Great Depression?" I asked.

"Yes," Ben replied. "In terms of the financial system, we have not seen anything like this since the 1930s, and it could get worse."

His answer clarified the decision I faced: Did I want to be the president overseeing an economic calamity that could be worse than the Great Depression?

I was furious the situation had reached this point. A relatively small group of people—many on Wall Street, some not—had gambled that the housing market would keep booming forever. It didn't. In a normal environment, the free market would render its judgment and they could fail. I would have been happy to let them do so.

But this was not a normal environment. The market had ceased to function. And as Ben had explained, the consequences of inaction would be catastrophic. As unfair as it was to use the American people's money to prevent a collapse for which they weren't responsible, it would be even more unfair to do nothing and leave them to suffer the consequences.

"Get to work," I said, approving Hank's plan in full. "We are going to solve this."

I adjourned the meeting and walked across the hallway to the Oval Office. Josh Bolten, Counselor Ed Gillespie, and Dana Perino, my talented and effective press secretary, followed me in. Ben's historical comparison was still echoing in my mind.

"If we're really looking at another Great Depression," I said, "you can be damn sure I'm going to be Roosevelt, not Hoover."

Almost exactly twenty-five years earlier, in October 1983, I was drinking coffee in Midland with a Harvard Business School friend, Tom Kaneb. We heard someone mention that a line was forming outside the doors of Midland's First National Bank. First National was Texas's largest independent bank. It had been a fixture in Midland for ninety-three years.

Recently, rumors had been flying about the bank's precarious financial position. First National had issued many of its loans when oil prices were rising. Then in the early 1980s, the price of crude dropped from almost forty dollars per barrel to under thirty dollars. The pace of drilling slowed. Loans defaulted. Depositors withdrew their cash. I transferred our exploration company's account to a big New York bank. I was not going to gamble on First National's solvency.

Tom and I hustled over to the bank. From the second-floor balcony, we watched people line up in the lobby to approach the tellers' windows. Some carried paper sacks. Amid the crowd was a prominent old rancher, Frank Cowden. Like other West Texas ranchers, Mr. Cowden was fortunate that his land overlay a lot of oil. He was a large shareholder of First National. He was working the line, telling people that the federal government insured every deposit up to $100,000. The people just stared back at him. They wanted their money.

On October 14, 1983, the FDIC seized First National and sold it to First Republic in Dallas. The depositors were protected, but the shareholders were wiped out and a Midland institution was gone. Mayor Thane Atkins spoke for a lot of folks when he said, "I feel like hanging a black wreath on my door."

I had read about the financial panics of 1893 and 1929. Now I had witnessed firsthand the bursting of a speculative bubble. First National, like all financial institutions, depended on the confidence of its customers. Once that confidence was lost, the bank had no chance to survive.

———

Sixteen years later, I was running for president. By nearly all measures, the economy was booming. America's GDP had increased by more than $2.5 trillion since the recession that had cost Dad the election but ended before he left office. Fueled by new Internet stocks, the NASDAQ index had shot up from under 500 to over 4,000. Some economists argued that the Internet era had redefined the business cycle.

I wasn't so sure. "Sometimes economists are wrong," I said in a speech outlining my economic policy in December 1999. "I can remember recoveries that were supposed to end, but didn't, and recessions that weren't supposed to happen, but did. I hope for continued growth—but it is not guaranteed. A president must work for the best case, and prepare for the worst."

The centerpiece of my plan was an across-the-board tax cut. I believed government was taking too much of the people's money. By the end of 1999, taxes accounted for a higher percentage of GDP than they had at any point since World War II. The government was supposedly running a large surplus. I knew where that money would go: Government would find a way to spend it. After all, Congress and President Clinton had agreed to increase nonsecurity discretionary spending by more than 16 percent in fiscal year 2001.

I had another reason for supporting tax cuts. I worried that we could be witnessing another bubble, this one in the technology sector. Larry Lindsey, my top economic adviser, believed the country was headed for a recession. If he was right, the tax cuts would act as a vital stimulus.

Sure enough, a recession officially began in March 2001. The *New York Times* considered the downturn a positive development for me. One article ran under the headline "For the President, a Perfect Time for a Recession." It sure didn't feel that way to me. I couldn't help but note a strange irony of history. In 1993, Dad had left behind an economy much better than the public realized. Now I had inherited one much worse.

With the economy tanking, the tax cuts took on a new urgency. I pressed Congress to move quickly. In June 2001, I signed a $1.35 trillion tax cut, the largest since the one Ronald Reagan signed during his first term. The bill reduced marginal tax rates for every income taxpayer, including millions of small business owners;* doubled the child tax credit from $500 to $1,000; reduced the marriage penalty; and eliminated the

---

*Many small business owners are sole proprietorships, limited partnerships, or Subchapter-S Corporations, meaning they pay their business taxes at the individual income tax rates.

lowest tax bracket, which removed five million low-income families from the tax rolls. The bill also phased out the death tax, a burden that was unfair to small business owners, farmers, and ranchers. I figured Americans had paid enough taxes while they were living; they shouldn't be taxed again when they died.

I was optimistic that consumers and small businesses would spend their tax relief to help pull the economy out of the recession. But we were in for another massive economic hit that no one expected.

The toll of 9/11 will always be measured by the 2,973 lives stolen and many others devastated. But the economic cost was shattering as well. The New York Stock Exchange shut down for four days, the longest suspension of trading since the Great Depression. When the markets reopened, the Dow Jones plunged 684 points, the biggest single-day drop in history—to that point.

The impact of the attacks rippled throughout the economy. Tourism plummeted. Several airlines filed for bankruptcy. Many restaurants sat virtually empty. Some hotels reported business being down as much as 90 percent. Manufacturers and small businesses laid off workers as skittish buyers canceled their orders. By the end of the year, more than a million Americans had lost their jobs. "The United States and the rest of the world are likely to experience a full-blown recession now," one economist predicted.

That was what the terrorists intended. "Al Qaeda spent $500,000 on the event," Osama bin Laden later bragged, "while America . . . lost—according to the lowest estimate—$500 billion." He outlined what he called a "bleed-until-bankruptcy" strategy and said, "It is very important to concentrate on hitting the U.S. economy through all possible means."

I saw it as my responsibility to encourage Americans to defy al Qaeda by keeping the economy moving. In late September 2001, I flew to Chicago's O'Hare Airport to promote the recovery of the airline industry. I walked onto a riser in front of 737s from American and United Airlines. With six thousand airline workers in the audience, I said, "One of the great goals of this nation's war is to restore public confidence in the airline industry. It's to tell the traveling public: Get on board. Do your business around the country."

Later, I would be mocked and criticized for telling Americans to "go shopping" after 9/11. I never actually used that phrase, but that's beside the point. In the threat-filled months after 9/11, traveling on airplanes, visiting tourist destinations, and, yes, going shopping, were acts of defiance and patriotism. They helped businesses rebound and hardworking Americans keep their jobs.

I was surprised by critics who suggested I should have asked for more sacrifice after 9/11. I suppose it's easy for some to forget, but people were making sacrifices. Record numbers of volunteers had stepped forward to help their neighbors. Even our youngest citizens pitched in. Students across the country donated $10 million—often one dollar at a time—to a fund we created to benefit Afghan children. In my 2002 State of the Union address, I launched a new national service initiative, USA Freedom Corps, and called on all Americans to devote four thousand hours to serving others over the course of their lifetimes.

The bravest volunteers were those who risked their lives by joining or reenlisting in the military, FBI, or CIA. Hundreds of thousands made that noble choice in the years after 9/11. Many served multiple tours of duty away from their families. Thousands of our finest citizens gave their lives. To suggest that this country didn't sacrifice after 9/11 is offensive and wrong.

Short of a military draft—a step I strongly opposed—I'm not sure what more I could have done to encourage sacrifice. This was a different kind of war. We didn't need riveters or victory gardens like we had during World War II. We needed people to deny the enemy the panic they sought to create.

I've always believed that the critics who alleged I wasn't asking people to sacrifice were really complaining that I hadn't raised taxes. "Taxes are more than a device to raise revenue," one *Washington Post* columnist wrote. "They are a statement of consensus on national purpose." I reject the premise that higher taxes would have led to stronger national purpose. I am convinced raising taxes after the devastation of 9/11 would have hurt our economy and had the opposite effect.

September 11, 2001, changed American life; it also transformed the federal budget. The projected surplus of early 2001 had been based on bullish forecasts for strong economic growth. The bursting of the tech bubble and subsequent recession significantly lowered those projections. The economic damage caused by the terrorist attacks drove them down even more. Then we faced the essential cost of securing the country and fighting the war on terror. In November 2001, Mitch Daniels, a fiscal hawk from Indiana who ably led my Office of Management and Budget, delivered the official report: The so-called surplus had vanished in ten months.

For years, I listened to politicians from both sides of the aisle allege that I had squandered the massive surplus I inherited. That never made sense. Much of the surplus was an illusion, based on the mistaken assumption that the 1990s boom would continue. Once the recession and 9/11 hit, there was little surplus left.

By the end of 2002, the recession was technically over, but the economy remained sluggish. In early January 2003, I called on Congress to accelerate the tax cuts from 2001, which had not fully taken effect, and to pass further tax cuts that would encourage business investment and job creation.

While the 2001 tax cuts passed with bipartisan majorities—as did a modest tax cut in 2002 focused on small businesses—the 2003 version ran into serious opposition. The left denounced the plan as "tax cuts for the rich." That charge was false. The Bush tax cuts, when fully implemented, actually *increased* the portion of the income tax burden that fell on the wealthiest Americans.*

Other critics opposed the tax cuts because they would drive up the deficit. It was true that tax cuts increase the deficit in the short term. But I believed the tax cuts, especially those on capital gains and dividends, would stimulate economic growth. The tax revenues from that growth, combined with spending restraint, would help lower the deficit.

The tax relief bill made it through the House by a vote of 231 to 200. The tally in the Senate was deadlocked at 50. Dick Cheney went to Capitol

---

*The top 1 percent of taxpayers went from paying 38.4 percent of overall taxes to 39.1 percent, while the bottom 50 percent saw their share decrease from 3.4 percent to 3.1 percent.

Hill to break the tie in his constitutional role as president of the Senate. Fortunately, he voted yes. He joked that he didn't get to cast many votes as vice president, but when he did he was always on the winning side.

I signed the tax cuts into law in late May 2003. By September, the economy had started adding jobs again. It didn't stop for 46 consecutive months. After reaching a peak of 6.3 percent in June, the unemployment rate dropped for five of the next six months and averaged 5.3 percent during my presidency, lower than the averages of the 1970s, 1980s, and 1990s. Some argued that the timing of the recovery right after the tax cuts was a coincidence. I don't think so.

———

Amid the economic growth, I was mindful that the country was running deficits. I took my responsibility to be a good fiscal steward seriously. So did my four budget directors—Mitch Daniels, Josh Bolten, Rob Portman, and Jim Nussle. As a wartime president, I told them I had two priorities: protecting the homeland and supporting our troops, both in combat and as veterans. Beyond those areas, we submitted budgets that slowed the growth of discretionary spending every year of my presidency. For the last five years, my budgets held this spending growth below the rate of inflation—in real terms, a cut.

I worked closely with Congress to meet my spending targets—or, as I called it, the overall size of the pie. I didn't always agree with how Congress divvied up the pieces. I objected to wasteful earmarks inserted into spending bills. But I had no line-item veto to excise pork barrel spending projects. I had to either accept or reject the bills in full. So long as Congress met my bottom line, which it did year after year, I felt that I should hold up my end of the deal and sign the bills.

The results have been a subject of heated debate. Some on the left complain that tax cuts increased the deficits. Some on the right argue that I should not have signed the expensive Medicare prescription drug benefit. It is fair to debate those policy choices, but here are the facts: The combination of tight budgets and the rising tax revenues resulting from economic growth helped drive down the deficit from 3.5 percent of the

GDP in 2004, to 2.6 percent in 2005, to 1.9 percent in 2006, to 1.2 percent in 2007.

The average deficit-to-GDP ratio during my administration was 2.0 percent, below the fifty-year average of 3.0 percent. My administration's ratios of spending-to-GDP, taxes-to-GDP, deficit-to-GDP, and debt-to-GDP are all lower than the averages of the past three decades—and, in most cases, below the averages of my recent predecessors. Despite the costs of two recessions, the costliest natural disaster in history, and a two-front war, our fiscal record was strong.

BUDGET COMPARISON TABLE*

| | Spending-to-GDP | Taxes-to-GDP | Deficit-to-GDP | Debt-to-GDP |
|---|---|---|---|---|
| Reagan ('81–88) | 22.4% | 18.2% | 4.2% | 34.9% |
| Bush 41 ('89–92) | 21.9% | 17.9% | 4.0% | 44.0% |
| Clinton ('93–00) | 19.8% | 19.0% | 0.8% | 44.9% |
| Bush 43 ('01–08) | 19.6% | 17.6% | 2.0% | 36.0% |

At the same time, I knew I was leaving behind a serious long-term fiscal problem: the unsustainable growth in entitlement spending, which accounts for the vast majority of the future federal debt. I pushed hard to reform the funding formulas for Social Security and Medicare, but Democrats opposed my efforts and support in my own party was lukewarm.

Part of the problem was that the fiscal crisis seemed a long way off to the legislative branch while I was in office. In early 2008, the Congressional Budget Office estimated that the debt would not exceed 60 percent of GDP until 2023. But because of the financial crisis—and spending

* Debt-to-GDP is the average measured at the end of each calendar year. Average spending, taxes, and deficits are calculated for fiscal years, which end September 30. Thus, the average of four or eight fiscal years excludes the effects of any policies implemented in the last three months and twenty days of a presidential term. If full-year FY '09 numbers were included in my averages, they would be: spending = 20.2%; taxes = 17.5%; deficits = 2.7%. This would incorporate spending for TARP and the initial auto loans as projected by Congressional Budget Office in January 2009. These figures overstate the additional spending, since the vast majority of TARP funding will be paid back.

choices made after I left office—debt will exceed that level by the end of 2010. A fiscal crisis that many saw as distant is now upon us.

———

"Wall Street got drunk, and we got the hangover."

That was an admittedly simplistic way of describing the origins of the greatest financial panic since the Great Depression. A more sophisticated explanation dates back to the boom of the 1990s. While the U.S. economy grew at an annual rate of 3.8 percent, developing Asian countries such as China, India, and South Korea averaged almost twice that. Many of these economies stockpiled large cash reserves. So did energy-producing nations, which benefited from a tenfold rise in oil prices between 1993 and 2008. Ben Bernanke called this phenomenon a "global saving glut." Others deemed it a giant pool of money.

A great deal of this foreign capital flowed back to the United States. America was viewed as an attractive place to invest, thanks to our strong capital markets, reliable legal system, and productive workforce. Foreign investors bought large numbers of U.S. Treasury bonds, which drove down their yield. Naturally, investors started looking for higher returns.

One prospect was the booming U.S. housing market. Between 1993 and 2007, the average American home price roughly doubled. Builders constructed homes at a rapid pace. Interest rates were low. Credit was easy. Lenders wrote mortgages for almost anyone—including "subprime" borrowers, whose low credit scores made them a higher risk.

Wall Street spotted an opportunity. Investment banks purchased large numbers of mortgages from lenders, sliced them up, repackaged them, and converted them into complex financial securities. Credit rating agencies, which received lucrative fees from investment banks, blessed many of these assets with AAA ratings. Financial firms sold huge numbers of credit default swaps, bets on whether the mortgages underlying the securities would default. Trading under fancy names such as collateralized debt obligations, the new mortgage-based products yielded the returns investors were seeking. Wall Street sold them aggressively.

Fannie Mae and Freddie Mac, private companies with congressional charters and lax regulation, fueled the market for mortgage-backed securities. The two government-sponsored enterprises bought up half the mortgages in the United States, securitized many of the loans, and sold them around the world. Investors bought voraciously because they believed Fannie and Freddie paper carried a U.S. government guarantee.

It wasn't just overseas investors who were attracted by higher returns. American banks borrowed large sums of money against their capital, a practice known as leverage, and loaded up on the mortgage-backed securities. Some of the most aggressive investors were giant new financial service companies. Many had taken advantage of the 1999 repeal of the Glass-Steagall Act of 1932, which prohibited commercial banks from engaging in the investment business.

At the height of the housing boom, homeownership hit an all-time high of almost 70 percent. I had supported policies to expand homeownership, including down-payment assistance for low-income and first-time buyers. I was pleased to see the ownership society grow. But the exuberance of the moment masked the underlying risk. Together, the global pool of cash, easy monetary policy, booming housing market, insatiable appetite for mortgage-backed assets, complexity of Wall Street financial engineering, and leverage of financial institutions created a house of cards. This precarious structure was fated to collapse as soon as the underlying card—the nonstop growth of housing prices—was pulled out. That was clear in retrospect. But very few saw it at the time, including me.

———

In May 2006, Josh Bolten walked into the Treaty Room with a guest he was trying to recruit to the administration, Goldman Sachs CEO Henry Paulson. I hoped to persuade Hank to succeed Secretary of the Treasury John Snow. John had been an effective advocate of my economic agenda, from tax cuts to Social Security reform to free trade. He had done a good job of managing the department and left it in better shape than he'd found it. He had been on the job for more than three years and both John and I felt it was time for a fresh face.

Josh told me Hank was a hard-charger—smart, energetic, and credible with the financial markets. Hank was slow to warm to the idea of joining my Cabinet. He had an exciting job on Wall Street and doubted he could accomplish much in the final years of my administration. He had a fine reputation and did not want his name dragged through the political mud. He was an avid conservationist who loved to fly-fish for tarpon and watch birds with his wife, Wendy—interests he might not be able to pursue. While Hank was a lifelong Republican, he was a party of one within his family. Wendy was a college friend and supporter of Hillary Clinton's. Their two children were disillusioned with the Republican Party. I later learned that Hank's mother cried when she first heard he was joining my Cabinet.

In his steady, low-key way, Josh eventually persuaded Hank to visit with me in the White House. Hank radiated energy and confidence. His hands moved as if he were conducting his own orchestra. He had a distinct way of speaking that could be hard to follow. Some said his brain was moving too fast for his mouth to keep up. That didn't bother me. People accused me of having the same problem.

Hank understood the globalization of finance, and his name commanded respect at home and abroad. When I assured him he would be my primary economic adviser and have unlimited access, he accepted the offer. I was grateful to Wendy and Hank's family for supporting him. At the time, none of us realized his tests as treasury secretary would rival those of Henry Morgenthau under FDR or Alexander Hamilton at the founding of the country.

———

When I took office, I became the fourth president to serve with Federal Reserve Chairman Alan Greenspan. Created under President Woodrow Wilson in 1913, the Fed sets America's monetary policy and coordinates with other central banks around the world. Its decisions have a wide-ranging impact, from the strength of the dollar to the interest rate on a local loan. While its chairman and board of governors are appointed by the president and confirmed by the Senate, the Fed sets monetary policy independently from the White House and Congress. That's the way it should be. An independent Fed is a crucial sign of stability to financial markets and investors around the globe.

I invited Greenspan to the White House for regular lunches. Dick

Cheney, Andy Card, and I would eat. Alan would not. He spent all his time answering our questions. His grasp of data was astounding. I would ask him where he saw the economy headed over the next few months. He would quote oil inventories, changes in freight miles in the railroad industry, and other interesting statistics. As he rattled off the figures, he slapped his left hand against his right fist, as if to jar more information loose. When his position came up for renewal in 2004, I never considered appointing anyone else.

When Alan sent word that he would retire in early 2006, we started the search for a successor. One name kept coming up: Ben Bernanke. Ben had served three years on the Fed board and joined my administration as chairman of the Council of Economic Advisers in June 2005. He was well respected by the staff and by me. Raised in a small South Carolina town, he was humble, down-to-earth, and plainspoken. Like me, he loved baseball. Unlike me, his team was the Boston Red Sox. He was able to distill complex topics into understandable terms. In contrast to some in Washington, the salt-and-pepper-bearded professor was not addicted to the sound of his own voice.

I liked to needle Ben, a sign of affection. "You're an economist, so every sentence starts with, 'On one hand . . . on the other hand,'" I said. "Thank goodness you don't have a third hand." One day in the Oval Office, I ribbed Ben for wearing tan socks with a dark suit. At our next meeting, the entire economic team showed up wearing tan socks in solidarity. "Look at what they've done," I said to Dick Cheney. The vice president slowly lifted the cuff of his pants. "Oh, no, not you, too!" I said.

What stood out most about Ben was his sense of history. He was a renowned academic expert on the Great Depression. Beneath his gentle demeanor was a fierce determination to avoid the mistakes of the 1930s. I hoped America would never face a scenario like that again. But if we did, I wanted Ben at the helm of the Federal Reserve.

As Fed chairman, Ben developed a close relationship with the other members of my economic team, especially Hank Paulson. Ben and Hank were like the characters in *The Odd Couple*. Hank was intense; Ben was calm. Hank was a decisive business leader; Ben was a thoughtful analyst who had spent much of his life in universities. Hank was a natural talker; Ben was comfortable listening.

Their opposing personalities could have produced tension. But Hank and Ben became perfect complements. In hindsight, putting a world-class investment banker and an expert on the Great Depression in the nation's top two economic positions were among the most important decisions of my presidency.

———

I began my final year in office the same way I had started my first, concerned about a bursting bubble and pushing for tax relief.

In mid-2007, home values had declined for the first time in thirteen years. Homeowners defaulted on their mortgages in increasing numbers, and financial companies wrote down billions of dollars in mortgage-related assets. Council of Economic Advisers Chairman Eddie Lazear, a brainy and respected Stanford professor, reported that the economy was slowing down. He and the economic team believed we might be able to mitigate the effects with well-timed tax relief.

In January 2008, I sent Hank Paulson to negotiate a bill with Speaker Nancy Pelosi and House Minority Leader John Boehner. They hammered out a plan to provide temporary tax incentives for businesses to create jobs and immediate tax rebates for families to boost consumer spending. Within a month, the legislation had passed by a broad bipartisan majority. By May, checks of up to $1,200 per family were in the mail.

The economy showed some signs of resilience. Economic growth reports were positive, unemployment was 4.9 percent, exports had reached record highs, and inflation was under control. I was hopeful we could dodge a recession.

I was wrong. The foundation was weakening, and the house of cards was about to come tumbling down.

———

Early in the afternoon of Thursday, March 13, we learned that Bear Stearns, one of America's largest investment banks, was facing a liquidity crisis. Like other Wall Street institutions, Bear was heavily leveraged. For every dollar it held in capital, the firm had borrowed thirty-three dollars to invest, much of it in mortgage-backed securities. When the housing bubble popped, Bear was overexposed, and investors moved their accounts. Unlike the run on First National Bank in Midland, there were no paper sacks.

I was surprised by the sudden crisis. My focus had been kitchen-table economic issues like jobs and inflation. I assumed any major credit troubles would have been flagged by the regulators or rating agencies. After all, I had strengthened financial regulation by signing the Sarbanes-Oxley Act in response to the Enron accounting fraud and other corporate scandals. Nevertheless, Bear Stearns's poor investment decisions left it on the brink of collapse. In this case, the problem was not a lack of regulation by government; it was a lack of judgment by Bear executives.

My first instinct was not to save Bear. In a free market economy, firms that fail should go out of business. If the government stepped in, we would create a problem known as moral hazard: Other firms would assume they would be bailed out, too, which would embolden them to take more risks.

Hank shared my strong inclination against government intervention. But he explained that a collapse of Bear Stearns would have widespread repercussions for a world financial system that had been under great stress since the housing crisis began in 2007. Bear had financial relationships with hundreds of other banks, investors, and governments. If the firm suddenly failed, confidence in other financial institutions would diminish. Bear could be the first domino in a series of failing firms. While I was concerned about creating moral hazard, I worried more about a financial collapse.

"Is there a buyer for Bear?" I asked Hank.

Early the next morning, we received our answer. Executives at JPMorgan Chase were interested in acquiring Bear Stearns, but were concerned about inheriting Bear's portfolio of risky mortgage-backed securities. With Ben's approval, Hank and Tim Geithner, the president of the New York Fed, devised a plan to address JPMorgan's concerns. The Fed would lend $30 billion against Bear's undesirable mortgage holdings, which cleared the way for JPMorgan to purchase Bear Stearns for two dollars per share.*

---

*The price was later renegotiated to ten dollars per share.

Many in Washington denounced the move as a bailout. It probably didn't feel that way to the Bear employees who lost their jobs or the shareholders who saw their stock drop 97 percent in less than two weeks. Our objective was not to reward the bad decisions of Bear Stearns. It was to safeguard the American people from a severe economic hit. For five months, it looked like we had.

————

"Do they know it's coming, Hank?"

"Mr. President," he replied, "we're going to move quickly and take them by surprise. The first sound they'll hear is their heads hitting the floor."

It was the first week of September 2008, and Hank Paulson had just laid out a plan to place Fannie Mae and Freddie Mac, the two giant government-sponsored enterprises, into government conservatorship.

Of all the emergency actions the government had to take in 2008, none was more frustrating than the rescue of Fannie and Freddie. The problems at the two GSEs had been visible for years. Fannie and Freddie had expanded beyond their mission of promoting homeownership. They had behaved like a hedge fund that raised huge amounts of money and took significant risks. In my first budget, I warned that Fannie and Freddie had grown so big that they presented "a potential problem" that could "cause strong repercussions in financial markets."

In 2003, I proposed a bill that would strengthen the GSEs' regulation. But it was blocked by their well-connected friends in Washington. Many Fannie and Freddie executives were former government officials. They had close ties in Congress, especially to influential Democrats like Congressman Barney Frank of Massachusetts and Senator Chris Dodd of Connecticut. "Fannie Mae and Freddie Mac are not facing any kind of financial crisis," Barney Frank said at the time.

That claim seemed more implausible as the years passed. In my 2005 budget, I issued a more dire warning. "The GSEs are highly leveraged, holding much less capital in relation to their assets than similarly sized financial institutions," the budget read. ". . . Given the very large size of each enterprise, even a small mistake by a GSE could have consequences throughout the economy."

That summer, we made another run at legislation. John Snow worked closely with Senate Banking Committee Chairman Richard Shelby on a reform bill that would create a new regulator authorized to reduce the size of the GSEs' investment portfolios. Senator Shelby, a smart, tough legislator from Alabama, pushed the bill through his committee despite unanimous Democratic opposition. But Democrats blocked a vote on the Senate floor. I am always amazed when I hear Democrats say the financial crisis happened because Republicans pushed deregulation.

By the summer of 2008, I had publicly called for GSE reform seventeen times. It turned out the eighteenth was the charm. All it took was the prospect of a global financial meltdown. In July, Congress passed a reform bill granting a key element of what we had first proposed five years earlier: a strong regulator for the GSEs. The bill also gave the treasury secretary temporary authority to inject equity into Fannie and Freddie if their solvency came into question.

Shortly after the legislation passed, the new regulatory agency, led by friend and businessman Jim Lockhart, took a fresh look at Fannie's and Freddie's books. With help from the Treasury Department, the examiners concluded the GSEs had nowhere near enough capital. In early August, both Freddie and Fannie announced huge quarterly losses.

The implications were startling. From small-town banks to major international investors like China and Russia, virtually everyone who owned GSE paper assumed it was backed by the U.S. government. If the GSEs defaulted, a global domino effect would follow and the credibility of our country would be shaken.

With Hank's strong advice, I decided that the only way to prevent a disaster was to take Fannie and Freddie into government conservatorship. It was up to Hank and Jim to persuade the boards of Fannie and Freddie to swallow this medicine. I was skeptical that they could do so without provoking a raft of lawsuits. But on Sunday, September 7, Hank called me at the White House to tell me it had been done. The Asian markets rallied Sunday night, and the Dow Jones increased 289 points on Monday.

I spent the next weekend, September 13 and 14, managing the government's response to Hurricane Ike. The storm pounded Texas's Gulf Coast early Saturday morning. The 110-mile-per-hour winds and 20-foot storm surge flooded Galveston, blew out windows in Houston, and killed more than 100 people. The worst storm to hit Texas since the Galveston Hurricane of 1900, Ike inflicted more than $24 billion in damage.

That same weekend, a different kind of storm was battering New York City. Like many institutions on Wall Street, Lehman Brothers was heavily leveraged and highly exposed to the faltering housing market. On September 10 the firm had announced its worst-ever financial loss, $3.9 billion in a single quarter. Confidence in Lehman vanished. Short-sellers, traders seeking to profit from declining stock prices, had helped drive Lehman stock from $16.20 to $3.65 per share. There was no way the firm could survive the weekend.

The question was what role, if any, the government should play in keeping Lehman afloat. The best possible solution was to find a buyer for Lehman, as we had for Bear Stearns. We had two days.

Hank flew to New York to oversee negotiations. He told me there were two possible buyers: Bank of America and Barclays, a British bank. Neither firm was willing to take Lehman's problematic assets. Hank and Tim Geithner devised a way to structure a deal without committing taxpayer dollars. They convinced major Wall Street CEOs to contribute to a fund that would absorb Lehman's toxic assets. Essentially, Lehman's rivals would save the firm from bankruptcy. Hank was hopeful that one of the buyers would close a deal.

It soon became clear that Bank of America had its eyes on another purchase, Merrill Lynch. That left Barclays as Lehman's last hope. But on Sunday, less than twelve hours before the Asian markets opened for Monday trading, financial regulators in London informed the Fed and SEC they were unwilling to approve a purchase by the British bank.

"What the hell is going on?" I asked Hank. "I thought we were going to get a deal."

"The British aren't prepared to approve," he said.

While Hank and I spoke all the time, those phone calls on Sunday—the supposed day of rest—always seemed to be the worst. It felt like we were having the same conversation again and again. The only thing changing was the name of the failing firms. But this time, we weren't going to be able to stop the domino from toppling over.

"Will we be able to explain why Lehman is different from Bear Stearns?" I asked Hank.

"Without JPMorgan as a buyer for Bear, it would have failed. We just couldn't find a buyer for Lehman," he said.

I felt we had done the best we could. But time had run out for Lehman. The 158-year-old investment house filed for bankruptcy just after midnight on Monday, September 15.

———

All hell broke loose in the morning. Legislators praised our decision not to intervene. The *Washington Post* editorialized, "The U.S. government was right to let Lehman tank." The stock market was not so positive. The Dow Jones plunged more than five hundred points.

A panic mentality set in. Investors started selling off securities and buying Treasury bills and gold. Clients pulled their accounts from investment banks. The credit markets tightened as lenders held on to their cash. The gears of the financial system, which depend on liquidity to serve as the grease, were grinding to a halt.

As if that weren't enough, the American International Group, a giant insurance company, was facing its own crisis. AIG wrote property and life insurance policies and insured municipalities, pension funds, 401(k)s, and other investment vehicles that affected everyday Americans. All those businesses were healthy. Yet the firm was somehow on the brink of implosion.

"How did this happen?" I asked Hank.

The answer was that one unit of the firm, AIG Financial Products, had insured large amounts of mortgage-backed obligations—and invested in even more. With mortgages defaulting in record numbers, the firm was facing cash calls for at least $85 billion that it did not have. If the company didn't come up with the money immediately, it would not only fail, it would bring down major financial institutions and international investors with it.

The New York Fed had tried to line up a private-sector solution. But no bank could raise the kind of money AIG needed in such little time. There was only one way to keep the firm alive: The federal government would have to step in. Ben Bernanke reported that AIG, unlike Lehman, held enough collateral from its stable insurance businesses to qualify for an emergency Fed loan. He laid out the terms: The New York Fed would lend AIG $85 billion secured by AIG's stable and valuable insurance subsidiaries. In return, the government would receive a warrant for 79.9 percent of AIG's shares.

There was nothing appealing about the deal. It was basically a nationalization of America's largest insurance company. Less than forty-eight hours after Lehman filed for bankruptcy, saving AIG would look like a glaring contradiction. But that was a hell of a lot better than a financial collapse.

---

With the AIG rescue, we had endured three weeks of financial agony. Day after day, the news kept getting worse. I'd go into a meeting with the Dow up two hundred points and come out thirty minutes later with it down three hundred. The markets were anxious, and so was I. I felt like the captain of a sinking ship. The Treasury, the Fed, and my White House team were working around the clock, but all we were doing was bailing water. I decided that we couldn't keep going like this. We had to patch the boat.

On Thursday, September 18—three days after Lehman declared bankruptcy—the economic team convened in the Roosevelt Room. Ben raised the possibility of another Great Depression. Then Hank and SEC Chairman Chris Cox laid out the plan: guarantee all money market deposits, launch a new lending vehicle to restart the commercial paper market, temporarily ban the short sale of leading financial stocks, and purchase hundreds of billions of dollars in mortgage-backed securities—the initiative that would become known as the Troubled Asset Relief Program, or TARP.

The strategy was a breathtaking intervention in the free market. It flew against all my instincts. But it was necessary to pull the country out of the panic. I decided that the only way to preserve the free market in the long run was to intervene in the short run.

"You've got my backing, one hundred percent," I told the team. "This is no longer a case-by-case deal. We tried to stem the tide, but the problem is deeper than we thought. This is systemic."

The conversation moved to a discussion of all the difficulties we would face on Capitol Hill. "We don't have time to worry about politics," I said. "Let's figure out the right thing to do and do it."

I had made up my mind: The U.S. government was going all in.

I reflected on everything we were facing. Over the past few weeks we had seen the failure of America's two largest mortgage entities, the bankruptcy of a major investment bank, the sale of another, the nationalization of the world's largest insurance company, and now the most drastic intervention in the free market since the presidency of Franklin Roosevelt. At the same time, Russia had invaded and occupied Georgia, Hurricane Ike had hit Texas, and America was fighting a two-front war in Iraq and Afghanistan. This was one ugly way to end the presidency.

I didn't feel sorry for myself. I knew there would be tough days. Self-pity is a pathetic quality in a leader. It sends such demoralizing signals to the team and the country. As well, I was comforted by my conviction that the Good Lord wouldn't give a believer a burden he couldn't handle.

After the meeting, I walked around the Roosevelt Room and thanked everyone. I told them how grateful I was for their hard work, and how fortunate America was that they had chosen to serve. In the presidency, as in life, you have to play the hand you're dealt. This wasn't the hand any of us had hoped for, but we were damn sure going to play it as best we could.

———

Hank and his team at Treasury pitched Congress hard on the financial rescue package. We proposed an appropriation of $700 billion—about 5 percent of the mortgage market, which we thought would be big enough to make a difference. Many legislators recognized the need for a large and decisive measure, but that didn't diminish their shock or anger. Democrats complained that the executive branch was seizing too much authority. One Republican senator said our plan would "take away the free market and institute socialism in America."

In some ways, I sympathized with the critics. The last thing I wanted to do was bail out Wall Street. As I told Josh Bolten, "My friends back home in Midland are going to ask what happened to the free-market guy they knew. They're going to wonder why we're spending their money to save the firms that created the crisis in the first place."

I wished there were some way to hold individual firms to account while sparing the rest of the country. But every economist I trusted told me that was impossible. The well-being of Main Street was directly linked to the fate of Wall Street.

If credit markets remained frozen, the heaviest burdens would fall on American families: steep drops in the value of retirement accounts, massive job losses, and further falling home values. On September 24, I gave a primetime address to the nation to explain the need for the rescue package. "I [understand] the frustration of responsible Americans who pay their mortgages on time, file their tax returns every April 15, and are reluctant to pay the cost of excesses on Wall Street," I said. "But given the situation we are facing, not passing a bill now would cost these Americans much more later."

A few hours before I went on the air to deliver the speech, my personal aide, Jared Weinstein, told me John McCain needed to speak to me immediately. I asked John how he was feeling about the campaign, but he went directly to the reason for his call. He wanted me to convene a White House meeting on the rescue package.

"Give me some time to talk to Hank," I said. I wanted to make sure a White House meeting wouldn't undermine my treasury secretary's efforts to structure a deal with Congress. John said he was going to issue a statement. Minutes later, he was on TV. He called for the meeting and announced he was suspending his campaign to work full-time on the legislation.

I knew John was in a tough position. He was trailing in the polls to Senator Barack Obama of Illinois, who had stunned Hillary Clinton in the Democratic primaries. No question the economic trouble was hurting John. Our party controlled the White House, so we were the natural target of the finger-pointing. Yet I thought the financial crisis gave

John his best chance to mount a comeback. In periods of crisis, voters value experience and judgment over youth and charisma. By handling the challenge in a statesmanlike way, John could make the case that he was the better candidate for the times.

I walked over to the Oval Office, where Josh Bolten was waiting with his deputy, Joel Kaplan, and Counselor Ed Gillespie. Nobody was keen on the idea of the meeting. Josh said Hank opposed it. But how could I say no to John's request? I could see the headlines: "Even Bush Thinks McCain's Idea Is a Bad One."

We notified Speaker Nancy Pelosi and Senate Majority Leader Harry Reid that the meeting would take place the next afternoon, Thursday, September 25. I called Senator Obama and told him I appreciated his interrupting his campaign schedule. "Anytime the president calls, I will take it," he said graciously. I extended the invitation to the meeting and made clear it was not a political trap. He agreed to attend.

At around 3:30 p.m. the next day, the participants began to arrive. Although I did not venture to the narrow parking strip between the White House and the Eisenhower Executive Office Building, I was told it looked like an SUV convention. Before the meeting started, I had a quick discussion with Senate Minority Leader Mitch McConnell and House Minority Leader John Boehner. We spent most of our time talking about how tough it would be to structure a deal that could garner Republican votes in the House. I told them it would be a disaster if Republicans killed the TARP bill and the economy collapsed.

Just before I sat down in the Cabinet Room, I had a moment with Speaker Pelosi. I told her I planned to call on her after Hank and I had made our opening remarks. She clearly suspected that my motive was to sabotage the Democrats. Like a volcano ready to erupt, she said, "Barack Obama will be our spokesman."

I took my seat at the center of the large wooden table Richard Nixon had donated to the White House. Hank Paulson, Dick Cheney, Josh Bolten, and I represented the administration. The party leaders and key committee chairmen represented Congress. Presidential candidates McCain and Obama took their seats at opposite ends of the table. Members of our staffs were sardined into the room. Nobody wanted to miss the marquee event in Washington's political theater.

I opened the meeting by stressing the urgency of passing legislation as soon as possible. The world was watching to see if America would act, and both parties had to rise to the challenge. Hank gave an update on the volatile markets and echoed my call for speedy passage.

I turned to the speaker. True to her word, she deferred to Senator Obama. He had a calm demeanor and spoke about the broad outlines of the package. I thought it was smart when he informed the gathering that he was in constant contact with Hank. His purpose was to show that he was aware, in touch, and prepared to help get a bill passed.

When Obama finished, I turned to John McCain. He passed. I was puzzled. He had called for this meeting. I assumed he would come prepared to outline a way to get the bill passed.

What had started as a drama quickly descended into a farce. Tempers flared. Voices were raised. Some barbs were thrown. I was watching a verbal food fight, which would have been comical except that the stakes were so high.

Toward the end of the meeting, John did speak. He talked in general terms about the difficulty of the vote for Republican members and his hope that we could reach a consensus.

After everyone had their chance to vent, I decided there was nothing more we could accomplish. I asked the candidates not to use the White House as a backdrop to issue political statements. I asked the members of Congress to remember we needed to show a united front to avoid spooking the markets. Then I stood up and left.

———

Early in the afternoon of Monday, September 29, the House of Representatives held a vote on the financial rescue bill. The previous two days, our fifth weekend in a row spent dealing with the financial crisis, had been packed with negotiations. Hank and his Treasury staff—joined by Dan Meyer, my cool-headed legislative affairs chief, and Keith Hennessey, my tireless National Economic Council director—had shuttled back and forth to Capitol Hill, working to resolve the remaining issues on TARP. Late Saturday night, Speaker Pelosi and John Boehner told me they had the outlines of a deal. On Monday morning, I stepped onto the South Lawn to congratulate Congress and urge the agreement's quick passage.

Back in the Oval Office, I started calling Republican House members to lock in votes.

"We really need this package," I told one congressman after the next. They all had reasons why they couldn't vote for it. The price tag was too high. Their constituents opposed it.

"I just can't bail out Wall Street," one told me. "I'm not going to be part of the destruction of the free market."

"Do you think I like the idea of doing this?" I shot back. "Believe me, I'd be fine if these companies fail. But the whole economy is on the line. The son of a bitch is going to go down if we don't step in."

At 2:07 p.m., the final vote on the bill was cast. It failed, 228 to 205. Democrats had voted in favor of the legislation, 140 to 95. Republicans had rejected it, with 65 votes in favor and 133 opposed

I knew the vote would be a disaster. My party had played the leading role in killing TARP. Now Republicans would be blamed for the consequences.

Within minutes, the stock market went into free fall. The Dow dropped 777 points, the largest single-day point loss in its 112-year history. The S&P 500 dropped 8.8 percent, its biggest percentage loss since the Black Monday crash of 1987. "This is panic . . . and fear run amok," one analyst told CNBC. "Right now we are in a classic moment of financial meltdown."

Shortly after the vote, I met with Hank, Ben, and the rest of the economic team in the Roosevelt Room to figure out our next move. We really had only one option. We had to make another run at the legislation.

My hope was that the market's severe reaction would provide a wakeup call to Congress. Many of those who voted against the bill had based their opposition on the $700 billion price tag. Then they had watched the markets hemorrhage $1.2 trillion in less than three hours. Every constituent with an IRA, a pension, or an E*Trade account would be furious.

We devised a strategy, lead by Josh Bolten, to bring the bill up in the Senate first and then make another run in the House. Harry Reid and Mitch McConnell quickly moved a bill with several new provisions intended to attract greater support, including a temporary increase in

FDIC insurance for depositors and protections for middle-class families against the Alternative Minimum Tax. The core of the legislation—the $700 billion to strengthen the banks and unfreeze the credit markets—was unchanged.

The Senate held a vote Wednesday night, and the bill passed 74 to 25. The House voted two days later, on Friday, October 3. I made another round of calls to wavering members. My warnings about the system going down had a lot more credibility this time. Thanks to strong leadership from Republican Whip Roy Blunt and Democratic Majority Leader Steny Hoyer, the bill passed 263 to 171. "Monday I cast a blue collar vote," said one member who changed his position. "Today I'm going to cast a red, white, and blue collar vote."

---

Days after I signed TARP, Hank recommended a change in the way we deployed the $700 billion. Instead of buying toxic assets, he proposed that Treasury inject capital directly into struggling banks by purchasing non-voting preferred stock.

I loathed the idea of the government owning pieces of banks. I worried Congress would consider it a bait and switch to spend the money on something other than buying toxic assets. But that was a risk we had to take. The plan for TARP had to change because the financial situation was worsening rapidly. Designing a system to buy mortgage-backed securities would consume time that we didn't have to spare. Buying shares in banks was faster and more efficient. Purchasing equity would inject capital—the lifeblood of finance—directly into the undercapitalized banking system. That would reduce the risk of sudden failure and free up more money for banks to lend.

Capital injections would also offer more favorable terms for U.S. taxpayers. The banks would pay a 5 percent dividend for the first five years. The dividend would increase to 9 percent over time, creating an incentive for financial institutions to raise less expensive private capital and buy back the preferred shares. The government would also receive stock warrants, which would give us the right to buy shares at low prices in the future. All this made it more likely that taxpayers would get their money back.

On October 13, Columbus Day, Hank, Tim Geithner, and Ben revealed the capital purchase plan in dramatic fashion. They called the CEOs of nine major financial firms to the Treasury Department and told them that, for the good of the country, we expected them to take several billion dollars each. We worried some healthier banks would turn down the capital and stigmatize those who accepted. But Hank was persuasive. They all agreed to take the money.

Deploying TARP had the psychological impact we were hoping for. Combined with a new FDIC guarantee for bank debt, TARP sent an unmistakable signal that we would not let the American financial system fail. The Dow shot up 936 points, the largest single-day increase in stock market history.

TARP didn't end the financial problems. Over the next three months, Citigroup and Bank of America required additional government funds. AIG continued to deteriorate and eventually needed nearly $100 billion more. The stock market remained highly volatile.

But with TARP in place, banks slowly began to resume lending. Companies began to find the liquidity needed to finance their operations. The panic that had consumed the markets receded. While we knew there was a tough recession ahead, I could feel the pressure ease. I had my first weekend in months without frantic calls about the crisis. Confidence, the foundation of a strong economy, was returning.

———

The financial crisis was global in scale, and one major decision was how to deal with it in the international arena. The turbulence came during France's turn as head of the European Union. Nicolas Sarkozy, the dynamic French president who had run on a pro-American platform, urged me to host an international summit. I grew to like the idea. The question was which countries to invite. I heard that some European leaders preferred that we convene the G-7. * But the G-7 included only about two thirds of the global economy. I decided to make the summit a gathering of the G-20, a group that included China, Russia,

*The United States, Japan, Germany, Great Britain, France, Italy, and Canada.

Brazil, Mexico, India, Australia, South Korea, Saudi Arabia, and other dynamic economies.

I knew it wouldn't be easy to forge an agreement among the twenty leaders. But with hard work and some gentle arm-twisting, we got it done.* On November 15, every leader at the summit signed on to a joint statement that read, "Our work will be guided by a shared belief that market principles, open trade and investment regimes, and effectively regulated financial markets foster the dynamism, innovation, and entrepreneurship that are essential for economic growth, employment, and poverty reduction."

It sent a powerful signal to have countries representing nearly 90 percent of the world economy agree on principles to solve the crisis. Unlike during the Depression, the nations of the world would not turn inward. The framework we established at the Washington summit continues to guide global economic cooperation.

———

The economic summit was not the biggest event of November. That came on Tuesday, November 4, when Senator Barack Obama was elected president of the United States.

My preference had been John McCain. I believed he was better prepared to assume the Oval Office amid a global war and financial crisis. I didn't campaign for him, in part because I was busy with the economic situation, but mostly because he didn't ask. I understood he had to establish his independence. I also suspected he was worried about the polls. I thought it looked defensive for John to distance himself from me. I was confident I could have helped him make his case. But the decision was his. I was disappointed I couldn't do more to help him.

The economy wasn't the only factor working against the Republican candidate. Like Dad in 1992 and Bob Dole in 1996, John McCain was on the wrong side of generational politics. At seventy-two, he was a decade older than I was and one of the oldest presidential nominees ever. Electing him would have meant skipping back a generation. By con-

---

*Responsibility for shaping the deal fell to Dan Price, a tenacious lawyer on the NSC staff, and Dave McCormick, the capable undersecretary of the treasury for international affairs.

trast, forty-seven-year-old Barack Obama represented a generational step forward. He had tremendous appeal to voters under fifty and ran a smart, disciplined, high-tech campaign to get his young supporters to the polls.

As an Obama win looked increasingly likely, I started to think more about what it would mean for an African American to win the presidency. I got an unexpected glimpse a few days before the election. An African American member of the White House residence staff brought his twin sons, age six, to the Oval Office for a farewell photo. One glanced up around the room and blurted out, "Where's Barack Obama?"

"He's not here yet," I deadpanned.

On election night, I was moved by images of black men and women crying on TV. More than one said, "I never thought I would live to see this day."

I called the president-elect to congratulate him. I also called John McCain to say he was a good man who'd given the race his best shot. Both were gracious. I told the president-elect I looked forward to welcoming him to the White House.

When I hung up the phone, I said a prayer that all would be well during my successor's time. I thought about one of my favorite presidential quotes, from a letter John Adams wrote to his wife, Abigail: "I pray Heaven to bestow the best blessings on this house and all that shall hereafter inhabit it. May none but honest and wise men ever rule under this roof." His words are carved into the mantel above the fireplace of the State Dining Room.

———

Months before the 2008 election, I had decided to make it a priority to conduct a thorough, organized transition. The first change of power since 9/11 would be a period of vulnerability, and I felt a responsibility to give my successor the courtesy of a smooth entry into the White House. The transition was overseen by Josh Bolten and one of his deputies, my talented former personal aide Blake Gottesman. They made sure the president-elect and his team received briefings, access to senior members of the administration, and office space in their new departments.

Part of the transition involved economic policy. The financial crisis brought one final decision point: What to do about the reeling American auto industry? The Big Three firms of Ford, Chrysler, and General Motors had been experiencing problems for years. Decades of poor management decisions had saddled automakers with enormous health-care and pension costs. They had been slow to recognize changes in the market. As a result, they had been outcompeted by foreign manufacturers in product and price.

When the economy took a hit, auto sales dropped. Then the freeze in the credit markets stopped almost all car loans. Auto company stocks were battered in the stock market collapse of September and October. Their cash balances dwindled to dangerously low levels. They had little hope of raising new funds in the private markets.

In the fall of 2008, GM CEO Rick Wagoner started pressing for federal help. He warned that GM would fail, and then the other automakers would follow. I didn't think it was a coincidence that the warnings about bankruptcy came right before the upcoming elections. I refused to make a decision on the auto industry until after the vote.

Six days after the election, I met with President-elect Obama in the Oval Office. Barack was gracious and confident. It seemed he felt the same sense of wonderment I had eight years earlier when Bill Clinton welcomed me to the Oval Office as president-elect. I could also see the sense of responsibility start to envelop him. He asked questions about how I structured my day and organized my staff. We talked about foreign policy, including America's relationships with China, Saudi Arabia, and other major powers. We also discussed the economy, including the auto companies' trouble.

Later that week, I sat down for a meeting with my economic team. "I told Barack Obama that I wouldn't let the automakers fail," I said. "I won't dump this mess on him."

I had opposed Jimmy Carter's bailout of Chrysler in 1979 and believed strongly that government should stay out of the auto business. Yet the economy was extremely fragile, and my economic advisers had warned that the immediate bankruptcy of the Big Three could cost more than a million jobs, decrease tax revenues by $150 billion, and set back America's GDP by hundreds of billions of dollars.

Congress had passed a bill offering $25 billion in loans to the auto companies in exchange for making their fleets more fuel-efficient. I hoped we could convince Congress to release those loans immediately, so the companies could survive long enough to give the new president and his team time to address the situation.

My point man on the auto issue was Secretary of Commerce Carlos Gutierrez. Born in Cuba, Carlos had immigrated to Florida as a boy. His parents moved to Mexico, where Carlos took a job driving a delivery truck for Kellogg's. Twenty-four years later, Carlos became the youngest CEO in that company's history and the only Latino CEO of a Fortune 500 company. He joined my administration in 2005 and did an outstanding job promoting trade, defending tax relief, and advocating for freedom in Cuba.

Carlos and the team pushed Congress hard to release the auto loans. We made progress in the House, but the Senate wouldn't budge. The only option left was to loan money from TARP. I told the team I wanted to use the loans as an opportunity to insist that the automakers develop viable business plans. Under the loans' stringent terms, the companies would have until April 2009 to become fiscally viable and self-sustaining by restructuring their operations, renegotiating labor contracts, and reaching new agreements with bondholders. If they could not meet all those conditions, the loans would be immediately called, forcing bankruptcy.

The deal drew criticism from both sides of the aisle. The head of the autoworkers' union complained that the conditions were too harsh. Grover Norquist, an influential advocate for fiscal conservatism, wrote me a public letter. It read, "Dear President Bush: No."

Nobody was more frustrated than I was. While the restrictive short-term loans were better than an outright bailout, it was frustrating to have the automakers' rescue be my last major economic decision. But with the market not yet functioning, I had to safeguard American workers and families from a widespread collapse. I also had my successor in mind. I decided to treat him the way I would like to have been treated if I were in his position.

———

One of the best books I read during my presidency was *Theodore Rex*, Edmund Morris's biography of Teddy Roosevelt. At one point near the end of his eventful tenure, Roosevelt exclaimed, "I knew there would be a blizzard when I went out."

I know what he meant. The period between September and December 2008 was the most intense, turbulent, decision-packed stretch since those same months in 2001. Because the crisis arose so late in my administration, I wouldn't be in the White House to see the impact of most of the decisions I made. Fortunately, by the time I left in January 2009, the measures we had taken had stabilized the financial system. The threat of a systemic collapse had passed. Once-frozen credit markets had begun flowing again. While the world still faced serious economic insecurity, the panic mentality was gone.

The following year brought a mixed picture. The stock market fell during the first two months of 2009 but ended the year up more than 19 percent. As banks rebuilt their balance sheets, they began to redeem government-owned shares. By the fall of 2010, the vast majority of the capital the Treasury injected into banks had been repaid. As the economy regains strength, more of that money will be repaid, plus dividends. A program derided for its costs could potentially end up making money for American taxpayers.

I've often reflected on whether we could have seen the financial crisis coming. In some respects, we did. We recognized the danger posed by Fannie and Freddie, and we repeatedly called on Congress to authorize stronger oversight and limit the size of their portfolios. We also understood the need for a new approach to regulation. In early 2008, Hank proposed a blueprint for a modernized regulatory structure that strengthened oversight of the financial sector and gave the government greater authority to wind down failing firms. Yet my administration and the regulators underestimated the extent of the risks taken by Wall Street. The ratings agencies created a false sense of security by blessing shaky assets. Financial firms built up too much leverage and hid some exposure with off–balance sheet accounting. Many new products were so complex that even their creators didn't fully understand them. For all these reasons, we were blindsided by a financial crisis that had been more than a decade in the making.

One of the questions I'm asked most often is how to avoid another financial crisis. My first answer is that I'm not sure we're out of the woods on this one yet. Financial institutions around the world are still unwinding their leverage, and governments are saddled with too much debt. To fully recover, the federal government must improve its long-term fiscal position by reducing spending, addressing the unfunded liabilities in Social Security and Medicare, and creating the conditions for the private sector—especially small businesses—to generate new jobs.

Once the economy is on firm footing, Fannie and Freddie should be converted into private companies that compete in the mortgage market on a level playing field with other firms. Banks should be required to meet sensible capital requirements to prevent overleveraging. The credit-rating agencies need to reevaluate their model for analyzing complex financial assets. And boards of directors must put an end to compensation packages that create the wrong incentives and reward executives for failure.

At the same time, we must be careful not to overcorrect. Overregulation slows investment, stifles innovation, and discourages entrepreneurship. The government should unwind its involvement in the banking, auto, and insurance sectors. As it addresses financial regulation, Congress should not infringe on the Federal Reserve's independence in conducting monetary policy. And the financial crisis should not become an excuse to raise taxes, which would only undermine the economic growth required to regain our strength.

Above all, our country must maintain our faith in free markets, free enterprise, and free trade. Free markets have made America a land of opportunity and, over time, helped raise the standard of living for successive generations. Abroad, free markets have transformed struggling nations into economic powers and lifted hundreds of millions of people out of poverty. Democratic capitalism, while imperfect and in need of rational oversight, is by far the most successful economic model ever devised.

———

The nature of the presidency is that sometimes you don't choose which challenges come to your desk. You do decide how to respond. In the final days of my administration, I gathered my economic advisers for a last briefing in the Oval Office. I had assembled a strong, experienced team that was capable of adapting to the unexpected and making sound recommendations. We had done what we believed was necessary, knowing it would not always be popular. For some in our country, TARP had become a four-letter word. I believe it helped spare the American people from an economic disaster of historic proportions. The government made clear it would not let the economy fail, and the second Great Depression that Ben Bernanke warned about did not happen.

As I looked into the tired faces of the men and women of my economic team, I thought about all my administration had been through. Every day for eight years, we had done our best. We had given the job our all. And through every trial, we had been honored to serve the nation we love.

# EPILOGUE

I began Tuesday, January 20, 2009, the same way I had started every day for the past eight years: I read the Bible. One of the passages that final day was Psalm 18:2—"The Lord is my rock, my fortress and my deliverer; my God is my rock, in whom I take refuge." Amen.

A little before 7:00 a.m., I took the elevator to the ground floor of the White House, walked down the Colonnade, and opened the glass-paneled door to the Oval Office for the last time. Josh Bolten was waiting inside. He greeted me with the same words he'd used every day as my chief of staff: "Mr. President, thank you for the privilege of serving."

On a normal morning, the West Wing would be bustling with aides. But that last day, the building was eerily quiet. There were no ringing phones, no television sets tuned to the news, no meetings in the hallways. The only sound I heard was the occasional buzz of a workman's drill, refitting the offices for a new team.

I left a letter on the Resolute desk. Continuing a presidential tradition, I had written to congratulate my successor and wish him well. The note was in a manila envelope addressed to "44."

"What an honor it has been to come to work in this office every day," I told Josh. Then I put my coat on, walked out the door, and took one last lap around the jogging track on the South Lawn, where Spot and I had walked the morning I gave the order to liberate Iraq.

My next stop was the East Room, where the White House residence staff had gathered. The packed room was a stark contrast with the emptiness of the West Wing. Nearly every member of the residence staff was there: the florists who put fresh bouquets in the Oval Office every morning, the butlers and valets who made our life so comfortable, the carpenters and engineers who keep the White House in working condition, the chefs who cooked us such fabulous meals, and, of course, the pastry chef who fed my sweet tooth.

Many on the residence staff had served not only for the past eight years, but during Mother and Dad's time in the White House as well. "You've been like family to us," I told the gathering, with Laura, Barbara, and Jenna at my side. "There are some things I'm not going to miss about Washington, but I'm going to miss you a lot. Thank you from the bottom of our hearts."

———

Barack and Michelle Obama arrived on the North Portico just before 10:00 a.m. Laura and I had invited them for a cup of coffee in the Blue Room, just as Bill and Hillary Clinton had done for us eight years earlier. The Obamas were in good spirits and excited about the journey ahead. Meanwhile, in the Situation Room, homeland security aides from both our teams monitored intelligence on a terrorist threat to the Inauguration. It was a stark reminder that evil men still want to harm our country, no matter who is serving as president.

After our visit, we climbed into the motorcade for the trip up Pennsylvania Avenue. I thought back to the drive I'd made with Bill Clinton eight years earlier. That January day in 2001, I could never have imagined what would unfold over my time in office. I knew some of the decisions I had made were not popular with many of my fellow citizens. But I felt satisfied that I had been willing to make the hard decisions, and I had always done what I believed was right.

At the Capitol, Laura and I took our seats for the Inauguration. I marveled at the peaceful transfer of power, one of the defining features of our democracy. The audience was riveted with anticipation for the swearing-in. Barack Obama had campaigned on hope, and that was what he had given many Americans.

For our new president, the Inauguration was a thrilling beginning. For Laura and me, it was an end. It was another president's turn, and I was ready to go home. After a heartwarming farewell ceremony at Andrews Air Force Base, Laura and I boarded Air Force One—now designated Special Air Mission 28000. We landed in Midland in the late afternoon of a beautiful West Texas winter day. We drove to a rally in Centennial Plaza, where we'd attended a sendoff ceremony eight years earlier. Many of the faces in the crowd were the same, a reminder of true friends who were with us before politics, during politics, and after politics.

"It is good to be home," I said. "Laura and I may have left Texas, but Texas never left us. . . . When I walked out of the White House this morning, I left with the same values I brought eight years ago. And when I look in the mirror at home tonight, I will have no regrets about what I see—except maybe the gray hair."

We flew to Crawford that night and were up at dawn the next morning for the first day of what Laura had termed "the afterlife." I was struck by the calm. There was no CIA briefing to attend and no blue sheet from the Situation Room. I felt like I had gone from a hundred miles an hour to about ten. I had to force myself to relax. I would read the news and instinctively think about how we would have to respond. Then I remembered that decision was on someone else's desk.

I had plenty to occupy my time. I went to work building the Bush Presidential Center on the campus of Southern Methodist University, which will include an official government archive, a museum, and a policy institute dedicated to promoting education reform, global health, economic growth, and human freedom, with a special emphasis on creating new opportunities for women around the world. I am blessed to be the only president to leave office with both parents alive, and I'm grateful for the chance to spend more time with them. In June 2009, Laura and I joined our extended family in Kennebunkport to mark Dad's eighty-fifth birthday, which he celebrated with another parachute jump. Mother quipped that his choice of a landing zone, St. Ann's Episcopal, was strategic. If the jump didn't turn out well, at least he'd be near a cemetery.

Every now and then, there are reminders of how much life has changed. Shortly after we moved to Dallas, I took Barney for an early-morning walk around our neighborhood. I hadn't done anything like that in more than a decade. Barney never had—he'd spent his entire life at the White House, Camp David, and Crawford. Barney spotted our neighbor's lawn, where he promptly took care of his business. There I was, the former president of the United States, with a plastic bag on my hand, picking up that which I had been dodging for the past eight years.

———

The day after I left office, I started writing this book. Working on it has been a great opportunity for reflection, and I hope you've enjoyed reading these thoughts as much as I've enjoyed writing them.

When I chose to structure this book around major decision points, I knew it would mean leaving out some aspects of my presidency. I don't fully cover foreign policy accomplishments such as the historic civil nuclear agreement with India or the Merida Initiative to fight drugs with Mexico. I devote just a few words to my record on energy and the environment, and I do not describe my decision to create the largest marine conservation areas in the world. I also omit an account of our successful efforts to improve services for veterans and reduce teen drug use and chronic homelessness. All these accomplishments are sources of pride, and I am grateful to those who helped make them possible.

Instead of covering every issue, I've tried to give the reader a sense of the most consequential decisions that reached my desk. As I hope I've made clear, I believe I got some of those decisions right, and I got some wrong. But on every one, I did what I believed was in the best interests of our country.

It's too early to say how most of my decisions will turn out. As president, I had the honor of eulogizing Gerald Ford and Ronald Reagan. President Ford's pardon of Richard Nixon, once regarded as one of the worst mistakes in presidential history, is now viewed as a selfless act of leadership. And it was quite something to hear the commentators who once denounced President Reagan as a dunce and a warmonger talk about how the Great Communicator had won the Cold War.

Decades from now, I hope people will view me as a president who recognized the central challenge of our time and kept my vow to keep the country safe; who pursued my convictions without wavering but changed course when necessary; who trusted individuals to make choices in their lives; and who used America's influence to advance freedom. And I hope they will conclude that I upheld the honor and dignity of the office I was so privileged to hold.

Whatever the verdict on my presidency, I'm comfortable with the fact that I won't be around to hear it. That's a decision point only history will reach.

# ACKNOWLEDGMENTS

I am fortunate to come from a family of bestselling authors. My mother and father wrote fine books, as did my sister Doro. Closer to home, Laura wrote a bestseller, Jenna wrote a bestseller, and they collaborated on another. Even my parents' dogs, C. Fred and Millie, authored their own works.

I was inspired by my family members' success and, more important, sustained by their love. I thank Laura for her constant love and for sharing in the experiences that made this book possible. I thank our daughters, Barbara and Jenna, for their hugs and laughter. I am glad to have Henry Hager as my son-in-law. I appreciate the unwavering support of Mother and Dad. And I thank Jeb, Neil, Marvin, and Doro for comforting their brother.

When I considered writing this book I knew the task would be a challenge. I did not realize how enjoyable it would be. The main reason is that I worked with Chris Michel. At the end of the administration Chris was my chief speechwriter. He knew how I talked and saw much of the history we made. His broad range of talents, from research to editing, has made the book project move smoothly. His upbeat personality was a constant joy. I will miss him as he heads off to Yale Law School.

This book took its first step toward publication when I hired Bob Barnett. Bob is a talented lawyer with sound judgment, unmatched experience, and great patience—which he showed by tolerating my frequent ribbing about his hourly rate. The truth is that Bob is the best in the business, and he was worth every penny.

I cannot imagine a better editor than Sean Desmond, a Harvard-educated son of Dallas, Texas. Sean knew where to add detail, when to cut words, and how to bring my decisions to life for the reader. He did it all with patience, professionalism, and a good sense of humor.

I am grateful to the superb team at Crown Publishing. Steve Rubin and Jenny Frost showed confidence in this project from the beginning. Maya Mavjee and Tina Constable capably saw it through to conclusion. I appreciate managing editor Amy Boorstein, copyeditor Jenna Dolan, creative director Whitney Cookman, editorial assistant Stephanie Chan, publicity director David Drake, production director Linnea Knollmueller, interior design director Elizabeth Rendfleisch, and the many others at Crown and Random House who helped make this book a reality.

Much of the research for this book was conducted by the brilliant and tireless Peter Rough. Peter spent the past eighteen months digging through archives, searching the Internet, and sifting through reams of paper. His insights and resourcefulness improved this book in countless ways. He also fact-checked every word of it, with assistance from four former members of my speechwriting staff: Staci Wheeler, Mike Robins, Mike Hasson, and Matt Larkin. Gabriel Gillett, Paul Langdale, Chris Papagianis, Sarah Catherine Perot, Kerrie Rushton, Sara Sendek, Josh Silverstein, and others added valuable research.

I am indebted to the professionals at the National Archives and Records Administration for their assistance on this book. I am grateful to Alan Lowe, director of the George W. Bush Presidential Library, and Supervisory Archivist Shannon Jarrett for making this project a top priority. Archivists Brooke Clement, Matthew Law, and Jodie Steck tracked down thousands of documents and photographs that helped refresh my memory and confirm details in my account. Sarah Barca, Tally Fugate, Peter Haligas, Neelie Holm, Bobby Holt, Elizabeth Lanier, David Sabo, and Ketina Taylor helped as well. I also thank the Presidential Materials staff of the National Archives in Washington—especially Nancy Smith, John Laster, and Stephannie Oriabure—who made many important, highly classified documents available for my use.

Many trusted friends contributed to this book. I am particularly grateful to those who reviewed the full manuscript: Steve Hadley, Josh Bolten, Andy Card, Blake Gottesman, Karen Hughes, Condi Rice, and Dana Perino, who also provided invaluable advice on publicity. Pete

Wehner read much of the book in its early stages and made insightful comments. Brent McIntosh and Raul Yanes carefully reviewed the final draft. Many others made suggestions on key chapters, including Dan Bartlett, Ryan Crocker, Mark Dybul, Gary Edson, Peter Feaver, Joe Hagin, Mike Hayden, Keith Hennessey, Joel Kaplan, Eddie Lazear, Jay Lefkowitz, Brett McGurk, and Hank Paulson. They are responsible for many of the book's strengths and none of its flaws.

Part of publishing a book as a former president is undergoing a declassification review. I was fortunate to have three capable lawyers help me navigate the process: Bill Burck, Mike Scudder, and Tobi Young. I am grateful to Bill Leary and his professional staff at the National Security Council, which helped expedite the review process. I also thank the dedicated men and women at the Central Intelligence Agency who helped check key facts.

Those who enjoyed the photo section can thank Emily Kropp Michel, who—along with the NARA team—sorted through many of the four million photographs digitally archived at the Bush Presidential Library. They received valuable guidance from Eric Draper, my chief photographer for all eight years, and former White House photographer Paul Morse.

The decisions I describe in this book would not have been possible without the service and support of many dedicated people over my fifteen years of public service. I thank Dick and Lynne Cheney for eight years of friendship. I appreciate the outstanding, selfless men and women who served in my Cabinet and on my White House staff, as well as on my campaigns and in the Texas governor's office. Laura and I will always be grateful to the fine agents of the Secret Service, the military aides who were always at my side, the incredibly generous White House residence staff, the doctors and nurses of the White House Medical Unit, the crews of Air Force One and Marine One, and the great team at Camp David. On behalf of Barney, Spot, and Miss Beazley, I extend special thanks to Dale Haney, Sam Sutton, Robert Favela, Cindy Wright, Robert Blossman, and Maria Galvan.

I am fortunate to be surrounded by a great team in Dallas, led by my talented and capable chief of staff, Mike Meece. I am grateful to Blake Gottesman and Jared Weinstein, two former personal aides who took months out of their lives to help me set up my office. Everyone in the Office of George W. Bush contributed to this book: Mike Meece, Brian Cossiboom, Logan Dryden, Freddy Ford, Ashley Hickey, Caroline Hickey, Caroline Nugent, David Sherzer, and Justine Sterling. I also thank Charity Wallace, Molly Soper, and Katie Harper for taking good care of Laura.

Aside from writing this book, I have spent the past eighteen months working to build my presidential center at Southern Methodist University in Dallas. I thank Mark Langdale for overseeing the endeavor, SMU President Gerald Turner for his close partnership, and Jim Glassman and Stacy Cinatl for their leadership at the George W. Bush Institute. I am particularly grateful to Don Evans, Ray Hunt, and Jeanne Johnson Phillips for all they have done to make the project a success.

I often tell people that I don't miss the politics of Washington, but I do miss the people. I am grateful to my many friends in Congress, fellow world leaders, and even members of the press corps.

Finally, I thank the men and women of the United States military. While I dedicated this book to Laura, Barbara, and Jenna, nobody did more to inspire me than those who wear the uniform of this country and their families. Their achievements will rank alongside those of the greatest generations in history, and the highest honor of my life was to serve as their commander in chief.

# INDEX